THE CANADIAN ENVIRONMENT IN POLITICAL CONTEXT

THE CANADIAN ENVIRONMENT IN POLITICAL CONTEXT

Andrea Olive

UNIVERSITY OF TORONTO PRESS

LIBRARY AND ARCHIVES CANADA CATALOGUING IN PUBLICATION

Olive, Andrea, 1980–, author
    The Canadian environment in political context / Andrea Olive.

Includes bibliographical references and index.
Issued in print and electronic formats.

ISBN 978-1-4426-0872-6 (bound).—ISBN 978-1-4426-0871-9 (paperback).—
ISBN 978-1-4426-0873-3 (pdf).—ISBN 978-1-4426-0874-0 (html)

    1. Environmental policy—Canada. 2. Canada—Politics and government.
3. Canada—Environmental conditions. 4. Environmentalism—Canada. I. Title.

HC120.E5O45 2015   363.700971   c2015-901112-4
                                       c2015-901113-2

We welcome comments and suggestions regarding any aspect of our publications—please feel free to contact us at news@utphighereducation.com or visit our Internet site at www.utppublishing.com.

North America
5201 Dufferin Street
North York, Ontario, Canada, M3H 5T8

2250 Military Road
Tonawanda, New York, USA, 14150

UK, *Ireland, and continental Europe*
NBN International
Estover Road, Plymouth, PL6 7PY, UK

ORDERS PHONE: 44 (0) 1752 202301
ORDERS FAX: 44 (0) 1752 202333
ORDERS E-MAIL: enquiries@nbninternational.com

Every effort has been made to contact copyright holders; in the event of an error or omission, please notify the publisher.

This book is printed on paper containing 100% post-consumer fibre.

The University of Toronto Press acknowledges the financial support for its publishing activities of the Government of Canada through the Canada Book Fund.

Printed in the United States of America.

Scientists have discovered that 1980 was the year humanity's collective demands first surpassed Earth's regenerative capacity. That is the year I was born. Since then, we have been living in debt—surviving today by borrowing from tomorrow. We need to find a different way.

This book is dedicated to Ella Spice, Jack Lindgren, and Roy Waller. If we get this right, you will never have to live on Mars.

Contents

Illustrations

Maps

Textboxes

Acknowledgements

THIS PROJECT HAS LARGELY been about my students. I have been teaching environmental policy since 2008—first at Purdue University; then at the University of Michigan-Dearborn and the University of Michigan, Ann Arbor; and now at the University of Toronto Mississauga. The students in those classes have played the largest role in shaping this book. Their questions, their essays and exams, and their keen sense of wonder about the world have inspired me on a daily basis.

Countless individuals' hard work has been poured into the creation of this book. I must thank my copy editor, Karen Taylor, for her patience, her close attention to detail, her expert research skills, and her kind sense of humour. (I am glad we can both laugh at spelling mistakes and government data.) I would like to thank my peer reviewers who provided excellent feedback and critical assessment. A special acknowledgement goes to Alice Cohen at Acadia University for kindly lending her expertise to Chapter 6. At the University of Toronto Press (UTP), I would like to thank Michael Harrison for having faith in this project right from the beginning (and maintaining that faith even when I lost it!). I would also like to thank Mark Thompson and Ashley Rayner for their assistance and quick response to my emails. Finally, I would like to thank the behind-the-scenes production staff at UTP because this book would never have been possible without them.

My mentors and colleagues have also contributed to the content of the book and to my creative process. At Purdue University, I would like to thank Leigh Raymond, as he was the first person to teach me about environmental policy. (Thanks again for lending me your POL223 lecture notes back in 2008.) At the University of Windsor, I would like to thank Stephen Brooks for teaching me so much about Canadian politics and enabling me to see the policy process up close (literally from the public gallery in the House of Commons). At the University of Toronto, I want to thank Graham White for reading and re-reading Chapters 9 and 10 so patiently. I also want to thank Barbara Murck and Monica Havelka for the countless conversations we have had over the past few years about environmental policy (or the lack thereof) in Canada. Similarly, I must acknowledge the contributions made by excellent teaching assistants in environmental policy—Andrew McDougall, Jodi Adams, David Houle, Nathan Lemphers, and Jerald Sabin. I have learned so much from each of you and hope we can continue to discuss environmental policy for years to come. I also want to thank Ed Schatz, Kathi Wilson, Matt Hoffmann, Linda White, Tenley Conway, and Grace Skogstad for their mentorship. Finally, the administrative staff at the University of Toronto Mississauga cannot be overlooked—Norma Dotto, Lorna Taylor, Terrie Winchester, David Linden, Sabrina Ferrari, Toni Luke-Gervais, and Maria Wowk. Thanks for keeping the lights on, the printer humming, the students organized, and generally making my job a thousand times easier (and more fun).

I particularly want to thank my family. Gratitude is all I have to give in return for making you read chapters of this book on the flight to Mexico for our Christmas vacation. And Mom and Dad, I want again to give you a special shout-out for having the foresight to build a cabin in the most beautiful place on earth. This book is about the nostalgia I have for all those summers during the 1980s and 90s, when I did not have to wear shoes, and I spent my days catching frogs and my nights looking at the stars. Finally, I cannot understate the role that Christopher Petrakos has played in the creation of this book. Every page tells the story of us.

Preface

GROWING UP SASKATCHEWAN, I became acutely aware of federalism at an early age. I knew my "capital city" was Ottawa in a faraway province called Ontario. In fact, Ottawa is 2,725 kilometres from Regina on the Trans-Canada Highway, nearly a 30-hour drive. However, the Legislative Assembly of the Province of Saskatchewan was only 3.5 kilometres from my parents' house—and my family would drive by it on the way downtown or on the way to swim practice in the early mornings. As far as I knew, that is where policy was made in my country. As it turns out, in terms of environmental policy, that is basically true. In Canada, provinces are extraordinarily powerful when it comes to the environment, especially in terms of natural resources.

At the heart of federalism is the issue of authority: who *should* govern the environment in Canada? The possibilities include not just Ottawa, provinces, and territories but also elected officials, appointed experts (such as scientists), industry, and the courts. It is likely true that all these actors have a role in safeguarding the environment. Finding the right balance of authority, however, is quite difficult. The balance of power between provinces and the central government in Ottawa has ebbed and flowed throughout Canadian history. The question of authority remains always in flux. Sometimes, all levels of government work together; at other times, the provinces and the federal government are at odds.

The Constitution Act of 1867 and the Canada Act of 1982 provide very little guidance on environmental stewardship across the country. Both Ottawa and the provinces have very important environmental powers. This book explores those powers and the relationship between the different levels of power, mainly between the federal and provincial governments, but municipal governments will also be considered. However, the book will not tell you who *should* govern the environment. That is a question for Canadians. I hope that, by the end of this book, you will have formed an answer to this question. It is often quite clear where one level of government is failing. What is less clear is how collaboration can evolve and be sustained, including collaboration with other important actors such as municipalities, international organizations, interest groups, citizen experts, and Aboriginal peoples.

The world of environmental policy is a crowded place, but the exchange of information and the constant pursuit of new answers to environmental problems in the face of economic development drive the overall policy system. The purpose of this book is to examine the different actors and motivations and the various policy outcomes in the Canadian environmental policy arena. It is intended primarily for students new to environmental policy and Canadian politics. However, scholars of Aboriginal politics, Arctic policy, climate change, pollution, biodiversity, or international politics will also find the book to be a good overview of procedures, challenges, and outcomes in these areas of interest.

This book is divided into 12 chapters. Chapter 1 is an introduction to Canada's environment and provides a brief synopsis of environmental quality across Canada and across different areas of the environment. The chapter offers an overview of environmental indicators including air and water quality as well as measurements of the state of Canada's forests, agriculture, biodiversity, and fisheries. Canada is adequately protecting the environment in some contexts, and, overall, the country is not polluted. But there are many places for improvement—and each calls for new policies, a recommitment to existing policy, or an entirely new policy approach. Overall, this chapter provides a quick snapshot of Canadian environmental policy, its strengths and its weaknesses. It sets the backdrop for understanding the issues discussed in greater depth in chapters 5 through 8. At the end of the chapter, a few possible reasons for Canada's weaknesses in environmental policy creation are examined—namely, the

country's dependence on resource extraction, urbanization, and affluence. These factors create numerous challenges for Canada's environmental policymakers. The country is quickly urbanizing, and the growing
economy is leading to an increase in affluence. This situation is good for
Canadians but a challenge for environmental protection.

   The subsequent two chapters are intended to provide a background
in the basics of government and public policy. Chapter 2 is a very brief
overview of political institutions and how they function inside Canada.
It is absolutely essential to understand the concept of federalism and
how it works in order to properly analyze environmental policy. Chapter
3 serves as an introduction to public policy. Here policy actors outside
of government are introduced, such as the media, interest groups, and
political parties. Different types of policies are discussed and specific
environmental policies are introduced for the first time. By the end of
Chapter 3, the reader should have a solid grasp on how Canada makes
environmental policy at the federal and provincial and territorial levels.
Though there are other very good textbooks on environmental policy in
Canada, these fail to connect the policies to the institutions and processes
that created those policies. The aim here is to put the environment into a
political context. For example, understanding environmental protections
and assessments for oil pipeline projects is difficult without linking these
to Aboriginal politics and the role of the judiciary in environmental law.
Similarly, omnibus bills and majority governments have been important in
recent environmental policy in Canada. This is all to say that students and
scholars of the environmental need to put politics at the centre of study.

   Chapter 4 is a very short history of environmentalism in Canada.
Canadians experienced a slow build toward environmental consciousness.
The first wave of environmentalism, which really began in the United
States, started at the turn of the twentieth century when the federal
government created national parks and started conserving forests and
wildlife. It was not until the 1960s, after two world wars, that a second wave of environmentalism occurred. During this wave and into the
1970s, Canada enacted most of its environmental legislation. The third
wave of environmentalism occurred in the late 1980s and early 1990s.
To analyze environmental policy in Canada, we must understand these
waves and the policies created within each era. Climate change is the
most significant challenge facing human beings in the twenty-first century.
Third-wave environmentalism was an international wake-up call to this
issue. However, unlike earlier issues such as deforestation or pollution,
climate change is far more complex. The policies that were created in the
third wave of environmentalism, such as the Kyoto Protocol, are inadequate. Canada will need a fourth wave of environmentalism to tackle

the problems of sustainable energy and climate change. This argument will not be taken up until Chapter 12.

Chapters 5 through 8 are centred on specific policy areas in Canada's environment. Each chapter explains what policy exists as well as who is responsible for implementation of said policy. Both the strengths and weaknesses of present policy are discussed, and the reader should be able to evaluate the effectiveness of governance in each case. Wildlife, particularly species at risk, is the focus of Chapter 5. Chapter 6 delves into pollution policy for air, water, and chemicals. Chapter 7 examines land policy for agricultural and forest lands as well as for cities. Chapter 8 is an introduction to energy policy in Canada, as well as a brief analysis of domestic climate change policy. Combined, these chapters critically examine some of the most important issues and policies in environmental policy today.

However, the book cannot and does not list or discuss every Canadian environmental policy in existence. There are far too many, as each province (and sometimes city) has created unique policy over the past 100 years. Instead, these chapters highlight the ways in which the federal and the provincial or territorial governments co-manage jurisdictional responsibilities by working with each other and with non-state actors such as private industry, citizens, municipal governments, and interest groups. In some countries, national environmental policy is the obvious focus, but, in Canada, provincial law provides the basis for environmental regulation and protection. Unfortunately, a comprehensive analysis of provincial environmental policy is extraordinarily difficult because each province not only operates or organizes itself differently from the others but also has a unique overall policymaking context in which environmental laws mix with other laws, such as those related to health, safety, and security. Moreover, the provinces vary on their level of commitment to implementing environmental protections and regulations. Consequently, chapters 5 through 8 will not present or discuss all existing environmental policy at the provincial level; rather, they will point to the processes of governance in these different issue areas as well as provide examples of how provinces are creating environmental laws and regulations.

Chapters 9 and 10 focus on Aboriginal policy as it relates to the environment. Chapter 9 is specifically about Aboriginal peoples and environmental policy and law, and Chapter 10 examines that policy in Canada's North, with a focus on Inuit governance and Aboriginal issues. Unlike in almost every other jurisdictional region discussed in this book, in the North, provincial authority, responsibility, and autonomy are limited. The Constitution gives clear federal jurisdiction over "Indians, and Lands reserved for Indians." Through time, that authority has evolved into a significant responsibility for environmental regulation and protection. Laws stemming from treaties and from the First Nations Land Management Act of 1999, as well as from the comprehensive land agreements in the North, include policies focused on the environmental protection of Aboriginal lands. Moreover, this area of environmental policy is defined not so much by Parliament or by bureaucratic regulation as by the Supreme Court of Canada. Since the 1970s, there have been almost a dozen legal cases with important ramifications for state-Aboriginal affairs. Almost all of these cases also affected environmental policy.

Canada is a northern nation. Roughly 40 per cent of the country's land mass lies in the North. Yet only about 1 per cent of the population lives there. Climate change, especially the series of warmer winters and longer summers recently experienced in the North, means not only melting ice caps but also new economic opportunities. Canada is prepared to exploit its northern natural resources—oil and gas, as well as industrial mining. As a sovereign nation, Canada can use its own land and resources in whatever way it sees fit. However, Canada is but one of eight countries with territory in the Arctic. Moreover, the Arctic Circle is a shared territory. The Canadian government and the international community acknowledge these facts. Through an intergovernmental organization called the Arctic Council, Canada governs environmental issues in the North collaboratively. This is the focus of Chapter 10, a focus that provides a fitting segue to the next chapter.

Chapter 11 is about international environmental policy and Canada's role in efforts to respond to global environmental problems. International institutions are introduced, as are specific policy areas, including those related to chemicals, biodiversity, and climate change. The United Nations is the primary focus because it leads many of the world's global efforts in the environmental arena. Other important institutions discussed include the World Bank and the Global Environment Facility. The effects of trade agreements on environmental policies are also examined. International norms dating to the UN Earth Summit in 1992, such as differentiated responsibility and the precautionary principle, are explored and linked to Canadian domestic policy. Finally, the chapter illustrates how policy is made and maintained globally by examining four international efforts: controlling ozone depletion, regulating harmful chemicals, preserving biodiversity, and reversing climate change through reducing greenhouse gas emissions. These efforts all respond to global environmental problems that require global action. Climate change is the most important problem facing the world, and it cannot be solved at the domestic level in any one or two countries. Overall, the chapter argues that, though Canada was once a global leader in environmental policy, in the past 10 years especially, the country has become a laggard. Canada's relations with the United Nations have diminished, and Canada has become a disappointment or, sometimes, a frustration to other countries at UN meetings.

The final chapter of the book looks forward into the twenty-first century and examines the future of environmental policy in the country. The final stage of the policy process, policy evaluation, is explained, allowing readers to reflect critically on the issues and policies discussed in the book. If Canada's policies are not working or are not being implemented, then how can changes be made? Different means and mechanisms of evaluating and amending policy are presented. The discussion then broadens to consider where environmental policy needs to be in the coming decades. Climate change and sustainable development are the primary focal points of this discussion. Whether a fourth wave of environmentalism will occur is considered. Can Canada overcome its apathy and begin to address serious environmental problems through a series of policy innovations and mixed policy approaches? That is a question for the citizens of Canada.

This book is not a comprehensive overview of every environmental policy or regulation that exists federally. Nor does it provide a laundry list of provincial policy and regulations. Canada has thousands upon thousands of laws that intersect with each other and affect the environment. Instead, this book discusses how environmental policy is made federally, provincially, and territorially. This discussion includes a detailed analysis of the different actors and institutions that are involved in the process. Many federal and provincial environmental policies are examined—sometimes at length and sometimes only briefly.[1]

Instead of explaining the different policies that exist and weighing the pros and cons of major legislation, this book pushes the reader to think critically about the drawbacks of present policies and policymaking processes and about the avenues for improvement. Federalism is full of twists and turns in Canada. You might find yourself thinking that the federal government should do more for water policy and less for forestry policy. Is that contradictory? Not necessarily, because the federal government interacts with different natural resources in different ways. For example, water moves across provincial and national borders whereas trees tend to stay in one place. Given these differences, one would not expect the federal government's relationship to natural resources and the environment to be consistent across issues or across provinces. Varying contexts, then, make it important for us to consider resources independently, as each chapter does, but also interdependently, as part of our national economy and our national heritage. The overall message of the book is that policy hurdles exist in creating and sustaining environmental regulation, but the problem is not federalism itself—instead, it is the interaction between federalism and economic regionalism.

Finally, this books serves as only an *introduction* to the varied policies and systems of governance for the environment in Canada. The point is to spark interest, generate debate, and provide the reader with the necessary background to begin a new avenue of research. There are hundreds, if not thousands, of books about specific Canadian environmental issues and policies in the Canadian context. As an introductory book aimed at students new to the field of Canadian environment policy, the book is designed to encourage further reflection and ways to master concepts and ideas. To that end, each chapter concludes with a list of suggested readings recommended for a more in-depth analysis. Each chapter also includes discussion questions and key terms to facilitate learning. As you read, the terms in bold are the key terms and concepts in the chapter. These terms, along with other important or complex concepts, can be found in the glossary at the end of the book.

COMPANION WEBSITE

You will find a companion website for this book at thecanadianenvironment .wordpress.com. The website includes updates on information in the book as well as a case studies, discussion of current issues and events, and debates in Canadian environmental policy. The political world sometimes moves quickly. New policies are made each year, and new guidelines are created and implemented often—even without public announcements or much fanfare. It is also likely that some of the policies discussed in the book have been amended or repealed. That is the policy process at work. And this ever-changing context of environmental policymaking is why a companion website is necessary.

Note

1 If you are interested in learning more about a specific environmental law, the Parliament of Canada website provides an online database of every single federal law passed since 1994. This database is called LEGISinfo and is free to the public. You can search by keyword to find any bill that exists. Once you find the bill, you will also get information about when it was passed and how (or when it failed). In fact, you can easily find out which committees in the House of Commons and Senate examined the bill and what amendments they proposed. This information includes the names of the parliamentarians who were involved with a bill's passage. Similar pages exist for provincial laws passed in legislative assemblies across the country.

Chapter 1

The Canadian Environment

CANADA WAS HOME to only about 35.5 million people in 2014, yet it is the second largest country in the world by landmass and the largest by coastline (Statistics Canada 2015b). Canada has fewer people than California even though California is smaller than Saskatchewan.[1] To show how thinly populated Canada is compared to its southern neighbour, we just need to know that there are more house cats in the United States than there are Canadians in the world.[2] Canada, then, is huge but sparsely and unevenly populated. Most Canadians (more than 85 per cent) live in one of Canada's four most populous provinces (Ontario, Québec, British Columbia, and Alberta), and, in 2014, about 35 per cent live in one of Canada's three largest census metropolitan areas: Toronto, Montréal, and Vancouver. More than two out of every three Canadians live close to the US border (Statistics Canada 2007), as though they are hugging the 49th parallel for warmth. This distribution pattern means that vast areas of the country are unpopulated.

Canadians often speak of their country as comprising five regions: the West (British Columbia, Alberta, Saskatchewan, and Manitoba), Ontario, Québec, the Atlantic provinces (New Brunswick, Nova Scotia, Prince Edward Island, and Newfoundland and Labrador), and the North (Yukon, Northwest Territories, and Nunavut). The four Western provinces have about 11 million people, Ontario's population is about 13.7 million, Québec's population is about 8.2 million, and the Atlantic provinces combined are only 2.7 million people (Statistics Canada 2014d). The remainder of the population lives in the three territories, comprising only about 117,000 people but almost 40 per cent of the country's land and freshwater area (Statistics Canada 2005).

Outside of the human element, the country has an absolute embarrassment of natural resources and beauty from coast to coast to coast. People from around the world travel to see Canada's splendour. The national and provincial parks of the Canadian Rockies are a large draw and have been declared World Heritage sites (UNESCO World Heritage Centre 2015). Millions of people flock to Niagara Falls every year to marvel at the breath-taking scenery. The Prairies offer a different type of beauty, as do the Arctic tundra and the rocky east coast of Newfoundland. In terms of wildlife, the most iconic Canadian animals include grizzly bears, polar bears, moose, beavers, and whales. But the country also has a wide array of other animals—upward of 70,000 species (Environment Canada 2014f). A country as big as Canada has much to offer in terms of ecosystem variation. Lastly, Canada has a huge coastline and touches three oceans: the Arctic, the Atlantic, and the Pacific.

In terms of natural *resources*, there is an uneven mix. British Columbia is known for forestry and hydroelectricity; Alberta for oil, coal, and some forestry. Also in the West, Saskatchewan contains vast stores of potash, uranium, natural gas, and some oil; and Manitoba has mining and some oil and forestry. Central Canada possesses hydroelectricity, minerals, and forestry resources, and the Atlantic provinces have the fisheries and some oil and minerals. The North has water, fisheries, oil, gas, and minerals such as diamonds and gold (Government of Canada 2012a). These natural resources first attracted Europeans to Canada (see MacDowell 2012). And Canada has been developing and exploiting these resources ever since it became an independent country.

The one environmental splendour and economic natural resource that is shared from the eastern to the western coast of Canada (although not by all of its northern coast) is the largest intact forest in the world: the boreal forest. A **boreal forest** includes a subarctic boreal region called a taiga, which begins where the tundra ends and has mostly spruce and fir trees. As a whole, the boreal forest is dominated by hardy trees that can withstand a cold climate, such as pines, larches, and spruces (La Roi 2015). However, the entire forest is not in the North, as you can see in Map 1.1. The forest extends far south into Canada and is mixed with wetlands and other types of ecosystems. Indeed, Canada's portion is so large that it makes up about 24 per cent of the circumpolar boreal forest that rings the Northern Hemisphere (all northern countries, such as Russia, Sweden, Norway, and Finland, have boreal forests; Natural Resources Canada 2014e, 16). Although the forest and other wooded lands in the boreal zone comprise almost one-third of Canada's landmass, only about

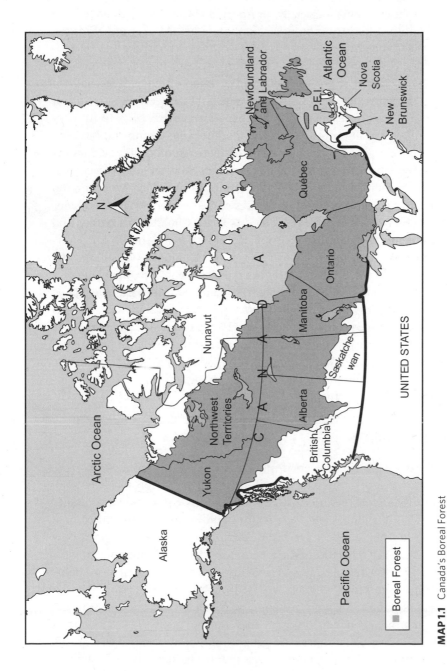

MAP 1.1 Canada's Boreal Forest

SOURCE: Boreal Songbird Initiative (2008). Reproduced by permission.

3.7 million Canadians live in the boreal zone (Natural Resources Canada 2014b). This forest is both an iconic Canadian symbol and a major backbone of the economy—especially for Aboriginal Canadians who rely upon it for hunting, forestry, ecotourism, and plant life (Marles and Northern Forestry Centre 2009).

Obviously, talking about *the* environment in Canada is very difficult because Canada is such a big place and contains so many different environments. This chapter sets out to provide a basic overview of different environmental issues across the country, from air quality to forestry health. But it is important to bear in mind that environmental quality varies from region to region and is affected by several factors, ranging from population density to climate change to political activity.

From a political standpoint, it is important to always keep in mind that Canada is divided into 10 provinces and 3 territories. Those divisions create real boundaries and jurisdictions when Canada's politicians and civil servants make decisions or policy about the environment. Canada also borders the United States by land and Denmark (Greenland) by water. The distance across the Nares Strait, which separates Nunavut from Greenland, is only 25 kilometres. Canada also shares the Pacific coastline with the United States and Mexico. Indeed this coast, with its numerous marine species, extends from Alaska to Mexico and into South America. Thus, Canada shares the continent and its natural resources with other countries. And international boundaries and jurisdictions, too, greatly affect environmental governance. Issues of international policy will be discussed in Chapter 11.

ENVIRONMENTAL QUALITY AND INDICATORS

Numerous aspects of the environment can be measured using **environmental indicators**. This chapter will focus on air, water, and ecosystem quality. Many of the indicators used to assess environmental quality and policy will be explored in greater detail in subsequent chapters of the book. This section serves as an introduction, an overview of how well Canada is managing in these common areas of environmental well-being. In 2008, the federal government passed the **Federal Sustainable Development Act** in which it mapped out sustainable growth across Canada's economy. For the purposes of that act, the government tracks nine environmental indictors and issues annual reports. Those indicators include assessments of greenhouse gas emissions, a weather warning index, and various air quality indicators; measurements of freshwater quality in rivers, of water quantity in rivers, and of the environmental quality of the Great Lakes; an appraisal of the number and extent of

Canada's protected areas; and measurements of the ecological integrity of national parks and of major fish stocks. You can find assessment reports for each of these indicators on Environment Canada's website—and most of the data in the following sections are drawn from those reports. Although these indicators are useful and important measures of environmental health, they are very narrow and tend to gloss over some larger issues while completely ignoring other ones, such as the state of Canada's forests and biodiversity. Thus, this section integrates the federal sustainable development indicators into a larger framework to provide a broader assessment of how well Canada is doing at managing the environment.

Air Quality

Air quality is measured by testing the levels of major pollutants in the air: nitrogen dioxide, sulphur dioxide, carbon monoxide, ozone, and particulate matter. These pollutants come mainly from vehicle emissions and industrial sources both inside Canada and outside, particularly from its neighbour to the south. The air quality in Canada is, on average, very good. In 2001, the World Health Organization ranked Canada third in an air quality index (after Estonia and Mauritius). However, quality varies by location. Whitehorse has the best air quality whereas Sarnia, followed closely by Toronto and Montréal, has the worst. Environment Canada provides an online Air Quality Health Index, a scale from 1 (low risk) to 10 (high risk), which allows anyone to find the air quality for most communities. Try it yourself at www.ec.gc.ca/cas-aqhi/.

Indoor air pollution is also a major concern for public health and the environment. Canadians now spend close to 90 per cent of their time inside (Health Canada 2015). Indoor pollutants fall into two categories: biological (e.g., mould, bacteria, and dust mites) and chemical (e.g., gases and particles). The government can and does regulate toxic chemicals linked to air pollution, such as ozone, but natural sources of pollution, such as radon (caused by uranium breakdown in the ground), are not regulated. To learn more about indoor air pollution in your home or workplace, look at Health Canada's website (http://www.hc-sc.gc.ca/ewh-semt/air/in/index-eng.php).

Is air pollution getting better or worse in Canada? It depends on where you live and what you measure. For example, in the United States carbon dioxide (CO_2) is considered a "dangerous pollutant" by the Environmental Protection Agency (EPA) and can be regulated by the federal government.[3] In Canada, CO_2 has not been listed as a toxic chemical, and it does not fall under federal chemical regulations. That said, the Canadian federal government can bring in CO_2 regulations—and has already done so through the new measure to limit CO_2 emissions from coal-fired power plants (see Chapter 8). This authority could conceivably be challenged in court, but that has not stopped federal regulation (albeit limited) action.

If you measure CO_2 levels in Canada, as illustrated below, you would see that air pollution is getting worse. However, if you measure other types of air pollution, such as ozone, you would see that things are getting better. As mentioned, air quality is pretty good across the country, with pockets of smog and pollution in large cities such as Toronto. **Sulphur dioxide** (SO_2) has been a problem for air quality in Canada. SO_2 is gas emitted when fuel containing sulphur is burned or used in an industrial process, such as electricity generation, or in the oil and gas industry. Per capita, Canada's SO_2 emissions are roughly 17 times those of Switzerland (Conference Board of Canada 2013c). However, SO_2 emissions have been declining steadily in Canada over the past two decades. Similarly, volatile organic compounds (VOCs) are declining, but Canada is not acting as quickly as other developed countries to reduce VOC emissions. VOCs are produced by vehicle emissions and chemical manufacturing. They combine with nitrogen oxides to produce smog and are a source of air pollution in large cities.

Like most areas of environmental concern, air pollution falls within the legal jurisdiction of both the federal and provincial governments. The federal **Canadian Environmental Protection Act (CEPA)** regulates toxic chemicals that cause air pollution, such as ozone and sulphur dioxide. But the provincial governments can also regulate air pollution as well as the industries that cause pollution (see McKitrick 2006 for a list of federal and provincial legislation for air quality). For example, in British Columbia, the provincial Environmental Management Act regulates contaminants that cause pollution in the air. The city of Vancouver also regulates and manages air quality—with delegated authority from the province. So, as you can see, air pollution is a shared concerned and a shared policy area in Canada, which is common because of Canada's federalism and the multiple levels of government this system encourages. Chapter 6 will discuss air pollution in Canada in more depth.

Climate change, another area of shared governance, is related to air pollution. Both involve greenhouse gases, which occur naturally but are also being added to the atmosphere through human activities such as driving a car or raising cattle. Carbon dioxide is the primary greenhouse gas that human action emits, and it is one air pollutant that is unquestionably on the rise in Canada. Figure 1.1 shows the amount of CO_2 in the atmosphere as measured in Alert, Nunavut, by Environment Canada. There is a seasonal decline in late May to early June due to the transport of air from southern latitudes that is depleted in CO_2 from photosynthetic uptake

FIGURE 1.1 CO_2 Emissions as Measured in Alert, Nunavut, 1975–2010

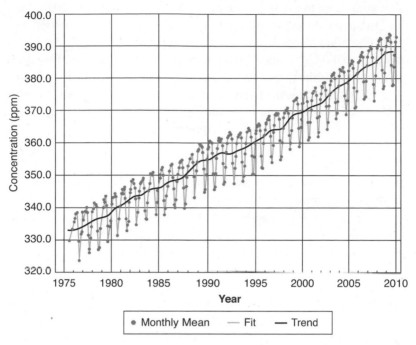

SOURCE: Environment Canada (2011). Reprinted with permission.

(Environment Canada 2011). The annual averaged CO_2 value at Alert in 1975 was about 333 ppm. Annual average CO_2 values were 384.12 and 386.9 ppm in 2007 and 2008 respectively. The annual change in CO_2 has increased from an average value of 1.35 ppm per year in the 1990s to nearly 2 ppm per year in the 2000s (Environment Canada 2011). This increase is due primarily to global increases in these emissions brought on by the burning of fossil fuels. And this trend is expected to increase unless dramatic action is undertaken in Canada and other parts of the world.

Other greenhouse gases include methane, nitrous oxide, and ozone. Collectively they are referred to as GHGs. The provinces have the authority to regulate some of the activities that produce these gases but only when these activities occur inside their own borders; the federal government also shares that authority. The CEPA could, but presently does not, include CO_2 as a toxic substance. If it did, Ottawa could regulate it under that law as opposed to discretionary policy created at the bureaucratic level (as it did through legislation limiting CO_2 emissions from coal-fired power plants). The federal government does, however, create national standards for car emissions through the CEPA. Under the On-Road Vehicle and Engine Emissions Regulations, added to the CEPA and updated in 2004, the federal government set emissions standards that align with those in the United States (Environment Canada 2013g). As this brief overview shows, however, setting and implementing national or international standards is complicated given Canada's federal system and constitutional division of powers. For example, although only the federal government has the power to sign international treaties, such as United Nations' climate agreements, to implement the treaties the government needs permission from the provinces. The issues of climate change and GHG emissions are discussed in chapters 8 and 11.

Water Quality

Similar to air quality, water quality is measured by testing the levels of pollutants—chemical, physical, and biological—in water. Water quality is assessed at the **watershed** level. In Canada, there are five main ocean watersheds: the Arctic, the Atlantic (including the Great Lakes), Hudson Bay, the Pacific, and the Gulf of Mexico (southern Prairies). Each of these massive land areas drains a network of lakes, rivers, and groundwater aquifers that channel water to an ocean. These large watersheds can be further divided into smaller sub- and sub-sub-watersheds that are referred to as drainage areas. To examine water quality across Canada or in your area, go to Environment Canada's website (http://www.ec.gc.ca/eau-water/).

What causes water pollution? Traditionally pollutants are divided into **point-source pollution** and **non-point-source pollution** (see EPA 2012b). In the first category are pollutants for which we know the exact source and point at which they enter the water. They could have been discharged from pipes, boats, or animal feed operations, for example. Non-point-source pollutants are chemicals that enter the water from either unknown sources or unknown points. They could be the result of fertilizer run-off, soil pollution, or chemicals leaching into soil or water (EPA 2012b). It is difficult to regulate non-point-source pollution because it can come from so many sources, or we might not know exactly how these pollutants get into the water.

Water guidelines are determined scientifically and only on the basis of intended use—meaning that there are different guidelines for a lake used for swimming and recreation than one used for livestock watering. Nationally, water pollution is not a pressing concern, but Canadians are dumping waste (human, animal, and chemical) into the environment quickly and at high volumes, so there is concern that the largest lakes and rivers, including the Great Lakes, will struggle to restore themselves. Environment Canada assesses national freshwater in rivers through 172 water quality stations set up across the country. Figure 1.2 illustrates that, in the 80 stations measured between 2009 and 2011, water quality was either mainly fair or good, with few stations reporting either poor

FIGURE 1.2 National Freshwater Quality Indicator, Canada, 2010–2012

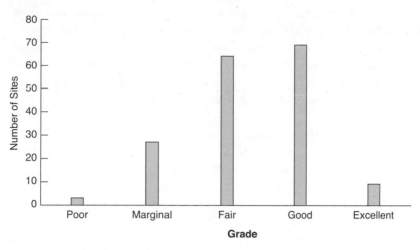

SOURCE: Environment Canada (2014d). Reprinted with permission.

FIGURE 1.3 Freshwater Quality by Land Use Category, Canada, 2010–2012

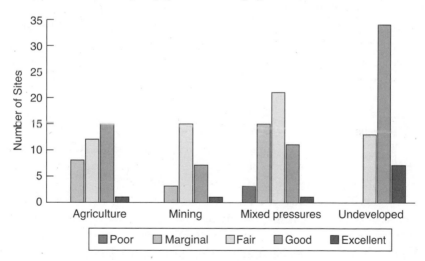

SOURCE: Environment Canada (2014h). Reprinted with permission.

or excellent water quality (Environment Canada 2014d). A poor rating
means that water pollution usually exceeds the national guideline by a
considerable margin, whereas excellent means water pollution almost
never exceeds national guidelines (Environment Canada 2014e).

Environment Canada also measures water quality in rivers as it relates
to geographical location and proximity to land use. Figure 1.3 illustrates
that water stations close to agriculture or mining had significantly more

results with a poor or marginal ranking for water quality. Rivers running through remote areas of the country are the cleanest while those in mixed areas (urban, suburban, and multi-land use) have a wider range of water quality (Environment Canada 2014h). In this introduction, the impact of urbanization and industrialization on environmental indicators will be discussed. However, in Chapter 6, where water pollution is a main topic, water quality in groundwater and lakes will be included (as here we are looking only at rivers).

Hypertrophication is threatening water quality in Canadians lakes and rivers (FPT Governments of Canada 2010). **Hypertrophication,** sometimes called eutrophication, happens when natural and human-generated pollutants and chemicals, such as nitrates, fertilizers, and sewage, enter water ecosystems. A body of water may respond by generating bloom or phytoplankton (algae) in the water. The environmental concern is hypoxia, or the depletion of oxygen in water, because that will have negative effects on aquatic species and human beings (Van Dolah 2000). Nutrient loading—the term used to describe these substances entering into bodies of water—is on the rise in Canada in over 20 per cent of the water bodies sampled by Environment Canada (FPT, Governments of Canada 2010; see also Hall et al. 1999). Nutrient loading is a major concern in the Great Lakes and Lake Winnipeg (Fuller, Shear, and Wittig 1995; Lake Winnipeg Stewardship Board 2006). In the case of the Great Lakes, Canada manages this problem collaboratively with the United States because the lakes and the sources of pollution are shared. Administration is co-regulated through the Great Lakes Water Quality Agreement, which was first signed with the United States in 1972 (amendments were made as recently as 2012).

The management of Canada's water quality is complicated and is an exemplary case of **multilevel governance**. All levels of government as well as organizations, citizens, and other countries, share responsibility for water. The provinces are considered owners of this natural resource, but the federal government is involved in regulating bodies of water that cross jurisdictions and international borders as well as the water that extends off the coastline over the continental shelf. Outside of Aboriginal communities, where water security remains a significant concern, Canada has had two major water quality public health scares in recent history—one in Walkerton, Ontario, in 2000 and one in North Battleford, Saskatchewan, in 2001 (see Chapter 6). Although overall water quality, especially of drinking water, is good across Canada, major problems are still to be resolved. One of particular importance and growing concern is safe drinking water on First Nation reserves (Duncan and Bowden 2009). This issue creates jurisdictional conflict because Aboriginal affairs are a federal responsibility whereas water supply is a provincial responsibility. Water quality as it relates to pollution will be examined carefully in Chapter 6.

Agriculture and Land

Canada grows a lot of food. In fact, Canada is the fourth largest exporter of agricultural and agri-food products in the world, and this industry is valued at $28 billion annually (Farm Credit Canada 2014). Canada's main grain crops are barley, corn, oats, rye, and, of course, wheat. Canadian oilseed production is concentrated in canola, soybean, and flaxseed. The ability to grow so much food is related not only to the sheer size of the country but also to its climate, water availability, and soil quality. Agricultural policy arises from the need to adequately manage and protect land as well as the need to ensure quality and safety in the form of environmentally sustainable products.

We use a lot of land for farming in Canada. Total farm area reported in the 2011 Census of Agriculture accounted for 7.2 per cent of the total land in Canada (Statistics Canada 2015a). As a percentage of the total land in each province, total farm area ranged from 0.1 per cent in Newfoundland and Labrador to just over 42 per cent in Prince Edward Island and Saskatchewan (see Figure 1.4). Cropland is the greatest component of agricultural land, comprising almost 55 per cent of the total farm area reported; pasture comprises just over 30 per cent (Statistics Canada 2015a). With so much land devoted to agriculture and because of agriculture's significance to the Canadian economy, Canada must maintain the ability to grow and raise food.

FIGURE 1.4 Percentage of Land Used for Agriculture, by Province and Total, 2011

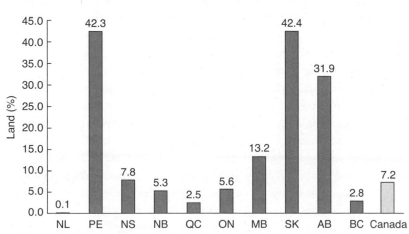

SOURCE: Statistics Canada (2015a, Figure 6)

Crop production requires healthy and nutrient-rich soil as well as hardy and biologically sound plants and seeds. Modern farming techniques are possible threats to both. The Green Revolution, following World War II, dramatically changed the way farmers grew food by introducing chemicals (pesticides, herbicides, and fertilizers) and biotechnology such as genetically modified crops and animals (see MacDowell 2012; Environment Canada 2014i). Most Canadian farms are large industrial operations that produce immense amounts of quality food for Canadians and many other countries in the world. Soil quality is a concern because of gaps in information regarding the impact of chemicals on soil and water systems (see Blanco-Canqui and Lal 2010). Soil can easily be contaminated by chemical build-up and the subsequent reduction in organic matter. At the national level, soil quality has been steadily improving in part because of the adoption of reduced-till or no-till farming practices through which farmers can grow food without disturbing the soil by removing weeds or creating furrows for irrigation (Environment Canada 2014i).

Soil and water quality, independently and in relation to each other, will be significantly challenged by climate change (see Blanco-Canqui and Lal 2010). Extreme weather events, such as droughts and flooding, will impact water runoff and the movement of water through soil. Consequently, it will be become harder for Canada to maintain the quality of soil needed to produce large quantities of food. Intensifying this problem is the possibility that farmers will respond by increasing the amount of fertilizer used in production to encourage growth and keep up with demand. More research is needed to understand the potential impacts of climate change on soil and the potential for hardier, climate-resistant crops (see Warren 2004).

Though agriculture relies on natural resources (e.g., soil, water, and clean air) and is an environmental product, it is also possible to see agriculture as a source of pollution that affects environmental quality (Conway and Pretty 2013). Since at least the 1940s, agriculture has become an industrial project. It requires large machinery, many chemicals, lots of water, and plenty of land. Thus, it impacts air and water quality as well as biodiversity. Farming competes for land. Sometimes the competition is with another industry, such as oil and gas, and sometimes agricultural land use competes with urbanization, as cities tend to sprawl out into rural areas. Similarly, farms compete with woodlands, wetlands, and native grasslands for space. Native grasslands, for example, are declining across the Prairies and may soon become extinct (Findlay 2010). Wildlife can survive on farmland in many instances, but the increase in machinery and chemicals is a threat to biodiversity because many species cannot coexist with intensive agriculture.

Policy related to agriculture includes federal legislation, such as the Canada Wheat Board Act and the Grain Act, as well as provincial laws, such as the Greenbelt Act and the Local Food Act in Ontario. Growing Forward 2 (GF2) is a recently launched policy framework (April 2013) that brings together multiple levels of governance for Canada's agricultural and agri-food sector. GF2 includes a $3-billion investment by federal, provincial, and territorial governments and is now the foundation for government agricultural programs and services over 2013–18 (see Government of Canada 2014b). Included in these programs is a focus on the environmental dimensions and impacts of agricultural. GF2 and agricultural policy will be discussed in Chapter 7, which tackles land use policy in Canada more broadly.

Fish and Fisheries

Canada has an abundance of water, so the country is well known for its marine life, especially wild fish such as salmon and cod. Unfortunately, Canada's fish are an overtapped resource and are not faring very well. Environment Canada measures the health of fish stocks by breaking them down into categories: marine mammals, groundfish, small and large pelagics (surface fish), salmon, crustaceans, and molluscs (Environment Canada 2015f). The quality of these stocks varies by type, as you can see in Figure 1.5. Most alarming is that over 28 per cent of the groundfish

FIGURE 1.5 Status of Major Fish Stocks, by Stock Group, Canada, 2013

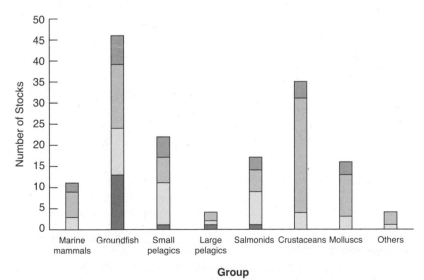

SOURCE: Environment Canada (2015f). Reprinted with permission.

stock is in the "critical zone," meaning that its stock level is below the point at which productivity is impaired but above that at which risk of extinction is a concern. A "healthy zone" indicates that spawning biomass is above the upper stock reference point as determined by the Department of Fisheries (Environment Canada 2015f).

The provinces of Atlantic Canada have been dependent on fish as a staple economic resource and have been greatly affected by fish management in Canada. The most famous example comes from 1992, when the federal government put a moratorium on fishing for northern cod, which had been central to the lives of Maritimers since North America was founded. The closure of the cod industry was the largest industrial closure in the country's history and put 35,000 Newfoundlanders out of work (see Harris 1998). The ramifications of this moratorium are still being felt today as the province struggles to stabilize its economy. Similarly, the northern cod stock struggles to recover and might never be a viable economic resource in the future. The northern cod crisis could be considered Canada's greatest environmental failure to date.

Freshwater fish are actually at a high risk of extinction globally. In Canada, about 10 per cent of freshwater fish stocks are either endangered or threatened with extinction in their natural range (Environment Canada 2015f). This number has been steadily increasing since the 1980s, and the causes are wide ranging: pollution, overfishing, habitat loss or degradation and fragmentation, invasive species, and climate change. The salt-water ecosystems are not faring much better—for many of the same reasons. And both fresh- and salt-water fish are increasingly contaminated with chemicals such as mercury (see Lourie and Smith 2013; Smith and Lourie 2009).

This situation presents environmentalists with two reasons to avoid fish completely: consuming fish endangers wild stocks and carries human health risks. However, not all fish are endangered and not all fish are a health risk. The trouble is in deciding which fish are safe to eat and when.

Managing fisheries is a challenge because the reasons for declining fish stocks include loss of habitat for spawning and rearing fish; changing food webs; shifts to warmer, less salty seawater (a result of natural climate oscillations and, possibly, climate change); and ocean acidification. That said, some stressors have been reduced successfully. Concentrations of contaminants now phased out of use, such as DDT and PCBs, are declining in wildlife and fish. In the past 15 years, federal, provincial, and territorial terrestrial protected areas have increased in number, area, and diversity of ecosystems represented (Environment Canada 2014c).

Fisheries are mainly the responsibility of the federal government through the Department of Ocean and Fisheries. Specific policy related to fish and fisheries will not be discussed as a stand-alone chapter in the book. Instead, biodiversity and wildlife management policy and water policy (chapters 5 and 6) as well as policies affecting Aboriginal peoples and the North (chapters 9 and 10) will intersect with the politics of fisheries in Canada. This approach is useful because the rationale for fisheries policy and for the overall management of aquatic species is largely driven by general environmental indicators, most notably biodiversity. Fisheries are discussed as an independent environmental indicator here so as to draw attention to this important environmental and economic natural resource before weaving it into other areas of policy in later chapters.

Forests

As noted, the boreal forest, stretching from the Yukon to Newfoundland and from the Arctic tree ring to the southern border, is the largest intact forest on earth—almost 3 million square kilometres are untouched by humans or human development (see Table 4.2 of Canada's National Forest Inventory at https://nfi.nfis.org/). When you think Canada, you should think forests. Nationally, forest health has changed little in the past few decades, but regionally there is great variation. Only 0.01 to 0.02 per cent of Canada's forest is lost annually to other types of land cover, and, even though old forests have shifted to young forests in some areas, old forests still make up 40 per cent of both Newfoundland and Labrador's boreal forest and British Columbia's coastal rainforest (FPT Governments of Canada 2010). That said, ecosystems near northern and mountain tree lines are changing because the climate is getting warmer. For example, trees are expanding northward along the Labrador coast, and tree growth and density are increasing near tree lines in the Yukon and northern Québec (FPT, Governments of Canada 2010).

How has Canada managed to maintain this precious environmental and economic resource? Despite having extensive forestry harvests, Canada has maintained its forests in large part because of environmental activists who have pushed successfully for provincial licensing systems and encouraged industry to ensure good practices through forest certification, as discussed in Chapter 7 (see Conference Board of Canada 2015a). Almost all of the forest land is **Crown land**—owned by the provinces (about 70 per cent) or the federal government. Management of this resources dates back to the founding of Canada and particularly to the turn of the twentieth century when the United States realized the importance of conservation and urged Canadian foresters to manage their resource better than the Americans had done in the eighteenth and nineteenth centuries (see MacDowell 2012; Dorsey 1998).

Even though Canadian forests are well managed, climate change, increasing international trade, and human activities have made forests vulnerable to threats by both native and alien organisms, including insects, fungi, and invasive plants (noxious weeds). According to the International Union for Conservation of Nature (IUCN), invasive alien species are the second most significant threat to biodiversity after habitat loss. In Canada, the genetic diversity of at least a dozen highly valuable hardwood species is under threat from invasive species damage (Aukema et al. 2009). Combined with the potentially harmful effects of climate change and increased global consumption of renewable resources, native and alien pests threaten the sustainability of forests in many parts of the country (Aukema et al. 2009). Forest health is an issue of major policy concern in the twenty-first century.

Forestry policy will be examined in Chapter 7 as it relates to land use policy in Canada. However, forest health will also be considered in Chapter 5 because habitat preservation and wildlife health are intertwined with forest preservation all across the country. The ability of the forestry sector to protect wildlife is controversial in places such as Ontario and British Columbia. The way forests intersect with, or compete with, urban sprawl and agricultural land use is part of the larger context of biodiversity management. As discussed in Chapter 5, the Ontario Endangered Species Act is supposed to protect Ontario's most vulnerable species, but the law exempts forestry from the main habitat protection provisions (Environmental Commissioner of Ontario 2009, 38–42). The tension between a resource industry, such as forestry, and an environmental goal, such as habitat protection, gets at the very essence of environmental policy in Canada.

Biodiversity and Species at Risk

In 2010 the federal government assessed biodiversity across the country with a focus on ecosystems as opposed to individual species. The report is called *Canadian Biodiversity: Ecosystem Status and Trends 2010*. There is both good and bad news. On the positive side, "much of Canada's natural endowment remains healthy, including large tracts of undisturbed wilderness, internationally significant wetlands, and thriving estuaries, particularly in sparsely populated or less accessible areas" (FPT, Governments of Canada 2010, 9). On the negative side, there has been a "loss of old forests, changes in river flows at critical times of the year, loss of wildlife habitat in agricultural landscapes, declines in certain bird populations, increases in wildfire, and significant shifts in marine, freshwater, and terrestrial food webs" (FPT, Governments of Canada 2010, 10). The ecosystems under the most stress in Canada, and, arguably, the ones for which new or amended policy is critical include those systems that support fish populations, prairie grassland birds, and forest-dwelling caribou.

Canada has a national committee in place to assess wildlife and determine which categories of species are at risk of extinction. The committee, known as the Committee on the Status of Endangered Wildlife in Canada (COSEWIC), comprises scientists and uses the best available science to determine the status of a species (Olive 2014b). All taxonomic groups are included—for example, mammals, plants, reptiles, fish, molluscs, birds, amphibians, and arthropods. COSEWIC assesses wildlife health and categorizes each species as one of the following: extinct, extirpated (no longer exists in the wild in Canada), endangered (facing imminent extirpation or extinction), threatened, special concern, data deficient (insufficient data to assess a species), or not at risk. See Table 1.1 for examples of Canadian species in each category. As of March 2015, COSEWIC has determined 312 species to be endangered across Canada (COSEWIC 2015). COSEWIC does not assess every single species that exists in Canada, so many more species would likely be added to the endangered category if they were assessed. Most endangered and threated species live in British Columbia or Ontario, which are the most biologically diverse places in Canada (Klinkenberg 2012). The reasons for endangerment are related to habitat loss or destruction,

TABLE 1.1 Examples of Canadian Species in Designated COSEWIC At-Risk Categories

COSEWIC STATUS	EXAMPLES OF SPECIES IN THIS CATEGORY
Extinct	Passenger Pigeon, Labrador Duck, Great Auk, Sea Mink
Extirpated	American Burying Beetle, Pacific Pond Turtle, Greater Prairie-Chicken, Oregon Lupine
Endangered	Atlantic Cod (except in the Arctic), Bashful Bulrush, Dakota Skipper, Eastern Foxsnake
Threatened	Olive-sided Flycatcher, Soapweed, Western Rattlesnake, Caribou (boreal population)
Special Concern	Atlantic Cod (Arctic Lakes), Baird's Sparrow, Buffalograss, Grass Pickerel, Polar Bear
Data Deficient	Atlantic Cod (Arctic Marine), Redbreast Sunfish, Fringed Bat, Black Buffalo, Bering Wolffish
Not at Risk	American Black Bear, False Mermaid, Northern Harrier, Redfin Pickerel

SOURCE: Data from the COSEWIC Database of Wildlife Species, http://www.cosewic.gc.ca/eng/sct1/searchform_e.cfm.

urbanization, industrialization, invasive species, and climate change (Venter et al. 2006).

In 2002 Canada passed national legislation, the Species at Risk Act, to protect and recover species at risk of extinction. However, the federal government has very limited jurisdiction in this area and can protect only migratory birds, aquatic species, and species found on federal lands (e.g., national parks, post office sites, or Aboriginal reserves). All other types of land and the species inhabiting it fall under the jurisdiction of provinces. As Chapter 5 will explain, the provinces offer a patchwork of protection as only 6 of the 10 provinces and 2 of the territories have legislation in place specifically to monitor and protect endangered species (Olive 2014a). The federal government has been steadily increasing the amount of protected land in Canada, but newly protected land tends to be in the North where the federal government has jurisdiction and conflicts over land use are less likely. Across the provinces, British Columbia has the most protected land but surprisingly lacks an endangered species policy (Olive 2014a).

FACTORS AFFECTING ENVIRONMENTAL QUALITY

It is difficult to pinpoint any one or two reasons why Canada's environmental performance on any of the quality indicators discussed previously might be weak. It is easy to target industry and attempt to blame our resource-based economy for pollution and environmental degradation. It is true that resource extraction and processing industries often use a lot of water and contribute to greater stresses on local environmental quality. The Alberta oil sands, discussed in Chapter 8, are a good example. However, other factors such as Canada's vastness make a difference because sizeable amounts of energy are required to transport people and to move goods to where they will be consumed, leading to high GHG emissions. Thus, one can argue that geography and industrial structure are hurdles to overcome—through technology, innovation, efficiency, and behavioural changes—in order to improve Canada's environmental performance (Conference Board of Canada 2015a, 2015b). But other explanations for Canada's poor environmental track record also warrant attention: urbanization, population growth, and affluence. Each of these will be discussed briefly here and raised again throughout the book.

Urbanization
You may not think of urbanization as an *environmental* issue, but urbanization has a significant impact on environmental quality. And

FIGURE 1.6 Percentage of Canadians Living in Urban Areas, 1871–2011

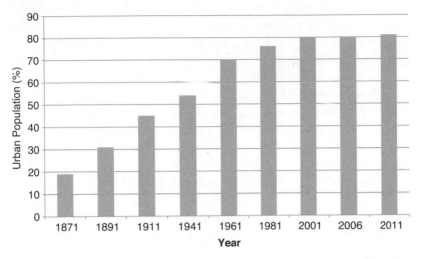

SOURCE: Data from Statistics Canada (2011a), Summary Table *Population, Urban and Rural, by Province and Territory (Canada).*

urbanization is becoming an increasing issue and environmental threat in Canada and across the world (United Nations 2004; National Research Council 2003; Wolman 1993). As Figure 1.6 illustrates, Canadians are moving from rural areas of the country into metropolitan areas. As of 2011, 81 per cent of Canadians live in a city. The environmental and public health concerns associated with urbanization involve not only people moving into a city but people moving very close to a city and creating urban sprawl. Urban sprawl is distinguished by low-density population, segregated land use, and an increase in automobile use (Fischler 2004). People move out of small apartments without parking spaces in the city into larger houses with two-car garages in the suburbs. The result is habitat destruction and fragmentation when open spaces or natural areas are turned into suburban communities, an increase in air pollution because of commuting and other human activities, the loss of agricultural land, and an increase in water use. And with so many people driving into the city for jobs, smog becomes a problem. According to Statistics Canada, the average commuting time was the longest (30 minutes or more) in the six largest census metropolitan areas of Canada (areas with at least 1 million residents): Toronto, Montréal, Vancouver, Ottawa-Gatineau, Calgary, and Edmonton (see Turcotte 2011). From a public health perspective, a lack of exercise and an increase in loneliness are also linked to urban sprawl (Fischler 2004).

Population and Immigration

Canada's population is increasing, and it continues to grow each year. In fact, immigration is the main driver of urbanization. In 1971, the country had over 21.9 million people while in 2012 that number jumped to almost 34.8 million (Statistics Canada 2014d). However, population growth is uneven across the country with some jurisdictions, such as Prince Edward Island and the Northwest Territories, growing very slowly, if at all, compared to Ontario and Alberta, which are growing very quickly. As Figure 1.7 illustrates, population growth between 1993 and 2013 was greatest in Alberta and Ontario, with most of Ontario's increase occurring in the greater Toronto area, thereby linking population growth to urbanization and urban sprawl (Employment and Social Development Canada 2015).

Population growth in the country is a result of immigration. Canada's immigration rate is twice that of the United States and one of the highest amongst all industrialized nations (Statistics Canada 2011b, 2014c). On average, Canada receives 249,000 immigrants each year (Green 2012), and this number is likely to increase as climate change and economic pressures encourage families in the Global South and Middle East to leave their homelands in search of new opportunities. Right now, Canada's immigrants come from all over the world, but particularly from Asian countries.

How is the environment affected by immigration? Recent immigrants tend to participate in politics at a lower rate than non-immigrants (see

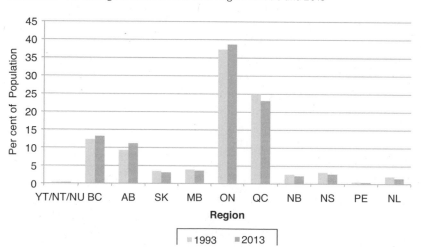

FIGURE 1.7 Percentage of Canadians in Each Region in 1993 and 2013

SOURCE: Based on Statistics Canada (2015b) *CANSIM Table 051-0005: Estimates of Population, Canada, Provinces and Territories.*

Elections Canada 2014). This can affect voter turnout and, thus, the types of policies that are created and implemented. Moreover, immigrants may bring to Canada attitudes about the environment that are not reflective of Canadian values (see Lovelock et al. 2013). Immigrants might take a few years to learn about Canadian laws and norms. They might also take a long time to become educated about Canadian wildlife and the environment at large. For example, recycling is a learned practice and value.

However, immigration does not necessarily have a negative impact on the environment. Indeed, the environment is one reason immigrants are attracted to Canada. And, as new citizens, immigrants have a vested interest in keeping Canada clean, healthy, and vibrant. The point is that an increasing population in Canada will put increasing pressure on ecosystems and give rise to urbanization and its related environmental threats. A growing Canadian economy cannot function without new immigrants, but environmental challenges are presented by this economic opportunity.

Affluence

Canada is getting richer. And, on average, Canadians are getting richer. Figure 1.8 illustrates that, in the six-year period between 1999 and 2005, the net worth of Canadian families increased from a median of $120,451 to $148,350 (Statistics Canada 2006). Why do environmentalists and public policymakers care about rising **affluence**? Affluence matters because rich people use more resources and cause more GHG emissions and pollution overall (Brown 2009).

At the end of the eighteenth century, British scholar Thomas Robert Malthus (1766–1834) hypothesized that population growth will always expand to the limit of subsistence. In other words, he thought that population growth would always tend to outrun increases in food production and would be repressed by "misery" (e.g., famine or plague) and "vice" (e.g., war and, for Malthus, contraception). The population crisis, or **Malthusian catastrophe**, a forced return to subsistence-level conditions, has been overshadowed by 150 years of rising living standards for a growing population. We have not been able to feed all our people, but our population has not continued to grow geometrically, as Malthus predicted. Canadian fertility rates have levelled off, new technologies and processes have increased food production, and we have witnessed a rise in affluence, at least in some parts of the world. Yes, there are more Canadians, but they also have more food and more money.

Population will always be important for environmental policy and as an environmental stressor. This issue has garnered a lot of international attention as it intersects with issues of poverty and public health. A high rate of population growth, such as that experienced by some African

FIGURE 1.8 Proxy Measure of Affluence in Canada: Measure of Median Net Worth of Canadian Families

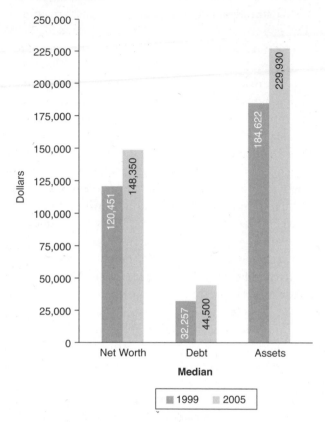

SOURCE: Statistics Canada (2006)

countries as well as India and other Asian countries, requires additional food and water, shelter, and energy. More people will also need more space and will encroach on land that sustains other types of biodiversity. And poor countries have a difficult time regulating activities that could cause irreparable harm to the environment, such as the slash-and-burn farming practiced in some countries where subsistence living justifies environmental damage (see Alam 2010; Myers and Kent 1995).

The critical thing to understand is that population does not matter as much as you might imagine—it is how much each individual consumes that is most important. For example, current agricultural practices worldwide could produce enough grain to feed about 2.5 billion people if we all ate like Canadians and Americans. But that grain could feed 10 billion or more individuals on a subsistence diet, a diet that includes only what is necessary for survival (Brown 2009). The average Canadian consumes more than an average Nigerian. The more money you have, the more ability you have to consume and pollute—fossil fuels, plastics, meat, and cell phones, for example. Richer people have larger ecological footprints. The richest 25 per cent of the world's population account for 90 per cent of the world's hazardous waste and 65 per cent of it green-house gases. A United Nations study found that one American child will consume and pollute more in his or her lifetime than 30 children born in a developing nation (Campbell, MacKinnon, and Stevens 2010). Thus, just because Canada has so few people does not mean it is a non-polluting, environmentally friendly country. Environmental impact is relative to a county's affluence.

If anything, being affluent has made Canada a throwaway society. We produce more waste than our population warrants. In 2008, Canada generated 777 kilograms of municipal waste per capita, well above the 17-country average of 578 kilograms per capita (Conference Board of Canada 2013b). Compared with Japan, Canada generated more than double the municipal waste per capita. Of the nearly 34 million tons of municipal solid waste generated in Canada in 2008, almost 26 million went to landfills or incinerators (Statistics Canada 2012). The rest was diverted through recycling or composting. Landfilling is the most common way to dispose of waste in Canada. But landfills emit methane (a GHG that contributes to climate change), and the leachate from landfills causes groundwater and surface-water contamination. Therefore, reducing the damage to the environment caused by municipal waste generation in Canada requires minimizing waste, increasing waste recycling and recovery, and disposing of any remaining waste in an environmentally benign manner (Conference Board of Canada 2013b). The creation and disposal of the waste caused by affluence and over-consumption contributes to environmental problems such as habitat destruction, surface and groundwater pollution, and other forms of air, soil, and water contamination. In Canada and across other developed countries, real gross domestic product (GDP) and average household disposable incomes have been steadily increasing since the 1980s, leading to increasing household consumption rates (Conference Board of Canada 2015a). Does Canada consume too much? Are we too rich? Affluence and population are part of sustainable development, which is discussed in Chapter 11.

QUALITY AND IMPACT ASSESSMENT

Researchers at Yale University (2015) publish an annual Environmental Performance Index that ranks every country, if data are available, on 10 quality indicators. Overall, based on 2014 assessments, Canada ranks 24th in the world out of 178 countries, and this ranking is largely because it receives high (per capita) scores on air quality, child mortality, and safe drinking water. However, on other indicators Canada scores lower, which brings down its overall average. For example, Canada is 104th for changes in forest cover and 97th for biodiversity and habitat. Keep in mind that the scale does not reflect current policies per se and that some rankings, such as the extent of terrestrial protected areas (part of the bio-diversity and habitat indicator), are influenced considerably by Canada's size relative to that of other countries. You can examine the "trending" score of each country to see if a country's performance in specific areas is improving or declining. Canada's trending score is 2.58 per cent, which suggests that, over the past 10 years, Canada's record has been "status quo" with very little change. Thus, on the basis of this index, one would conclude that Canada is a fairly "strong performer" environmentally but is trending so slowly that improvements are not expected. For compara-tive purposes, note that Canada's 24th place is behind the ranking for Greece and Italy, and that the United States is 33rd and Mexico is 65th, to put Canada in its North American context (for data, see http://epis. yale.edu).

In January 2015 the Center for Global Development (in Washington, DC) released its Commitment to Development Index for 2014 in which it ranked 27 of the world's richest countries on policies that affect poorer nations (Center for Global Development 2015). There are seven areas on which the countries are assessed, including environmental policies. The environment component examines how rich countries are tackling their disproportionate exploitation of the global commons. Are they reining in greenhouse gas emissions and fossil-fuel production? Do they subsidize fleets that deplete fisheries off the coasts of Senegal and India? Do they control imports of illegally cut tropical timber? In this envi-ronmental component, Canada ranked dead last in 27th place and was the only country not to have made progress in the past five years. Why did Canada rank so poorly? It is because Canada backed out of the Kyoto Protocol and continues to have high greenhouse gas emissions with low gas taxes (for current data, see http://www.cgdev.org/initiative/commitment-development-index).

Finally, and more locally, a domestic think-tank called the Conference Board of Canada makes an annual assessment of the environmental performance of 17 countries. In 2014, Canada ranked 15th (Conference Board of Canada 2015a). The study applauded Canada for its "A" grades on indicators related to water quality, threatened species, use of forest resources, and low-emitting electricity production but had to give Canada a low overall assessment because of its GHG, nitrogen oxides, and VOC emissions; its poor stewardship of freshwater resources; and its municipal waste generation. The countries that scored worse than Canada were the United States (16th) and Australia (17th), also because of their poor records on climate change initiatives. By and large, no matter who is assessing Canada's environmental performance, the numbers never stack up in its favour. Assessment of different environmental indicators suggests Canada has work to do in the environmental realm. Whatever challenges lie ahead, they will have to be met in the context of urbanization, immigration, and growing affluence.

CONCLUSIONS

When it comes to using environmental indicators for change, we should think about each indicator as pinpointing some political problem that requires a practical policy solution. Water quality is not just an "environmental problem" in the sense that pollution contaminates lakes and rivers. Water quality is a problem of politics and governance. What policy can we create to minimize that problem? And what type of policy mechanisms should we employ to produce the necessary changes in human behaviour? The desired policy might involve more education and awareness, but it could also involve regulation, economic incentives, or voluntary actions. In fact, the best policy probably is a mixture of all three. But Canada's water is not going to clean itself up—public policy is required.

In some areas, Canada has a good environmental track record and is managing problems or resources very well. However, environmental policy across the country is quite disappointing, and Canadians need new or amended policies. Subsequent chapters of this book map out environmental indicators in greater detail while trying to get at what policy already exists and what level or levels of government are responsible for implementing that policy. The book also highlights possible areas for policy elevation and improvements. Although specific policies are not recommended, the book does provide the reader with the tools necessary to think about different policy solutions in areas where Canadian federal or provincial policy is lacking. But first, chapters 2 and 3 will provide a quick overview of how public policy is made in Canada and present an in-depth discussion of institutions, interests, and actors.

Key Terms

boreal forest; environmental indicators; Federal Sustainable Development Act; carbon dioxide; sulphur dioxide; Canadian Environmental Protection Act (CEPA); watershed; point-source pollution; non-point-source pollution; Crown land; affluence; Malthusian catastrophe

Discussion Questions

1. If a friend asked you whether he or she should be concerned about air pollution in Canada, what would you tell your friend and why?
2. What is the difference between point-source and non-point-source water pollution? Why is one more difficult to regulate than the other?
3. What effect does affluence have on the environment?
4. Does urban sprawl affect your life? How so?
5. Why does Canada consistently score so poorly in studies measuring environmental regulation or environmental well-being?

Suggested Readings

Chertow, M. R. 2001. "The IPAT Equation and Its Variants." *Journal of Industrial Ecology* 4 (4): 13–29. http://dx.doi.org/10.1162/10881980052541927.
Harriot, Trevor. 2010. *Grass, Sky, Song: Promise and Peril in the World of Grassland Birds*. Toronto: HarperCollins Canada.
Parson, Edward A. 2000. "Environmental Trends and Environmental Governance in Canada." *Canadian Public Policy* 26: S123–43. http://dx.doi.org/10.2307/3552575.
Parson, Edward. 2001. *Governing the Environment: Persistent Challenges, Uncertain Innovations*. Toronto: University of Toronto Press.
Suzuki, David. 2007. *The Sacred Balance: Rediscovering Our Place in Nature*. Vancouver: Greystone.

Notes

1 California had an estimated population of 38.8 million in 2014 and a land size of 423, 967 square kilometres, including water (US Census Bureau 2010, 2015). Saskatchewan has a total land area of 651, 900 square kilometres (Statistics Canada 2005).

2 It is estimated that there are upward of 70 million stray cats in the United States and 95.6 million house cats—that is 165.6 million cats (Humane Society of the United States 2014; Mott 2004).

3 Note, however, that the EPA did not say that CO_2 is, by itself, a pollutant but rather that the high concentrations in the earth's atmosphere are human caused and in need of regulation. (See EPA 2015a for a description of how the EPA is regulating CO_2.)

Chapter 2

Canadian Politics and Institutions

CANADA IS A constitutional monarchy and a **parliamentary democracy** in which elected representatives have the authority, and responsibility, for making laws to protect individuals and communities. To the extent that Canada has laws in place to protect national parks, limit toxic substances, reduce air pollution, or control water pollution, elected politicians likely made those laws. In this sense, to study the environment is to study **politics**. But what is politics? The most common definition is Harold Lasswell's classic statement that politics is the art of deciding "who gets what, when, [and] how" (Lasswell 1936). The existence of scarcity produces conflict and necessitates "politics," or the governing of decision making. At some level, politics is conflict. Not all people get what they want, when they want it, or how they want it. Whether we recognize it or not, there are limits to water, oil, wealth, and other environmental and social goods. So we need to decide who gets what, when, and how, as Lasswell puts it. These decisions are almost always controversial and involve competing claims. In Canada, because we have a well-established and stable parliamentary democracy, officials make decisions about the allocation of resources on our behalf. These decisions fall into the realm of public policy.

Public policy is an attempt to appease conflict either through direct action or, sometimes, through inaction. If, for example, a government decides not to regulate carbon dioxide (CO_2) emissions, then the government's policy toward climate change could be summarized as "indifferent" or "lax." However, when a government decides to monitor and cap CO_2 emissions, then that government is creating a "carbon pollution policy."

Public *policy* is technically different from *law*, but the two words are often used interchangeably. Law refers to rules created and passed in Parliament prohibiting or determining behaviour. Law is also backed up with the full force of police authority, including the possibility of punishment for non-compliance. Policy, on the other hand, is more like government objectives. A government may create and implement a policy without that policy being passed in Parliament. But the policy would not be backed by police force or the threat of punishment. The distinction between law and policy is important and will be further explored in Chapter 3. Of critical importance here is that not only government or elected officials create and implement environmental policy or law. A whole network of actors is involved, ranging from political parties and interest groups to the media to citizens. These policy actors will be discussed in the next chapter. This chapter focuses on the idea that environmental policy and law decide who gets what, when, and how, and that such decisions are made in the realm of politics and result in a public policy.

In Canada, studying politics and the environment requires a careful examination of **federalism**. Political authority is divided between the national central government in Ottawa and the 10 provincial governments. The three territorial governments are technically under federal responsibility, but more and more authority is being devolved to them, as this book will discuss (see also Yukon Legislative Assembly 2012; Northwest Territories Executive 1999). Ottawa does not have the power to make policy in all environmental areas—in fact, in most cases, the provinces decide who gets what, when, and how. And, in some circumstances, Aboriginal groups or cities make decisions about competing claims and scarce resources. Policymaking is a complex field of shared authority. It is crucial to understand not only how our representatives make policies but also how different actors share this responsibility. Thus, this book centres on federalism and the question of who governs the environment in Canada. Throughout the text, you will be challenged to think about not only who *does* govern but also who *should* govern environmental matters across the nation. Because of the way federalism is organized by the Constitution, figuring out who has the authority to make decisions is difficult. If that were not complex enough, it is also not always clear who is best equipped to make decisions: the public, the experts, or the elected officials? And at what level or scale should decisions be taken: the local, the provincial, or the federal? To examine these questions, each chapter explores the idea of multilevel governance and discusses what level of government is best suited to dealing with a specific policy issue, such as species at risk or electricity consumption.

The concept of **governance** will be used throughout the text to examine public policy and the question of who *should* govern. As mentioned, more actors are invested in public policy outcomes than just elected officials and state organizations. Governance is about the process of governing and decision making. It examines how elected officials are influenced and mobilized by citizens, the media, or interest groups to act in certain ways at certain times.

To investigate governance also means considering how rules and different procedures affect policy outcomes (Enderlein, Walti, and Zurn 2010). For example, we can say that Parliament determines climate change policy in Canada. However, if we examine the governance of air pollution and energy management closely, we could argue that a complex network of actors, both domestic and international, influences elected politicians, political parties, and perhaps even bureaucrats. We know that the United States pressures Canada to provide low-cost bitumen (oil) just as we know that Alberta's politicians, concerned about the economy, make land, air, and resource policy with international actors in mind. It is far too simple to say the "government" makes policy. Still, we need a general understanding of how decisions are made in Canada and of Canada's various political institutions before we can move to an examination of the environment and the policies we have in place to manage that environment.

CANADA'S POLITICAL INSTITUTIONS

Canada is a constitutional monarchy as well as a parliamentary democracy. The country is a former British colony and a current member of the Commonwealth with Queen Elizabeth II as the head of state. However, the monarch serves only a symbolic and ceremonial role; the Constitution and Parliament are responsible for law and policy in Canada. A **constitution** is the supreme or fundamental law in a political system, and it determines not only the relationship between the state and the citizens but also the distribution of powers among different state actors. The Canadian Constitution defines the responsibilities of the federal government and the provincial governments. Consequently, it has wide-ranging implications for environmental policymaking.

Inside Canada's parliamentary democracy, there are three branches of government: executive, legislative, and judicial (see Figure 2.1). The executive comprises the monarch as head of state; her representative in Canada, the governor general; and the prime minister and his or her cabinet and officers, including the bureaucracy. The legislative branch of government is more informally known as "Parliament" and comprises both the

FIGURE 2.1 Branches of Government

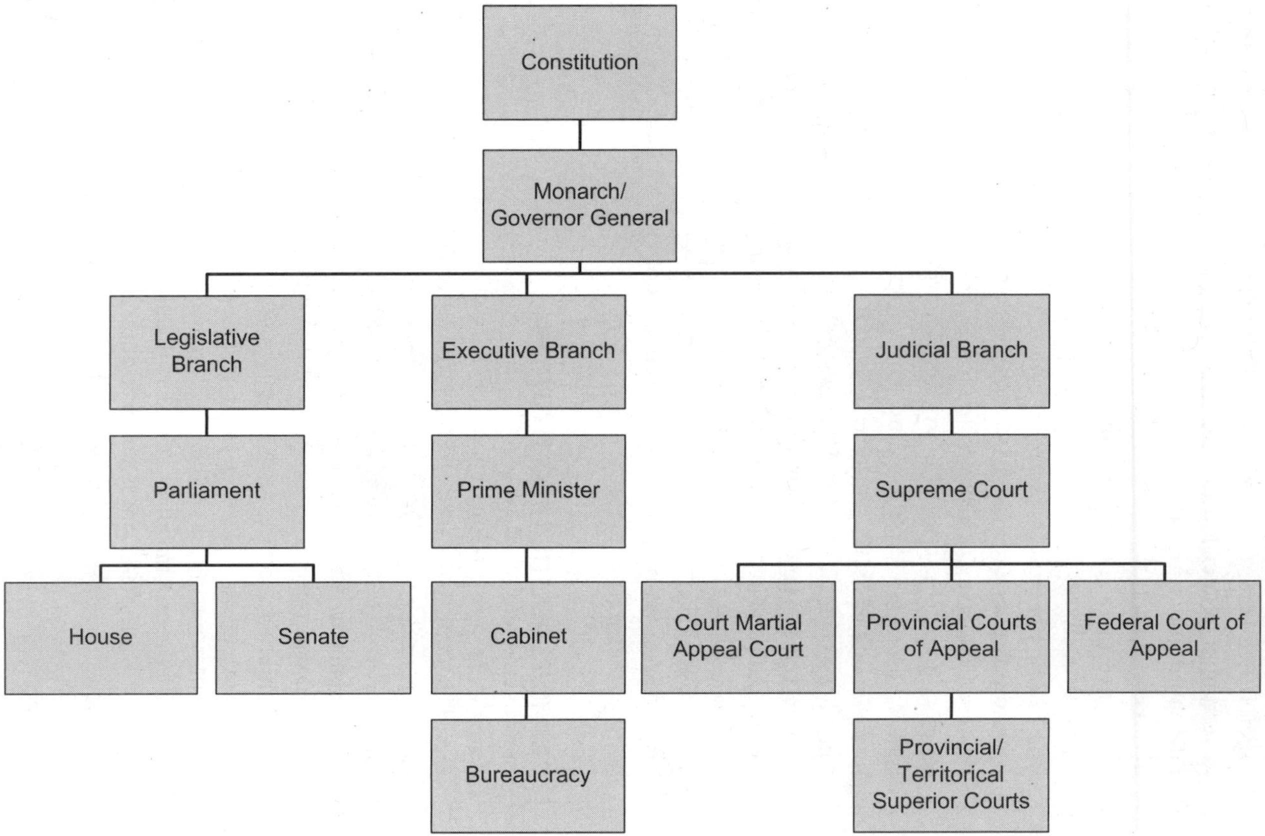

House of Commons and the Senate. Although the judicial branch does not legislate and is not part of Parliament, it does interpret laws and policy and checks the constitutionality of both, making it significant in Canadian governance. The judiciary is not just the Supreme Court of Canada but also the federal and provincial court systems as well as military courts. Each function of Canadian government will be quickly reviewed here before we move to a discussion of federalism.

Executive Branch

The role of the **executive branch** is to implement laws and ensure that public business is carried out efficiently and effectively. The prime minister (PM) and his or her cabinet are the only elected members of the executive branch. Other members, such as the governor general, are appointed by the Queen on the recommendation of the prime minister. And the bureaucracy is neither elected nor appointed but hired in a merit-based system. In 2015, Stephen Harper was the prime minister and David Johnson was the governor general. Queen Elizabeth will remain the head of state until Prince Charles or Duke William assumes the throne.[1] As mentioned, the monarch and her appointed representative, the governor general, perform mainly a symbolic role in Canada. Policymaking and governing authority rests with the prime minister and Parliament.

In fact, it is fair to say that the PM and his or her cabinet are at the centre of making policy and law in Canada. Once a party leader becomes prime minister, the first thing he or she does is choose members of cabinet. The cabinet comprises 20 to 40 other members of Parliament in the same party as the PM (there are exceptions, as senators have been cabinet members in the past, and, on rare occasions such as in coalition governments, members have been drawn from another party). The cabinet, modelled after the Queen's Privy Council in the United Kingdom, advises the PM on specific areas of policy importance in Canada. The PM and cabinet also have power over the budget and public spending because any legislation that involves raising or spending public dollars (such as taxes or royalties from resource extraction) must be introduced into the House of Commons by a member of cabinet.

In 2015, Prime Minister Harper had 39 members of cabinet, which is one of the larger cabinets in Canada's history. The higher-profile placements include the ministers of finance, defence, justice, and foreign affairs, as well as the president of the Treasury Board of Canada. A list of cabinet members and short biographies of each minister can be found at the prime minister's website (http://pm.gc.ca/eng/ministers). These individuals are given the title "Honourable." Note that judges, senators, and past cabinet ministers also carry the "Honourable" title.

Beyond the PM and cabinet, the executive branch also comprises the bureaucracy, which includes all federal agencies and departments, for example, the departments of health, finance, education, and the environment. We refer to the individual Canadians who work for these departments and agencies as **civil servants**, and their jobs are not dependent on the PM or the parties in government. When elections occur and new governments are formed, civil servants are not directly affected—they keep their jobs and continue to work inside the federal bureaucracy. The role of the bureaucracy is to administer federal programs and agencies. So when a government creates new policy or Parliament passes a new law, the bureaucracy must implement that law across the country.

Environment Canada is the primary bureaucratic agency for environmental policy. It was established in 1971 and has a mandate to "preserve and enhance the quality of the natural environment, including water, air, soil, flora and fauna; conserve Canada's renewable resources; conserve and protect Canada's water resources; forecast daily weather conditions and warnings, and provide detailed meteorological information to all of Canada; enforce rules relating to boundary waters; and coordinate environmental policies and programs for the federal government" (Environment Canada 2014a). Other pertinent bureaucratic agencies with overlap in the environmental sector include Natural Resources Canada and Fisheries and Oceans Canada, which will both be discussed throughout the book. Starting in late 2013, the Honourable Leona Aglukkaq was appointed to serve as minister of the environment, and, in that role, she was responsible for overseeing Environment Canada. She was also minister of the Canadian Northern Economic Development Agency (appointed in 2011) and for the Arctic Council (appointed in 2012). The Honourable Aglukkaq was first elected to the House of Commons in 2008 and re-elected in 2011. Cabinet positions are at the discretion of the prime minister, and he or she is free to shuffle members in and out of different cabinet positions at any time.

Legislative Branch

The **legislative branch**, or Parliament, is intended to represent the people of Canada. Members of the House of Commons (called the "House" or the "Commons") are accountable to Canadians through regular elections. The governor general, at the request of the prime minister, appoints members of the Senate. Together, these two chambers of Parliament enact our nation's laws. All national **environmental laws** in Canada have passed through these two houses, so it is important to understand how each chamber functions (although it is important to understand that not all environmental *policy* passes through the two chambers, as policy can be made at the executive level).

The House of Commons comprises elected members known as members of Parliament (MPs). The House is designed to represent Canadians by population and by region, meaning that Canada is divided into ridings. Between 2011 and 2015 there were 308 ridings across the country—so 308 seats in the House. Due to growth in the Canadian population and to constitutional agreements regulating the distribution of seats amongst Canadian provinces and territories, the number of ridings increased to 338 for the first general election after May 1, 2014, with a corresponding rise in the number of seats in the House. The number of people represented by each riding varies considerably depending upon a province or territory's population. For example, in the 2011 election, each of the 4 ridings in Prince Edward Island represented approximately 35,000 individuals, whereas each of the 106 ridings in Ontario represented about 120,000 people. Why? The representation formula is designed so that not only a province's population but also its geographic and historic significance in Canada's union are considered. Representation by population is the main principle followed, however, so that Manitoba, with close to 13 per cent of the combined provincial population of voters, was allotted 14 ridings or 12.54 per cent of the provincial seats in the 2015 election, and Ontario, with almost 40 per cent, was given 42 ridings or 36.12 per cent of the provincial seats (see Elections Canada 2015). This distribution may seem unfair from a provincial standpoint, but it means that Canadians can be more equally represented in Canada. If Manitoba and Ontario had the same number of ridings, this would mean the approximately 13.5 million people in Ontario would have the same amount of representation as the almost 1.3 million people in Manitoba. That would not be fair representation from a population perspective.[2]

When you vote for an MP, you vote in the riding in which you live. You can find your riding on Election Canada's website (http://www.elections.ca). At the end of an election, all the votes are tallied and which MPs are elected to the House of Commons is determined. In Canada, we use a **first-past-the-post system** whereby, to win a seat in the House, an individual needs to win the most votes in a riding, although not necessarily a majority of votes. Only one candidate from each party can run in a single riding, so, for example, a Liberal, a Conservative, a New Democrat, and a Green candidate could all contest a single seat. The winner must get the most votes. Therefore, the Liberal could win 30 per cent of the popular vote, the NDP 20 per cent, the Green Party 10 per cent, and the Conservative 40 per cent. In this case, the Conservative would be elected MP for the riding because he or she has more votes than any other candidate—although a majority of the total vote (60 per cent) went to others. You can find the MP for your riding on the Parliament of Canada website using your postal code (http://www.parl.gc.ca/).

Whichever political party has the most MPs in the House of Commons gets to form government. And here is where the executive branch and the legislative branch connect. On May 2, 2011, Canadians elected 166 MPs from the Conservative Party, 103 MPs from the New Democratic Party, 34 MPs from the Liberal Party, 4 MPs from the Bloc Québécois, and 1 MP from the Green Party (Parliament of Canada 2011). The result was that the Conservative Party formed the government, and its leader, Stephen Harper, became prime minister. Stephen Harper is an MP from the Calgary Southwest riding, and Canadians from that riding elected him to be their MP (75 per cent of voters in the Calgary Southwest riding voted for Harper). Because the Conservative Party elected him as its leader, Harper also became prime minister. It is important to remember, then, that Canadians do not vote for their prime minister directly; the PM is simply the leader of the party with the most seats in the House of Commons.[3]

Because there were 308 seats in the House of Commons in 2011, the Conservatives, who won more than 154 seats, formed a **majority government**. Majority governments can easily pass legislation because, each time the House votes on a bill, the governing party already has enough votes to pass that bill. For example, in April 2015, the Conservatives had 160 seats in the House. If they decided to pass a bill declaring the second week of March as "National Spring Break," they could introduce that legislation in Parliament and call a vote. If all 160 Conservative MPs voted "yes" that bill would become law. Even if every other MP voted "no," there would be only 145 votes against. (Yes, that makes only 305 votes; 3 of the 308 seats were vacant in April 2015. For these and other statistics on current MPs, see the Parliament of Canada website: http://www.parl.gc.ca/parliamentarians/en/members.) The point is that, typically, all members of a party vote the same way. Each party has someone called the **party whip** whose responsibility it is to ensure that each and every MP in a party votes according to that party's policies in all but designated "free votes." Importantly, the party whip also ensures that each MP attends the House of Commons to vote, especially when the vote might be close. Usually, then, a majority government can pass legislation easily.

But can a majority government pass any law it wants? Technically, yes. In practice, however, the government is responsible to voters and would not jeopardize its popularity and risk losing the next election by straying too far from voter expectations. Voters expect an elected government to implement its party platform, policies that the MPs in the party campaigned on and made election promises about. The broad themes of each party's platform are outlined in its policy book or on its website. Moreover, a governing party does not pass just any law it wants because the courts can rule legislation unconstitutional or enforce the Charter of Rights and Freedoms; both the Constitution and the Charter hold governments in check.

What happens if no party wins a majority in the House? There are really only two options. First, the party with the most seats can form a **minority government**, as happened in 2008 when the Conservative Party had only 143 MPs in the House. In this case, the governing party does not have enough votes to pass legislation, so it must get MPs from another party to vote for a bill or abstain from voting against it. Consequently, minority governance often requires a lot of compromise and deal making between the governing party and other parties that might be willing to vote with the government.

Second, two or more parties can form a **coalition government**. What this entails is the cooperative governance by two or more parties that, when their seats are combined, have at least a majority. Federally, this has happened only once in our history since Confederation—Prime Minister Borden's Union Government of 1917. Coalition governments occur more often at the provincial level and in other parliamentary democracies. The United Kingdom, for example, was governed by a coalition government from 2010 to 2015. There was almost a coalition government in Canada after the 2008 election. The Liberal Party, with 77 seats, and the New Democratic Party, with 34, reached an accord to form a coalition government. With only 114 MPs combined, these parties needed the support of the Bloc Québécois (BQ), with 49 seats. The BQ offered 18 months of support. However, before the non-confidence vote that could have brought down the Conservative minority government, Governor General Michaëlle Jean granted Prime Minister Stephen Harper's request to suspend (or prorogue) Parliament. The Conservatives compromised with the Liberals and maintained power after Parliament was reconvened, thus avoiding a coalition government that would have ousted them from power (see Brooks 2013 for more information about coalition governments).

Beyond making federal law, MPs also fill a representative role and spend a lot of time in their home ridings dealing with local issues. Any Canadian can reach out to the MP in his or her riding to ask questions, raise important issues, or voice criticism and complaints. Social media and the Internet make finding out what your MP is doing or communicating with him or her very easy. Because an MP's job is to represent Canadians, each MP must respond to the issues of the riding. Moreover, interest groups, as discussed in Chapter 3, also reach out to MPs or lobby them to get issues raised in Parliament.

Each MP is to attend Question Period in the House of Commons Monday through Thursday afternoon. With all members present (give or take occasional absences), the House discusses the important issues of the day and works to make legislation. When not in Question Period, members may be in a committee meeting or taking time to meet with visiting dignitaries or to answer correspondence. Because members also live in their ridings, they must spend a lot of time travelling. Most MPs return to their home ridings on Thursday night for the weekend. You can imagine how difficult this is for MPs from the North, the West, or the Atlantic provinces to travel each weekend. During the summer months, when the House is not in session, MPs will spend the majority of their time in their home ridings with their families.

Finally, MPs also serve on legislative committees that are formed around specific policy areas. The committee topics vary, but there are several permanent standing committees such as those for national defence, the status of women, natural resources, and the environment and sustainable development. (Consult the Parliament of Canada's website for a list of committees.) The Senate has a similar committee structure. Members of Parliament are assigned to different committees, and most committees have between 6 and 10 members. At the start of each fall session, the House of Commons Standing Committee on Procedure and House Affairs establishes a membership list for each legislative committee, and the list is approved by the House. Party distribution on committee reflects party distribution in the House (see Parliament of Canada 2014).

The main purpose of the committees is to research, discuss, and debate proposed legislation. After an MP introduces a bill into the House (or the Senate), the bill is normally referred to a committee. In committee, the MPs from different parties will discuss and debate the legislation. They are responsible for closely analyzing the need, purpose, and feasibility of a piece of legislation. Often, committees will interview experts as part of their research for new policy or their evaluation of already existing policy. A bill frequently "dies" at the committee stage because, for example, a committee never gets around to discussing it or cannot agree on the need or purpose of the legislation—so there is never a full report to the House for open debate and a vote.

The Senate has 105 appointed members and was designed by the founders of Confederation to protect regional and minority interests. Each province and territory is entitled to a specific number of Senate seats, but, for the purpose of regional representation, these seats are grouped into four main areas, each of which is granted 24 seats: Ontario and Québec are each a division as are the Maritimes and the Western provinces. Beyond these regions, the three territories are each granted one senator and Newfound and Labrador has six seats. So, when the prime minister chooses which people to recommend for appointment to the Senate, the regional design must be respected. Political party affiliation does exist in the Senate whereby each senator is a member of a political party (except in the case of the Liberal Party starting in 2014; see below). Because the prime minister chooses whom to recommend for Senate appointment, he or she will select members from his or her own party. And because senators are appointed until the age of 75, rather than to four- or six-year terms, a prime minister can have a big impact on the party make-up of the Senate. For example, between 2006 and 2014, Stephen Harper appointed 59 individuals to the Senate, and all are members of the Conservative Party (see Parliament of Canada 2012). Not surprisingly, the Conservative Party now has a majority in the Senate, meaning that Conservative-sanctioned bills pass through the Senate upon a vote.[4]

The Senate has the same legislative responsibility as the House, except no bills pertaining to the use of public spending can originate in the Senate. In Canada, a bill has to pass through the House and the Senate before it becomes law. Consequently, every piece of environmental law that exists at the national level in Canada has passed through the House of Commons and the Senate. For the most part, the Senate is known as the "chamber of sober second thought" and is responsible for a close reading of a House bill to ensure feasibility of implementation upon passage.

Canadians have discussed and debated reforming or abolishing the Senate. Often, the public, and to some extent the House MPs, are critical of the Senate because members are appointed as opposed to elected. However, the Senate provides some legislative advantages to Parliament. For example, senators do not have to spend time campaigning or raising money, so they can instead focus on long-term issues. Each MP is elected for a term of a maximum of only five years and then needs to be re-elected to stay in office. Thus, MPs often try to pass legislation hurriedly or focus too much on short-term problem solving and policy benefits due to the short duration of their term. They also need to raise funds for their re-election constantly, which is time consuming and often necessitates promises and commitments to campaign donors—something that senators are not concerned with because of the length of their appointments (see Brooks 2013).

Some also criticize the Senate's representation as unequal because there are 24 members from each region as determined over a hundred years ago before population grew out West (the six from NL and one from each territory were added later). Alberta especially would like to have more senators to balance out the power of Ontario and Québec. This problem could be addressed by moving to a representation formula similar to that used for the House, which includes the principle of representation by population. Any such change would come at the cost of smaller provinces such as Prince Edward Island, as it would have almost no representation in the House or the Senate—yet PEI is 1 of Canada's 10 provinces, which implies that it should have influence on laws affecting the country. This issue of what constitutes fair representation in the Senate may never be settled in Canada.

Finally, the Senate scandal that began in late 2012 leaves many MPs and Canadians wondering if the Senate should be abolished. Because of a 2012 auditor general's report, the public learned that a few senators had been misspending public money and using their Senate housing allowance for personal travel or personal benefit (Boyer 2014). Each senator is supposed to reside in the home province he or she is representing, so senators are given a housing allowance for time spent in Ottawa and a travel allowance for trips back and forth. It turns out that Prince Edward Island Senator Michael Duffy, although listing a PEI cottage as his primary residence, was living only in Ottawa and had claimed over $90,000 in expenses. Similarly, Saskatchewan's Senator Pamela Wallin claimed travel and housing expenses unrelated to Senate business; she lived and worked in Toronto while still a senator, listing a community near her summer cottage in Saskatchewan as her primary residence. Senator Wallin paid back her expenses, but Duffy's were covered indirectly by a personal cheque to Duffy written by Nigel Wright, the prime minister's chief of staff. The cheque led to further scandal and Wright's resignation (Boyer 2014). This scandal is ongoing, so its full impact cannot be assessed.

Thus, recent years have not been good to the Canadian Senate. In 2013, Prime Minister Harper asked the Supreme Court to determine whether Parliament could independently make changes to the Senate (e.g., changing term limits or making senators elected officials) or whether such changes required a constitutional amendment, which would necessitate approval from the provinces as well as the two chambers. The Supreme Court determined that the House cannot make amendments to the Senate—that such reforms would require approval from the majority of the provinces. (See *Reference re Senate Reform*, 2014 SCC 32 [2014] 1, S.C.R. 704 for the official court decision.)

In January 2014, Justin Trudeau, the leader of the Liberal Party of Canada, announced that senators appointed by the Liberal Party, of which there were 32 in the Senate, are no longer "Liberal" senators.

In other words, senators appointed under Liberal governments are no longer part of the Liberal caucus, which effectually makes these senators independents inside the Senate. Why? Trudeau (2014) is trying to make the Senate of Canada a non-partisan institution "separate from political or electoral concerns." Likely, however, Trudeau is only adding fuel to a long-burning debate on the Senate, as this move is more symbolic than practical.

Judicial Branch

The role of the **judicial branch** is to be a non-partisan interpreter of law in Canada (see Figure 2.2). Judges in superior courts are appointed by the governor general on the advice of the prime minister and the federal cabinet. They are not elected, but an advisory committee and, recently, an ad hoc review committee are involved in selecting judges for Canada's Supreme Court. Appointments to provincial courts are made by each province's lieutenant governor on the recommendation of the provincial government. Just as it affects other areas of policymaking, federalism influences which level of government can make what kind of laws. The Constitution grants the federal government the right to make criminal law, but the responsibility for the administration and implementation of laws lies with the provinces.

FIGURE 2.2 Canada's Judicial System

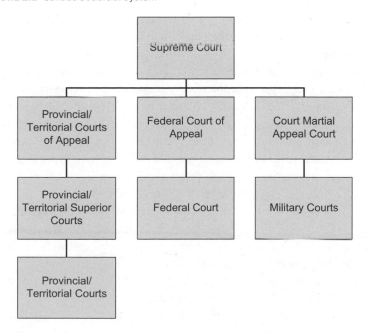

Consequently, each province has established its own system of courts to perform this role—applying and interpreting both federal laws and provincial laws.

Since 1949, the Supreme Court of Canada has been the highest court of appeal. It comprises nine judges, and, by custom, three of those judges are from Québec to ensure the appropriate interpretation of Québec's civil law. The court primarily hears between 40 and 70 appeal cases per year from the lower courts. For example, if a provincial court's decision is appealed, the Supreme Court can hear the case and either overturn or uphold the lowers court's decision. The Supreme Court's ruling is the final ruling and cannot be appealed to another level or body of courts. The Supreme Court can also be asked to provide constitutional interpretation—even regarding the division of powers between Ottawa and the provinces. As mentioned, Prime Minister Harper asked the Supreme Court to determine whether the federal government could unilaterally reform the Senate.

Interpreting and applying Canadian law is a big responsibility. The courts oversee everything from parking ticket disputes to terrorist allegations to interpreting the constitutionality of environmental laws across the country. In fact, the judicial branch has a large impact on environmental policy in Canada and can influence it through **constitutional litigation**, the **judicial review of administrative action**, and ruling on **civil action** for environmental harm cases and **class action suits**. And there are plenty of examples of each of these in Canadian history. To note one, the Supreme Court of Canada's decision in *MiningWatch Canada v. Canada (Fisheries and Oceans)* is an example of environmental litigation that impacts federal environmental assessments and public participatory rights. The court decided that the federal government cannot split projects into small parts and avoid the rigorous environmental assessment requirements, including meaningful public consultation, intended by Parliament (Mitchell 2010). Essentially, the Supreme Court had to interpret Parliament's intentions in creating environmental assessments. After reviewing the matter carefully, the court decided that Parliament wanted public consultation to be part of the overall assessment process. Thus, the Department of Fisheries and Oceans cannot sidestep the intended process of consultation or assessment more broadly by sending parts of large projects through the less rigorous channels of smaller projects. Here the Supreme Court did not make a law—it just changed the way an existing law (environmental assessments) was being implemented by the federal government.

It is important to note the judges are not elected and do not make policy or law in Canada. Instead, judges interpret law made by Parliament or provincial legislative assemblies and can shape the way legislation is implemented. If the legislative branch wants to change a law or make a new law, it is free to do so at any time. That said, the legislative branch cannot alter legal precedent or change the Constitution or Charter without due process. Thus, there is a balance between the branches of government. And all three function together to make, implement, and enforce law in Canada.

FEDERALISM

Federalism is perhaps the defining political feature of Canada. Negotiating the relationship between the provinces and the central government dates back to the creation of Canada as a separate country from the United Kingdom (see Smiley 1987). In the eighteenth century, North America looked much different than it does today, as most of the continent was claimed by the British, Spanish, or French. Since that time, colonial empires have been replaced by nations. For example, British territory shrank after the American Revolutionary War (1775–83). More significantly for Canada's development, France lost all of its territory in mainland North America with the treaty that ended the Seven Years' War (1763).

By the 1860s, British colonies and territories in North America included most of the land that is now Canada, but these were divided by history, language, and religion. For example, a substantial part of the newly unified Province of Canada, composed of Lower Canada (Québec) and Upper Canada (Ontario), had been a French colony until 1763. Its population was predominantly French speaking and Catholic. These Canadians favoured federalism so as to ensure they had jurisdiction over linguistic and cultural matters. On the other hand, English Canadians, who were generally Protestant, loyal to Britain, and concerned about interference from the newly created United States, favoured a strong unitary state.

The Maritimes also favoured federalism and feared a unitary state with a national government in Ontario that would dictate regional policy out East (see Brooks 2013). As part of a compromise, the Canadian Constitution, originally the British North American Act of 1867, establishes two levels of government: national and subnational (or provincial). Both levels have important law-making powers as well as taxation powers, and neither level can alter the other level's power. The result is a federal country with a constitution that sets out the powers of the central government in Ottawa and the powers of the provincial governments. The Constitution cannot be changed without consent of Parliament and consent of the provinces.

The Constitution Act of 1867 does not spell out powers too carefully in the environmental realm (Library of Parliament 2013), partly because the founders of Canada could not have foreseen the complicated political, economic, and social conditions related to the environment today. That said, the Canadian federal government has some clear authority over the environment. That authority comes from **Section 91 of the Constitution** and includes powers such as those related to international borders, international relations, trade and commerce, navigation and shipping, seacoasts and fisheries, and criminal law. The federal government also has primary jurisdiction over federal works and undertakings; for example, it regulates the land and activities of the federal government, its agencies, and corporations; the armed forces; and a variety of other entities such as railways, aviation, interprovincial transport, and grain elevators (see Table 2.1).

Last, the 1867 Constitution Act grants the federal government general authority to make laws for the "peace, order, and good government of Canada" (POGG). Generally, POGG-preserving laws are considered appropriate only when there is an emergency (e.g., national defence) or when a matter is of national concern (i.e., affecting all provinces or all Canadians). The Judicial Committee of the Privy Council, a British board that served as Canada's court of final appeal until 1949, decided in 1896 that the POGG clause could be used by the federal government to override the power of the provinces only in matters of a "national dimension" or at times of "national crisis." However, Canadian constitutional law on this matter remains unclear. Instead, the Supreme Court has wrangled with the issue. In 1975, for example, the court was asked to rule on the constitutionality of the Anti-Inflation Act, a temporary measure designed to control high unemployment and inflation, and found that the POGG clause could be used in such a circumstance to encroach on provincial powers (MacDonald 1977). Nevertheless, since that 1975 ruling, the federal government has never used POGG justification outright to intrude

TABLE 2.1 Environmental Powers as Described in the Canadian Constitution

FEDERAL POWERS (SECTION 91)	PROVINCIAL POWERS (SECTION 92)
Taxation	Taxation within Provinces
Regulation of Trade and Commerce	Education
Aboriginal Canadians	Private Property
Criminal Law	Provincial Crown Lands
Military and Defence Treaty Making	Natural Resources
Peace, Order, and Good Government	
Navigation and Sea Shipping	
Territories	

on provincial jurisdiction. In fact, it is difficult to imagine a case in which the federal government would invoke POGG to make law for a province.

For the provinces, **Section 92 of the Constitution** grants jurisdiction over the management and sale of public lands, property and civil rights, and matters of a merely local or private nature. However, when the Constitution was updated in 1982, the provinces gained jurisdiction over non-renewable natural resources, forestry, and electric energy. Until 1982, an act of the British Parliament, the **British North America Act of 1867**, was Canada's constitutional document. Through another act of the Parliament of the United Kingdom, the **Canada Act** of 1982, Canada patriated the Constitution, which meant that the consent of Britain was no longer required for constitutional amendments. That same year, Canada's major constitutional document, the **Constitution Act**, was proclaimed on April 17; it includes a **Charter of Rights and Freedoms**. The province of Québec did not sign the patriated 1982 Constitution, but formal consent of all provinces was not necessary. Today, the Constitution does apply to and in Québec. Consequently, Québec and the other nine provinces have the same environmental jurisdiction as outlined in Table 2.1.

Thus far, federalism has been laid out as a neat and tidy relationship between Ottawa and the rest of Canada. However, it is important to understand how complicated and unsettled this relationship is in practice. This is especially true when it comes to the environment. All these jurisdictional distinctions, including POGG, are legally very important but also somewhat vague. For example, provinces clearly have jurisdiction over non-renewable resources, such as oil, and other resources, such as electricity generation and forestry. This reality has played out in the handling of the Alberta oil sands and British Columbia's forestry. But when it comes to resources such as water, the Constitution is less helpful in terms of guidance. Why? Constitutional powers related to water regulation are divided and overlapping. Fisheries, navigation, and international waters are federal responsibilities while water resources and supply are provincial and territorial responsibilities. So who governs water in Canada? As Chapter 6 will explain, water is managed by multiple levels of government, but, over the last two decades, there have been "diminished federal government focus" (Bakker 2007, 3) and revised or innovated provincial management schemas, including the creation of Saskatchewan's Water Security Agency (known before October 2012 as the Saskatchewan Watershed Authority), Québec's watershed-based management organizations (which include environmental groups and citizens), and Manitoba's new ministry, Manitoba Conservation and Water Stewardship. All of this leads to a "patchwork of provincial and federal laws, with inconsistencies and gaps in important areas of responsibility and oversight" (Bakker 2007, 7). Thus, the question of who does and who *should* govern water is raised in Chapter 6.

As you can probably guess, understanding federalism is about more than reading the Constitution. How Canada functions on a day-to-day or yearly basis is about complex relationships and commonly accepted rules. **Norms,** or patterns of behaviour established over time and accepted by society at large (Axelrod 1986), create real constraints on governments because "norms can have tremendous power" (Axelrod 1986, 1095). There are unwritten rules that guide relations between spheres of power in Canada. In a sense, norms signify constitutional change not through formal amendments but through the development of policy, programs, and practices that are accepted as legitimate. For the purposes of understanding environmental policy, we must consider three relationships: those between (1) Québec and Canada; (2) the provinces and Canada; and (3) Aboriginals and Canada. These will be taken up briefly here and explored in the other chapters of the book—specifically, the third relationship is outlined in Chapter 9, which deals exclusively with Aboriginal environmental law and policy. Each of these three relationships is critical because the norms that have developed in them constrain environmental policy today.

Québec and Canada

There is no denying that Québec is unique compared to Canada's other nine provinces. In 2007, Stephen Harper and the Parliament of Canada formally recognized Québec as a "nation" within Canada. The social, political, and cultural context inside this former French colony has made a mark on Canadian federalism. The province is also large and populous, which has an undeniable pull on federalism, especially with a House of Commons in which representation by population is a fundamental principle. In 2011, the province was allotted 75 seats in the House and 24 seats in the Senate. Beginning with the 2015 election, the province is allocated 78 seats in the House and 24 in the Senate. That amounts to 102 out of 443 possible seats, or 24 per cent of the total legislative branch coming from Québec, which has slightly more than 23 per cent of Canada's population (Elections Canada 2015).

Moreover, Canada's historic relationship with Québec has created operating norms that today can stand in the way of cooperation and law-making. The source of friction may date back to the 1848–67 period, when Upper Canada (Ontario) and Lower Canada (Québec) formed the united Province of Canada governed by a single legislature that provided equal representation to the two colonies. At the time, English-speaking Upper Canada had a much smaller population than did French-speaking Lower

Canada, but a convention developed quickly that a bill had to be passed by a majority of members from each of the now-united colonies before it became law (see Brooks 2013). Perhaps this deal-making tradition set a precedent that Canada has yet to overcome. Québec, quite famously, did not sign the 1982 Constitution Act, as mentioned. Nor did Québec agree to the 1997 Calgary Declaration, which was an agreement that "all provinces, while diverse in their characteristics, have equality of status" (Calgary Declaration 1997).

Similarly, in environmental policy, Québec has always set itself apart from Ottawa and the other provinces. The examples are diverse and many. Perhaps most well known is Québec's attempt to regulate water pollution inside the province. Instead of recognizing this regulation as a provincial right, the Supreme Court upheld the federal law (the Canadian Environmental Protection Act) regulating pollution. In the 1997 case *R. v. Hydro-Québec*, the court decided that "the stewardship of the environment is a fundamental value of our society and that Parliament may use its criminal law power to underline that value" (*R. v. Hydro-Québec*, [1997] 3 S.C.R. 213, para 127; see Muldoon and Lundgren 1997). That said, the province has enacted successful environmental regulations, including being the first province to have a "right to a healthy environment," which it put into its Environmental Quality Act in 1978. Québec was the first province in Canada to pass endangered species legislation (in 1989). Québec, however, was also the first province to object to the passage of a federal endangered species act.

In fact, when creating national environmental policy, the federal government always has to tread lightly where Québec is concerned. It is difficult for the central government in Ottawa to create national policy in environmental matters because Québec does not always recognize its authority and often rejects national policies. Also, Québec has a history of strongly protecting provincial rights and its identity as a unique political entity within Canada. In the case of water pollution, Ottawa won the right to enforce the Canadian Environmental Protection Act and assert the federal government's right to make environmental policy (McKenzie 2002). However, Québec has responded by consistently rejecting national efforts and creating its own (often quite progressive) environmental law. This issue will be discussed in chapters 5 through 8 as we look at specific environmental policies.

The Provinces and Canada

Canada is a large country with a small population. Almost 60 per cent of that small population is concentrated in the two provinces known informally as **central Canada**: Ontario and Québec. These two provinces, consequently, have a greater impact in Canadian federalism than do the other eight **periphery provinces**. Often, central Canada's interests act as a centripetal force in Parliament, where Ontario and Québec hold a majority of seats and have a long history of guiding Canadian policy. The West has always lamented its periphery status, leading political analysts to discuss **western alienation**. The East lives out a reality similar to that of the West. The consequence of a centre-periphery dynamic is that periphery provinces have tended to look toward provincial governments to meet their needs instead of to a distant central government (Brooks 2013).

This provincial reliance has also been exacerbated in the past 50 years by economics. Each province has a regional economic resource or **economic staple**: forestry in British Columbia, oil in Alberta, natural gas and potash in Saskatchewan, and so on. Such **economic regionalism** turns federalism into a conflict over regional economic interests. During the 1970s "government resources became increasingly constrained, economic growth slowed and spurted, and federal-provincial bickering over responsibilities and money increased" (Simeon and Robinson 1990, 213). The provinces began to expand their jurisdiction by growing programs and even won the battle to be consulted on international negotiations. It was really during the 1990s that power started shifting toward the provinces—a trend that continues today. Faced with "mounting public debt and deficits," Ottawa handed over more responsibility and less funding to the provinces, which created a provincial "sense of ownership and independence" (Brock 2008, 153). This history helps us understand Alberta's reluctance to let Ottawa get more involved in oil sands regulations, even for the purposes of climate change policy.

Luckily for Alberta, Stephen Harper and the Conservative Party ushered in an era of **open federalism** in 2006. Open federalism, as opposed to collaborative federalism in which some or all of the 11 governments act collectively, means a shift in the federal-provincial balance toward the provinces, reigning in federal spending power, and a greater respect for the division of powers as stated in the Constitution (Brock 2008; Brooks 2013). To be clear, open federalism does not create a formal change to the Constitution but instead is an informal and unwritten set of guiding principles. The Conservative Party is changing the rules of the game and bending federalism toward the provinces. A specific example is provided in the discussion of water policy and the Navigation Protection Act in Chapter 6.

Aboriginal Peoples and Canada

The word "**Aboriginal**" serves as an umbrella term for three distinct groups of Canadians: First Nations, Inuit, and Métis peoples. The First Nations have occupied Canada, outside of the northern territories, since time immemorial (as discussed in Chapter 4). In the United States, these original inhabitants of North America are called Native Americans. In both countries, the people referred to by these two categorical descriptions are often treated as homogenous when, really, hundreds if not thousands of different First Nations people or Native Americans historically occupied North America. Aboriginal Affairs and Northern Development Canada recognized 617 Canadian First Nation communities in 2015 (AANDC 2015c). The Inuit represent the people who have occupied northern Canada since before remembered history (as discussed in Chapter 10). Last, the Métis are a unique people who emerged in the historic Rupert's Land and have a lineage of one First Nation parent and one European (often French) parent. The Métis, however, were not considered Indians under the Indian Act, so the federal government did not have responsibility for them. Because their existence did not predate European colonization, they were considered not to have a historic claim to land or resources. The Constitution Act of 1982 did recognize the Métis as an Aboriginal people, although it left undefined what rights and claims were theirs as a consequence of this new status.

First Nations signed treaties with the federal government or, historically, with Britain, such as the Royal Proclamation of 1763. The treaty relationship places First Nations' land or reserves inside the "federal house." This means First Nations have the unique status of falling under the complete jurisdiction of the federal government as "discharged primarily but not solely" through Aboriginal Affairs and Northern Development Canada (AANDC) under the Indian Act (Phare 2011).

The Inuit in Canada also have a special place inside federalism. Inuit are the Aboriginal people of northern Canada. About 45,000 Inuit live in 53 communities in Nunatsiavut (Labrador), Nunavik (Québec), Nunavut, and the Inuvialuit Settlement Region of the Northwest Territories. Each of these four Inuit groups has settled land claims with the federal government. When these land claims are combined, the Inuit-held area equals one-third of Canada's landmass (AANDC 2013c). The federal government, through the Indian Act as administer by AANDC, is responsible for programs and services pertaining to the Inuit. These include economic development programs and postsecondary education as well as negotiating and implementing self-government and land claims agreements with Inuit communities (AANDC 2013c).

As Indians under the Indian Act, both the Inuit and First Nations have a right to consultation from the federal government when federal action, environmental or otherwise, could impact treaty lands or rights or land claims agreements. According to the federal government guidelines on consultation, "the common law duty to consult is based on judicial interpretation of the obligations of the Crown ... in relation to potential or established Aboriginal or Treaty rights of the Aboriginal peoples of Canada, recognized and affirmed in section 35 of the *Constitution Act, 1982*" (AANDC 2011a). This right has been reaffirmed in recent Supreme Court cases (discussed in Chapter 9), such as in the *Haida Nation v. British Columbia* and *Taku River Tlingit First Nation v. British Columbia* decisions in 2004 and the *Mikisew Cree First Nation v. Canada* decision in 2005, which determined that that the government has a duty to consult and, where appropriate, accommodate when "the Crown contemplates conduct that might adversely impact potential or established Aboriginal or Treaty rights" (AANDC 2011a). The implications of these decisions for environmental policymaking are substantial and are investigated in Chapter 9. Suffice to say here that, provincially or federally, Canada cannot make environmental policy without considering the country's special relationship with its indigenous peoples.

MULTIPLE LEVELS OF GOVERNANCE

Clearly, at least two levels of government have policymaking power in Canada: federal and provincial. That is at the heart of federalism. However, other levels of power are important for our understanding of policymaking in Canada: international power and local power. The international institutions and actors that have policy implications for Canada, including the United Nations, the North American Free Trade Agreement, and the North Atlantic Treaty Organization, will be discussed in Chapter 11. Canada is a sovereign country and makes its own laws. No other country can make laws for Canada. However, Canada exists inside a complex international arena and as an industrialized nation, so it is influenced by international organizations and trade agreements. Canada is also heavily influenced by the United States, which is both its closest neighbour and its largest trading partner. The Canada-US relationship will be highlighted throughout this text because it is so significant for environmental politics. In fact, understanding energy or water policy in Canada is very difficult without thinking about policymaking within the context of Canada-US relations.

Governments at the city or municipal level also influence or make policy. A **municipality** is an administrative division with political jurisdiction over a populated place, such as a village, town, or city. Provinces can extend certain powers to cities, so these vary across the country. Large cities such as Vancouver, Toronto, and Montréal have a lot of policy power and make some extraordinarily important environmental decisions. The power of larger municipalities is especially felt in the context of transportation, energy use, and water use. For example, the City of Toronto, home to about 2.6 million people in 2011, has reduced greenhouse gas emissions from its own operations by 40 per cent since 1990 through programs such as energy retrofits in city-owned buildings and using cool lake water to air condition Union Station and Old City Hall (Kebe, Bellassen, and Leseur 2011). Similarly, the City of Vancouver is implementing environmental programs to reduce its emissions. Vancouver City Council has already adopted a climate change strategy that guides building codes, city maintenance, infrastructure, parks, and related city business (City of Vancouver, 2014). Cities contain many people, thus both what cities do and what their powers are in the environmental policy arena matter.

We must understand, then, that various levels of government in Canada either directly make or directly influence environmental policy. As Parson (2000) points out, "the environment is extreme in the extent that it is characterized by overlapping and shared authority between governments, and between state, non-state, and inter-state actors" (S130).

CONCLUSIONS

Canada is a constitutional monarchy and a parliamentary democracy. The Canadian Constitution divides power between the federal government and the provincial and territorial governments. In the case of the environment, power is overlapping and jurisdiction is often vague. In practice, the provinces might seem to hold the balance of power because they are responsible for natural resources and for public or provincial Crown land as well as for private property. However, the federal government can, and does, get involved in environmental issues, as the rest of this book will detail.

The three branches of government work separately, but together they are responsible for the creation, implementation, and evaluation of our national and provincial laws. Chapter 3 will define public policy and explain the process of making policy and laws in Canada. Keep in mind that the executive and legislative branches of Canadian government are joined, as the prime minister and the cabinet (the executive branch, which sets policy aims) sit inside Parliament (the legislative branch, which makes laws). Also important to the Canadian system, especially in the realm of environmental politics and policy, is the involvement of other actors such as cities, non-governmental organizations, and citizens. The next chapter will introduce these other actors in the policy-making process and outline the different levels at which policy is made in Canada.

Key Terms

constitutional monarchy; parliamentary democracy; politics; federalism; governance; constitution; executive branch; civil servants; Environment Canada; legislative branch; environmental laws; first-past-the-post system; majority government; party whip; minority government; coalition government; judicial branch; constitutional litigation; judicial review of administrative action; civil action; class action suits; Section 91 of the Constitution; Section 92 of the Constitution; British North America Act of 1867; Canada Act; Constitution Act; Charter of Rights and Freedoms; norms; central Canada; periphery provinces; western alienation; economic staple; economic regionalism; open federalism; Aboriginal; municipality

Discussion Questions

1. What environmental issues matters most to you? Which level of government (federal or provincial) do you think is most responsible for overseeing policy in that area?
2. Why might an elected Senate be beneficial in Canada's parliamentary democracy?
3. The Constitution divides power between the provinces and the federal government in many environmental realms. What are the pros and cons of this reality?
4. What is the difference between government and governance?
5. Which is the most powerful branch of government? How do the branches of government balance each other and serve as a check against absolute or concentrated power?
6. Do you think open federalism might be good for the environment? Why or why not?
7. Canada is defined by economic regionalism. What does this mean, and what influence does economic regionalism have over how federalism works across the country?

Suggested Readings

Banting, Keith, Roger Gibbins, P. M. Leslie, Alain Noel, Richard Simeon, and R. Young. 2006. *Open Federalism: Interpretations, Significance.* Kingston, ON: Institute of Intergovernmental Relations, Queen's University.

Cameron, David, and Richard Simeon. 2002. "Intergovernmental Relations in Canada: The Emergence of Collaborative Federalism." *Publius* 32 (2): 49–72. http://dx.doi .org/10.1093/oxfordjournals.pubjof.a004947.

Harrison, Kathryn. 1996. *Passing the Buck.* Vancouver: UBC Press.

Harrison, Kathryn. 2000. "The Origins of National Standards: Comparing Federal Government Involvement in Environmental Policy in Canada and the United

States." In *Managing the Environmental Union: Intergovernmental Relations and Environmental Policy in Canada*, edited by Patrick Fafard and Kathryn Harrison, 49–80. Kingston, ON: School of Policy Studies, Queen's University.

Harrison, Kathryn. 2002. "Federal-Provincial Relations and the Environment: Unilateralism, Collaboration, and Rationalization." In *Canadian Environmental Policy: Context and Cases*, edited by Debora L. VanNijnatten and Robert Boardman, 123–44. Toronto: Oxford University Press.

Hoberg, George. 1997. "Governing the Environment: Comparing Canada and the United States." In *Degrees of Freedom: Canada and the United States in a Changing World*, edited by Keith G. Banting, George Hoberg, and Richard Simeon, 341–88. Montréal: McGill-Queen's University Press.

MacDowell, Laurel Sefton. 2012. *An Environmental History of Canada*. Vancouver: UBC Press.

McKenzie, Judith I. 2002. *Environmental Politics in Canada: Managing the Commons into the Twenty-First Century*. Oxford: Oxford University Press.

Skogstad, Grace. 2003. "Who Governs? Who Should Govern?: Political Authority and Legitimacy in Canada in the Twenty-First Century." *Canadian Journal of Political Science* 36 (5): 955–73. http://dx.doi.org/10.1017/S0008423903778925.

Skogstad, Grace, and Paul Kopas. 1992. "Environmental Policy in a Federal System: Ottawa and the Provinces." In *Canadian Environmental Policy: Ecosystems, Politics and Process*, edited by Robert Boardman, 43–59. Toronto: Oxford University Press.

Smiley, D. V. 1987. *The Federal Condition in Canada*. Toronto: McGraw-Hill Ryerson.

Valiante, Marcia. 2009. "The Courts and Environmental Policy Leadership." In *Canadian Environmental Policy: Prospects for Leadership and Innovation*, 3rd ed., edited by Debora L. VanNijnatten and Robert Boardman, 30–45. Oxford: Oxford University Press.

Notes

1 Technically the British Parliament maintains the right to determine succession and could choose anyone as king or queen. In modern history, Parliament has not used this power, and succession has proceeded through the reigning royal family.

2 However, even with the system in place, rural areas and PEI are significantly over-represented in terms of the number of MPs per population.

3 Or, in the case of a coalition government, the PM can be the leader of the party that has been chosen to form government.

4 However, even without a majority of seats in the Senate, the governing party in the House usually gets its bills passed in the Senate because it is generally not seen as legitimate for the Senate to block the will of the people, represented by the House of Commons.

Chapter 3

Making Policy in Canada

PUBLIC POLICY is intentional action or intentional inaction by the government that influences the lives of citizens (Peters 1999). As discussed in Chapter 2, deciding not to create speed limits would still be considered creating automotive and transportation policy—just as deciding to make seat belts mandatory for all passengers is also automotive policy. Generally, public policy is made in response to some sort of problem, it is goal oriented, and it is usually on the "public's" behalf (Birkland 2011)—although it can be made on behalf of particularly powerful interests (such as interest groups, as will be discussed). There are literally thousands of policies in existence in Canada today. Some were created by Parliament and are national law. Some were made by provincial legislative assemblies and are provincial law. All laws are public policies, but not all policies are laws. Remember from Chapter 2 that only law is formally passed through Parliament and is backed up by the authority of the courts. Policy can be made by the executive branch and implemented by bureaucracy without going through Parliament. Moreover, private institutions can also create policy. For example, the university or college you attend has policies in place regarding everything from registration deadlines to tree maintenance. The university, but not the police, enforces these policies. Everywhere you turn in all aspects of your life, you confront public policy.

Because the environment encompasses the entire natural world and how it is affected by human activity, it is a broad policy category. Hessing, Howlett, and Sumerville (2005) distinguish between **resource policy** and **environmental policy**. Resource policy is regulation of the "how, when, and where" of primary resource extraction. For example, oil is a resource produced by nature and used by human beings for energy. Canada has policies and regulations in place to manage or guide the entire oil extraction process, right from granting access to the land where the oil can be found, through to guidelines on the emissions from the production and end use of oil. All these policies would fall under natural resource policy.

Environmental policy, on the other hand, is policy aimed at *protecting* the environment as a result of development, resource extraction, or consumption (Hessing, Howlett, and Sumerville 2005). An example is the Species at Risk Act of 2002, which seeks to protect and recover endangered species in Canada, such as the burrowing owl in Saskatchewan or the Lake Erie watersnake in Ontario. Other examples are the policies in place to protect air quality and water quality—and Canada does have many of these types of environmental policies. This book examines both types of policy, natural resource and environmental, with more focus given to the latter and to *how* such policy is made in Canada. This chapter will explain who makes policy (the actors), how they make policy (the process), what policy tools are available to policymakers, and what types of policies exist in Canada at the national and provincial levels.

POLICY ACTORS

The main actors in Canada's policy arena were introduced in Chapter 2: the prime minister and the cabinet, Parliament (the House of Commons and Senate), and the judiciary. However, other policy actors must be discussed before we can understand Canadian policymaking. These include political parties, interest groups, the media, and citizens.

Political Parties

A **political party** is a group of citizens united by a similar ideological outlook and seeking control of government to promote their ideas and politics (Barbour and Wright 2013; Brooks 2013). These ideas are frequently grouped to form an ideology, a particular worldview or a set of values. People who share an ideology often interpret the world and politics in a similar way. Typically, we think about broad ideologies such as conservative, liberal, socialist, or communist. Environmentalism can be considered an ideology, but concern about the environment is something shared by other ideologies as well. Thus, individuals joined by a conservative or a liberal worldview, for example, could have deep concern for pollution or climate change. The difference between these ideologies is in how adherents see a problem and how they want to solve it.

Political parties are generally formed around ideologies and, as the definition states, they pursue control of government so they can promote their worldview and offer their solutions to problems. In some instances, however, a political party can be formed around a moderate, centrist set of values and aims in an attempt to win the most votes. This sort of party is sometimes referred to as a "catch-all" party. Arguably, the Liberal Party of Canada is an example because it positions itself in the ideological centre and is therefore quite open to a broad range of social and economic views. But it is unfair to label only the Liberal Party of Canada as being a "catch-all" party because, historically, other political parties have moved from their ideological principles in an attempt to "catch" votes (Clarkson 2011; Eaves and Owen 2012).

Canada has five main political parties, and each represents a unique and fairly coherent set of policies to voters. Each party's platform is fairly consistent with its ideology and clearly different, at least in some aspects, from the platforms of the other parties. Thus, voters can make a decision based on which party's platform most closely represents their own ideas and beliefs about how government and society should function. The political parties with representation in the House of Commons are the Conservative Party, Liberal Party, New Democratic Party (NDP), Bloc Québécois (BQ), and Green Party. The BQ exists only inside Québec and is not traditionally considered a "national party," even though its leader participates in the televised national party debates during election period. Outside of these five parties, other parties do exist in Canada, and new parties are always able to form and run candidates in an election (see Brooks 2013).

It is common to speak of political parties as existing on a left-right continuum where the left represents social democracy or socialism and the right represents conservatism or even fascism. In such a model, the Liberal Party is considered a centre party, the NDP a left-wing party, and the Conservative Party a right-wing party. The Green Party is harder to pin down on this traditional left-right continuum, as it seems to draw support from across the political spectrum. More often than not, however, the party is considered to be closer to the left than the right. One might think that only left-wing parties would make environmental policy because the "environment" is often considered a left-wing issue. This is not true. All political parties in Canada have an environmental platform.

Political parties may all agree about a problem or share a priority, but they often differ in their proposed solution. For example, all five parties in Canada support "clean energy," but how each party wants to create and support clean energy varies. The Green Party and the NDP would use tax dollars to invest in research and development supporting clean energy, for example, encouraging initiatives such as windmills. The Liberal Party would rather provide incentives, such as tax breaks, to industries that develop and use green technology. The Conservative Party has a history of providing subsidies with tax dollars to promote the use of biofuels and carbon capture and storage. Thus, the stated program goal is the same, but the process or method of arriving at the goal is different (Pembina Institute 2011). Moreover, in addition to different methods and policies, parties have different priorities. "Clean energy" is a much bigger priority and issue for the Green Party than for the Conservative Party, for example.

Each political party in Canada has a party website that describes its ideology and provides a policy platform on different issues ranging from education to health care to the economy to the environment. Perusing each website to get a good sense of where the parties say they stand on environmental issues is worthwhile. However, seeing what political action members of each party have taken on specific issues is perhaps an even better gauge. How have certain party members voted on environmental issues? What have parties done for the environment while in office? Which parties introduce environmental legislation in the House or Senate? Which parties have supported or enacted legislation that has harmed Canada's environment? Finding answers to these questions is more time consuming but more telling than accessing "party platforms" on party websites. As the expression goes, "The proof is in the pudding."

Finally, we must remember that, although a provincial political party is related to its federal counterpart, each is a separate entity in many ways (see Brooks 2013). The federal Conservative Party has a specific ideology and set of policy preferences. The Ontario or New Brunswick Conservative Party will share a similar ideology and many policy preferences but will not be exactly the same. A Canadian might even be a member of one national party but a different provincial party. These differences partly result from regionalism and the nature of local politics. Thus, you should spend time familiarizing yourself with the parties in your home province, as they might not share all the same goals or strategies of the national party.

Elizabeth May and the Green Party of Canada

The Green Party of Canada (GP) was founded in 1983 and ran 60 candidates in the 1984 general election. But it was not until 2004 that the GP ran a candidate in each of Canada's 308 ridings—becoming only the fourth federal party in history to have a full slate of candidates. Despite being excluded from televised national debates during all but the 2008 election campaigns, the GP has risen in popularity since its founding. Elizabeth May is a Canadian environmentalists, activist, lawyer, and politician. She was the executive director of Sierra Club of Canada from 1989 to 2006, when she became leader of the Green Party. On May 2, 2011, she became the first elected Green Party MP by winning the Saanch-Gulf Islands riding in British Columbia.

It is not necessary to join a party to vote in Canada. So why join a party? Membership allows you to participate in the creation of a party's policy platform and to run or vote for party leader. For example, in April 2013, when the federal Liberal Party held a leadership race to replace Michael Ignatieff, only registered members of the Liberal Party of Canada were allowed to run or vote. Ultimately, the members voted for Justin Trudeau to lead the party. Essentially, party members choose the various possible prime ministers because they select the leaders of the parties.

Interest Groups

Interest groups are "private associations which promote their interests by attempting to influence government rather than by nominating candidates and seeking responsibility for the management of government" (Barbour and Wright 2013). Interest groups are not part of government. They are like clubs or clusters of individuals banded together by a single interest or set of interests and working actively to change public policy. They are also called **non-governmental organizations** (NGOs), which is a broader category encompassing all organizations that are not formally part of government but work in the public sphere. Not all NGOs are interest groups as some are charities or think tanks. A simple example of an interest group is MADD: Mothers Against Drunk Driving. Anyone can join this group, including men, but no one inside the group is running for public office. Instead, everyone works together to influence politicians to make stricter regulations about driving under the influence of alcohol and drugs. In this sense, interest groups play a large role in policymaking. Members of an interest group are not necessarily bound by ideology or a common worldview; rather, they share concern for a specific issue. MADD will have members across a broad political spectrum, and political party affiliation is not important for group membership.

Traditionally, interest groups have five different functions in society: representation, education, agenda setting, lobbying, and serving a watchdog role (Barbour and Wright 2013). Not all citizens can be members of government nor can elected officials always represent all members of their ridings on all issues. So interest groups fill a "representation void" that exists in society. For example, my MP may represent most of my political views, but she does not adequately capture my attitudes toward biodiversity. I can join the David Suzuki Foundation and allow that organization to reflect my values in the federal political arena. Thus, a political party as well as a variety of interest groups can represent me.

Interest groups also fulfil an educational role, as they spend most of their time informing Canada's public and politicians about their cause. An interest group use its resources (i.e., time and money) to research its cause and gather statistics and evidence to make a case as to why policy should be changed. MADD, for example, has a page of "statistics" on its website that presents cumulative data pertaining to fatalities, injuries, property damage, and the societal cost of impaired driving crashes (www.madd.ca). This information is used to try to persuade the public and politicians to change the Criminal Code of Canada by making penalties more stringent and testing more vigorous. The information and data collected by MADD, or any interest group, serve a useful educational purpose because, otherwise, citizens and politicians might not be aware of specific issues.

The goal of any interest group is to get its issue on the government agenda so that legislation will be tabled and passed in Parliament to benefit or promote the group's cause. To get an issue on the government agenda, interest groups will lobby government. The term "lobby" comes from the British system, which saw elected officials and peers gathering in the hallways (or lobbies) of Parliament before and after debates, where members of the public could approach them with concerns, questions, or special requests. Thus, "lobbying" is now the term used to capture the process by which groups or individuals appeal to politicians. However, this practice is no longer confined to the lobbies of Parliament Hill. Lobbying now involves social media, lunches and dinners, golf tournaments, hockey games, and other methods of attracting the attention of individual MPs. And lobbying can be conducted by professional "lobbyists" hired to represent particular interests to Parliament. As of March 31, 2014, almost 3,000 lobbyists were listed in the Canadian Registry of Lobbyists: 2,144 consultant lobbyists, 489 in-house lobbyists representing organizations, and 302 in-house lobbyists representing corporations (Office of the Commissioner of Lobbying of Canada 2014, 4).

In a federal system such as Canada's, the divided spheres of power mean there are more levels of government to lobby. However, the strong party discipline of MPs and of members of provincial parliament or legislative assemblies (MPPs or MLAs) members of the provincial legislatures means that lobbying has a more limited potential to affect policy. As explained in Chapter 2, each party has a party whip responsible for ensuring that all members of a party vote in line with party policies and preferences. Thus, many individual MPs do not have much say, so lobbying them as individuals is not the most effective way to influence policy outcomes. At most, a lobbyist might be able to convince an MP to introduce a private members bill, but that bill would still need to pass a vote in the House of Commons and the Senate to become public policy. Instead, a lobbyist would approach members of the upper party echelon (party leader and cabinet ministers, for example) who could then influence the way all MPs in the party would vote on a specific ballot measure.

Finally, interest groups also play an important watchdog role in society. Sometimes interest groups are even called "watchdogs" by the media or government. The idea is that interest groups watch government actors and policy outcomes to ensure that politicians are fulfilling their promises and that laws and organizations are functioning as intended. Members of the public will vote, but they often do not have the time (or interest) to monitor government action and see if all politicians are living up to their campaign promises. So, generally speaking, all interest groups perform these five tasks but their success hinges on several other factors. According to Brooks (2013), successful interest groups are well organized, have numerous resources at their disposal (people as well as money), have electoral influence, have group cohesion (something that really binds members together), and have the capacity to inflict damage on the economy (through their influence).

There are upward of 20,000 Canadian organizations that fit the description of an interest group (Brooks 2013). The Canadian Council of Chief Executives (CCCE), an economic interest group of Canadian CEOs and entrepreneurs, is one of the most resource rich in Canada, with members controlling over $6 trillion in assets. CCCE represents large companies that, combined, employ about 1.5 million Canadians (CCCE 2014, 4). Environmental interest groups do exist in Canada. The most important ones, which Wilson (1992) calls "the majors," include Nature Canada (formerly the Canadian Nature Federation), the Canadian Parks and Wilderness Society, the David Suzuki Foundation, Ducks Unlimited Canada, Greenpeace Canada, the Nature Conservancy of Canada, Sierra Club Canada, and World Wildlife Fund Canada. These groups spend their resources educating Canadians on environmental issues and lobbying the government to enact stricter environmental legislation. Chapters 5 through 8 explore the role of interest groups and environmental non-governmental organizations in more detail and provide examples of recent interest group work.

The Media

The media plays a very important role in society and politics. Social media, which enables the sharing of user-generated information through Internet-based tools, is an increasingly popular means of political communication. But more traditional forms of media are significant as well. Print media includes newspapers and magazines, and commercial media

includes radio and television broadcasting by privately owned corporations. All these types of media play a role in the policy process and are
worth discussing here.

There are still several print newspapers in Canada even though print
media is declining in North America (Communic@tions Management
2013; Pew Research Center 2015). Canada's national newspapers are *The
Globe and Mail* and the *National Post*; some larger newspapers include the
Toronto Star, *The Vancouver Sun*, the *Montreal Gazette*, and the *Calgary
Herald*. It used to be common for Canadian households to get a daily
paper delivered to the door every morning. I grew up in a house where the
Regina Leader-Post was on our doorstep before I left for swim practice in
the morning. It is unlikely that many of you read a print edition newspaper
in your own home on a regular basis. Instead, you are more likely to
gain access to some or all of these newspapers through the Internet. It is
a good idea to follow one or two of these papers on Twitter or Facebook
to stay abreast of current Canadian issues.

Canadians can get international and national news through the
Canadian Broadcasting Corporation (CBC), a state-supported public
radio and television broadcaster that also provides online content. Its
programming is in English, French, and Aboriginal languages. Privately
owned broadcasters provide television news, including CTV, Global,
City, and TVA. This last is a privately owned French-language television network. Aboriginal Peoples Television Network (APTN), a public
television network for indigenous people, also provides national news.
However, similar to print media, television is struggling to compete
with the Internet. According to the Canadian Radio-television and
Telecommunications Commission *Communications Monitoring Report*
for 2013, 79 per cent of Canada's 13.9 million households had an
Internet subscription in 2012, which is slightly more than the US average. Roughly 33 per cent of Canadians watched Internet television in
that same year, with typical users watching 3 hours per week—up from
2.8 hours the previous year. Internet consumption of radio is also increasing, with about 20 per cent of Canadians streaming an AM or FM signal
over the web in 2012 (CRTC 2013).

So, how does all this media affect public policy? In the most straightforward way, we can argue that media informs the public about politics
and everyday events. To a certain extent the media shapes knowledge
and public opinion in society. Some events, such as auto accidents and
elections, occur in the public realm and the media "covers" them. Other
times, journalists become watchdogs and investigate government claims,
analyze complex data or details, and evaluate public policy. The media,
then, can shape public opinion by influencing what issues are given

attention and how those issues are presented (McCombs 1977). Or as Bernard Cohen famously pointed out, "The press ... may not be successful in telling its readers what to think, but it is stunningly successful in telling its readers what to think about" (Cohen 1963, 13).

In communications and media studies, **priming** and **framing** are often used to describe the media's influence (Cox 2013). Priming is influencing the public's perception of certain people, events, and issues by the emphasis given to their particular characteristics. It can even refer to the amount of attention or the kind of attention that events or political candidates receive in the media (Cox 2013; Scheufele and Tewksbury 2007). For example, an ideologically right-leaning newspaper might feature articles and photographs that present Liberals as irresponsible spendthrifts while emphasizing the stability and trustworthiness of Conservatives as fiscal managers. A left-leaning blog might focus on the recent Conservative government's "heartless" cuts to programs and services while emphasizing the NDP's commitment to social equality. Closely related is framing, or the process through which the media emphasizes particular aspects of a news story, thereby influencing the public's perception of the story (see Cox 2013; Scheufele and Tewksbury 2007). For example, the phrase "youthful indiscretion" has a different meaning than "moral transgression" even though both phrases could be used to describe (or frame) the same action—such as Miley Cyrus twerking on television with Robin Thicke.

Relaying facts and events is a crucial part of the public policy process. However, the media is not always a positive or beneficial influence. "Horserace" journalism is political journalism that focuses on the competitive aspects of politics rather than on actual policy proposals and political decisions (Barbour and Wright 2013). It can emphasize image instead of content.

A related tendency is scandal watching, or the concentration on developing scandals to the exclusion of other, possibly more relevant, news events (Barbour and Wright 2013). In fall 2013, Toronto Mayor Rob Ford completely dominated Canadian news because police had recently located a video that apparently showed him smoking crack cocaine. Every media outlet in Canada was reporting on this singular event, despite the fact that other events of political significance were also occurring—such as the announcement of a Canada-EU free-trade agreement (the Comprehensive Economic Trade Agreement); the release of a recovery strategy for the North Pacific humpback whales; agreement on a climate pact between California, Washington, Oregon, and British Columbia; and countless other important events that were underreported because of the Ford scandal.

The media helps citizens learn about new issues and policies, stay informed about ongoing policies, and evaluate public policy, making it a critical part of the policy process. It is important to consider not only these different aspects but also the priming and framing of issues when you are thinking about government and policy. Where do you get your news? How are the stories framed? It can be easy to think that a newspaper is reporting "facts," but this is not the case. Instead, the media presents narratives, and the consumer needs to reflect on multiple sources and types of media before coming to decisions about public policy.

Citizen Experts

Citizens play an indispensable role in the policy process, and experts, such as scientists, medical doctors, PhDs, and other credentialed and respected members of society, make up an important subset of citizens. **Citizen experts** are not elected to hold any government office or official government position. That said, such individuals can sometimes be asked to serve as an advisor to the prime minister or premier, such as when Dr. Tom Flangan, a political science professor at the University of Calgary, served as a senior communications advisor to Stephen Harper during the 2006 election campaign. Normally, however, the influence of experts in the policy process comes through their research or professional agenda. The media or Parliament, for example, might ask medical doctors about the health risks associated with certain chemicals or air pollutants. Scientific research carried out by non-government scientists in areas of water pollution, deforestation, biodiversity loss, or other environmental issues is almost always used by political actors to make policy decisions. Economists, sociologists, historians, and political scientists, for example, might be asked to give evidence or a statement in Parliament, such as during a formal review of policy during the evaluation stage. The point is that non-elected citizens get involved in essential policymaking decisions by way of their expert knowledge on a specific issue or in a specific field.

Is this democratic? Yes. Our elected officials cannot be experts in all fields and must rely upon the best available information to make important decisions affecting the public. They must, therefore, seek information from citizen experts. However, a consequence is that certain citizens play a larger role than others in the policy process. Experts are trusted by the public to be unbiased, factual, and fair—instead of pushing their own agendas or fudging facts.

Citizens

You are among the last set of actors. Citizens also play an important role in public and environmental policy. As voters, individual Canadians select their members of Parliament (at least in the House of Commons) as well as members of their provincial legislative assembly and their municipal council. Citizens are also members of political parties, members of interest groups, and consumers of media. In all these ways, citizens are indirectly involved in the policymaking process. Whom you vote for matters for environmental policy. What interest groups you donate money to matters for environmental policy. The news you choose to watch will have an effect on the salience of particular issues and pieces of information (the extent that you are aware of and concerned about specific events, places, and people) and your attitude toward policy.

Citizens are also economic consumers. Through buying products, citizens signal to the market and to the government what is important and what is worth paying (more) money for. Do you buy organic food? If so, that tells your grocery store to continue to sell organic food. That signals suppliers and farmers that organic food is a viable economic good. It signals the government that organic food might need to be regulated or at least certified, so you know you are buying a quality and genuine organic apple. Thus, because enough citizens buy organic apples every day, environmental policy must be made to certify and regulate organic apple production. Our power as consumers is profound. In some senses, you vote every time you purchase something. For this reason, you should never underestimate your power as a citizen and as a participant in the economy.

As Figure 3.1 makes apparent, various actors interact in society to influence public policy. This chart does make it seem as though each

FIGURE 3.1 Actors Influencing Environmental Policy

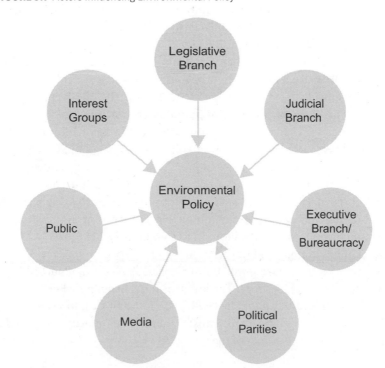

group has an equal weight and representation in the process. However, as this chapter has made clear, different groups influence policy differently—and some groups matter more than others (especially at certain times of policymaking). Although MPs draft, debate, and pass laws, citizens, through interest groups, media, and political parties, influence MPs. The role different actors play in the overall process will be discussed further as we examine the process of policymaking.

THE POLICY PROCESS

The process of making policy in Canada is not always straightforward. The classic model, or narrative, of how *law* as policy is made has five stages: agenda setting, formulation, legitimization, implementation, and evaluation (see Figure 3.2). According to this process model, an issue will get on the government *agenda*, and, in response to the issue, an MP or group of MPs will *formulate* a policy and write a bill to address the issue. After the bill has moved through three readings in the House and Senate, it will be voted on and *legitimized* by Parliament and then given royal assent. At this point, the bureaucracy will *implement* the law and allow the public, media, interest groups, politicians, and perhaps even the Supreme Court to *evaluate* the effectiveness or legitimacy of the law. After evaluation, the law might be terminated, whereupon it exits the cycle; kept until circumstances require another evaluation; or amended, which moves it back to the agenda-setting or policy-formulation stage.

A good example of a Canadian law that went through each stage of the policy cycle is the Canadian Environmental Protection Act (CEPA). This law provides a systematic approach to assessing and managing chemical substances in the environment. During the 1980s, pollutants, especially toxic chemicals, were of public interest across North America (see Chapter 4). The "toxic blob" found near Windsor, Ontario, on the St. Clair River created national concern, and the ongoing Love Canal disaster near Niagara Falls added more fuel to the public fire. In response to public concern, the federal government put the issue on its *agenda* and created a task force in 1985 to examine policy approaches to toxic substances. Based on the findings of the committee, the government drafted legislation and introduced it in the House of Commons in 1986. Bill C-74, the Canadian Environmental Protection Act, went through major revisions in the committee stage (*formation*) but was passed (*legitimized*) in 1987 and came into force in June 1988. The law was implemented by Environment Canada and Health Canada. In 1994, the House of Commons Standing Committee on Environment and Sustainable Development conducted a five-year review (*evaluation*) of the CEPA and recommended amendments.

In 1996, Bill C-74 was introduced in Parliament but died on the order of paper when the general federal election was called. Bill C-32 was introduced in 1998 and received royal assent on September 14, 1999. It came into force in March 2000. Thus, you can see that the classic policy cycle can adequately capture the macro level of policymaking in Canada.

When a Model Is Only a Model

It is important to keep in mind that the policy cycle is just a model and not always a reflection of reality. Not all policy follows the path to law that the CEPA did. And not all policies are or become laws. Moreover, law does not just sail through each stage, but progress can happen in fits and spurts, sometimes skipping stages completely. For example, the 2002 Species at Risk Act was originally introduced in the House of Commons in 1996 (as Bill C-65, the Canada Endangered Species Protection Act), but it kept failing to get legitimization so was stuck at the formulation stage for years. And even today, some would argue, the law is stuck at the implementation stage because parts of the law have not been fully or properly implemented (e.g., the safety net provision discussed in Chapter 5).

Furthermore, the model does not adequately capture the agenda-setting stage of the process and, consequently, much has been written in political

FIGURE 3.2 The Policy Process in Five Stages

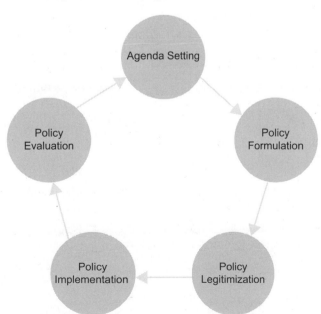

science and public policy literature about this stage. Perhaps the most well-known model for agenda setting is John Kingdon's three streams model, which suggests that a focusing event occurs and gets everyone's attention (Kingdon 2010). A focusing event is something such as the 2011 tsunami in Japan, which led to the meltdown at the Fukushima Daiichi nuclear station. That event led the US government to slow the development of nuclear facilities initially (although recently the United States has reconsidered nuclear energy as a way to reduce GHG emissions across the country). Essentially, a tsunami in Japan got everyone's attention and focused it on nuclear power. Arguably, the toxic blob and the Love Canal disaster were the focusing events for the CEPA. But do we always have to wait for a big event to occur before policy can be made? No. Policy is made under several different conditions. An election can easily trigger a series of new policies because a new party in power can have different goals or strategies for achieving them. Likewise, a government might need a few years to implement its party platform, so long-standing party aims may seem to surface out of the blue as policy.

Perhaps most important, the model does not capture the other ways in which policy can be made in the country. The governing party can implement regulations or guidelines that create new ways of doing things in the policy realm. These policies do not pass through Parliament and are not law. For example, the Conservative Party implemented the Chemicals Management Plan in 2006, which is a set of guidelines for how the Canadian Environmental Protection Act will be implemented by the bureaucracy (see Chapter 6). The Chemicals Management Plan did not come into existence as spelled out by the policy process. Instead, the prime minister and cabinet ministers for Health Canada and Environment Canada created (with consultation from citizen experts and government bureaucrats) the management plan and announced its implementation (see Prime Minister of Canada 2006). Thus, the Chemicals Management Plan is a policy but not a law. It is a set of guidelines, and the next party to form government is free to change these guidelines at any time without consent of Parliament. There are hundreds if not thousands of policies that exist federally and across the 10 provinces and 3 territories.

The governing party can also create policy through omnibus bills. An **omnibus bill** is any bill that covers a wide range of unrelated topics. It has been common for the Harper government to create budget bills as omnibus bills. The government included things related to the budget in the bill and received approval for everything at once. For example, in 2012 the Harper administration introduced a budget bill that made changes to the Navigable Waters Protection Act. The changes, which passed with the budget, reduce federal oversight on Canada's waterways (see

Chapter 6). Because the Harper government has enough votes to pass a bill in Parliament, the omnibus bill passed, and consequently changes were made to environmental policy. There was no debate per se on the newly named Navigation Protection Act, and the law itself did not go through the stages of the policy process as laid out neatly above.

Administrative Decision Making and Implementation: Tribunals

Administrative tribunals can be established by federal or provincial legislation (i.e., by Parliament or a provincial legislature) to function as specialized agencies responsible for policy implementation. The individuals who make up the tribunal are appointed by government and are often considered "experts." Once created, tribunals may conduct research and make recommendations, as in law reform commissions. However, some tribunals make rules and develop national or provincial policy. The Canadian Radio-television and Telecommunications Commission is an example of an administrative tribunal with the power to make rules governing Canadian communications. Other types of tribunals include those that adjudicate labour relations or make decisions about grant allocations. The most important type of tribunal for environmental policy are the environmental assessment boards that carry out environmental assessments for the government or a third party before the initiation of a project that will impact the environment. All tribunals are expected to be non-partisan, even those whose members are appointment by the government in power. The superior courts have jurisdiction to review the function of any administrative tribunal to ensure fairness and constitutionality (Kuttner 2006).

As discussed in Chapter 2, the court system can also alter policy in Canada. This has been particularly true in the area of Aboriginal law and the environment, as discussed in Chapter 9. The courts have unquestionably changed the way the federal government interacts with Aboriginal lands and Aboriginal groups for the purposes of natural resource extraction. Since the Haida Nation case, the "duty to consult" has placed responsibility on the federal government to conduct formal consultations with Aboriginal groups when government decisions or even government-authorized actions (such as environmental assessments) potentially impact Aboriginal lands or Aboriginal rights to resources. Thus, Canada's Parliament did not create a federal law that says the government has a duty to consult. Instead, the duty, which is an important piece of environmental policymaking today, comes from the Constitution Act and the courts' interpretation of that act.

Actors and the Process

Different actors are important at different stages of the policymaking process—which itself involves making laws and regulations, guidelines and targets, and general policy aims. However, let's concentrate here on the policymaking process as outlined. In terms of general agenda setting, all actors can be involved, especially interest groups and the media, but, when it comes to putting something on the legislative agenda in the House or Senate, a member of Parliament must introduce the issue into one of the chambers. At the bare minimum, their participation is required. In the formulation stage, members of Parliament set about writing a new policy. They require information from a variety of sources: news media, interest groups, citizens' letters, public opinion polls, think tanks, government studies, and academic scholarship. Often lobbyists play a large role here as they write letters, make phone calls, and meet with MPs so as to influence the intent and language of the bill. Similarly, bureaucrats at various agencies might also write policy briefs to help shape policy at this stage. However, very few people are involved in actually writing the law, usually just the committee to which the bill was referred, but many different actors indirectly contribute to the process.

At the legitimization stage, only members of Parliament and the executive branch participate. The House and Senate pass a new law through a majority vote. The governor general then signs the bill into law, giving it "royal assent." The bureaucracy becomes involved again in the policy process at the implementation stage, as it must now implement the new policy. If the House and Senate pass a new law protecting endangered species, then Environment Canada must implement this law on federal lands and territory. Federal Environment Canada offices exist throughout the country in regional branches, and the minister of the environment must see that each office is working together to implement a national endangered species law (this specific example will be discussed in Chapter 5).

Finally, the evaluation stage, like the agenda-setting stage, is open to participation by everyone in a broad sense. The public can speak out about policies they do or do not like. For example, there was a large public outcry about the long-gun registry in rural Canada. People did not like the way this law was implemented. By voicing their complaints, they were evaluating the law. The media obviously plays a large role, as you can imagine. *The Globe and Mail* has a "daily poll" enabling readers to express opinions regarding a political or policy issue. This and similar polls can often gauge public opinion on an issue and provide evaluation of a policy. Interest groups evaluate policy by collecting data on the success or outcomes of a law once it has been implemented. Likewise, elected politicians will speak out about their assessment of specific law. They can stand in the House or Senate and voice a concern, or they can go to the media and relay that concern to the public. Almost any actor, then, can participate in the evaluation stage.

The policy cycle is a useful description of how policy is often made in Canada. However, a more nuanced understanding of the process, of its variety and contexts, is necessary. Thinking about what kind of policy is being made is also important, as the next section demonstrates.

POLICY INSTRUMENTS AND TOOLS

Policies come in different shapes and forms. Most policy is meant to change individual or group behaviour to benefit the public good (or, in some circumstances, to benefit private corporations). How a policy actually works to change behaviour varies from policy to policy. Generally speaking, the government can take a very hands-off approach or a very direct approach. For example, public education can be a policy employed by the government to change attitudes and behaviour. Other tools include **voluntary instruments, economic instruments,** and **regulatory instruments** (see Table 3.1). Each is worth briefly reviewing here because Canada has employed all of these tools, sometimes in combination, in environmental policy.

Voluntary policy tools ask individuals or companies to change their behaviour but do not provide direct incentives for their doing so (no penalty or payment). Recycling programs are voluntary tools to reduce consumer waste. The government provides bins and asks us to recycle. When you are walking down Yonge St. in Toronto, the garbage receptacles all have a recycling option. No police officer hovers to ensure we recycle

TABLE 3.1 Policy Tools

TYPE OF POLICY	EXAMPLES OF TOOL OR STRATEGY
Voluntary Outreach/Education	Pollution release inventories, environmental report cards, eco-labelling, performance awards (non-monetary)
Economic	Emissions trading, user fees, pollution taxes, product fees, deposit refund systems, environmental subsidies, performance awards (monetary)
Regulatory	Product or substance ban or limit, design-based standards, performance-based standards, permit systems

our Tim Hortons paper bag—it is up to us to take action. Similarly, the government can ask companies to recycle or to produce less plastic in the first place. This style of policymaking is quite popular and frequently used—mainly because it is a low-cost way to change behaviour. Unfortunately, it is not always effective.

Voluntary programs are usually combined with public education or outreach. The government provides information and data about a specific problem in hopes that, if we learn about a problem, we will change our personal behaviour to alleviate that problem. For example, statistics and information about the amount of pollution caused by automobiles can affect individual behaviour. Or, if the government provides society with information about plastic bottle pollution and also provides a way to recycle plastic bottles, individuals might voluntarily decide to recycle. Such an approach means the government does not have to use penalties or payment. For example, did you know that it can take three litres of water to make one litre of bottled water?[1] Does that information make you more likely to think twice about buying bottled water? If so, then information has altered public behaviour. However, sometimes information and education are not enough to make a significant difference, so the government turns to economic or regulatory policy tools.

Economic tools use money to alter behaviour and come in the form of taxes, charges, or subsidies and payment incentives. The government does not prohibit cigarette smoking, but, by levying large taxes on cigarettes, the government alters behaviour because fewer people smoke, and those who do smoke less than they would if cigarettes were cheaper. Chapter 8 will discuss the idea of taxing carbon dioxide as a way to make companies produce less greenhouse gas. Charges can also be attached to specific behaviours. Companies might have to pay to dump waste or individuals might have to pay an extra charge on plastic bottles.

Although taxes and charges are both disincentives, the government can also incentivize behaviour through subsidies or reward payments. The government can pay individuals to return their plastic bottles, for example, thereby encouraging recycling. So, instead of fining people who do not recycle plastic, the government rewards people who do. What difference does choosing an incentive rather than a disincentive make? Fining individuals who do not recycle would be very time intensive and costly for the government. Essentially, it would require garbage police who inspect what individuals throw away and then fine non-compliance. Incentives, on the other hand, allow individuals to seek out the government for reward—saving government time and, arguably, money. Of course, fewer people may recycle, but, if the incentive is set high enough, more people might recycle. At the end of the day, the government decides which tool to use (and this decision usually happens during the formulation stage of policymaking).

Finally, regulatory tools are probably the easiest to understand. These are the simple "do" and "don't" policies that come with consequences. A fine for failure to comply with speed limits or seat belt policies is a regulatory tool that you may recognize. Such an approach prohibits a specific behaviour, such as speeding or unsafe driving. Or a regulatory tool can also be permit based, whereby an individual or a company requires permission from the government to do something, such as fish or dump pollution into a waterway. The easiest way to remember how regulatory tools are used to associate them with penalties for violation. These tools always require monitoring and governmental enforcement to be effective.

DEFINING ENVIRONMENTAL POLICY

We tend to associate the environment with pollution and wildlife (or "nature"), but, today, it covers a much larger and more complicated landscape. Likewise, many different public policies relate to the environment. Aspects of environmental policy are included in the governance of public health and safety, science and technology, agriculture and forestry, and waterways, for example. In fact, I challenge you to think of something that is not "environmental." It is hard! But if almost anything can be construed as an environmental issue, then is all public policy environmental policy? Not quite. What is meant by environmental policy in Canada is policy that governs human behaviour toward the environment. And this definition explains why, as John Dryzek argues, environmental problems are so tangled—they are found at the intersection of ecosystems and human social systems, and are thus "doubly complex" (2013, 9).

In Canada, we have hundreds of environmental policies at the federal level, and each varies according to the policy tools used to alter behaviour. Canada is a young nation, but environmental policy dates back to its founding inception, as Chapter 4 will discuss in detail. Below is a list of some of the most significant federal environmental policies created in Canada's history. The policies in bold were enacted when the Liberal Party was in power while the others were enacted under the Conservative Party. No other party has formed government in Canada, so they cannot be credited with specific policies—although they likely played a major role in the formulation and legitimization of various environmental laws.

Fisheries Act, 1868, 2012
Navigable Waters Protection Act, 1882, 2012[2]
*Migratory Birds Convention Act, 1916, **1994***

National Parks Act, 1930, 2000
National Wildlife Week Act, 1947
Arctic Waters Pollution Prevention Act, 1970
Canada Water Act, 1970
Canadian Environment Week Act, 1971[3]
Clean Air Act, 1971
Department of the Environment Act, 1971
Canada Wildlife Act, 1973
Ocean Dumping Control Act, 1975
Canadian Environmental Protection Act, 1988,[4] *1999*[5]
Canadian Environmental Assessment Act, 1992, 2012
Canada Foundation of Sustainable Development Technology Act, 2001
Species At Risk Act, 2002
Federal Sustainable Development Act, 2008
Environmental Enforcement Act, 2010

These are all federal laws made by the federal government (passed through Canada's Parliament). It is important to understand that some federal policies pertain to process and affect the way environmental policy is made or implemented across a wide sector of society. For example, under the former Canadian Environmental Assessment Act (CEAA), any economic project falling under federal jurisdiction required an approved environmental assessment before it could begin. Under CEAA 2012, an assessment is no longer automatically triggered whenever a federal authority intends to participate in a project. An **environmental assessment (EA)** is a significant undertaking as it must determine the extent to which a project will cause adverse environmental effects. This determination involves the use of the "best available science." The assessment also includes the mitigation efforts of the parties willing to offset the effects. The minister of environment must make the final decision as to whether the effects are justified in the particular circumstance—does the benefit of the project outweigh the environmental costs? An assessment is warranted when the project involves federal lands, migratory birds, aquatic species, and initiatives that cross provincial or international boundaries and Aboriginal lands. Those seeking project approval to build a dam or drill for oil, for example, must provide a description of their project to the Canadian Environmental Assessment Agency to verify if a formal EA is required. The agency has 45 days to decide if an EA is necessary and a subsequent 365 days to complete one. The public may provide comment during the 45-day period as well as during the formal EA, if one is conducted. One reason an EA may not be conducted is if the minister of the environment believes the substantive requirements of an EA can be met at the provincial level or if a province is willing to undertake the assessment (see Ecojustice 2012c for a legal background on the Canadian Environmental Assessment Act).

Another federal law that influences environmental policy across the country is the Environmental Enforcement Act. Passed in 2010, this federal law amends the enforcement tools and penalty regime across 10 different existing federal acts: the Antarctic Environmental Protection Act (AEPA); the Canada Water Act; the Canada National Marine Conservation Areas Act (CNMCAA); the Canada National Parks Act (CNPA); the Canada Wildlife Act (CWA); the Canadian Environmental Protection Act (CEPA), 1999; the International River Improvements Act (IRIA); the Migratory Birds Convention Act (MBCA), 1994; the Saguenay–St. Lawrence Marine Park Act (SSLMPA); and the Wild Animal and Plant Protection and Regulation of International and Interprovincial Trade Act (WAPPRIITA). Essentially, the 2010 law changes the way all these laws are enforced by creating new monetary penalties. Obviously, this law affects policy across the country and across all environmental areas, from air pollution to wildlife. The law does not, however, change the way provinces enforce their own laws.

Last, the **Federal Sustainable Development Act** (FSDA) of 2008 has wide ramifications for 30 departments and agencies in the federal government. As will be discussed in many chapters of this book, sustainable development is about meeting the needs of today without compromising the needs of future generations. The FSDA aims to balance economic development and resource extraction in Canada, on the one hand, with preserving a safe and sustainable environment, on the other (Environment Canada 2013f). We must, for example, conserve our forests if we want to continue to have a profitable forestry industry. The FSDA calls for a Federal Sustainable Development Strategy (FSDS) that is updated every three years (the FSDA is a law and the FSDS is a policy). These strategies require every federal agency that is related to the environment and the economy to create goals and set targets for growth and conservation/protection. So, again, the FSDS is an example of a single federal policy that has wide-ranging ramifications for how environmental policy is created and implemented in Canada.

POLICYMAKING IN THE PROVINCES

Provinces function similarly to the national government. Each provincial government has an executive and legislative branch and a judiciary. One important difference is that provinces have **unicameral legislatures**, meaning their legislative assemblies have one chamber: the lower chamber. Provinces do not have a senate. A bill has to move through only one chamber before becoming law, consequently. Each province has a premier, who is the leader of the party with the most seats in the provincial legislative assembly. Like the federal system, the provincial system is also flooded with policy actors—political parties, interest groups, media, and citizens. As a responsible citizen, you should familiarize yourself with your provincial legislative assembly and with the political parties in your province.

Canada's provinces have also enacted many environmental laws and regulations over time. In fact, most environmental regulation is a provincial responsibility, as provinces have jurisdiction over many natural resources, wildlife, and land. A policy would undergo the same stages as it would at the federal level, except provincial legislative assemblies have no upper chamber to get through. Provinces also use a wide variety of policy tools, and this produces different kinds of policies across the country. For example, Nova Scotia may decide to use a regulatory approach to recycling, whereas Ontario may use a voluntary approach. In areas of provincial jurisdiction, the federal government and other provinces cannot infringe on a province's authority. So in any given environmental area, policy varies from coast to coast to coast. As you will see, this variety is indeed the case for most policy areas discussed in this book.

POLICYMAKING IN THE TERRITORIES

Constitutionally, territories and provinces have different powers. Like provinces, territories do have jurisdiction over education, social welfare, health, local government, transportation, and civil law. Each territory also has its own government. There is a premier and a legislative assembly with a single chamber (a lower house) that makes policy (Yukon Legislative Assembly 2012). In terms of environmental policy, however, the most significant difference between provinces and territories comes down to land and natural resources. The provinces own and control most Crown land (public or government land), with the exception of land reserved for national parks and the like. But in the territories, the federal government retains ownership and control of all Crown lands—this includes extensive natural resource rights. This federal ownership has huge environmental and economic implications because the vast majority of land in the North is Crown land, so the federal government is a substantial economic player and responsible for significant environmental oversight.

In 2003, the federal government transferred administrative responsibility, but not ownership, of land and non-renewable resources to the Yukon government. In 2012, the Northwest Territories also received administrative responsibility for land and resources. Nunavut is hoping to establish a similar arrangement in the next few years. In fact, seeing these three territories become official provinces in the next decade would not be surprising.

What complicates policymaking in the North are the various land claims agreements, modern-day treaties between the federal government and the Aboriginal peoples (Inuit) residing in the North. The relation between these agreements and environmental policy will be discussed in Chapter 10, but it is important to mention here that these agreements create new institutions of government, such as co-management boards, to administer wildlife, land, and environmental regulation. In areas where an agreement exists, such as parts of Nunavut, Québec, and Newfoundland and Labrador, the Inuit have retained some level of control over policymaking.

Territories can make their own environmental policy, but only for land not owned by the federal government or not co-managed by the Inuit. Often, a territorial government is forced to make policy in conjunction with other levels of government. And because territories control less land, they have less power in the environmental realm (Yukon Legislative Assembly 2012).

CONCLUSIONS

Policymaking in Canada is a complicated process with a variety of actors entering and exiting the process at various times. A straightforward, simplistic description is that environmental law is made by our elected officials and implemented by our bureaucracy. But, as should be clear, the process is rarely straightforward, and, even when it is, numerous outside influences affect policy, including media, interest groups, and citizens. Policy can be regulatory, voluntary, or economic, and it can impact behaviour directly or affect the overall process of how a rule is carried out. Each level of government—the national government, the provincial governments, and, to a lesser extent, the territorial governments—has the power to create environmental policy. The next chapter provides an overview of the history of the environmental movement in Canada. This chapter sets the context for understanding how environmental problems developed and why wildlife, pollution, and climate change continue to be pressing issues across the country.

Key Terms

public policy; resource policy; environmental policy; political party; interest groups; non-governmental organizations; citizen experts; omnibus bill; voluntary instruments; economic instruments; regulatory instruments; environmental assessment; Federal Sustainable Development Act; unicameral legislatures

Discussion Questions

1. What are the major differences between political parties and interest groups?
2. The media plays a big role in the policy process. Do you think the media has a larger negative or a larger positive effect on environmental policy in Canada?
3. What role do you play in policymaking in Canada?
4. How is policymaking different in the territories than the provinces?
5. Which set of policy tools (voluntary, economic, or regulatory) do you think is most effective at altering public behaviour? Why?

Suggested Readings

Hessing, Melody, Michael Howlett, and Tracy Summerville. 2005. *Canadian Natural Resource and Environmental Policy*. Vancouver: UBC Press.

Howlett, Michael. 2013. *Canadian Public Policy: Selected Studies in Process and Style*. Toronto: University of Toronto Press.

Lorimer, Rowland, and Mike Gasher. 2001. *Mass Communication in Canada*. 4th ed. Toronto: Oxford University Press.

Muldoon, Paul, Alastair Lucas, Robert B. Gibson, and Peter Pickfield. 2014. *An Introduction to Environmental Law and Policy in Canada*. Toronto: Emond Montgomery Publications.

Orsini, Michael, and Miriam Smith, eds. 2007. *Critical Policy Studies*. Vancouver: UBC Press.

Notes

1 The Pacific Institute (2007); this estimate includes the water used in the manufacture of plastic bottles. The Canadian bottled water industry reportedly requires 1.3 litres of water to produce a litre of bottled water (AAFC 2013b).

2 The 2012 title is the Navigation Protection Act.

3 Although this act was passed when the Liberals were in power, the legislation was the brainchild of Conservative John Diefenbaker, prime minister between 1957 and 1963.

4 This law subsumed and replaced the Environmental Contaminants Act of 1975, the Clean Air Act, and the Ocean Dumping Act.

5 This law, passed during the tenure of Liberal Jean Chrétien, replaced the 1988 act and expanded it to include not just pollution management but pollution prevention.

Chapter 4

The History of Environmentalism in Canada

CANADIANS ARE NOT HISTORICALLY ENVIRONMENTALISTS. The country is vast, natural resources are abundant, and human population is low. Thus, on the surface, there seems to be little incentive to conserve resources or reduce waste for environmental reasons. When Europeans first colonialized North America, the "environment" was not part of the cultural lexicon. Scientific discoveries about biodiversity loss, water pollution, and greenhouse gases, for example, were to come later in the nineteenth and twentieth centuries. Canadians today are more aware of globalization's implications and better understand that economic growth has environmental trade-offs and that environmental limits exist. Canadians first confronted some of those limits at the turn of the twentieth century when North American forests were in decline and species such as the bison were becoming extinct.

This chapter will trace the rise of the environmental movement in Canada. After describing the colonization of Canada, the chapter moves to the development of national parks and conservation policy. This history is quickly summarized, but, for readers with a deeper interest in our natural history, two recent books are worth further consideration: *Canadians and the Natural Environment to the Twenty-First Century* (Forkey 2013) and *An Environmental History of Canada* (MacDowell 2012). After our brief foray into history, we then jump to the 1960s and second-wave environmentalism. This second wave, as well as the third wave, are outlined and discussed. The possibility of a fourth wave of environmentalism will be taken up in the concluding chapter of the book. Before we look at where we are headed, however, we need to consider where we have been.

NATURAL HISTORY PRE-1867

Science tells us that dinosaurs inhabited what is now Canada millions of years ago but that human beings stepped upon North America relatively recently. Evidence from the Northwest Territories and northeastern Yukon suggests that small hunting groups occupied Canada as far back as 25,000 BCE (Cinq-Mars 1979; Morlan et al. 1990). It is believed that North America's first people crossed over the Bering Land Bridge and then spread southward (MacDowell 2012). These indigenous peoples were met by migrants from Europe 500 years ago, and the environment of Canada was forever changed. The first Europeans to travel to North America came for trade and exploration. The Norse peoples arrived between 800 and 1000 CE in the Arctic and Newfoundland and Labrador (Diamond 2011). The Norse, originally from the Scandinavian countries of Europe, did not establish permanent colonies in North America, but they did establish permanent settlements in Iceland and Greenland (Diamond 2011).

The story of Christopher Columbus "discovering" America is very well known. His ships arrived in the Bahamas in October 1492, and his crew probably sighted Cuba in the same month. John Cabot's voyage of 1497 is commonly held to be the first European "discovery" of the mainland of North America since the visits of the Norse. Of course, neither of these men actually discovered the Americas, as both regions were already inhabited by indigenous peoples. The Europeans changed the North American environment. Indigenous peoples were already fishing across the continent, but Europeans sent hundreds of fishing and whaling fleets to the area each year during the sixteenth century. Of course, disease was one of the most significant environmental changes Europeans brought; a smallpox epidemic wiped out thousands and thousands of indigenes across the continent (see also Crosby 2004 for a discussion of European expansion in North America).

Europeans also brought agricultural goods—both animals and plants—that forever altered North America. Europeans had an almost insatiable appetite for furs and established commercial hunting in seventeenth- and eighteenth-century Canada and the United States. Beaver, buffalo, and sea otter were among the most hunted wildlife in the New World. The Hudson's Bay Company got its start in Canada as a fur-trading corporation, receiving its royal charter in 1670. From its early posts and forts on the Hudson and James bays, the company went on to control the fur trade in a vast area of North America (see Bothwell 2007 and Morton 2006 for histories of Canada more broadly). Unfortunately, active hunting

severely comprised wildlife populations as traders killed millions of animals in a short period. The stress on ecosystems is not measurable, but
trade has had long-lasting impacts on Canada (Innis 1930).

Permanent settlers who cleared the land of trees for farming also
affected Canada's environment. The indigenous people who had occupied
the land before European settlement were mainly hunters and gathers
and did not engage in any large-scale forestry or farming. However,
Europeans quickly began deforestation for the purposes of farming and
homesteading (Tchir, Johnson, and Nkemdirim 2012). Crop production had a slow rise, but, by the nineteenth century, Canada's farmers
were producing crops and raising cattle and hogs. The Prairies were also
transformed into agricultural lands, and, with directed effort by Britain's
government, people from Eastern and Western Europe settled in the
region and established farms (Bothwell 2007; Morton 2006). Finally,
the last change brought by the Europeans in the short time between 1500
and 1800 was forestry. Trees were initially cut down to make room for
farming, and a symbiotic relationship developed between the sawmills
and the settlers. However, by 1850, the lumber industry was moving into
areas without settlers. Deforestation happened virtually everywhere that
had trees. The result was wealth because deforestation created space for
infrastructure such as roads and villages, as well as providing a resource
for the manufacture of timber products and paper (Tchir, Johnson, and
Nkemdirim 2012).

Private Property Rights and the Landscape

Indigenous peoples of North America had no formal system of private property. The idea of "owning" land was not part of their cultural
lexicon. Many tribes were nomadic and followed food sources around
the continent without much thought as to who "owned" the land.
They did have notions of territory, however, and tribes would either
respect each other's claim to a specific geographical area or fight
over land and resources. Yet territorial claims were in flux, and there
was certainly no way to buy or sell territory—it was simply used, and
sometimes the ability to use the land had to be won through negotiation or battle (see Dickason and Newbigging 2010).

The Canadian (and more significantly, the American) love affair
with private property is evident in the works of John Locke and Adam
Smith—European thinkers of the seventeenth and eighteenth centuries. John Locke (1632–1704) wrote in *Two Treatises on Civil Government*

that individuals have a natural right to ownership of property. When a man has "mixed his labour with" something in nature, "he ... thereby makes it his property" (Locke [1690] 1988, sec. 27). The role of government, then, is to help protect an individual's right to ownership. Adam Smith helped refine this theory by arguing that secure property rights ensure the best possible allocation of resources. These theories were applied in the British colonies such that land was no longer passed down through feudalism (as had been precedent in Great Britain). In North America, any hardworking pioneer could secure a right to land.

But were the indigenous peoples of North America not already using the land? Why did they not "own" it on the basis of Locke's theory? Indigenous peoples were often nomadic and did not settle the land or use their labour to "improve" it, to make it more productive, for example. So, according to the European view, they failed to secure their right to it. Essentially, the colonists used Locke's labour theory to justify the privatization of land in North America in a way that excluded indigenous peoples. In some instances, treaties were created between the colonial powers (e.g., the British and French governments) and the specific tribes who were determined to have property rights (see chapters 9 and 10). But, for the most part, Europeans implemented their system of private property across North America and forever changed the map and the landscape (Olive 2014a).

Thus, Canada's environment was radically altered, for the better and the worse, through European contact. Fishing, hunting, farming, and forestry remain important contributors to Canada's economy, and all four industries were developed commercially around the same time by Europeans who saw Canada as a vast and indestructible place. It appeared to the early settlers that the land had more to give than any peoples could ever take. Unfortunately for us, that did not turn out to be true.

For indigenous North Americans, the environment and their relationship to it were marked by European settlement. Migrants themselves, from Siberia during the last ice age over 15,000 years ago, indigenous people had learned to survive in hunter-gatherer tribes across present-day Canada (Goebel, Waters, and O'Rourke 2008). As survivalists, they were neither pro- nor anti-environmentalists. They killed what they wanted to eat, and they gathered food from wherever they wanted without much thought toward ecosystem health or biodiversity (which are modern scientific concepts). To survive, indigenous peoples "adapted various ecosystems to fit their needs; they manipulated the natural world to subsist and constructed complex trading nexuses" (Forkey 2013, 7). European settlers, on the other hand, "altered the land to fit their own way of living" (Forkey 2013, 7) and colonized land at different times with varying impact (see the text box on private property).

Where was the federal government in all of this? Remember that "Canada" did not exist until 1867 and that, even after Confederation, when Canada had its own federal government, some decisions were still made by Britain. The twentieth century ushered in economic and environmental realities for the British and American governments. As a consequence, conservation principles took root in the United States and travelled north to Canada (Dorsey 1998). The history of environmentalism in North America, then, begins with the conservation of forests and the creation of national parks by federal governments, first in the United States and then in Canada. This initiative is often seen as the **first wave of environmentalism**. For the first time, North Americans saw the continent as a destructible place and realized that resources, especially wildlife and forests, were not limitless.

NATIONAL PARKS

The Rocky Mountains Park Act of 1887 established officially what is now called Banff National Park, the first of a large system of parks in Western Canada. These parks, however, were not just for preserving wilderness or protecting forestry. One of the main forces driving the creation of Banff and similar parks was tourism (Forkey 2013). The federal government wanted people to travel out West. If people could see the land and enjoy the parks, then perhaps they would want to settle in the West and turn the land to productive uses, such as agriculture or forestry. If not, the tourists would still spend money during their visits to the western part of the country. In a similar fashion, the Dominion Forest Reserves and Parks Act of 1911 aimed to establish parks across Canada in order to protect land and generate tourism; it also placed all Canadian national parks under the administration of the world's first national parks branch (Dorsey 1998; Forkey 2013).

The bison was the first animal to come under park protection in Canada. These huge animals had been hunted almost to extinction during the years of European settlement, expansion, and trade. It is estimated that it took fewer than 100 years for bison to disappear from the Prairie provinces (Foster et al. 1992). Nevertheless, bison were exactly the type of animal that park tourists wanted to see. Thus, tourism added impetus to efforts to protect bison and the land they needed to survive. In 1906–07,

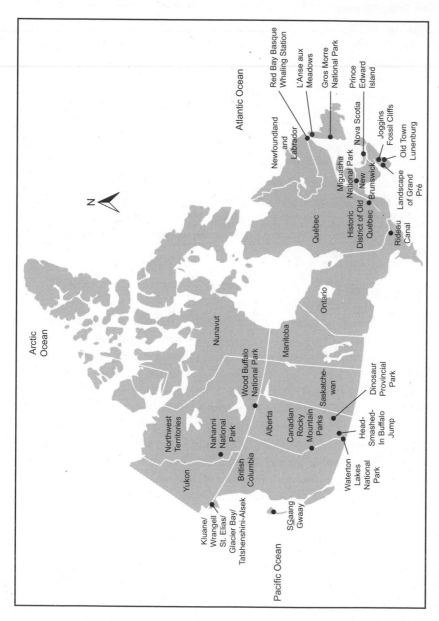

MAP 4.1 World Heritage Sites in Canada, 2013

SOURCE: Adapted from Parks Canada (2014), *Canada's Existing World Heritage Sites*. Ottawa: Parks Canada. http://www.pc.gc.ca/progs/spm-whs/-/media/progs/spm-whs/maps/WHS-2013-08-01_e.ashx.

the Canadian federal government purchased bison from the United States and had them shipped to Buffalo National Park near Wainwright, Alberta; this park is no longer in existence. (The federal government was already responsible for a surviving herd, which lived in the area that would become Wood Buffalo National Park.)

The bison and the national parks were a tourism sensation. In 1887, only 3,000 people visited parks in Alberta, but by 1912, that number had jumped to 73,000 people in a single year. Although not all of this increase can be attributed to the bison (the park system was expanding at the same time that automobile and transportation improvements were being made), it is fair to say that the bison were big sellers (Forkey 2013). This story suggests that ecotourism, as we know it today, is actually a relatively old concept. Canadians have long been dealing in the ecotourism business as a way to expand the economy by protecting the environment.

During the early twentieth century, the federal government reserved land for national parks and forest or game reserves from coast to coast (northern parks came later): Jasper (AB) in 1907, Elk Island (AB) in 1906, Mount Revelstoke (BC) in 1914, Kootenay (BC) in 1920, Prince Albert (SK) in 1927, Cape Breton Highlands (NS) in 1936, Fundy (NB) in 1948, and Georgian Bay Islands (ON) in 1929. Today we have 44 national parks and national park reserves in Canada (for a list, see Parks Canada 2008). Although they cover less than 3 per cent of our total land, they do represent a vast wilderness that is protected for Canadians and future Canadians (Dearden and Rollins 2008). Actually, these parks are enjoyed the world over, as 12 of our national parks are part of designated UNESCO World Heritage Sites: the 6 parks of the Rocky Mountains, Gros Morne National Park, the Gwaii Haanas National Park Reserve, the Nahanni National Park Reserve, the Kluane National Park Reserve, Wood Buffalo National Park, and Waterton Lakes National Park. (See Parks Canada 2014 and Map 4.1.) This means they are recognized by the United Nations as having significant physical (and cultural) importance to the world. They are visited and cherished because of their intrinsic value and not their economic or natural resource value.

THE ENVIRONMENTAL ERAS

Even though the twentieth century began as an era of conservation and park creation, by the time World War II began, both Canada and the United States were settled into a period of substantial economic growth and resource extraction (Dorsey 1998). Not surprisingly, during World War I and World War II, very little attention was paid to environmental concerns. It would be over a decade after the end of World War II before a second wave of environmentalism began. However, from the 1950s until today, Canada has created and implemented a vast array of public policies aimed at the protection of the environment and the regulation of natural resources.

In the United States and Canada, the 1960s is known as the "environmental era"—part of the **second wave of environmentalism**—because during this decade the public became critically aware of environmental problems. Consequently, in the early 1970s, both countries passed major and long-lasting environmental legislation (Parson 2001). Rachel Carson's book *Silent Spring* is often credited with starting the environmental era (McKenzie 2002; Zelko 2013). The book was published in 1962 and spent 31 weeks on the *New York Time's* best-seller list. Chemicals and their widespread use are at the heart of the book. As a marine biologist, Carson used her ecological viewpoint to detail the changes in the environment—including the human environment—that resulted from the use of chemicals such as DDT (Carson 1962). However, the book alone did not compel action across Canada. Other events also happened during the 1960s that led to an environmental culture. In 1967, the first photos of Earth from outer space were published, providing humans with a snapshot of their home. In the United States, 20 million people gathered in different cities and towns to celebrate the first Earth Day on April 22, 1970.

Garrett Hardin published his famous "Tragedy of the Commons" essay in *Science* in 1968. He argued that individuals acting according to rational self-interest behave so as to get the most out of land, water, or other resources held in common as quickly as possible, that they lack an incentive to conserve or manage these resources. What does this mean? Imagine a community owns land in common as public land, and people are allowed to let their cattle graze upon this land free of charge. Hardin argues that the land would soon be overgrazed because each person would try to maximize the benefit (free grazing) by keeping as many cattle as possible and spread the costs to others (the community, a future generation). Thus, Hardin argues, "Freedom in a commons brings ruin to all," an idea he called the **tragedy of the commons** (Hardin 1968, 1244). His narrative became a metaphor for all types of environmental ills—from dumping waste in the oceans to air pollution to deforestation. The "tragedy of freedom in a commons" calls for a regulated commons. Hardin's idea was, for many people, a call to policy action and regulation in North America.

During the 1960s, environmental groups arose across the country. The most famous is probably Greenpeace, which was founded in Canada in 1971 by a group of Canadian and American activists in Vancouver protesting nuclear-weapons testing (Zelko 2013). But, before that, two environmental groups started in 1969: Pollution Probe in Toronto and the Society Promoting Environmental Conservation in Vancouver (O'Connor 2014). These events and these organizations were all part of the second wave of environmentalism in Canada. Today, all three environmental groups remain important interest groups in the Canadian environmental policy arena. Greenpeace and Pollution Probe maintain a national focus, but the Society Promoting Environmental Conservation deals primarily with British Columbia's environment.

During the 1960s and 1970s, the United States passed major pieces of environmental legislation, including the National Environmental Policy Act (1970), the Clean Water Act (1972), the Endangered Species Act (1973), the Safe Drinking Water Act (1974), and the Department of Energy Organization Act (1977). As an issue, the environment cut across party lines, and presidents from both parties signed environmental bills into law during the 1970s (see Rosenbaum 2013; Vig and Kraft 2012). In Canada, legislation was slower to develop because of the unique challenge of managing regional differences within the country's federal system (Parson 2001). The national government of the United States had more federal powers and was able to pass "command and control" policies administered at the federal level. For example, the Endangered Species Act applies to all land parcels across the United States, whereas the Canadian Species at Risk Act applies only to federal lands, migratory birds, and aquatic species. Federal powers in the United States made it easier for the federal government to quickly create major legislation to address environmental issues such as pollution and biodiversity loss.

In Canada, one federal politician stands out among others as vocally pro-environment during the second wave of environmentalism: Pierre Elliott Trudeau. In his 1969 Throne Speech, Prime Minister Trudeau announced five new environmental laws, taking a federal law-making approach similar to that of the United States. No prime minister before or since has laid out such an ambitious environmental agenda in a Throne Speech. Unfortunately, his government was not able to bring this agenda to fruition as quickly as planned. Trudeau, who was prime minister from 1968 to 1979 and then from 1980 to 1984—Progressive Conservative Joe Clark held that office from June 1979 to March 1980—did establish the Department of the Environment in 1971. This is a milestone in Canadian environmental history. And the federal government enacted the Clean Air Act (1971) and the Canada Water Act (1972) under Prime Minster Trudeau. The federal government also passed, in 1976, the Environmental Contaminants Act to control chemicals such as PCBs. Keep in mind that, even with the Department of the Environment established, most of its projects were limited to federal jurisdiction or to discretionary assessment processes for the provinces to follow.

Third Wave

The late 1980s and early 1990s is referred to as the **third wave of environmentalism**. Once again, widespread public awareness led to genuine demands that government officials enact environmental legislation. If the 1960s and 70s were predominately about pollution and energy, the third wave was about the ozone layer, wildlife, acid rain, and, more recently, sustainable development and climate change (McKenzie 2002). Prime Minister Brian Mulroney's Progressive Conservative government (1984–93) was more active in the environmental realm than was Prime Minister Jean Chretien's Liberal government (1993–2003), although the latter did sign the Kyoto Protocol, committing Canada to reduce greenhouse gas emissions. Under Mulroney, Canada took serious action on acid rain, and Mulroney and President George H. W. Bush signed an acid rain treaty in 1991 (the Air Quality Agreement). Moreover, the Canadian Environmental Protection Act of 1988, passed during Mulroney's term, brought many of Trudeau's environmental goals into legal existence. Mulroney is arguably Canada's "greenest" prime minister given the number of environmental treaties and laws made during his time in office (CBC 2006b).

The 1990s were important for environmental policy both federally and provincially. Although American policy had been pushing the envelope for years on the issue of public participation in environmental matters, Canada was slower to catch on. The Northwest Territories was the first jurisdiction to adopt environmental rights legislation (Environmental Rights Act, 1988), followed by the Yukon (Environment Act, 1991) and Ontario (Environmental Bill of Rights, 1993). The National Pollutant Release Inventory was created in 1992 to increase public access to information. The provinces and Canadian citizens were calling for a more direct role in environmental policy. Today, the provinces have extraordinary jurisdictional responsibility for most natural resources and related environmental issues. Regionalism and the democratic process of local governments are of critical importance because of the institutional and governance shifts that began in the third wave of environmentalism.

At the federal level, the 1990 "Green Plan" of the Progressive Conservative government was a noble aspiration that fell completely flat in implementation. The plan, which endorsed sustainable development principles (discussed below), promised $3 billion in federal spending on environmental protection over five years. The money was not spent. The plan was eventually pushed to the side in light of federal budget cutting and neoliberal policies. Here "neoliberal" is meant to signify an attempt to balance budgets, decrease public debt, and reduce the regulatory and policy roles of government. Policies derived from **neoliberalism** were introduced by the Mulroney government's shift in monetary policy in the early 1980s and cemented by its implementation of the free-trade deal in 1989; these neoliberal policies were largely carried forward by the Liberal government that followed in the 1990s.

In 1992, Canadian representatives attended the United Nations Conference on Environment and Development in Rio de Janeiro, more commonly known as the Rio Summit or the **Earth Summit**. This conference marks a significant turning point in both international and Canadian environmental governance. In total, 172 countries participated, and the key issues involved economic growth and environmental protection worldwide. Specific themes centred on climate change, water, alternative energy, and indigenous rights (Axelrod and VanDeveer 2014). At this conference, Canada signed the Convention on Biological Diversity, discussed in chapters 8 and 11, the UN Framework on Climate Change Convention, discussed in Chapter 11, as well as Agenda 21 and the Rio Declaration on Environment and Development. The **Rio Declaration** contains 27 principles and is intended to guide the implementation of sustainable development on our planet (United Nations 1992).

What is **sustainable development**? The concept rose to fame after it was used in the 1987 report of the Brundtland Commission, entitled *Our Common Future*. Here the concept was defined as "development that meets the needs of the present without compromising the ability of future generations to meet their own needs" (World Commission on Environment and Development 1987). Essentially, sustainable development aims to reconcile economic growth, social welfare, and environmental protection. The concept is strongly anthropocentric in that human needs must be met before environmental needs within the sustainable development framework. Since third-wave environmentalism, sustainable development has become part of the worldwide discourse on environmental protection, as discussed in Chapter 11 (Conca and Dabelko 2010). What sustainable "development" means domestically for Canada is not always clear, as Canada is already considered a developed country. However, even a country categorized as industrialized or developed continues to experience economic and industrial growth or development. Thus, for countries such as Canada, the United States, and those of Western Europe, sustainable development means a realistic inclusion of environmental considerations when making economic and social decisions (see Environment Canada 2014k for Canada's conception of the term and policy goal).

Sustainable development, like other environmental policies, is difficult to implement because of federalism. The provinces and the federal government often have not only overlapping jurisdictions but also oppositional goals. For instance, Saskatchewan might want to grow its potash industry quickly so as to create new jobs and wealth for the province. However, because the federal government is responsible for overseeing sustainable development, as outlined in the 2008 Federal Sustainable Development Act, Ottawa might have to push Saskatchewan to think long term and consider all the environmental ramifications of intensive potash mining, such as water consumption or air pollution. Part of what makes it difficult for Ottawa to dictate policy is that the province has the constitutionally defined authority to control the exploitation of its own natural resources. This situation plays itself out across the country, as economic regionalism pushes and pulls the centre of authority in federalism. Thus, even though the federal government has signed various UN conventions and has the responsibility of adopting international norms when it comes to sustainable development and precautionary measures, federalism often puts Ottawa and the provinces on different sides of the negotiating table. So although the third wave of environmentalism has seen a worldwide effort to adhere to sustainable development principles, Canada has not been as successful at this domestically (or internationally, as Chapter 11 explains).

Another aspect of sustainable development at the forefront of the third wave of environmentalism is **green consumerism**, which rests on an awareness of our purchasing power as individual consumers. Green consumerism is the consumer deciding to purchase or not based at least partly on environmental criteria (Peattie 1995). It is an example of the individualization of responsibility or the belief that individual actions can repair the environment. Thus, celebrities quite commonly extoll the virtues of the latest "green product," from make-up to fair-trade coffee to organic clothes. Consumerism can be seen as a form of participatory democracy. In a way, buying is voting. (Although, in a democracy, the system is based on formal equality in that one person gets one vote, whereas consumerism is much more unequal because each person has a different purchasing power.) However, we still speak to the economy and to our politicians through our purchases. If all Canadians started to buy hybrid vehicles, the market would respond—as would government policy around areas of transportation and gasoline subsidies. In the 1980s and 1990s, as affluence grew in Canada, more people started to think about the environmental consequences of their purchases. Green consumerism tends to fluctuate with the market—when Canadians feel financially stable, they tend to care more about the environment and spend money accordingly. But when the economy falters, as it did during the 2008 recession, Canadians tend to focus more on the economy and jobs than on environmental issues and green products (for critique of this type of consumerism, see Tidwell 2009).

The End of the Third Wave and the Rise of the Green Party

The Green Party of Canada (GPC) was technically founded in 1983, but it did not start gaining significant vote counts until the early 2000s. In the 2004 federal election, the GPC ran a candidate in every riding across Canada and earned 4.3 per cent of the total vote (Jansen and Lambert 2013). In 2006, that percentage was 4.48, a slight increase. It was 6.78 per cent in 2008. This increase may seem small, but the party was almost always relegated to less than 1 per cent of the vote through the 1980s and 1990s (Jansen and Lambert 2013). Support dropped in the 2011 election—the party took only 3.91 per cent of the vote. It did, however, elect an MP, party leader Elizabeth May, to the House of Commons (see Green Party of Canada n.d.). As noted in Chapter 3, she is the first member of the GPC to win a seat in Parliament. The party is primarily concerned with the environment but does have a policy platform that explains its stance on issues across the social and economic spectrum. The vision of the party is to integrate the environment into the social and economic realm, thereby creating greener jobs and a healthier democracy and society. The party platform can be found on the party website (www.greenparty.ca), and an explanation of May's support for specific policies can be found on her own webpage (http://elizabethmaymp.ca).

Every province in Canada now has a provincial Green Party. New Brunswick was the last province to create one in 2008. The British Columbia and Ontario GPs, which are the oldest in Canada, have been the most successful as well. In fact, in the 2007 provincial election the GP of Ontario won just over 8 per cent of the total vote. However, as we saw federally, the Ontario vote count dropped to 2.9 per cent of the popular vote in the 2011 provincial election (CBC 2011a; Green Party of Ontario 2015), which might be a response to the recession that signals a prioritization of other issues. In British Columbia, the GP continues to poll strong, and, in the 2013 election, it won just over 8 per cent of the popular vote and elected its first member to the legislative assembly, Andrew Weaver (Bailey 2013; CBC 2013a).

As mentioned in Chapter 3, not only the Green Party reflects environmentalism in politics. The rise of environmental concern in all national parties is an outcome of third-wave environmentalism, which ended in the mid-1990s. In 2006, "the environment" was listed as the most important issue facing the country and remained ahead of health care and economic issues for 18 months (Brown 2010). Since 2008, "the economy" has been the most important issues for the majority of Canadians, usurping both the environment and health care. Nevertheless, all national parties continue to engage with environmental issues, albeit to vastly different extents, and, in the past few years, much debate has ensued around climate change, oil and energy policy, species at risk, food and GMO policy, and chemical management. In the twenty-first century, the world is such a complex place that avoiding a discussion of environmentalism when making decisions about the economy, public health, foreign aid, national defence, or public safety is difficult. For example, how can we untangle the severe rise in cases of childhood asthma, a health-care cost, from issues of smog and transportation, which are both environmental and economic concerns?

ENVIRONMENTALISM AND IDEOLOGY

The liberal democratic tradition is founded on the ideas of individualism, capitalism, technology and progress, representative democracy, and freedom. Alongside conservative values of hierarchy, tradition, order, and monarchy, these are the founding principles of Canada. We see human beings as having dominion, or at least stewardship, over nature. The pursuit of happiness is commonly conceived as the ownership of property, and acquiring property and other material goods is the driving force of the economy. Generally, we do not question these values as a society. However, our attitude toward the environment and other living things can force us to evaluate our behaviour and ideology, to strive to make changes, opening up the possibility of accepting limitations on our freedoms and our spending habits. This is what happened during the three waves of environmentalism—each of which occurred within our liberal democratic political system and our capitalist economy.

Alongside the growing evolution of environmental consciousness and scientific discovery, Canadians' philosophy about our place in the environment has grown into distinct worldviews. We do not agree on environmental philosophies, just as we do not all vote for the Green Party of Canada. Generally, political ideology exists on a socialism—liberalism—conservatism continuum, as presented in Chapter 3. But paralleling these political ideologies is an environmental or ecological continuum that ranges from ecocentrism to anthropocentrism (see Table 4.1 and McKenzie 2002). Eco-philosophies do not map well onto the socialist–conservative paradigm because they take into

TABLE 4.1 Comparing the Liberal Tradition to Eco-philosophies

LIBERAL DEMOCRATIC CAPITALISM	ECO-PHILOSOPHIES
Anthropocentric	Ecocentric
Representative Democracy	Direct Democracy
Individualism and Self-Interest	Community Based
Capitalistic	Sustainable
Federal or Unitary States	Decentralization/Ecoregions

SOURCE: Based on McKenzie (2002), Table 1.4.

consideration not simply collective versus individual values but the world at large. That is to say, eco-philosophy is concerned with non-human values and human-nature interaction. Thus, these philosophies can sometimes act as a critical framework—a way to understand our place in the world as well as that of other living things. To that end, they can help guide our everyday decisions.

Ecocentrism, as the name suggests, puts nature at the centre of the value system whereas anthropocentrism places human beings there. The former argues that all of nature has intrinsic worth and should be considered in economic and political decisions whereas the latter prioritizes the value of human beings. You can easily see that the two camps would disagree about specific economic decisions. For example, the clear-cutting of a forest for campsites might strike someone who ascribes to ecocentrism as deeply problematic because trees have intrinsic worth, so the human desire for a campground should not trump their value. Someone taking an anthropocentric view could disagree, possibly arguing that trees can grow elsewhere or that we have enough forestland but not enough campsites. This argument places a human need above an environmental one.

Deep ecology takes ecocentrism one step further. It is an environmental philosophy founded by Norwegian thinker Arne Naess in 1973. It is predicated on the idea that all living things have intrinsic value *and* inalienable (possibly legal) rights to existence. Consequently, in the previous example, the forest would have a *right to exist* that the human creation of a campground could not violate. Of course, in deep ecology, human beings are also part of nature, and they too have a right to exist. But a human right does not de facto trump another living thing's right. Human beings are not at the centre of existence. This view is fairly radical, and not many Canadians subscribe to deep ecology. However, many individuals find themselves somewhere between ecocentrism and anthropocentrism when it comes to making political and economic decisions with environmental impacts (James 2015; Weston 2003).

CANADIAN ENVIRONMENTAL POLICY AND POLICY TOOLS

As illustrated, throughout the first three waves of environmentalism, federal and provincial governments made numerous policies to protect natural resources and the environment. Historically, Canada's problem has not been the development of policy so much as the lack of implementation and enforcement (Parson 2001). The environmental eras did establish several impressive policies—federally and provincially—but Canadian governments have, since the country's inception, favoured business and economic interests, or natural resource exploitation, over the environment. This orientation partly results from the push and pull of economic regionalism mixed with a weak central government. The provinces want to develop economically, and the federal government does not have the power to dictate environmental stewardship.

Since the 1960s, the tools and style of policy have largely involved **closed bargaining** and cooperation between government and business interests over the enactment of environmental standards, their implementation, and the level of compliance expected of corporate actors or polluting parties (Howlett 2002). Governments have been largely unwilling to regulate industry in the command-and-control fashion of much US policy. Instead, in Canada, a **memorandum of understanding**— an agreement between governments and the private sector—is commonly used to achieve a particular goal, such as the reduction of emissions. These agreements allow governments to achieve pollution targets without passing specific regulations (Henriques and Sadorsky 1999) and are examples of voluntary policy instruments, as discussed in Chapter 3.

The result is that environmental legislation in Canada has been primarily enabling rather than mandatory. Unlike in the United States, where regulations passed by Congress generally require the implementation of specific policies, in Canada, officials are authorized to develop regulations but rarely have the obligation to act (Field and Olewiler 2002). In addition, lack of information on pollution sources and environmental science continues to handicap policymakers. Although information flows between industry and government are improving, Canadian governments still rely on the polluting industries themselves for much information (Henriques and Sadorsky 1999). Traditionally, government has worked with industry to protect the environment in a manner that is collaborative and not confrontational. Industry is expected to record and report its actions honestly and then implement the agreed-upon policies to reduce pollution or otherwise protect a resource.

Corporate Social Responsibility in Canada

Corporate social responsibility (CSR) is a form of voluntary self-regulation that corporations engage in so as to meet government or international standards of business conduct (Beal 2013). More specifically, the Canadian government presently defines CSR as "the voluntary activities undertaken by a company to operate in an economic, social and environmentally sustainable manner" (Government of Canada 2014a). The benefit of CSR is twofold: government can avoid the (costly) monitoring of industry, and industry can avoid (costly) regulation through transparent good behaviour.

However, CSR often surpasses government policy aims by trying to exceed standards, set new business goals, or meet international norms of business. For example, in 2012, the Bank of Montreal's board diversity policy aimed to have women represent at least a third of the bank's independent board of directors (Bank of Montreal 2012); the government target, announced in 2014, is 30 per cent over five years (Canada's Advisory Council for Promoting Women on Boards 2014). As another example, TD Bank's "TD Forests" has helped to protect 13,000 hectares of critical forest habitat across North America as of 2014; that's more than two football fields per day (Toronto-Dominion Bank 2015). There is no Canadian law or even a national guideline requiring banks to conserve forests. Similarly, Tim Hortons requires its Canadian millwork suppliers to use only wood certified by the Forest Stewardship Council in Canadian restaurants. Also, by expanding recycling and waste-diversion programs at its distribution centres in 2012–13, it diverted 80 per cent of its waste from landfill (Maclean's 2013).

Why would companies voluntarily enact environmental standards? In part, they do so to avoid government regulation and to "green" their image so as to obtain **social licence** or community acceptance. A company can build a socially acceptable image and create a good working relationship with a community (big or small) such that the community will be willing to accept the company's less desirable practices because of the good the company is otherwise engaged in (see Fletcher 2003). For example, Canada will tolerate the mass production of Tim Hortons coffee cups because the company is making its best efforts at recycling. Similarly, a community might tolerate an oil company's pollution because the company supports local sports events, donates money to nature groups, and has promised to reclaim the land once the oil is tapped. Social licence must be earned, and it can be lost if a company crosses the line or breaks (too many) Canadian laws.

Although, as discussed, voluntary policy instruments are frequently used in the twenty-first century, different policy tools are being and have been used since the 1960s. Early environmental laws at the provincial level were more regulatory in tone. In the early 1990s, several pilot studies involving a variety of proposals to replace regulation with market- and tax-based financial incentives were undertaken (Henriques and Sadorsky 1999). However, due to fiscal cutbacks, most of these studies were not concluded. In the latter half of the 1990s, the Liberals implemented some voluntary tools based on self-reporting and cooperation. Examples include the Canadian Industry Packaging Stewardship Initiative, the Voluntary Challenge and Registry Programme, and the Accelerated Reduction/Elimination of Toxics (ARET) program, as well as sector-specific arrangements such as eco-labelling and certification in the forest sector. Measuring the success of these programs is difficult because self-reporting is rarely enforced or monitored by a third party or non-state actor, beyond an informal and non-scientific assessment by an interest group.

During all three waves of environmentalism, incentive-based policies have rarely been used. There are a few examples of specific taxes or of tax write-offs for investment in pollution abatement or control. As mentioned, however, governments have been reluctant or unable to impose specific standards. Thus, without relying on regulation or economic policy mechanisms, most regulation has been in the form of guidelines that suggest a range of pollution targets. The Canada Water Act is an example. Will this approach continue to work in the future? Addressing climate change issues presents Canada with an important challenge and opportunity to experiment with a host of regulatory, market-based, incentive-based, and voluntary initiatives to determine the instruments best able to achieve goals. Much has been written on the possible policy tools that could be used in climate policy across Canadian jurisdictions (see Bernstein et al. 2008). At the end of the day, it will be important for Canada to buck historical trends established during the different waves of environmentalism and adopt a willingness to engage with a variety of policy tools that function independently and collaboratively across different sectors of environmental and natural resource issues.

ENVIRONMENTAL POLICY UNDER CONSERVATIVE PARTY LEADERSHIP, 2006-15

The Conservative Party, led by Stephen Harper, came to power in 2006, forming a minority government. In the 2008 election, Harper was elected once again and led a minority government until the party won a majority of House of Common seats in the 2011 election. It is fair to say that Prime Minister Harper is not an environmentalist. Quite famously, he refused to support the Kyoto Protocol and, in 2011, led Canada's withdrawal from Kyoto. This move was expected, as, in 2003, he referred to the protocol as a "socialist scheme." Also, Harper has been accused of muzzling Canadian scientists who study climate change (Turner 2013), and he has been one of Canada's strongest advocates for Alberta oil sands development and a vocal supporter of Arctic resource exploration.

However, to say that the Conservative Party has done nothing to benefit the environment since 2006 would be unfair. On the contrary, the federal government has committed to increasing funding for public transportation (especially in Vancouver, Toronto, and Ottawa), for clean energy (e.g., for hydroelectricity in Manitoba), and for parks such as the Rouge National Urban Park in Toronto. In 2009, the government also introduced more environmentally related spending in terms of clean energy research around capture and storage; renovations and energy retrofits for housing (costs will be split with the provinces); Artic research stations; the clean-up of federal contaminated sites; and the improvement of government reporting and data management on environmental indicators such as GHG emissions, water, air pollution, and chemical management. Some of these initiatives have been implemented; others have not. In general, however, Conservative environmental policy under Prime Minister Harper has emphasized "responsible resource development" over environmental protection.

The 2011 platform of the Conservative Party, entitled *Here for Canada*, focuses on five key priorities: (1) creating jobs through training, trade, and lower taxes; (2) supporting families by cutting taxes and providing more monetary support for caregivers; (3) eliminating the deficit by 2014–15 by cutting spending; (4) improving community safety and creating news laws to protect children and the elderly; and (5) increasing national security and defence by investing in Canada's North and strengthening the Canadian Armed Forces. As you can see, the environment is not a key priority for the party.

In some senses, then, the Conservative Party is taking a **Promethean approach** (Dryzek 2013) to natural resources and the environment in Canada. Prometheus was the mythical Greek Titan who stole fire from the gods and gave it to humans, so they could progress into advanced civilizations. In the environmental world, Prometheans are those individuals who believe in unregulated and unlimited human development. From their vantage point, there are no "finite resources," and "natural resources" are just resources created by humans transferring matter into productivity. A tree is not a natural resource so much as lumber is a human product and a symbol of ingenuity and progress. The main idea behind this worldview is that humans will always find solutions to their problems, and all of human history has been a story of progress. We use the resources we have, and when we run out of something, we will find a way to meet our needs through other resources. Perpetual economic growth is within human reach, and concern about the "environment" is unnecessary. The earth simply provides tools for progress; human energy and ingenuity are the only resources humanity needs to survive and develop (Dryzek 2013, 52–72). As outlandish as this worldview might seem to some, it is actually widely accepted in Western societies. According to John Dryzek (2013), "Promethean discourse resonates with the interests of both capitalist market zealots and Christian conservatives, not to mention miners, loggers and ranchers ... such constituencies are smaller or absent in other countries, save Canada and Australia (67).

CONCLUSIONS

Canada was once considered a leader in environmental policy, as Chapter 11 will discuss. First-wave environmentalism created national parks across the country and turned much needed attention to the reality of finite resources and the wise use of Canada's nature. During the second and into the third wave of environmentalism, Canada was a "trailblazer" in environmental law and took a progressive stance on environmental matters (Wood, Tanner, and Richardson 2010). However, during and after the third wave of environmentalism, Canada increasingly struggled to implement its ambitious environmental policies, particularly sustainable development. The third wave was washed ashore by neoliberal values that favoured the economy over the environment. Little action for climate change occurred in the third wave of environmentalism. Consequently, some scholars label Canada an "environmental laggard" (Parson 2000, Wood, Tanner and Richardson 2010). We struggle to implement the policy we have, and we fail to innovate when creating new policy.

The federal election of 2015 saw the Liberal Party, led by Justin Trudeau, and the NDP, led by Tom Mulcair, vying with Stephen Harper's Conservatives for leadership of the country. Similar to the Conservatives, the Liberals have a primary focus on the economy and creating jobs and prosperity for Canadians. Trudeau supports the Keystone XL pipeline that will see further exploitation of the oil sands in Alberta and the subsequent continual rise in Canada's greenhouse gas emissions. The Liberals do not support the Northern Gateway Pipeline, however, and have pledged to pursue a national carbon-pricing plan with the provinces. Nevertheless, the Liberal Party platform on energy and the environment is anthropocentric in that it "supports projects that offer responsible and sustainable ways of getting our resources to market—while at the same time respecting Indigenous rights, our natural environment and earning the trust of local communities" (Liberal Party of Canada 2015). Also, based on past Liberal governments, it is likely that environmental policy under Liberal Party leadership will be remarkably similar to that experienced under Conservative Party leadership. Arguably, the Liberal Party base (its core of loyal supporters) is more supportive of environmental action than is the Conservative Party base. Liberals would advocate oil and gas regulation and freedom of speech for government scientists, for example.

The NDP has an even more ambitious environmental platform, which includes moving away from fossil-fuel dependence, establishing binding targets to cut greenhouse gas emissions, and strengthening laws to protect biodiversity, water quality, and food security. Still, its environmental plan rejects "the claim of a fundamental contradiction between environmental health and economic growth" (NDP 2013).

Fourth-wave environmentalism will be discussed in Chapter 12. Once we discuss policy around energy, pollution, land, and wildlife, we will have a better sense of why a fourth wave might be needed and what challenges it will face. To some extent, the question will hinge on our attitude toward economic growth. Media often portrays politicians talking about the link between Canadian prosperity and economic growth. Rarely are the environmental impacts of this growth discussed or debated in a public forum. There is an unquestionable tension between our desire to protect the environment and our desire to exploit natural resources. More important, the trade-offs are too often ignored, glossed over, or ill considered. As Laurel MacDowell has written, "balancing the needs of the planet and public health with economic growth and private initiative is the issue of the twenty-first century" (MacDowell 2012, 264).

Key Terms

first wave of environmentalism; second wave of environmentalism; tragedy of the commons; third wave of environmentalism; neoliberalism; Earth Summit; Rio Declaration; sustainable development; green consumerism; ecocentrism; deep ecology; closed bargaining; memorandum of understanding; social licence; Promethean approach

Discussion Questions

1. What events led to the second wave of environmentalism?
2. How were the second and third waves of environmentalism different? Was policymaking different in the two eras? How so?
3. Do you engage in green consumerism? If so, how and why?
4. What makes "sustainable development" so difficult to implement in Canada?
5. Describe Canada's approach to environmental policymaking in broad terms. Has the Harper government altered the path of policy in the country—how so?

Suggested Readings

Biro, Andrew. 2010. "Environmental Prospects in Canada." *Environmental Politics* 19 (2): 303–9. http://dx.doi.org/10.1080/09644010903576934.

Boyd, David R. 2003. *Unnatural Law: Rethinking Canadian Environmental Law and Policy*. Vancouver: UBC Press.

Erickson, Bruce. 2014. *Canoe Nation: Nature, Race, and the Making of a Canadian Icon*. Vancouver: UBC Press.

Friesen, Gerald. 1987. *The Canadian Prairies*. Toronto: University of Toronto Press.

Howe, Joshua P. 2014. *Behind the Curve: Science and the Politics of Global Warming*. Seattle, WA: University of Washington Press.

MacDonald, Douglas. 2007. *Business and Environmental Policy in Canada*. Toronto: University of Toronto Press.

MacDowell, Laurel Sefton. 2012. *An Environmental History of Canada*. Vancouver: UBC Press.

May, Elizabeth. 2006. *How to Save the World in Your Spare Time*. Toronto: Key Porter Books.

May, Elizabeth. 2014. *Who We Are: Reflections on My Life and Canada*. Vancouver: Greystone Books.

McKenzie, Judith I. 2002. *Environmental Politics in Canada: Managing the Commons into the Twenty-First Century*. Oxford: Oxford University Press.

O'Connor, Ryan. 2014. *The First Green Wave: Pollution Probe and the Origins of Environmental Activism in Ontario*. Vancouver: UBC Press.

Toner, Glen. 2002. "Contesting the Green: Canadian Environmental Policy at the Turn of the Century." In *Environmental Politics and Policy in Industrialized Countries*, edited by Uday Desai, 71–120. Cambridge, MA: MIT Press.

Turner, Chris. 2013. *The War on Science: Muzzled Scientists and Willful Blindness in Stephen Harper's Canada*. Vancouver: Greystone Press.

Weyler, Rex. 2004. *Greenpeace: How a Group of Ecologists, Journalists and Visionaries Changed the World*. Vancouver: Raincoast Books.

Chapter 5

The Conservation of Species at Risk

THE STORY OF DEVELOPING CANADIAN WILDLIFE POLICY, specifically policy for species at risk, is perhaps the best example of the challenges posed by federalism to environmental policymaking. The Constitution gives the federal government very limited power when it comes to these issues. Beyond migratory birds, aquatic species, and federal lands, Ottawa's power is limited. As with other areas of environmental policy, the provinces have the real power to regulate. Each province in Canada has jurisdiction over not only wildlife but also provincial Crown lands and the regulation of private lands. And regulating land use is extremely important because to safeguard wildlife is to protect the habitat, or land, where various species live.

As mentioned in Chapter 4, when Europeans arrived on the continent, wildlife was bountiful. In fact, the fur trade put Canada on the world map. There was simply no reason to worry about the health of Canada's wildlife or ecosystems. Worry about both did begin, however, when the bison started to decline and the passenger pigeon became extinct in the early twentieth century. In response, the federal government started to create national parks and to enact some wildlife legislation, as will be discussed. It was not until the 1960s, however, that **biodiversity**, meaning genetic variation in life forms, became an international issue. At the time this book was written, Canada was still struggling to legislate for the protection of biodiversity and species at risk.

As Chapter 1 illustrated, some of our ecosystems are thriving while others are in serious decline. Although it is true that species go extinct naturally, the reality is that artificial extinction (caused by humans) is rapidly increasing (Pimm et al. 2014). There are five main causes: habitat loss or fragmentation, toxic pollutants, human persecution, the introduction of invasive species (Kerr and Cihlar 2004; Venter et al. 2006; Wilcove et al. 1998), and climate change (Office of the Auditor General of Canada 2013b). To address artificial extinction, society must think carefully about how best to conserve biodiversity and recover already endangered species. This chapter will focus on species at risk (SAR) legislation in Canada. The federal government enacted the Species at Risk Act (SARA) in 2002, and six provinces and one territory have stand-alone species at risk legislation. Where SARA is deficient, the provincial laws are supposed to fill the gaps. This chapter will explain how the patchwork of Canadian laws is allowing species to fall through the gaps, as there is extremely weak protection for habitat everywhere in the country.

WHY CARE?

Any Canadian might ask, "Why should I care about biodiversity loss and species at risk?" It is hard to imagine that, in such a large country with so few people, other species are struggling to survive. Can't they just move north somewhere? Or can't we just put them in a national park? Canada's population is only part of the concern. The fact that most Canadians live close to the border with the United States does put pressure on southern ecosystems, particularly in heavily populated places such as Vancouver and Toronto. Ironically, those areas are among the most biodiverse in Canada. Other species also like to live close to the southern border where it is a bit warmer (Chu et al. 2015; Office of the Auditor General of Canada 2013a, chap. 6). Beyond just people pushing out wildlife, what we choose to do with our land, air, and water poses a problem for maintaining biodiversity. Canadians may not inhabit all of Saskatchewan, but using large tracts of land for agriculture and mineral extraction means less room for other living things. Similarly, Ontario and Québec are huge, but both sustain a major forestry industry in their northern lands. Because humans disturb the ecosystem through this sort of resource extraction, some species are finding it harder and harder to coexist with human development.

When it comes down to it, human beings value other species for intrinsic or instrumental reasons (see Beazley 2001). We either value animals, plants, insects, and birds because they have inherent worth as living creatures (**intrinsic value**) or because they provide human beings with necessary goods and services (**instrumental value**). Some species are essential to our existence—trees clean the air, wetland plants clean the water, bees pollinate our plants (food), certain insects clean the soil, and so on. All these tasks that other creatures complete for their own survival end up helping human beings a lot. Thus, some animals are used directly as food or medicine, both instrumental, while others are needed for "ecosystem services."

To put this discussion into the context of moral philosophy, Canadian researcher Karen Beazley (2001) explains that there are really five different perspectives or rationales for valuing species:

1. Species are rivets in spaceship earth;
2. Species are awe-inspiring;
3. Species provide ecosystem services;
4. Species are created by God; and,
5. Species have intrinsic worth.

Each of these is worth brief contemplation, as discerning why you value other species will be important in understanding why you think laws should or should not be put in place. In this list, numbers 1, 2, and 3 are instrumental while numbers 4 and 5 are intrinsic.

To argue that species are "rivets in spaceship earth" is to say that all living things are part of the same world and that we do not know how important one part is until we lose it. We know that Earth functions as a complete system, that we are all connected together on this plant by air and water. What will happen to that whole if we lose one species at a time? At some point, the whole system could come crashing down. Maybe it is okay from an ecosystem standpoint that a species of frogs goes extinct and a species of bird as well. The outcome may be more insects because they have fewer predators. Perhaps the ecosystem will find a balance again—or perhaps not. The problem is that we may not know until it is too late which species or combination of species is critical to the system's survival.

That various species inspire awe may not seem complicated as a reason for conservation. Humans have always looked at the natural world with awe. To get close to a giant moose in Banff National Park is to be in awe. To see a humpback whale or a snowy owl in its habitat is to experience the mystery, power, beauty, and humbling inspiration of nature. Can you imagine a world without other species? That is the stuff of science-fiction movies. But do we really need all species to feel awe? The answer is "maybe" for two reasons. First, not all people find the same species awe-inspiring. For some, the sight of a polar bear is the most romantic notion of Canada they hold, but others are inspired by the wild trillium, sturgeons, salamanders, or, for lots of children, spiders and snakes. Beauty in nature is in the eye of the beholder. Some Canadians love the forest and its wildlife while others respond to the flora and fauna of the Prairies or of the Atlantic's rocky shores. Different people will want to conserve different species and different landscapes. Second, some of the species that are more universally acknowledged as awe inspiring, for example, bears, birds, and whales, depend on less inspiring species for survival. There can be no grassland birds without grasslands. Thus, various species have instrumental value because they are the potential "instruments" of inspiring awe or of holding the system together, as a rivet would.

Canadian species also have instrumental value because they provide Canadians with numerous ecosystem services. Biodiversity is a public good, and all Canadians benefit when biodiversity flourishes. The estimated value of ecological goods and services ranges from $2.6 billion per year from Ontario's Greenbelt, to $5.4 billion from British Columbia's lower mainland, to $703 billion per year from Canada's boreal forests (Kenny, Elgie, and Sawyer 2011). Biodiversity provides anthropocentric goods such as food, medicine, pollination, and protection of water quality, as well as numerous cultural and recreational benefits such as hunting, hiking, birding, photography, and spaces for spirituality. We need other species for our economy, especially agriculture and tourism. We may not need *all* species for these reasons, but, as already explained, we do not know which species are "essential."

The argument that species are created by God and the argument that species have intrinsic worth are two sides of the same coin. If one believes in God as creator of the world, then this belief provides a solid reason for stewarding Earth and all its creatures. However, if one does not believe in God or does not believe that God created Earth, then the idea that species have intrinsic worth is a solid ethical reason for stewarding Earth and all its creatures. There is some evidence that Canadians do believe that other species have intrinsic worth. As SARA states in its preamble, "wildlife, in all its forms, has *value in and of itself* and is valued by Canadians for aesthetic, cultural, spiritual, recreational, educational, historical, economic, medical, ecological and scientific reasons" [emphasis added]. Newfoundland and Labrador goes one step further, stating in its Endangered Species Act (2001) that other species "have a right to exist"— perhaps no stronger intrinsic value claim exists in North American legislation. Overall, the five reasons, both instrumental and intrinsic, provide a good argument as to why we should care about biodiversity.

FEDERAL CONSERVATION OF WILDLIFE

The earliest attempts by the federal government to protect wildlife include the 1911 North Pacific Fur Seal Convention (between Great Britain on behalf of Canada, Russia, the United States, and Japan), the 1916

Migratory Birds Convention Act (with the United States), and the 1927 Provincial Parks Act that placed logging bans on shorelines to protect watersheds and wildlife (MacDowell 2012). But it was not really until the second wave of environmentalism that momentum for biodiversity and species at risk picked up pace in the policy world.

In the United States, the Endangered Species Preservation Act was passed in 1966, followed quickly by the Endangered Species Conservation Act of 1969. In 1973, the Convention on International Trade in Endangered Species Wild Fauna and Flora (CITES) was agreed on by 80 states in Washington, DC, and the US Endangered Species Act of 1973 was signed (see Olive 2014a, chap. 2). Canada was slower to act, but pressure on wildlife was less significant in this less (industrially) developed and urbanized country. The Canadian Wildlife Service was established in 1947 to conduct scientific research, educate the public about wildlife, and work with national parks to manage and promote wildlife and implement federal wildlife policy. The Canadian Wildlife Act did not come into being until 1973, and, as a federal law, it was only able to lead by example and set standards and goals for the provinces. Canada also signed CITES in 1974, although the convention entered into force internationally only in 1975, and an international agreement to protect polar bears in 1973 (see Olive 2014a, chap. 3).

At the 1992 UN Conference on Environment and Development (the "Earth Summit" in Rio de Janeiro), the **United Nations Convention on Biological Diversity** (CBD) was opened for signatures; by 1993, it had received 168 signatures representing 196 countries (or "parties"). As discussed in greater detail in Chapter 11, Canada was the first industrialized country to ratify the treaty (the prime minister and cabinet have to approve a treaty before it is considered "passed" in Canada). The CBD has three key priorities: (1) to conserve biological diversity, including not just living species but also their genes; (2) to promote the sustainable use of biological diversity; and (3) to promote the fair and equitable sharing of the benefits derived from biological diversity (e.g., genetic resources, including pharmaceuticals and technology). Over the past 20 years, Canada has been working toward progress in these three areas.

All signatories to the convention must create biodiversity strategies and action plans at the national level (see biodivcanada.ca). Each strategy is then to be streamlined into all government sectors and activities that have an impact on biodiversity domestically. In addition, each country must prepare reports on the status of biodiversity at the national level. Canada developed a biodiversity strategy in 1995, which was a joint effort by the federal, territorial, and provincial governments. In 2006, Canada released an outcomes framework, formally known as A *Biodiversity*

Outcomes Frame for Canada. Both initiatives, as well as Canada's 2020 biodiversity goals and targets, aim at fulfilling UNCBD commitments. Similarly, Canada's most recent report on the status of biodiversity, its fifth since 1992, was released in March 2014 and offers an assessment of all Canada's ecosystems (follow the link on biodivcanada.ca to access the full report). The cornerstone of federal biodiversity policy, however, is the Species at Risk Act. After discussing that policy, the next section will move to an overview of provincial legislation, or lack thereof, in Canada.

The Federal Government and the Species at Risk Act

After Canada signed the UNCBD in 1992, it took four years for Bill C-65, the Canada Endangered Species Protection Act, to be introduced in Parliament. Industrial interests immediately rejected it, concerned that the bill would impose excessive costs on the private sector (Amos, Harrison, and Hoberg 2001; Illical and Harrison 2007; Olive 2014a). The provinces also objected to Bill C-65 on the grounds that it gave too much power to the federal government. The bill died in 1997 when a federal election was called. In 1998, the legislative initiative was rekindled by the creation of the Species at Risk Working Group (SARWG), a coalition of environmental and business organizations forged by Elizabeth May, the current leader of the national Green Party. The group recommended that the federal government create financial support for voluntary stewardship programs as an alternative to regulation (Amos, Harrison, and Hoberg 2001).

After spending two years redrafting Bill C-65, the government reintroduced the legislation in 2000 as Bill C-33, the Species at Risk Act. However, that bill died with the calling of a federal election in 2000. A third version, C-5, was introduced in 2001 and passed in the House of Commons in June 2002, but it too died when Parliament was prorogued that year. The Senate then invoked a special parliamentary procedure to reinstate the bill without it having to go through three more readings in the House. The upper chamber finally approved SARA in October 2002, and the bill received royal assent on December 12, 2002 (Illical and Harrison 2007; Olive 2014a). This story shows that the policy process is not always neat and tidy with a clear progression of steps from the agenda-setting stage to the evaluation stage. SARA was created in fits and spurts over a 10-year period.

SARA is a federal law with limited reach into the provinces. SARA applies automatically only to endangered species on federal lands in Canada, which is about 5 per cent of the country's total territory outside of the North (Boyd 2003, 184). The law is intended to recognize and protect all scientific classifications of species (and their habitats) that are at risk of becoming extinct in Canada or around the world. It prohibits the killing of species and protects critical habitat. SARA makes it an offence to "kill, harm, harass, capture, or take individuals of a wildlife species that is listed as an extirpated species, an endangered species or a threatened species" (SARA, S.C. 2002, c. 29, s. 32). Moreover, it is illegal to "damage or destroy the residence of one or more individuals of a wildlife species that is listed as an endangered species or a threatened species" (SARA, S.C. 2002, c. 29, s. 33). These prohibitions automatically apply to all listed aquatic species, all birds listed under the Migratory Birds Convention Act of 1994, and all other species found on federal lands. The responsibility for implementing SARA is shared between the minister of Fisheries and Oceans Canada, which oversees matters concerning aquatic species, and the minister of Environment Canada, who is responsible for Parks Canada and oversees matters concerning all other terrestrial species on federal lands.

Under SARA, species become protected once they are added to the list of wildlife species at risk. The head of the Canadian Endangered Species Conservation Council and the environment minister are advised regarding which species should be added by (the Committee on the Status of Wildlife Endangered (COSEWIC) in Canada), which is a non-government body consisting of 31 independent scientists who are drawn from each of the 13 provincial and territorial government wildlife agencies, 4 federal agencies, 3 non-government science members, 10 co-chairs of the Species Specialist Subcommittees, and 1 co-chair from the Aboriginal Traditional Knowledge Subcommittee (Government of Canada 2015a). It makes recommendations based on the "best science available," which includes Western science, Aboriginal traditional knowledge (discussed in Chapter 9), and community knowledge.

At first glance, the process for deciding whether a species should be protected seems remarkably streamlined. All COSEWIC species assessments received by the environment minister are posted publicly on the Species at Risk Public Registry. The minister has 90 days to publish (and make public) a response statement and provide timelines for action. Within nine months of receiving the assessment, the government must decide whether to accept or reject it. Sometimes, the government will refer the species back to COSEWIC for further information. If no decision is made within nine months, the species is automatically added to the list in accordance with COSEWIC's recommendation (Environment Canada 2009, 6–7; Government of Canada 2015b; Olive 2014b).

In practice, however, long delays are possible. The government has interpreted the receipt of a COSEWIC assessment by the environment minister to be different than its receipt by government, citing SARA itself, which says that the nine-month countdown to listing a species automatically if no decision is taken starts when the "Governor in Council" receives an assessment. So environment ministers can respond in 90 days but not send a COSEWIC assessment on to cabinet, leaving the status of many species in limbo. Indeed, *The Globe and Mail* reported that, between 2009 and 2013, 92 of the 141 COSEWIC assessments were never officially transmitted (Otto, McKee, and Whitton, 2013).

Thus, although the assessment for listing is a scientific decision made by COSEWIC, the listing of the species for SARA protection is a political decision made or delayed by the government. Once a species is listed, Environment Canada assembles a recovery team to draft and implement a recovery plan in collaboration with the appropriate federal, provincial, and Aboriginal entities.

SARA includes a **safety net** provision that enables the federal government to act inside provinces if or when a province fails to protect an at-risk species. In Canada, the federal government has virtually exclusive authority over marine life and over most wildlife north of 60 degrees longitude (which has been delegated to the territorial governments), but the provincial governments have near-comprehensive authority over terrestrial wildlife, lands, and resources. Only 6 of the 10 provinces and 1 of the 3 territories have stand-alone species at risk legislation. Ontario, Québec, New Brunswick, and the Northwest Territories have updated their policies since the federal government passed SARA in 2002. Presently, listed endangered species (and their identified habitats) are granted mandatory protection only on federal lands across the country and in all lands inside Ontario and the NWT. In all other places, species are afforded discretionary protection, which often means little to no protection.

The provinces are not forced or even incentivized to create and update legislation, and things move slowly as a result. The creation of a "safety net" provides a way for the federal government to provide "a residual power to protect species and habitat on non-federal lands" (Wojciechowski et al. 2011, 206). The law states that if the federal government has reason to suspect that a province or territory is not protecting a species or its habitat effectively, then it can apply federal prohibitions to non-federal lands in that province or territory (Smallwood 2003, 56). Doing so is called issuing an emergency order and is a rare example of the federal government regulating wildlife and habitat inside provinces—where the province has clear jurisdiction (SARA, S.C. 2002 c. 29, s. 80). However, there are no clear guidelines in place that establish when a province is considered to have "failed" or when it is appropriate for the federal government to act inside a province. The federal safety net is entirely discretionary.

In September 2013, Environment Canada invoked the safety net for the greater sage grouse (*Centrocercus urophasianus urophasianus*) in Alberta and Saskatchewan. The sage grouse is a sagebrush bird on the Prairies. The bird has experienced a 98 per cent decline since 1988 (Environment Canada 2014g). The largest threat is habitat loss through the oil and gas industry. The sage grouse has a very specific mating dance, and the bird will not dance within a few miles of oil mining. Neither Alberta nor Saskatchewan has stand-alone species at risk legislation, and neither province was working actively to protect the habitat of the sage grouse. Thus, the federal government invoked an emergency order (the safety net) to protect the bird on federal and provincial Crown lands in the provinces. This strategy might be too little too late for the bird, but it creates a legal precedent for using the safety net. The federal government's use of an emergency order will make using this power again in the future for similar cases easier. (Also, environmental groups could find it easier to sue Environment Canada for not applying the safety net in similar cases, of which there are many across Canada—especially in areas of proposed pipelines).

Finally, it is important to note that SARA embraces a precautionary approach to species and habitat protection. This approach is in line with that of the UNCBD, with Canada's commitment to sustainable development, and with the use of the precautionary principle in many areas of environmental policy (such as the chemical legislation discussed in Chapter 6). The preamble of SARA says "if there are threats of serious or irreversible damage to a wildlife species, cost-effective measures to prevent the reduction of loss of the species should not be postponed for a lack of full scientific certainty (SARA, S.C. 2002, c. 29). Thus, Canada is prepared to protect species in cases where there is imperfect scientific information about the status of the species in the wild. Instead of waiting for more Geological Information Systems (GIS) data or biological status reports, Canada will list, protect, and attempt to recover a species that is suspected to be at risk on the basis of the best information available at the time. This commitment to endangered species is serious and has been adopted by all signing parties to the UN Convention on Biological Diversity.

PROVINCES AND SPECIES AT RISK

Because provinces have jurisdiction over their natural resources (including wildlife) and over private property as well as provincial Crown lands, most endangered species protection happens (or fails to happen) at the provincial level. In 1996, shortly after the federal government signed the UN Convention on Biological Diversity, the federal, provincial, and territorial ministers responsible for wildlife met and signed the Accord for the Protection of Species at Risk (Québec participated but did not sign the accord). As of 2015, only six provinces and one territory have stand-alone species at risk legislation. The three most western provinces and Prince Edward Island have wildlife acts that offer only some protection to endangered wildlife. Nunavut and the Yukon also have wildlife acts that provide some protection—although very few species are listed in the territories as endangered or threatened. The other six provinces do have legislation that specifically addresses species at risk. However, it should be noted that Manitoba, Nova Scotia, and Newfoundland and Labrador all have endangered species acts (ESAs) that predate SARA (see Table 5.1). Thus, little coherence exists among Canadian policies (see Olive 2014a).

Ideally, all provinces and territories would have legislation in place to protect at-risk species and their habitats. As of 2015, only Manitoba's ESA offers mandatory protection to a listed species *and* its habitat. In the case of the other provinces and territories, the identification and protection of habitat is discretionary, meaning the government can decide if and when to protect habitat. In other words, protecting habitat is not

TABLE 5.1 Provincial Endangered Species Policy

PROVINCE/TERRITORY	ENDANGERED SPECIES POLICY	WILDLIFE POLICY WITH ENDANGERED SPECIES PROTECTION
British Columbia		Wildlife Act, 1996
Alberta		Wildlife Act, 1980
Saskatchewan		Wildlife Act, 1998
Manitoba	Endangered Species and Ecosystems Act, 1990	
Ontario	Endangered Species Act, 2007	
Québec	An Act Respecting Threatened or Vulnerable Species, 2002	
New Brunswick	Species at Risk Act, 2012	
Nova Scotia	Endangered Species Act, 1998	
Prince Edward Island		Wildlife Conservation Act, 1988
Newfoundland and Labrador	Endangered Species Act, 2001	
Nunavut		Wildlife Act, 2003
Northwest Territories	Species at Risk, 2009	
Yukon		Wildlife Act, 2002

Note: Legislation is dated from the first year during which it was enacted.

Source: Adapted from Olive (2014a), Table 3.1

legally required—it is optional. This is true even in Ontario where the ESA is touted as the strongest law of its kind in Canada.

Overall, this messy patchwork of protection has too many holes. No two provinces have the same law, and shared ecosystems or even shared species get limited attention. The provinces do not communicate about protection and recovery—not with each other and not with the federal government. The 1996 meeting was the only time all jurisdictions came together to discuss species at risk legislation. The provinces must do better as they are the ones with the power to create and implement regulation on most land parcels across the country.

THE ROLE OF CITIES

Cities play a limited role in the protection of species at risk in Canada. Because there are virtually no federal lands inside city limits, SARA applies only to migratory birds or aquatic species that live or pass through these areas. Provincial policy, as noted, is quite weak across the country and has few implications for cities. However, a growing international movement aims to include cities in the protection of green space and wildlife; see the United Nations Environment Programme's urban biodiversity project, the Global Partnership on Cities and Biodiversity (UNEP 2014). The UN notes that cities comprise just 2 per cent of the world's surface, but their inhabitants use about 75 per cent of the world's resources. These people depend on healthy ecosystems and biological diversity for three main services: "provisioning of food, fibre and fuels; regulating through purification, detoxification and mitigation of droughts and floods; and enriching the spiritual, aesthetic and social life of urban dwellers" (UNEP 2014). Because cities draw on the resources of surrounding regions and because their waste and emissions can affect these regions, the policies of Toronto, Vancouver, Montréal, and Canada's other large urban centres have a significant impact on healthy ecosystems in Canada.

THE ROLE OF NGOs

Many non-governmental organizations (NGOs) are also involved with species at risk and wildlife protection in Canada. At the federal level, the largest groups are the David Suzuki Foundation, Nature Canada, Sierra Club Canada, the Canadian Wildlife Federation, Ducks Unlimited Canada, the World Wildlife Fund Canada, and the Nature Conservancy of Canada. At the provincial level, hundreds of groups exist, and some federal groups, such as Sierra Club Canada, have provincial branches. These groups all have websites, Facebook pages, and Twitter feeds. If you want to stay informed about the status of species at risk in Canada, follow a few of these NGOs.

The most important functions of NGOs devoted to protecting species at risk are education, outreach, and research. Canada is a huge country with thousands of species. The federal government cannot possibly oversee conservation on all the land or monitor the health and vitality of all species. This massive effort requires the assistance of NGOs, think tanks, private research firms, and public universities. Hundreds of examples exist of such efforts by NGOs.

One took place in Saskatchewan, a province that lacks strong environmental legislation. An organization called Nature Saskatchewan provides citizens and land managers with a wealth of information about wildlife and species at risk in the province. The "useful resources" section of the website includes factsheets about the values of biodiversity to ranchers and farmers, information about conservation easements, and descriptions of endangered species that people might come across on the landscape (see www.naturesask.ca). The group also provides links to other websites and organizations.

NGOs are also important watchdogs. In 2012, Ecojustice published a report entitled *Failure to Protect: Grading Canada's Species at Risk Laws* in which it analyzed and graded all SAR legislation in Canada. (See Figure 5.1.) British Columbia, Alberta, Saskatchewan, and the Yukon each received an F grade. The Northwest Territories, PEI, and New Brunswick (before its 2012 legislation) earned D-range grades, while the other provinces and the national government all earned grades in the C range. Not an inspiring report card! One consistent problem shared by all jurisdictions is a failure to identify and protect critical habitats for species. For this reason, Ecojustice recommends stronger laws, better implementation of the laws, and stronger federal oversight.

The David Suzuki Foundation (DSF), with support from other organizations, has often sued the federal government for failing to implement SARA. For example, the DSF and other environmental groups took the federal government to court in 2012 for failing to protect four endangered species along the proposed (and now approved) Northern Gateway pipeline and shipping route. According to the DSF, the Pacific humpback whale, the Nechako white sturgeon, the marbled murrelet, and the southern mountain caribou are all put at risk by the pipeline (Ecojustice 2013b; Moore 2012). Each of these species was listed as endangered or threatened under the Species at Risk Act when the Northern Gateway project was seeking approval; their recovery strategies, to which the government is legally bound, were at least three years past their due dates. (Note, however, that in 2014 the

FIGURE 5.1 The Report Card of Provincial and Federal Species at Risk Legislation as Graded by Ecojustice, 2012

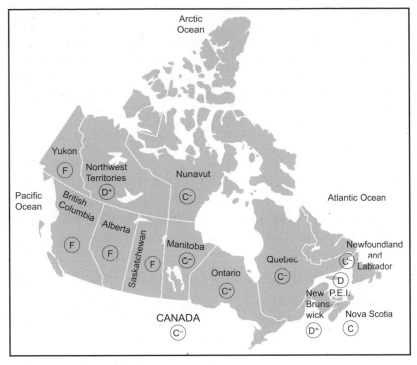

SOURCE: Ecojustice (2012a), 7. Reprinted with permission.

federal government removed the Pacific humpback whale from the list of threatened species, as discussed in Chapter 12.) These recovery strategies detail the habitat the species require to survive and how it will be protected. By delaying recovery strategies and, by extension, delaying identification of the critical habitats that must then be protected, the federal government eases the way for projects to speed through regulatory review, projects that could destroy critical habitat and cripple species recovery.

Ecojustice filed the litigation against the Harper government on September 26, 2012, in federal court, acting on behalf of the David Suzuki Foundation, Greenpeace Canada, Sierra Club of British Columbia, the Western Canada Wilderness Committee, and Wildsight (Ecojustice 2013b). In 2014, the ruling came back that the government had "acted unlawfully in failing to post proposed recovery strategies" for these four species. The judge also noted that "the delays encountered in these four cases are just the tip of the iceberg," as there were, at the time, some

167 species at risk for which recovery strategies had not been developed (*Western Canada Wilderness Committee v. Canada*, 2014 FC 148).

Some of these species at risk with overdue recovery strategies will also be affected by the Northern Gateway project, for example, the boreal caribou and the northern goshawk. In total, the *Report of the Commissioner of the Environment and Sustainable Development* listed 146 recovery strategies as being overdue as of March 31, 2013, the majority by over three years (Office of the Auditor General of Canada 2013a, chap. 6).

THE ROLE OF CITIZENS

As in other areas of environmental management, citizens have a large and important role to play in endangered species and wildlife conservation. Canada is a big country with plenty of land and a lot of biodiversity. However, the government, whether provincial or federal, cannot monitor or manage all land and water across the country at all times. It is up to everyday people to take note of wildlife and report concerns and problems.

Citizens who are landowners and land managers have a particularly important responsibility for wildlife and the protection of endangered species (Olive 2014a). At the end of the day, decisions made by land managers have a huge effect on wildlife. The choice to use pesticides, put up a fence, cut down trees, build a house, or put in a backyard pool has ramifications for the species that share habitats with humans.

In order for SARA or provincial policy to be successful, stewardship by Canadians is necessary. The Habitat Stewardship Program (HSP) for Species at Risk, a federal program created in 2000, provides millions of dollars to protect habitat, but other programs exist that bring together citizens, organizations, and conservation (Environment Canada 2014g). The Aboriginal Fund for Species at Risk supports projects contributing to species recovery on Aboriginal lands or carried out by Aboriginal organizations or communities (see Environment Canada 2015a). The Natural Areas Conservation Program "helps non-profit, non-government organizations secure ecologically sensitive lands to ensure the protection of our diverse ecosystems, wildlife, and habitat" (Environment Canada 2013b). Unlike prior programs, this one works through an agreement between the government and the Nature Conservancy of Canada. It enables federal matching funds for the projects of this organization and its non-government conservation partners, such as Ducks Unlimited Canada.

Even if you are not a landowner or manager, there are still countless ways to get involved in biodiversity protection. For example, in Toronto, citizens are encouraged to participate in a 48- or 24-hour "BioBlitz." In teams led by experts, citizens go to a specified location and count all the different species they can find in certain period. These counts help researchers measure biodiversity in a huge area of land and can provide an annual assessment of biodiversity decline (or increase). The first two BioBlitzes were held in Toronto's Rouge Park, but the program is spreading across Ontario and has plans to launch nationally in 2017 (see www .ontariobioblitz.ca).

Another, somewhat similar program is the North American "Christmas Bird Count." On any one day between December 14 and January 5, teams of citizens count every bird found within a circle having a 24-kilometre diameter (the circles stay the same year to year). These counts are organized at the local level, and anyone can participate. Data from this census are maintained by Bird Studies Canada, which partners with the Avian Knowledge Network to provide access to bird-monitoring statistics; these data are also used in species at risk recovery and action plans. The two citizen-based projects mentioned here provide just a sample of the important ways in which individuals can connect with the environment and the biodiversity that lives close to home. No matter where you live, you share your habitat with other species. Learning to live together is a requirement if life itself is to be sustained.

CONCLUSIONS

Federalism poses many challenges to managing biodiversity in Canada, especially when it comes to protecting species at risk. The federal government has the constitutional authority to enter into international treaties. To preserve biodiversity, the federal government has exercised this authority through the Migratory Birds Convention Act, the international Agreement on Conservation of Polar Bears, CITES, and the UNCBD (to name a few). The federal government is also responsible for the protection of aquatic species, and Ottawa safeguards wildlife and species at risk on federal lands, including on Aboriginal reserve lands.

Federalism means that the provinces carry the bulk of the regulatory power for wildlife and habitats, as they control natural resources and private property as well as manage provincial lands. Unfortunately, the provinces are not taking their role seriously enough. The Western provinces and PEI need legislation to protect endangered species and their habitats. Ontario, which has the strongest endangered species law in Canada, was sued by Ecojustice lawyers on behalf of the Ontario Nature and Wildlands League over regulatory changes that exempted the forestry industry (among others) from the main provisions of this law; the case was heard in January 2015.

When the provincial record is added to the federal "pattern of unfulfilled commitments and responsibilities," discussed previously, the news is disheartening (Max Paris Environment Unit 2013). The protection of Canada's endangered flora and fauna should be a case of shining multilevel governance, one in which municipalities, provinces, and the federal government work together with the First Nations and Inuit, as well as with NGOs and community groups, to implement meaningful species at risk legislation. This is not the case.

Key Terms

biodiversity; artificial extinction; intrinsic value; instrumental value; United Nations Convention on Biological Diversity; safety net

Discussion Questions

1. Of the five listed reasons to value biodiversity, how would you personally rank them from most to least important? If you were trying to convince your MP to protect biodiversity, in what order would you provide the reasons? Are the lists different—why or why not?
2. What is the federal government's role in protecting species at risk in Canada?
3. Does your province have species at risk legislation? How many species does the law protect?
4. If you were an endangered species, a bird for example, what part of the country would you most want to live in and why?
5. Why is the discretionary protection of habitat problematic?

Suggested Readings

Beazley, Karen, and Robert Boardman, eds. 2001. *Politics of the Wild: Canada and Endangered Species.* Don Mills, ON: Oxford University Press.

Burnet, J. Alexander. 2003. *A Passion for Wildlife: The History of the Canadian Wildlife Service.* Vancouver: UBC Press.

Findlay, Scott C., Stewart Elgie, Brian Giles, and Linda Burr. 2009. "Species Listing under Canada's Species at Risk Act." *Conservation Biology* 23 (6): 1609–17. http://dx.doi.org/10.1111/j.1523-1739.2009.01255.x.

Garner, Robert. 2004. *Animals, Politics, and Morality.* Manchester, UK: Manchester University Press.

Illical, Mary, and Kathryn Harrison. 2007. "Protecting Endangered Species in the US and Canada: The Role of Negative Lesson Drawing." *Canadian Journal of Political Science* 40 (2): 367–94. http://dx.doi.org/10.1017/S0008423907070175.

Loo, Tina. 2006. *States of Nature: Conserving Canada's Wildlife in the Twentieth Century*. Vancouver: UBC Press.

MacDonald, Cameron. 2013. *Endangered Species Road Trip*. Vancouver: Greystone Books.

McGregor, Deborah. 2002. "Traditional Ecological Knowledge and the Two-Row Wampum." *Biodiversity* 3 (3): 8–9. http://dx.doi.org/10.1080/14888386.2002.97 12586.

Olive, Andrea. 2014. *Land, Legitimacy, and Stewardship*. Toronto: University of Toronto Press.

Smallwood, Kate. 2003. *A Guide to Canada's Species at Risk Act*. Toronto: Sierra Legal Defense Fund.

Suzuki, David. 2011. "Beyond the Species at Risk Act: Recognizing the Sacred." *Journal of Environmental Policy and Practice* 22 (3): 239–54.

Wilson, E. O. 1992. *The Diversity of Life*. Cambridge, MA: Harvard University Press.

Chapter 6

Water, Air, and Chemical Pollution

MOST CANADIANS do not think of their country as being polluted. And, for the most part, it is not. The largest exception to that, and likely the most polluted environment in Canada, is in southern Ontario. A corridor of industry just south of Sarnia's downtown core has been named **Chemical Valley** because of the 62 large industrial facilities located there. These facilities comprise about 40 per cent of Canada's chemical industry, hence the name. The city of Sarnia has some of the worst air pollution in the industrialized world (MacDonald and Rang 2007). Water quality and public health are other related issues for this area. The pollution here would be rivalled by that near the oil sands in Alberta, but far fewer people live in northern Alberta than in Sarnia. Not surprisingly, the oil sands and Sarnia are connected—by way of a pipeline that brings bitumen to a refinery in Sarnia. Although Sarnia and the oil sands are extreme examples of pollution in Canada, there are other reasons to be concerned about water quality, air pollution, and chemical pollution all across the country.

Natural and unnatural contaminants can cause pollution (Saier 2006). Too much nitrogen oxide from natural sources, such as lightning strikes, biological decay, and volcanoes, can cause air pollution; and too much naturally occurring arsenic in groundwater is poisonous. Human sources of pollution or unnatural contaminants, however, are an ever-increasing concern. These occur when we dump waste in waterways, drive cars, raise large herds of cattle, flush pharmaceuticals down the toilet, generate nuclear waste from power plants and toxic chemical waste from manufacturing plastics or cellphones, and so on. Today pollution is ubiquitous and deeply tied to our consumerist lives.

This chapter examines the policy and politics of water, air, and chemical pollution. Today, many Canadian communities, and particularly those near the Great Lakes and on First Nation reserves, are concerned about water quality. Air quality is a worry in only a few cities, but CO_2 emissions, a form of air pollution, are a serious concern throughout the country and the world because of their relation to climate change. Chemical pollutants produced by the manufacture of consumer goods ranging from plastics to make-up but also by agriculture, electricity generation, smelting, and the incineration of waste pose a danger because they bioaccumulate when in the food chain (e.g., mercury or pesticide levels get higher as animals eat other animals that have eaten contaminated plants). Clearly, examining existing federal and provincial policy to control these three types of pollution, as well as the role of cities, NGOs, and citizens in this arena of policymaking, is an important task.

THE POLITICS OF WATER

Everyone knows that Canada has a lot of water. You often hear that Canada has a fifth of the world's total **freshwater supply** (Sprague 2007). But what people do not think about too often is that much of this water is a non-renewable resource. The Great Lakes, Canada's largest supply of fresh water, are not renewable—only 1 per cent of the water in the lakes is renewed on an annual basis (from snow melt and precipitation); the remainder is water left over from glaciation and is not renewable (De Loë and Kreutzwiser 2007). Without this distinction, people tend to overestimate how much water there is in Canada. So which countries have the largest renewable water supplies? Brazil and Russia come out on top. Canada, with 6.5 per cent of the world's renewable supply, is tied with Indonesia for third place, although the United States and China (each with 6.4 per cent) are close behind (Sprague 2007, 25).

Moreover, people do not tend to think about the location of Canada's water. Most of the country's vast water supplies are not in heavily populated areas. In fact, more than half of Canada's fresh water flows north into Arctic or sub-Arctic regions where it is not available for most Canadians (Environment Canada 2013h). And water resources and rainfall vary greatly across the country. The result is that some places have access to a lot of fresh water—for example, in large lakes or rivers—while other places rely on groundwater for their drinking supply. Managing water quality is a challenge in both cases as pollution can easily enter surface water or seep into groundwater. The water Canadians need is not always where we want it to be, and even when it is, it may not be very clean because of industrial and agricultural pollution.

Last, it is important to think about varieties of water use. Canadians either withdraw water from a source (e.g., from a lake or river or the ground) for use in homes and businesses, or they use water at its source for recreation or industry (e.g., generating hydroelectric power). In both cases, Canadians use a lot of water. In 2004, the average Canadian used 329 litres per day for personal use (cooking, showering, and drinking) while the average European used a little over half that amount (Environment Canada 2007, 2013h). A Canadian lifestyle, then, is water intensive. Only Americans consume more water per capita. Though Canadians seem unlikely to run out of water, some places are already experiencing droughts (think southern Alberta) and having to conserve water and access more sources. Thus, both water conservation and water quality are important issues for some Canadians (see Bakker 2007).

Water withdrawal for business and industry is also substantial. For example, the Prairies use a lot of water for agriculture and most of that water is drawn from the ground or from rivers and lakes. You may think that water is just returned to the ground through farming, but remember that this water is mixed with the herbicides and pesticides used on cropland. Moreover, agriculture "consumes" the water that is then stored in plants or animals. According to Environment Canada, 44.6 billion cubic metres of surface water—from rivers and lakes—is withdrawn for agriculture and manufacturing each year (Harker et al. 2004). Agriculture withdrew only 9 per cent of the total amount, but, of the water it withdrew, it consumed 71 per cent of it—meaning that this water was not returned to the watershed (Harker et al. 2004).

Ontario uses a lot of water for manufacturing, as does Alberta in oil sands production. And water use for manufacturing purposes has huge implications for water management and quality in the country. When industry or mining uses water, there is always something left over—a type of polluted water that is returned to the watershed or stored apart from it. For example, in the oil sands, water is used for heating the bitumen underground. After that process is complete, the water that is left has been heavily polluted with chemicals and mixed with heavy metals from the deep layers of soil. Because it is too polluted to return to the Athabasca River system, the water is stored in "tailing ponds" or large containment areas (Flanagan 2015; Royal Society of Canada 2010). This form of pollution is very serious and a significant risk for wildlife (birds can mistake the ponds for clean water, for example) and for the larger watershed as tailing ponds can seep into the ground or leak into the river (Royal Society of Canada 2010).

Groundwater is water in the pores and fractures of rock formations under our feet. Aquifers are large deposits of groundwater that are recharged from water at the surface. About 30 per cent of Canadians rely on groundwater for their drinking water—mostly in rural areas. In fact, approximately two-thirds of those who use groundwater live in rural areas (Environment Canada 2013e). See Map 6.1 for a province-by-province indicator of population reliant on groundwater. Industry, mining and fracking, and agriculture use groundwater. To draw groundwater in Canada requires a permit, and the process of obtaining one varies from province to province. Unfortunately, no level of government in Canada has been good about measuring or monitoring groundwater withdrawal (Bakker 2007). Consequently, we do not have a good sense of how much groundwater we have in Canada or of who is using what, at what rates, or for what purpose. Perhaps more important, we do not understand how climate change will affect our groundwater supply. This lack of knowledge makes creating sound public water policy very difficult.

Water Management

Canada has no legally enforceable national water quality standards. It also has poor monitoring of water quality and use, as well as a lack of data about water supplies (Nowlan 2007). Chapter 3 noted that the quality of Canada's water tends to be very good overall (at least in rivers as measured by Environment Canada). But there have been exceptions, most notably on First Nation reserves and in Walkerton, Ontario, in 2000 and North Battleford, Saskatchewan, in 2001.

Aboriginal Affairs and Northern Development Canada (AANDC) released the results in July 2011 of the National Assessment of First Nations Water and Wastewater Systems. The report indicated that over 70 per cent of the drinking water on reserves posed a risk to human health—in fact, 39 per cent of the drinking water systems in First Nation communities are considered "high risk," and 34 per cent are "moderate risk" (AANDC 2011b, 16). Water issues remain an ongoing crisis on reserves across the country (see also MacIntosh 2008). This topic is discussed again in Chapter 9.

On non-reserve land, there have been at least two major recent public health scares. Both are a good example of Environment Canada's mandate crossing paths with that of Health Canada. Water quality is an environmental issue, but also a public health issue. Health Canada bears some responsibility for water safety. In Walkerton, E. coli contaminated the town's water supply and infected nearly half the population—eventually killing seven people. In North Battleford, cryptosporidiosis polluted the water and infected more than 6,000 people. No one died, but many

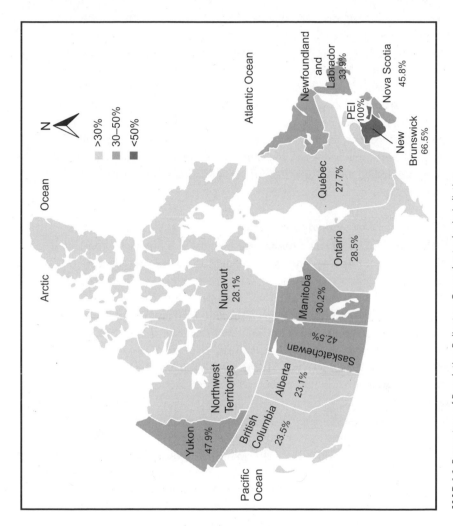

MAP 6.1 Percentage of Population Reliant on Groundwater by Jurisdiction

SOURCE: Environment Canada (2013e). Reprinted with permission.

people suffered prolonged illness, and everyone in the town had to boil their water before use for many long weeks before the problem was handled. These stories are certainly not the norm in Canada. But they warn Canadians to keep water quality a salient issue.

Who is responsible for water management in Canada? That is not an easy question to answer. No one can "own" water in Canada—instead, the provinces manage water on behalf of the public. As with other natural resources, such as oil, the provinces are seen as the rightful managers, a right laid out in Section 92 of the Constitution. However, the federal government also plays a large role in water management because Ottawa is responsible for navigation and shipping on all Canadian waters and for the fisheries, trade and commerce, international relations, and treaty making. More so than in the case of energy, water is a shared responsibility across multiple levels of government—from the federal government to the watershed boards and the municipal and community councils and agencies (Saunders and Wenig 2007).

The Federal Government and Water

Water is a difficult resource to manage because it is not easily controlled. Water does not respect political boundaries, so its use as well as its management must be shared across jurisdictions—even across countries. This transnational and transjurisdictional nature of water might lead you to think the federal government is best situated to managing water. However, just the opposite is happening in Canada: a devolution of power from the federal government to the provinces in the management of water (this is another example of open federalism). This shift has largely been driven by a federal neoliberal agenda but also by the increasing complexity of water management.

During the second wave of environmentalism in the 1970s and 1980s, the federal government was more active in water policy. In 1970, Ottawa passed the Canada Water Act. The 1984–85 Inquiry on Federal Water Policy led eventually to the release of a Federal Water Policy in 1987. Although these initiatives sound very bold and heavily regulatory—in fact, they sound very much like American command-and-control legislation, such as the Clean Water Act of 1972 or the Safe Drinking Water Act of 1974—this is the not the case. The most important thing to know about this Canadian federal legislation, however, is that it was non-binding on the provinces. These federal policies served as guidelines and not requirements. So they are part of federal water policy but not of the federal water law that *regulates* or *mandates* provincial compliance. (Of course, the water pollution laws outlined in the Canadian Environmental Protection Act, which serves as a catch-all law for various types of pollution, do restrict the provinces). In 1985, the federal government passed the Arctic Waters Pollution Prevention Act, which is regulatory but does not over-step provincial rights, as the territories and the Arctic Ocean are part of the federal government's jurisdiction.

More recently, and certainly since the Conservative Party rose to power in 2006, we have seen the federal government defer to the provinces in matters of water management that are regional in nature. Perhaps the best example of this deference is the Navigation Protection Act that was amended by Parliament in 2015. The Navigable Waters Protection Act (NWPA) was originally enacted by Parliament in 1882, making it one of Canada's oldest federal environmental laws. As mentioned, the federal government has exclusive jurisdiction over navigation and shipping in Canada. The NWPA controlled logging operations, dams, pipelines, and bridges so as to protect Canadians' right to navigate waterways without interference. How is this an environmental law? The NWPA was a federal tool to protect the overall quality of Canadian waterways. Essentially, the federal government dictated who could use Canada's waterways and for what purposes. If an industry wanted to develop a project on a waterway, it needed to get a permit from the federal government—granted under the pretense that such development would not impede navigation on the water. The NWPA acted as a stopgap on development and the subsequent pollution caused by industry in Canada's waterways. It was a type of "federal oversight" on Canadian waterways.

In 2012, the federal government amended the NWPA, renaming it the Navigation Protection Act (NPA). The amendments came through Bill C-45, which was an extensive omnibus budget bill. The newly named NPA was designed to protect *navigation* and not navigable *water*. Thus, 99.7 per cent of Canada's lakes and 99.9 per cent of Canada's rivers are now excluded from federal oversight, meaning that industrial activity, dams, and bridges will no longer require federal permits or federal environmental assessments because the federal government only regulates navigation *on* the water and not the water itself (Ecojustice 2012b). The result is that the NPA leaves protections in place for just 97 of the roughly 32,000 lakes previously protected under the NWPA and effectively leaves matters of water quality and of protecting nearshore habitats to others (FOCA 2014).

Although the **devolution of powers** to the provinces is the current trend in federal water policy, Ottawa maintains sole responsibility for both water on First Nation reserves and **transboundary water**—water that is shared by Canada and the United States. In fact, managing transboundary water is perhaps the most important environmental issue shared by the two countries and has been part of the US-Canada relationship since

Confederation. The Canadian federal government signed the Boundary Waters Treaty with the United States in 1909. The treaty sets out the core legal principles necessary to govern shared water, and it creates the institutional framework to implement policy. This treaty deals exclusively with surface water that is shared; it is silent on the issue of groundwater. Thus, it would not be a violation of the Boundary Waters Treaty if North Dakota were to use too much of its groundwater for fracking and unintentionally pump some from Saskatchewan, its neighbour. Although the issue of shared groundwater has not been on the federal agenda, it would be a federal responsibility because Ottawa deals with transboundary water (Norman, Cohen, and Bakker 2013).

Canada and the United States also have an International Joint Commission for protecting shared waters, which was created through the Boundary Waters Treaty (Fischhendler and Feitelson 2005; LeMarquand 1993; Schwartz 2006). This commission has a quasi-judicial capacity, as it is intended to approve permits that affect water flow. Recommendations of the commission are technically non-binding, but in only a handful of instances have its recommendations not been followed (Clamen 2013). The commission is also responsible for investigating and reporting on the quality of shared water. However, it looks at an issue only if requested to do so by both national governments, which means that the most contentious issues might never make it to review. Finally, the Great Lakes Water Quality Agreement, first signed in 1972, is another joint Canada-US agreement. Its stated purpose is to protect the quality of shared water in the five Great Lakes (Linton and Hall 2013). The Great Lakes are a precious resource for public drinking water, industrial uses, and aquatic ecosystems. The five lakes combined create a water basin that represents 18 per cent of the world's fresh surface water (Environment Canada 2013d).

As well as the NPA and the governing of water shared with the United States, the Canadian federal government does have other environmental laws that give it power to regulate water pollution. These include the Fisheries Act, the Canadian Environmental Protection Act, the Canadian Environmental Assessment Act, and any spending programs agreed to by the provinces under the Canada Water Act and the Federal Water Policy. However, none of these include the regulatory power to set quality standards or to manage water supply. Those powers are entirely provincial.

The Provinces and Water

The provinces are the primary managers of water in Canada. Section 92 of the Constitution grants them jurisdiction over drinking water, municipal treatment and sewage, and water taking—including for industrial and agricultural uses. However, similar to the way the federal government leaves responsibility for protecting water to the provinces, the provinces leave it to the municipalities. Often, managing water quality and pollution falls to authorities at the city or community level. Therefore, it is necessary to discuss two separate but related provincial issues: water permits and water quality control. The first is handled mostly at the provincial level, but the latter is more a municipal responsibility.

Water Permits

Because provinces consider themselves resource owners, they naturally see themselves as the proper judges of who gets water and when. Provinces allocate water to private or public users within their borders, which is one of the most important environmental decisions because ecosystems and biodiversity also rely on well-managed water supplies. Unfortunately, the provinces are not doing a particularly good job of managing this responsibility. Provincial water allocations are inconsistent, and no province has a serious hold on how much water is at stake because groundwater is not adequately measured by the provinces. Provinces issue use permits, or **allocations**, without knowing exactly how much water there is or how many permits should exist. There is a risk that a province will give out too many permits and not save enough for ecosystems or for times of drought. This problem has already occurred in some places in Canada, such as southern Alberta.

All across Canada, in each province and territory, you need permission to withdraw or divert water. For example, if a farmer wants to draw water from the ground to irrigate his or her fields, a permit from the provincial government is needed. That permit gives the landowner a water right. In some provinces, a water market allows permit holders to engage in water rights transfers—one permit holder, for example, gives his or her right to access water to a different person or party to use in a different place or for a different purpose (see Bakker 2007; Hill et al. 2008).

As mentioned, no one can "own" water in Canada—the provinces are legally considered the "owners," but that simply means they manage water on behalf of the public. A water right is not private ownership of water but instead a use right. A water permit gives someone the right to a certain amount of water under certain conditions. The system of water rights varies across the country. For example, in the Western provinces a permit holder gets an exclusive right to use water from the date of application. The system is based on the seniority of the permit and is often called a **first-in-time, first-in-right system**. During shortages, the first permit holder gets the most water. Permits are usually for a stated purpose and time and cannot be traded. However, since 1999, Alberta does have a water market in the southern part of the province where droughts are most common. And Saskatchewan is looking into creating a water market system but no trades or permit sales have occurred yet.

In Ontario and the Maritimes, rights to water are established based on **riparian rights,** a system in which owners of land that borders water enjoy certain water rights. Landowners have non-transferable rights to access water flow on or bordering their property. Ontario has a statutory limit that caps any given landowner at no more than 50,000 litres of water a day. Anything above that, and the landowner would need a separate permit to draw or divert adjoining water. Riparian rights cannot be traded because they are attached to parcels of land. However, the system is flexible enough to enable a landowner to sell a property's "water right" without selling the property. Examples of severing the selling of a water right from the sale of land exist in the western United States. (For information on water regulations and water allocation schemes across all Canadian jurisdictions, see Hill et al. 2008; Brandes, Nowlan, and Paris 2008).

Climate change, an increase in agriculture, and the loss of wetlands will put intense pressure on provincial permitting processes. It is absolutely essential for provinces to undergo scientific data gathering such that groundwater levels are assessed and hydrologic systems are more fully understood. Poorly regulated pumping of groundwater or of any freshwater system today spells disaster for future generations of Canadians. There is no reason that we should be so poorly implementing this part of the water management equation. All 10 provinces and 3 territories would benefit from creating allocation systems based on a scientific assessment of water quantity so as to ensure sustainability (especially in light of projected urban growth). The provinces have been more than willing to accept the *right* to allocate water, but they are failing to take on this *responsibility*.

A better way to manage water would be collaboratively—not just across the provinces but across different levels of government and with the involvement of different sectors of society. Non-state actors, such as private industry, farmers, environmental groups, and municipal users, must be involved in water planning and allocation. Procedural justice, or the inclusion of all actors, is important because sound management requires buy-in and participation from multiple sectors of civil society. Environmental groups should be able to ensure that ecosystems have their fair share of allocations, and city users should be able to make a claim to adequate amounts of water regardless of drought-like conditions (see box "Water, Business, and the Environment"). Canada has enough water for all its users, but if provinces continue to hand out allocations to industry and agriculture without fully understanding how much ecosystems need and when, then problems will quickly arise.

Water Quality

In response to one of the largest public health scares in Canada, the Walkerton tragedy of 2000, Ontario passed a Safe Drinking Water Act in 2002 and a Clean Water Act in 2006. In many ways, these laws followed the policy process presented in Chapter 3. Water quality was put on the government's agenda because of the Walkerton tragedy. After consultation with experts and the Ontario public, a bill was drafted for each act and passed through the Legislative Assembly of Ontario. The Ministry of Environment and Climate Change oversees the implementation of both laws. Because water authority in Ontario is exercised at the watershed level, these acts provide mandates, regulations, and funding for local governments and watershed authorities to implement the legislated provisions. However, watershed authorities do not cover the whole province, and all data collection at the watershed level is funded and overseen by the province. So, if a given watershed authority makes any recommendations, these can be enacted only when approved by the province.

The Safe Drinking Water Act is meant to regulate quality standards for drinking water, create licensing for water-testing laboratories, and grant approval for private water-supply systems (see CELA 2011 for an in-depth discussion of the major provisions). The Clean Water Act is meant to help protect drinking water from the source (such as a lake or an underground reservoir) to the tap. In Ontario, the province creates "Source Protection Committees" that assess existing threats and potential threats to water. This assessment requires public participation, and the planning process for source protection is open to anyone in a community (but the public only gets a third of the seats on any given protection committee). The Clean Water Act also created the Ontario Drinking Water Stewardship Program, which offers financial assistance to landowners, farmers, or businesses that want to reduce threats to local drinking-water sources. The evaluation of these policies is ongoing. Ontario has not had another water scare since Walkerton, and, in some ways, that is the test that matters most. Water quality has improved for Ontarians. That said, problems still exist on First Nation reserves in the province, but that is a federal issue and not within Ontario's jurisdiction.

Water, Business, and the Environment

The Nestlé Waters Canada corporation has a water-bottling operation outside of Guelph, Ontario. The company obtained a permit from the province to draw groundwater. The permit allows Nestle to withdraw 1.13 million litres of water each day; it pays $3.71 for every million litres it pumps. (Remember that water is "free" because no one "owns" it, so the company pays to pump the water rather than paying for the water itself.)

In 2012, the province attached a new condition to Nestlé's permit whereby the company was forced to cut back on the volume of water it pumps during times of drought. Of all users in the watershed, including farmers, Nestlé is the only one to have restrictions placed upon its permit. In response, the company appealed these drought restrictions to the Ontario Environmental Review Tribunal. Nestlé argued that it should not be singled out or treated differently than other permit holders. Environmentalists argued that Nestlé's permit is already unique because it is the only user to withdraw water completely and not return a single ounce to the watershed.

While the tribunal was deliberating, Nestlé made a deal with the Ontario government to remove the conditions on its permit. However, before the company could withdraw its appeal and end the preliminary public hearing, conservationists launched their own appeal.

Bruce Pardy, who presided over the tribunal, sided with the conservationists. The tribunal concluded that the motion to approve the deal between Nestlé and the province was "not consistent" with Ontario law or in the public interest and ordered a full hearing (Kerr 2013). Nestlé withdrew its objections and has agreed to abide by the conditions placed upon its permit. For details, see Environmental Commissioner of Ontario, "1.7.1: The Importance of Public Participation in Environmental Appeals," in *Managing New Challenges: Annual Report 2013/2014* (Toronto: Environmental Commissioner of Ontario, 2014), 38.

The water crisis in North Battleford, Saskatchewan, in 2001 has had less effect on water quality management in the province. But that is not to say water management is stagnant in the province. In fact, Saskatchewan is undergoing so many rapid changes that its water supply system must adjust. Saskatchewan is a growing place, an international hub for agriculture and a source of potash, natural gas, and oil. The province is struggling to keep up with the changing and increasing demands on water. Two provincial Crown corporations share responsibility for water—SaskWater and the Saskatchewan Water Security Agency (SWSA). In 2012, the Saskatchewan Watershed Authority was converted into the SWSA, a move by the Saskatchewan Party government that came as a surprise to the public. There were no public consultations and no discussion or debate in the Legislative Assembly of Saskatchewan. Instead, the provincial government created the SWSA and announced a new 25-year strategy for water in the province.

SaskWater is a commercial Crown corporation, which means it generates its own revenue. It is responsible for providing water to municipalities and industry. The real power over water takings and allocations, water quality, and environmental protection comes from the SWSA, which has legislative responsibility for existing legislation in the province related to water: the Watershed Authority Act, the Watershed Associations Act, the Water Power Act, and the Conservation and Development Act. Moreover, the SWSA is in the process of reviewing all water uses and permits in the province as well as overall water quality and ecosystem health. With this information, Saskatchewan likely will create new regulations. It is not clear if new policy will pass through the legislative assembly or if the SWSA will simply proceed unilaterally. Either way, water quality and water allocations are changing in the province. We may see other provinces make significant changes to the way water is managed and allocated, especially given the challenges posed by the increases in urbanization and industrialization.

Transprovincial Water

The runoff from snow on the Rocky Mountains is a significant source of water for the Prairie provinces. The water generated by runoff flows into rivers that move eastward through Alberta, Saskatchewan, and into Manitoba. Who owns the snow? Who owns water in rivers? If Alberta and Saskatchewan, both thirsty agricultural centres, take all the water then Manitoba would get none. Recognizing potential conflict and wanting to ensure fairness, the provinces of Manitoba, Alberta, and Saskatchewan and the federal government created the **Prairie Provinces Water Board** (PPWB) in 1948 and updated its operating procedures in 1969 under the Master Agreement on Apportionment. Board members and consultants are drawn from Environment Canada, Agriculture and Agri-Food Canada, Alberta Environment and Sustainable Resource Development, the Saskatchewan Water Security Agency, Manitoba Transportation and Infrastructure, and Manitoba Conservation and Water Stewardship. The board itself is composed of two representatives from the federal government and one member from each of the three provinces. This is multilevel governance at work. The mission of the PPWB is to "ensure that transboundary waters are equitably apportioned and protected" and to "provide a forum for exchange of information in order to prevent and resolve transboundary water management conflicts" (PPWB 2012). Although this board is primarily concerned with the allocation of water, protecting the quality of the water is also part of the overall agreement. The board oversees the monitoring and assessment of water quality and provides a meaningful forum for information exchange and cooperative behaviour to address immediate or long-term issues.

Similarly, the **Mackenzie River Basin Board** provides multilevel governance for the Mackenzie River watershed, which is one of the most important watersheds in the world. Covering 1.8 million square kilometres, the Mackenzie River Basin is almost one-fifth of Canada's total landmass. Given its northern location, it has a population of roughly 500,000 people, mainly Aboriginal—most of whom depend on the basin's rivers, lakes, and waterways for their livelihood (MRBB 2013). In 1997, the federal government, the Northwest Territories, Yukon, British Columbia, Alberta, and Saskatchewan signed the Mackenzie River Basin Transboundary Waters Master Agreement. Similar to the PPWB's Master Agreement on Apportionment, this agreement deals with the equitable allocation of water, sustainable development, and water quality issues.

Thus, the provinces cooperate to handle water quality and allocations rather than just working independently. Water does not respect political boundaries, so, when it crosses a border, collaboration is necessary. The federal government works with provinces to oversee the equitable sharing of water and of the responsibility to protect water quality. Both initiatives are hindered by lack of monitoring and data. Canada will need to address these issues in the twenty-first century if the country is to adapt to urbanization and the pressures of climate change adequately.

The Role of Cities in Water Policy

Although each province exercises rights over water on behalf of its citizens, municipalities manage water in the Canadian provinces. They are the frontline for its quality control and delivery. How do cities manage this task? For many cities, water has been a costly headache. Infrastructure, such as household pipes built in the nineteenth century, is old and in need of an update, but the costs are more than cities can afford. As a result, Canadian cities have dabbled in **water privatization**. Privatization does not mean the buying and selling of water; rather, it is about supply management. It means allowing private companies to manage water supply and sewerage. In these scenarios, municipalities retain ownership of the water supply but contract out its management to private companies (often American or European companies) to improve efficiency and lower costs. Private management often entails municipalities overseeing the quality of the water that is being managed by the private company.

Historically, private companies were the first to supply water in most world cities from London to Boston to Toronto. These companies would supply good, clean water to those who could pay. Cholera and typhoid outbreaks in the nineteenth century lead to government management of universal water and the tight regulation of private companies. Many municipalities today manage water as a public utility; the government owns the water supply infrastructure and provides water to the public for a small free. That is how SaskWater, mentioned previously, supplies and manages water in Saskatchewan. However, some cities use a public-private partnership (a P3) in which the government retains rights over the water, but a private company is contracted to design, build, and sometimes manage the water supply system. In some rural parts of the country, it is not economically or politically feasible for the government or a P3 to manage water, so instead water supply is a community-run service (Bakker 2007).

Regardless of how water is managed, the municipal government is responsible for ensuring its quality. The Walkerton and North Battleford episodes are extreme examples of poor water quality management. The federal government does not have a national policy or strategy to reduce water pollution and ensure water quality. The provinces set regulatory standards and oversee pollution discharge into waterways as well as manage chemical pollution that could affect ground or surface water. Nevertheless, municipal water systems are undermined by lack of funding and insufficient scientific data to properly manage the resource. Some cities have started to hand some of the responsibility over to the private sector, which subsequently raises water prices to reflect the cost of building and maintaining adequate infrastructure and water delivery. Some Canadians are deeply concerned about private management because for-profit businesses lack accountability and might guarantee water quality only at the lowest level necessary so that profit can be maximized.

The Role of NGOs in Water Policy

Water is becoming an ever more important issue for Canadians. Water quality for human beings is one of the most significant human health issues in the world. There are thousands of NGOs dedicated to the cause, and the United Nations has been working on water quality and water supply for decades. In Canada, countless community groups and regional NGOs champion water quality issues, which is not surprising given the regional nature of water quality management in the country. At the national level, the David Suzuki Foundation often fulfils the watchdog role and leverages its national profile when necessary to bring attention to local issues.

The case of trihalomethanes (THMs) in the water supply of Newfoundland communities is a good example. THMs are a by-product of industrial solvents or refrigerants and are known carcinogens. They can also be formed as a by-product of using chlorine to clean water for drinking, as many communities in Newfoundland do. Essentially, the chlorine reacts with organic matter in the water to produce THMs. Since 2000, the level of THMs in Newfoundland drinking water has doubled, and more than 160 water supplies in the province exceed Canadian recommendations (White 2013). The province and Health Canada argue that health risks from THMs are less than those posed by not treating water with chlorine. The David Suzuki Foundation brought attention to the issue nationally and has been lobbying the federal and provincial government to invest in water technology for the province. Updated filtration systems would help to ensure safer water but are too costly for most Newfoundland communities (Boyd 2006; White 2013).

Another Canada-wide NGO, although not an interest group, is the Canadian Association on Water Quality (CAWQ). It was established in 1967 as a non-governmental and non-profit voluntary organization that brings together experts interested in water quality. CAWQ includes engineers, scientists, and water managers who are directly involved in water quality research and protection. Lobbying government is not the intent of CAWQ. Instead, the goals of the organization are to promote research, which is then shared through the *Water Quality Research Journal of Canada* and at regional and national water quality conferences.

One perhaps surprising advocate of water quality is the Ontario Federation of Agriculture (OFA), which is the largest voluntary farm organization in Canada and represents more than 37,000 farm families across the province. Originally established in 1936, OFA is based in Guelph, Ontario. The organization has had a Water Quality Working Group since 1992, which is dedicated to ensuring that rural water is maintained—if not enhanced—through farm practices. This goal is accomplished by promoting well-water testing and the use of licensed well contractors for the proper construction and maintenance of wells. The group also lobbies the government to create a water take and permit system that documents water budgets and ensures that the necessary tools are in place to protect and allocate water—especially during times of shortage. Related to this, the OFA also encourages farmers to obtain and abide by water permits and participate in programs designed to establish water budgets at a regional level. Finally, it helps farmers to implement the Clean Water Act and to obtain funds through the Ontario Drinking Water Stewardship Program discussed previously (for information on this lobby group, see www.ofa.on.ca).

Outside of public health and human concerns, water quality for ecosystems and wildlife is starting to get more attention. In November 2013, Ecojustice lawyers, on behalf of Sierra Club BC and the Wilderness Committee, filed a lawsuit against the British Columbia Oil and Gas Commission for allowing oil and gas companies to withdraw significant quantities of water from lakes and rivers without going through the proper long-term approval process (Campbell 2014). The government has been issuing fracking operations with short-term (annual or two-year) permits to withdraw the necessary water. The short-term permits provide a "go-around," so industry does not need the environmental assessments required by the process of obtaining long-term water licences. Environmentalists also argue that short-term water approvals allow companies to draw larger volumes of water than would be allowed by the licences. They see the repeated granting of short-term permits as illegal because the intent of water permit laws is to ensure environmental assessments are conducted so the environment is protected.

The Role of Citizens in Water Policy

Canadians do not give much thought to water. The **myth of abundance** has lulled them into a false sense of security about Canada's water supply and water quality (Sprague 2007). In reality, the everyday habits of citizens in industrialized countries likely put water quality at an unnecessary risk. Remember that, in August 2013, the employees of Thames Water, a British utility company, discovered a huge, bus-sized lump of congealed fat, rotting food, and baby wipes in the sewers of London. Weighing nearly 14 tons, it was the biggest "fatberg" ever recorded in the country until one the length of a Boeing 747 was discovered in 2014 (CBC 2013b; Webb 2014). This story is a reminder that anything you flush down the toilet is going back into the water supply. Sure, it gets cleaned. But can technology advance as quickly as our ability to throw new objects, products, and chemicals into the bowl?

One problem in Canada is dealing with the accumulating amount of trace drugs found in water (CBC 2014a). How do drugs get into the water supply? The most common way is that medications we take (medicinally or recreationally) pass through our bodies and are excreted. Livestock animals in Canada, because they are administered drugs in the form of antibiotics and hormones, also contribute. Drugs also commonly enter the water supply as discarded unused medication (flushed down the toilet) and hospital waste that ends up in landfills and seeps into groundwater. There is good reason to be more conscientious about what you put down the drain or flush down the toilet.

Other substances can contaminate the water supply. For example, Ontario's Grand River is full of artificial sweeteners. Treated waste in the municipal water supplies still contains trace elements of sucralose, cyclamate, saccharin, and acesulfame potassium, which end up in the natural environment. Roughly 500,000 people rely on the Grand River for drinking water so these substances pose a threat to water quality. Moreover, because the Grand River also flows into Lake Erie, the watershed and every associated ecosystem are affected (Semeniuk 2013). This problem is not isolated to Ontario as Canadians across the country consume diet pop and other artificially sweetened foods. Statistics Canada reports that, in 2008, Canadians aged 19–30 consumed about 38 grams of diet pop on average each day. In the 31–50 age group, this number jumps to 65 grams a day (Garriguet 2008). Again, it is important to be conscientious about what we consume as human beings, because, chances are, it will end up in our local water supply, which we and other living things need to survive.

AIR POLLUTION

A human being breathes about 26,000 times a day and so inhales a mixture of oxygen, nitrogen, water, argon, carbon dioxide, and trace amounts of other substances in the surrounding air. As discussed in Chapter 3, Canada's air quality is good overall. However, air pollution *is* a problem in Canada. Pollutants get into the air from various sources—both natural and human. Natural events such as volcanic activity and forest fires release carbon dioxide, particulate matter, and other pollutants into the air. Wind can blow contaminated air toward fragile ecosystems or areas of human settlement, endangering life. Even something as natural as vegetation or plant growth can affect air quality by releasing carbon dioxide, nitrogen oxide, or methane into the air. Human sources are just as wide ranging and involve large industrial sources (e.g., power plants that emit sulphur dioxide) and smaller sources (e.g., cars that emit carbon dioxide).

The quality of the air we breathe affects our lungs and heart. Poor air quality is linked to allergies, asthma, headaches, and a myriad of other public health risks (Bates 1995; Shprentz 1996). But we are not the only ones being affected. Poor air quality affects ecosystem health too (EEA 2014). For example, pollutants from the air can enter plant life either directly through pores on the plant's leaves or through uptake from the soil and water. The health of these plants will then affect wildlife that come into contact with them. Air pollution can also be deposited in the water system—leaching from soil into groundwater, running off from agriculture into lakes and streams, or even from air coming into contact with rivers.

Second-wave environmentalism was fairly effective at addressing air pollution. Today, however, problems remain—particularly with greenhouse gases (see Chapter 8) and sulphur dioxide. Though you might not realize it, sulphur dioxide is a dangerous chemical. Petroleum refineries, power plants, and other large industries produce it as a by-product.

It is linked to asthma, and, as an ingredient in acid rain, it is also linked to harmful effects on aquatic ecosystems, forests, and agriculture. Canada produces more than two times the average of sulphur dioxide per capita in advanced industrial countries. Only Australians produce more per capita emissions than Canada, and only the United States produces a higher total amount of emissions. Luckily, Canada's performance is improving. In 2012, its emissions of sulphur dioxide were 59 per cent lower than in 1990 (Environment Canada 2014j). However, 14 of the 17 peer countries against which Canada's progress is measured achieved larger reductions between 1990 and 2009 (Conference Board of Canada 2013c).

Air quality is the responsibility of all Canadians. All levels of government, from the federal government to the municipalities, have responsibilities in ensuring Canadians have clean air to breathe. Non-state actors are also deeply involved. For example, the role of private industry is complicated. A lot of companies, especially those directly involved in producing alternative energy such as wind or solar power, are focused on greening their operations and reducing air pollution (and other types of pollution). However, private industry is also a major source of air pollution all across the country. Two examples that readily come to mind are the oil sands in Alberta and chemical manufacturing in Chemical Valley in Ontario. However, there are countless examples of private industry contributing to immense air pollution, such as fracking for unconventional oil and gas, coal-fired power plants, and the transportation industry. Thus, it is not surprising that so many and various NGOs, from both the environmental and public health arenas, are also committed to improving air quality in Canada. Although Canada's biggest problem is its level of CO_2 emissions, it does face many regional challenges that need to be addressed.

The Federal Government and Air Pollution Policy

The federal and provincial governments both have some legal jurisdiction over air pollution control. As mentioned in Chapter 1, air quality standards set at the national level are non-binding guidelines. In 1971, the federal government passed a Clean Air Act to regulate asbestos, lead, mercury, and vinyl chloride. The Canadian Environmental Protection Act of 1999 subsumed the earlier act, both of which became law under Liberal governments. In 2006, the minority Conservative government led by Stephen Harper introduced another Clean Air Act, but the policy was never passed in Parliament. Opposition parties, led by the NDP, claimed the law did little to prevent climate change and would not meet the Kyoto Protocol targets or other Canadian commitments to reduce GHG emissions (CBC 2006a). Nevertheless, some of the proposed Clean Air Act regulations have seeped into policy created by the majority Conservative government since 2008. For example, the proposed Clean Air Act emphasized harmonizing Canada's emission standards with those of the United States—something that the federal government has been working on in recent years.

In May 2013, the federal government announced new ambient air quality standards for particulate matter and smog. Table 6.1 illustrates the new and projected standards. The federal government is increasing quality standards to better reflect current public health and medical research. These standards are voluntary guidelines established by the federal government under the authority of the Canadian Environmental Protection Act of 1999. Still, provinces and territories are expected to take action to meet these new guidelines.

Not all federal action on air quality is reduced to creating guidelines. Ottawa has considerable power in the area of air pollution control because it signs bilateral agreements with the United States and international treaties, such as the Copenhagen Agreement discussed in Chapter 11. In 1991, Canada and the United States signed the Canada-United States Air Quality Agreement to address transboundary air pollution and reduce acid rain. The specific pollutants targeted by the agreement are sulphur dioxide and nitrogen oxides, the precursors to acid rain. In 2000, the "Ozone Annex" was added to this agreement to reduce smog

TABLE 6.1 Federal Ambient Air Quality Standards

		NEW STANDARDS	
POLLUTANTS	OLD STANDARDS	2015	2020
$PM_{2.5}$ Annual	N/A	10 µg/m^3	8.8 µg/m^3
$PM_{2.5}$ for 24-hour	30 µg/m^3	28 µg/m^3	27 µg/m^3
Ozone for 8-hour	65 parts per billion	63 parts per billion	62 parts per billion

SOURCE: Environment Canada (2013a). Reprinted with permission.

in both countries. Every two years, a progress report summarizes the key steps taken to meet the commitments established by the agreement (these can be found on Environment Canada's website). The 2014 report states that Canada's total emissions of sulphur dioxide have decreased by 58 per cent from 1990 levels while the United States has reduced total sulphur dioxide emissions from covered sources by 78 per cent from their 1990 emission levels. Between 2000 and 2012, Canada reduced total emissions of nitrogen oxides by 45 per cent in the transboundary ozone region while US total nitrogen oxide emissions decreased by 47 per cent in the region (International Joint Commission 2014, 1). This progress is significant and an environmental and public health victory for the federal government.

The Provinces and Air Pollution Policy

Provincial policy for air quality is extremely varied because of the nature of air pollution. This kind of pollution is relevant to both public health departments and environmental departments. Regulations will also come from departments of energy, natural resources, and agricultural and even from departments of commerce or trade. Policies, guidelines, and standards may come from all these departments in a single province. Thus, determining which province is doing the most for air quality is very difficult.

For example, in 1945, a section of Alberta's Public Health Act was amended to addressed air quality, but only as a public health concern. In 1971, the province created its first environment department and passed the Clean Air Act, which was then replaced by the Environmental Protection and Enhancement Act in 1992. The purpose of this act is very broad: "to support and promote the protection, enhancement and wise use of the environment" (Environmental Protection and Enhancement Act, RSA 2000, ch. E-12, s. 2). Regulations in the act apply to environmental areas ranging from recycling to wastewater drainage to air quality. The act is not specific to air pollution but does give the province some room to regulate industry and set standards in the province.

Of course, in Alberta today, the big air polluters are the oil sands companies and coal-fired power plants. The 1992 Environmental Protection and Enhancement Act is far too outdated to keep up with the ever-expanding development in the province. Therefore, in 2012, Alberta announced a Joint Canada–Alberta Implementation Plan for Oil Sands Monitoring. Designed to be fully in place by 2015, the plan aimed to improve monitoring of the environment in Alberta's oil sands region. New air monitoring sites in upwind and downwind locations of the oil sands were planned, along with new monitoring techniques that rely on remote imagery, mobile monitoring systems, and refined networks. Right now monitoring is a priority because no one really knows how much air pollution oil sands development causes or what the effects are for public health and regional ecosystems. There is also the need to track air pollution as it moves from the oil sands into other provinces and even into the United States.

With all 10 provinces enacting a variety of air pollution measures—either directly or via other public health or environmental laws—keeping track of what is going on from a policy standpoint is challenging. In an attempt to create better collaboration, the federal, provincial, and territorial governments decided to work together to fight some types of shared pollution, including air pollution. Early in 1998, all environmental ministers (except Québec's) signed the Canada-wide Accord on Environmental Harmonization to improve cooperation and environmental protection across the nation. The accord has led to Canadian environmental standards in six priority areas related to air pollution: particulate matter, ground level ozone (smog), benzene, mercury, dioxins and furans, and petroleum hydrocarbons. Though progress has been made in all these areas, the provincial and territorial governments have worked very successfully with each other and with the federal government in creating and implementing consistent policy for ozone-depleting substances. Following the Federal Halocarbon Regulations of 2003 and the Ozone-Depleting Substances Regulations of 1998, all Canadian jurisdictions have mandatory requirements for the handling of ozone-depleting substances. This will be discussed again in Chapter 11.

As mentioned, these **Canada-wide standards** (CWSs) that recommend levels or concentrations of substances in the environment have been developed under the Canada-wide Accord on Environmental Harmonization and provide a framework for federal, provincial, and territorial environment ministers to address environmental concerns and public health risks cooperatively. The goal is to create common environmental standards across the country. However, each government is responsible for implementing the standards in its own jurisdiction. Governments report to the public and to each other on progress toward achieving agreed-upon standards.

The Role of Cities

Cities create a lot of air pollution, mainly because urbanization increases energy use and transportation needs. The World Health Organization (2011) compiled air pollution data for 1,100 cities in 91 countries for the years 2003–10. As a country, Canada ranked fourth best overall in terms of air quality. The worst Canadian cities for air pollution were

Sarnia and Montréal. Sarnia is an industrial area, so, not surprisingly, air quality there is low. It is somewhat surprising, however, that Montréal scored lower than the more populated city of Toronto.

As mentioned, Québec did not sign the Canada-wide Accord on Environmental Harmonization nor did it agree to Canada-wide standards as targets. Instead, Québec regulates its own air pollution and sets its own standards. The Clean Air Regulation associated with the province's Environmental Quality Act is an important regulatory mechanism in this process. It is designed to "establish particle and gas emission standards, emission opacity standards, air quality standards and monitoring measures to prevent, eliminate, or reduce the emission of contaminants into the atmosphere" (Environment Quality Act, CQLR, c Q-2, r. 4.1). Perhaps Montréal's relatively poor showing in the WHO study could have been avoided if the new Clean Air Regulation, which came into force July 2011, had been adopted sooner.

But even before the WHO study, Montréal began taking matters into its own hands. In 2010, it launched the Montréal Community Sustainable Development Plan 2010–15; the first key theme is "improving air quality and reducing greenhouse gas emissions." A second significantly related theme is "ensuring the quality of residential living environments" (Gagnon 2010, 2). The specific air quality goals for the city are to reduce Montréal's greenhouse gas emissions to 30 per cent below 1990 levels by 2020 and to achieve the Canadian standard for fine particulate concentrations in the ambient air by 2020. Aside from creating a general GHG reduction strategy, the initiatives developed to achieve these goals are to reduce dependence on cars, promote electric transportation (electricity is hydroelectricity in Québec), increase awareness of climate change, reduce the use of firewood in the urban area, reduce the use of fuel oil for heating, and experiment with alternatives to mineral abrasives (Gagnon 2010, 4).

One way to assess the plan's efficacy is through measuring air quality at Montréal's air quality monitoring stations. In 2011, the number of poor air quality days had decreased at 11 stations out of the 13 then operational and increased at 2 (including at the station monitoring the downtown core, where most people spend their time). By 2012, the number of poor air quality days was at its lowest number since 2008 (when technology to measure fine particles changed). Specifically, in 2008, Montréal experienced 67 poor air quality days while, in 2012, the city had 49 poor air quality days (Boulet and Melançon 2013). Does this improvement mean the Montréal Community Sustainable Development Plan is working? Maybe. Assessing air quality trends in a short period of time is difficult. It appears that, for a few years, air quality was getting better in the city, which could be related to an increase in the use of public transportation that the city has witnessed in recent years. However, air pollution is a difficult thing to pinpoint and contain. For example, in 2013, air quality decreased in Montréal to 53 poor air quality days, and this worsening was largely attributed to forest fires in the region. And, in 2014, the number of poor air quality days crept up to 64 days (CBC 2014b). The 2012 finding could be an outlier, or a new upward trend may be beginning. Either way, air quality remains a vital issue in cities such as Montréal, which must balance sustainable development as its population increases.

The Role of NGOs

There are surprising few air pollution–specific NGOs in Canada; one is the Ontario Clean Air Alliance. Instead, many environmental and public health groups share an interest in clean air, such as the David Suzuki Foundation, the Ecology Action Centre, Friends of the Earth Canada, Pollution Probe, and the Lung Association. Because air pollution cuts across so many environmental and public health issues, and because its sources range from cars to the oil sands, NGOs that advocate for clean air as part of a broad environmental and health strategy are somewhat forced to create coalitions and address the issue from multiple angles and perspectives.

The Role of Citizens

It can be hard to relate to air pollution because its causes seem so pervasive and industrial—far removed from our everyday actions. But, as individuals, we cause air pollution, so we have a role to play in its reduction. Making greener transportation decisions is one significant contribution.

As responsible citizens, we should also pay attention to the Air Quality Health Index and heed warnings about limiting outdoor activity during high-exposure times. But even those living far from the more polluted cities should keep air pollution in mind. Reducing GHG emissions is our only hope at preventing (or slowing down) the devastating effects of climate change. The City of Toronto has many tips on its website for cutting energy and vehicle use by 20 per cent so as to improve city air quality. This advice is part of the city's Live Green Toronto initiative. Some of the suggested strategies include using the city's growing public transportation network more frequently, keeping car tires inflated, reducing engine idling (in fact, you can be fined up to $5,000 dollars for idling your car for more than three minutes in Toronto), and reducing home energy use (which is less of an issue now that Ontario has phased out coal energy and relies on cleaner hydroelectric and nuclear sources). Canadian citizens living in other large cities can adopt some of these recommendations.

CHEMICALS AND POLLUTION

Chemicals are everywhere in our lives. We touch chemicals every day; they are present in the food we eat and the pillowcases we sleep on each night. Chemical substances are in the environment, our food, clothes, and even our bodies. Many of these chemical substances are used to improve the quality of our lives. Luckily, most are not harmful to the environment or to human health. However, some have the potential to cause harm, in certain doses, and should be used only when the risks are appropriately managed.

According to Canadian scientists and activists Rick Smith and Bruce Lourie (2009), chemical pollution is worse today than in the 1960s in three ways. First, chemical pollution is now global because of what is known as the **grasshopper effect**. This term refers to the "jumping" of toxic organic chemicals from warmer regions to colder ones, such as the Arctic and the Antarctic. These chemicals move through the atmosphere in a series of short hops—cycles of evaporation and condensation. The grasshopper effect has been used to explain why Inuit have some of the highest levels of chemical pollution in their bodies (Johansen 2002). Of course, chemical pollution dumped in the ocean is also carried thousands of kilometres around the world, ending up in faraway places. Whether the wind or the waves pick up a chemical and carry it "away"—the problem is that there is no such place as "away." Our planet is a closed system, and we are now beginning to understand the ramifications of our interconnectedness.

Second, unlike litter or other visible pollution eyesores, most chemical pollution is invisible. You cannot see the toxic chemicals that exist in plastics or in your mascara. You cannot see or taste the Teflon that sticks to your food and is digested in your body. When you drink water, you cannot see the chemicals that might be swirling around in the glass. When you cut into a piece of BBQ salmon, you do not see the mercury or the brominated flame-retardants inside the meat. The invisibility of chemicals makes them easy to ignore; technically, we do not see a problem. And it also makes addressing the problem more difficult because people cannot judge for themselves what is in their food, make-up, or everyday household products. Moreover, even when people do know that a toxic chemical such as mercury is in fish, many do not have the scientific background to judge how much is safe or what the trade-offs are between eating the fish and forgoing a good source of protein and omega-3 fatty acids.

Third, chemical pollution now has chronic and long-term effects. Many commercial chemicals share a common property: they persist—they do not break down in the environment, so they bioaccumulate in living organisms. Bioaccumulation means the storage of a growing amount of a substance in an organism, for example, the accumulation and storage of toxins in the human body, usually in fatty tissue. If a chemical is a persistent organic pollutant (POP), it is resistant to being broken down so it persists in the environment. While some POPs can eventually be broken down, this process takes a very long time; furthermore accumulation is often cyclic, meaning that while you are breaking down POPs you acquired earlier, you are adding more of the substance to your system—and your body can never fully eliminate it. Over time, you accumulate more and more, which might cause major health problems eventually. And, if you breastfeed a child, you will pass your accumulated toxins to the baby through your fatty breast milk. This thought is scary, and, without a scientific background, weighing the risks of breastfeeding against using formula is difficult.

Together, these three reasons illustrate the importance of governmental regulation of chemicals to keep society and wildlife safe (although you may be able to bottle-feed a baby, a whale does not have that option and must rely on milk potentially contaminated by toxins that the mother whale has accumulated by eating fish). Both the federal and provincial governments regulate chemicals in Canada. Even more so than water or air pollution regulation, chemical pollution policy requires direct participation by countless experts who have the necessary scientific background. Also, the chemicals that pollute our air, water, and soil are often important to the Canadian economy. Again, compromising between economic development and protecting the environment presents a challenge for policymakers, who want to promote the economy and mitigate risks to the public. Often the risks are unknown or uncertain, and legislators must make decisions based on the information at hand.

Before discussing the actions (or the inaction) of legislators within government, we should understand two types of processes used in decision making for chemical policy: risk assessment and risk management. First, **risk assessment** is an estimation, conducted by experts and analysts, of the magnitude of risk posed to public health or to the environment. Risk is generally considered to be the product of the probability of an event or exposure and the consequences of that event or exposure. The basic question being answered through risk assessment is this: "How much risk *is* there?" Second, **risk management** is an evaluation of the costs and benefits of a risk, usually conducted by politicians or bureaucrats, and a decision regarding how society will manage those trade-offs. The basic question being answered: "How much risk *should* there be?" Keeping the two questions separate is important because risk assessment relies strictly on science and expert knowledge whereas risk management relies on a set of political values and economic trade-offs. The first one is scientific, but the second is political.

What happens when science cannot produce the answer needed to make a sound decision? Determining risk is probabilistic and never an exact science. That risk is expressed as inexact probability makes a lot of people uncomfortable. They want to know the exact effects of specific chemicals, for example. But often science is only able to say, "If you eat more sugar, your risk of diabetes increases." It is a risk and not a certainty. Lots of people eat a sugary diet and never develop diabetes. How then do we make policy? When is a risk great enough for our government to take action? Determining when to act is the greatest challenge facing policymakers in the area of pollution. One approach has been to use the precautionary principle (see Chapter 11 for its international origins). The idea has its roots in the German word *Vorsorgenprinzip*, which means "forecaring principle." This principle can be translated into the dictum "better safe than sorry." In the policy world, it suggests that we do not need to be 100 per cent certain of an outcome before regulation is created. Thus, if good scientific reasons exist for believing that a chemical or pollutant is going to cause harm, policymakers should act and implement regulations (or even an outright ban). The federal government and the Supreme Court of Canada have both endorsed the use of the precautionary principle in the area of chemical policy.

Federal Chemical Policy

The 1999 Canadian Environmental Protection Act (CEPA) is the keystone legislation for chemical management. The act is jointly administered by Environment Canada and Health Canada, as both agencies have numerous reasons to regulate chemicals. The CEPA specifies that new substances manufactured or imported into Canada (since 1994) must undergo government-led human health and environmental assessments. If a substance is found to have the potential to pose risks to the environment or to human health, control measures may be put in place before it is allowed into the Canadian marketplace. If the risks are judged to be too great or not sufficiently manageable, the substance may be prohibited in Canada. The Government of Canada assesses approximately 600 substances new to the Canadian marketplace each year.

In 2006, the Conservative government introduced the Chemicals Management Plan (CMP). This policy works in tandem with the CEPA to set priorities and timelines for action on chemicals of concern. CMP also seeks to integrate chemical management activities across federal departments. Additionally, the CMP provides funding for research, monitoring, and surveillance, as well as a commitment to communicate data about potential risks to Canadians. Finally, the plan is part of a larger effort to collaborate internationally on chemical assessment and management, as discussed in Chapter 11.

Remember that the Canadian Environmental Protection Act was passed by Parliament (as discussed in Chapter 2) whereas the Chemicals Management Plan is a policy initiative developed by the federal government to address chemical regulation. The CMP was designed at the bureaucratic level and never passed through Parliament to become an official law. Thus, the CEPA is legislation, and the CMP offers regulations and sets out procedures for implementing the CEPA. In 2011, after the Conservatives and Stephen Harper were re-elected, the Government of Canada announced the renewal of its Chemicals Management Plan. Thus, the federal approach to chemical pollution and risk continues to be twofold. First, the CEPA requires that Canada examine all chemicals in commerce. The CMP streamlines this process by categorizing the chemicals and then setting a timeline to assess and create management plans.

Other laws relevant to chemical pollution include the Pest Control Products Act, the Food and Drug Act, the Hazardous Products Act, the Cosmetic Regulations, and the Consumer Product Safety Act. However, these laws do not fall under the jurisdiction of Environmental Canada. For example, the Pest Control Products Act is administered by Health Canada's Pest Management Regulatory Agency. The purpose of the law is to prevent unacceptable risks to people and the environment from the use of pest control products, so it regulates pesticides imported into Canada and sold or used here. This act obviously has important ramifications for the environment and non-human species. Health Canada, nevertheless, remains the lead agency.

The Provinces and Chemicals

All provinces and territories have legislation and regulations to manage air quality, toxic substances, and pesticides. Similar to air pollution control, chemical management is found at different intersections of public policy. Because chemicals are so pervasive, regulations exist for their use in food, drugs, cosmetics, lawn-care products, and commercial goods. Occupational health and safety legislation regulates the use of hazardous chemicals on the job. The transportation and disposal of chemicals is also controlled. In each province, legislation exists in all of these areas. As discussed, Canada-wide standards are in place for air pollutants, many of which are toxic chemicals, but the provinces (except Québec) have harmonized standards for both the emission and disposal of only one toxin: mercury. For other chemicals, such as halogens and pesticides, there are no nationally agreed-to regulations.

This section focuses predominately on chemical management policy in Ontario because it is the most populated province in Canada with the largest provincial economy. Therefore, when Ontario creates new legislation, the law has repercussions for the Canadian economy at large. If a specific chemical can no longer be used in baby bottles in Ontario, chances are companies will not use that chemical in baby bottles at all. Creating one type of bottle to sell in Ontario and another for sale elsewhere would be too costly for a commercial company.

Ontario and Québec were the first two provinces to restrict the use and sale of cosmetic pesticides. Ontario's Pesticides Act of 1990, last amended in 2009, legislates one of the most comprehensive restrictions on lawn and garden pesticides in all of North America. Over 250 chemical pesticides have been banned inside the province (see Ontario 2015). The origins of this ban are explained in the section on the role of cities because Toronto was the first jurisdiction to create by-laws banning the chemicals. But it is important to note that Canada has now surpassed the United States and the European Union in the area of lawn-care regulations. At first glance, this small achievement might seem unimportant, but when we remember who comes into contact with lawns (mostly children and pets), it is reassuring to know that commercially valuable products were not prioritized in this case.

Ontario also acted early on a synthetic compound called bisphenol A (BPA), one of the most commonly produced chemicals in the world. Most people know little about BPA, but it is used to make plastics hard or flexible, and durable. Commercially, it has been used in baby bottles and water bottles as well as in computers, cell phones, DVDs, and thousands of other plastic products.

Is it dangerous? You bet. The hormone-disrupting properties of BPA were discovered in 1930, but market demand put the product into commercial use and sales skyrocketed. BPA is an extraordinarily useful chemical. Unfortunately, it has been linked to early puberty, decline in testosterone, breast and prostate cancer, and interference with cell structure and function (Smith and Lourie 2009, 234).

If you were born in the 1990s, you have reason to be concerned about BPA. A Statistics Canada study, conducted in partnership with Health Canada, found that, although 9 out of 10 Canadians aged 6 to 79, or 91 per cent of the population, have BPA in their urine, "young people aged 12 to 19 had an average level of 1.50 parts per billion—higher than the overall average of 1.16 parts per billion" (Bushnik et al. 2010; Schmidt 2010).

Premier Dalton McGuinty of Ontario agreed to regulate BPA in baby bottles in 2008, after immense pressure from NGOs, led predominately by mothers with a deep need to ensure the safety of baby bottles and children's toys. Federally, BPA was put at the top of the list of chemicals to assess under the Chemicals Management Plan. In 2010, BPA was declared a "toxic substance" in Canada, and it is now banned from use in baby bottles nationally. In fact, Canada was the first country to declare BPA toxic. Subsequently, the EU also banned BPA in baby bottles. So how was this policy made? A risk assessment of BPA led policymakers in Canada to manage the chemical through regulation. Science illustrated how much risk there might be, and Canadian policymakers decided how much risk to tolerate. The answer is none when it comes to baby bottles.

The Role of Cities

The charge against cosmetic pesticides was led at the municipal level by grassroots NGOs, for example, the Toronto Environmental Alliance, the Pesticides Action Group Kitchener, and Citizens for Alternatives to Pesticides. Subsequently, the Supreme Court of Canada granted municipalities the right to regulate in the area of lawn care; moreover, the Court legitimatized the use of the precautionary approach being taken by cities and NGOs. By 2010, over 170 municipalities had banned the cosmetic use of pesticides (Christie 2010; Pralle 2009; Smith and Lourie 2009).

Cities are also directly involved in chemical pollution control by way of water and air quality management, as already discussed. Chemicals in our water supply become the responsibility of municipalities because they control water quality. As an example, cities in the Grand River watershed will draw water from the river to ensure that the artificial sweeteners found in drinking water do not harm the public. Moreover, cities such as Toronto, Vancouver, and Montréal have taken direct action to reduce chemicals in air pollution. Cities have far fewer responsibilities, though, when it comes to ensuring food quality and reducing the amount and types of chemicals on the dinner table or in breakfast cereal. Moreover, cities have little control over commercial and consumer goods that contain chemicals. City councillors and municipal governments are simply not involved in those decisions. Thus, more often than not, chemical pollution control falls to the provincial and federal levels of government.

The Role of NGOs

Chemical policy really calls into question the role of science in public policymaking. What is the role of scientists, who are not elected by the public, in decision making? What is the role of the public, who are not scientists, in determining risk? Is chemical policy undemocratic? Should it be undemocratic? Let's say the drinking water in Mississauga, Ontario, has 11.5 µg/L of chlorine. Is that too much? Too little? Should we take a vote, or should we let scientists determine what amount of chlorine is "safe" for us to drink?

The underlying assumption in our society is that science is objective, rational, and standardized. But we often overlook how political and economic the process and outcome of science can be. In reality, science is often uncertain and even more frequently contested (Young and Matthews 2010). Moreover, it can be tied to powerful interests or inaccessible to the public. Given the very scientific nature of the debate over chemical pollution, there is a large role for NGOs to play in education and awareness as well as in mobilizing independent researchers and other experts to serve as watchdogs over government policy.

Environmental Defence Canada has become the leading NGO on matters of chemical pollutants in Canada. Under the leadership of Rick Smith, who was the NGO's executive director from 2003 to 2012, the organization spread awareness about the chemical pollutants in everyday household products. *Slow Death by Rubber Duck*, published in 2009 by Rick Smith and Bruce Lourie, further publicized the debate over toxins. Their follow-up book, *Toxin Toxout*, became a bestseller in just a few weeks early in 2014. Today, Environmental Defence Canada remains committed to lobbying the government to tighten regulation on chemicals in make-up, household cleaners, children's toys, food, and other commercial goods.

Toxins and chemical pollution are becoming serious environmental and health threats in Canada's North. The grasshopper effect, explained earlier in this chapter, is partly responsible for the accumulation of these substances in the North, as is the fact that most of Canada's rivers flow north, thereby carrying pollutants through the water to the Arctic Ocean and into northern ecosystems. No Canadian NGO has focused exclusively on this issue. Instead, public awareness has been generated through media outlets, especially CBC North and northern newspapers. Because so few people live in the North, the issue has not yet caught national attention. However, it is likely that, in the next few years, the David Suzuki Foundation, Greenpeace Canada, World Wildlife Fund (WWF) Canada, and Sierra Club will champion this issue. Presently, both Greenpeace Canada and WWF Canada have a focus on the Arctic because of climate change and potential of shipping through the Northwest Passage. As increased attention turns to the North, more people will become aware that chemical pollution in the south threatens northern environments.

Outside of domestic NGOs, the Inuit Circumpolar Council (ICC) leads the charge against persistent organic pollutants in the Arctic. The ICC was founded in 1977 in Alaska. In 2015, it represented over 160,000 Inuit in the United States, Canada, Greenland, and Russia (see www.inuit.org for current information). This organization, especially its role in the Arctic Council, is discussed in greater detail in Chapter 10. As a major international NGO, the ICC spreads awareness and lobbies government across the world regarding issues that concern Inuit populations, chemical pollution included. In 2003, the ICC co-authored a book entitled *Northern Lights against POPs: Combatting Toxic Threats in the Arctic* as a way to tell the POP story from a Northern perspective. The ICC also participated in the Stockholm Convention to eliminate POPs, as discussed in Chapter 11. This issue remains central to the work of the ICC because Inuit depend on marine life for nutritional intake—and when toxic chemicals pollute that food, both wildlife and the Inuit are threatened.

The Role of Citizens

Chemicals are so pervasive that it is hard to know when they are being used. In fact, you have probably come into contact with hundreds upon hundreds of potentially dangerous chemicals already today. As citizens and consumers, we trust the government to keep us safe from unnecessary risk. This approach is reasonable, yet each of us is responsible for being an educated and informed consumer and citizen. At the end of their book *Slow Death by Rubber Duck*, authors Rick Smith and Bruce Lourie present a list of "action items" for citizens to incorporate into their everyday lives. These include avoiding fragrances, vinyl, Teflon, antibacterial products, and air fresheners; eating fewer fatty foods and less fish (in which chemicals bioaccumulate); reading all product labels before use; installing hardwood floors; and shopping organic. The list is overwhelming, and it suggests that, given a policy void, citizens must look out for themselves.

Politicians respond to voter demands. Politicians also care a great deal about the economy and the large industries that employ Canadians and contribute to economic stability. Many chemical companies fit into that category. Thus, politicians will likely try to keep these companies in business and avoid restricting their commercial products unless they pose serious (and scientifically documented) risks to human health or unless voters demand regulatory action. Unfortunately, citizens are easily and perhaps happily ill-informed about the dangers posed by commercial chemicals. However, much information is available regarding the safety of our food and products—you just have to dig a little to educate yourself about the possible risks.

CONCLUSIONS

Pollution in the twenty-first century is a more challenging problem than it has ever been in human history. Our water, air, and chemical pollutants are largely products of our own making, but, in so many ways, managing pollution eludes us. Are things getting better or worse? We hardly know. As a country, Canada has made significant strides in cleaning up the air and water and in reducing exposure to chemical risk. However, ensuring ongoing water quality requires further action—especially as new chemicals seep into our water supply. An uphill battle is also being fought against the release of GHG emissions in cities and from oil sands mining. And keeping control of industry's chemical pollution is difficult because companies produce new chemicals for commerce faster than science can test those chemicals for environmental safety. Thus, framing pollution policy so as to protect the environment will likely be as challenging in the future as it is today.

Pollution management is largely a government-led effort. We have national standards, Canada-wide agreements, provincial legislation, and municipal participation. But gaps in the intersecting mishmash of policies allow for pollution to seep into our everyday lives and our environment. Shared governance should be the model Canada strives toward in pollution management. The critical role played by non-state actors, such as NGOs and citizens, cannot be overlooked, nor can the potential role played by other non-state actors, such as the private sector. Some of the most important non-state actors in pollution policy are scientists. As discussed in Chapter 3, scientific information has undergone a democratic revolution since the 1960s. So one of the biggest challenges facing pollution management is finding credible peer-reviewed science and not relying on industry or NGO science, or expecting industry to keep citizens safe.

It is absolutely necessary for Canadians to fund peer-reviewed, expert, and unbiased science conducted in university and government research facilities. To be able to *manage* the risks posed by pollution to human health and the environment, we must accurately *measure* those risks.

Key Terms

Chemical Valley; freshwater supply; groundwater; devolution of powers; transboundary water; allocations; first-in-time, first-in-right system; riparian rights; Prairie Provinces Water Board; Mackenzie River Basin Board; water privatization; myth of abundance; Canada-wide standards; grasshopper effect; risk assessment; risk management

Discussion Questions

1. If you were to conduct a risk assessment for how much risk is involved in taking a night course at your university or college,

what types of questions would you ask? What about if you were conducting risk management?

2. Why is it easier for the federal government to regulate chemical pollution in Canada than water pollution?

3. Why is water management a good case study in "governance" of the environment?

4. Does it make more sense for the federal government or the provincial governments to take the lead in regulating air pollution? Defend your answer.

5. Are you worried about chemical pollution in your everyday life? What can you do about it?

6. Why is pollution becoming a less manageable issue over time?

Suggested Readings

Bakker, Karen, ed. 2007. *Eau Canada: The Future of Canada's Water*. Vancouver: UBC Press.

Christensen, Randy. 2006. "Water Proof 2: Canada's Drinking Water Report Card." *Ecojustice*. http://www.ecojustice.ca/waterproof-2-canadas-drinking-water-report-card/.

Johns, Carolyn, and Mark Sproule-Jones. 2009. "Water Pollution Policy in Canada: Cases from the Past and Lessons for the Future." In *Canadian Environmental Policy and Politics: Prospects for Leadership and Innovation*, 3rd ed., edited by Debora L. VanNijnatten and Robert Boardman, 216–35. Toronto: Oxford University Press.

MacFarlane, Daniel. 2014. *Negotiating a River: Canada, the US, and the Creation of the St. Lawrence Seaway*. Vancouver: UBC Press.

Smith, Rick, and Bruce Lourie. 2012. *Toxin Toxout: Getting Harmful Chemicals out of Our Bodies and Our World*. Toronto: Knopf Canada.

Chapter 7

The Politics and Policy of Land: From Agriculture to Forests to Cities

LAND POLICY IN CANADA is of utmost importance to the environment. To make this huge topic more manageable in the context of an introductory book on environmental policy, this chapter divides it into three areas of separate focus: agricultural policy, forest policy, and urban land policy. As in chapters 5 and 6, this chapter first examines who governs and how, outlining existing land policy, and then discusses the roles of other actors (cities, NGOs, and citizens) in policymaking.

Landownership in Canada is mainly vested in the Crown. And, historically, this land was "owned" by the British monarch and passed along hereditarily. Today, the federal and provincial governments actually own Crown land, but the authority for this ownership still rests with Canada's monarch, presently Queen Elizabeth II. Almost 90 per cent of Canada's land is Crown land, with 41 per cent federal and 48 per cent provincial. The rest is privately owned (Neimanis 2011). The majority of federal land is in the three territories and is administered mainly through Aboriginal Affairs and Northern Development Canada. Only about 4 per cent of the land in the provinces is federal land, which consists mostly of national parks, First Nation reserves, and military bases. It is through leasing rights to the natural resources of Crown lands that the provincial and federal governments profit. Crown lands can be leased for logging and mineral or oil extraction. Because most land in Canada is Crown land and the provinces own so much of it, they are significantly responsible for developing land use policies.

Land is such an important environmental issue because Canada is the second largest country in the world by landmass. In other words,

Canadians manage a lot of the earth's total area—9,984,670 square kilometres of land and fresh water, to be exact. So how that land is used matters a great deal. Canadians manage countless ecosystems and a vast area of different topographies. As mentioned in Chapter 1, Canada has the largest intact boreal forest in the world, some of the most productive agricultural land, and is home to North America's fourth largest city by population. There is no escaping the fact that Canadians are land managers, as are all the world's citizens. We shape the ground beneath our feet in countless ways, and our footprints will have lasting impacts on future generations.

AGRICULTURAL POLICY

A significant impetus in the development of modern Canadian farming was Canada's role in supplying wheat to Britain. Wheat was a prairie staple, and a main driver of economic growth between the mid-nineteenth and mid-twentieth centuries (Friesen 1987; Russell 2012). To grow food, Canada needed many people (immigrants) and considerable infrastructure. You cannot grow food in Saskatchewan (or the North West, as it was referred to the nineteenth century) and expect it to end up in Britain without a lot of roads, railways, and people. Today, the Prairies are still a food powerhouse, supplying grains, oilseeds, and beef to the world. Thus, the politics of food are complicated but of critical importance.

Within the Canadian Constitution, both levels of government have responsibility for agricultural policy (Hessing, Howlett, and Summerville 2005; Skogstad 2008). Provincial and federal jurisdictions do not just overlap; Ottawa and the provinces truly share powers. Generally speaking, the Constitution assigns to the provinces responsibility for any activity confined within them, leaving the federal government responsible for national and international issues such as trade. At times, responsibilities overlap, as they do for parts of the farm income safety net. Where there is joint responsibility, the governments at these two levels must work together to develop and deliver agriculture policy.

One of the biggest environmental challenges facing agricultural policy-makers in Canada is the management of chemicals. North America (and the world) experienced the **Green Revolution** beginning in the 1940s, so government policies were designed to encourage engagement with the global agricultural market through the development of technologies, infrastructure, and management techniques that increased agricultural production. Increased production came at the cost of decreasing plant diversity (growing only a few popular plants) and of introducing chemicals into ecosystems and the human food chain (MacDowell 2012). Using pesticides dramatically increased crop production, making food cheaper and more widely available on the global market.

When James Watson, Francis Crick, and Maurice Wilkins discovered DNA in 1953, it revolutionized the food industry. Understanding the molecule that is the basis of heredity meant scientists could modify DNA to produce a desired result (MacDowell 2012, 221–22). Human beings could now control animal reproduction in a whole new way. We could create the best turkeys or cows for meat or milk production through the manipulation of DNA. We could produce genetically altered canola that resists insects and tolerates herbicides. The ethical implications are still debated, but those concerns have not slowed the food industry's mass production of genetically modified plants and animals (Peekhaus 2014). Canada now grows a few crops and raises a few animals very well. Monoculture (growing a single crop) has altered the Prairies, where wheat and corn have replaced native grassland. Agricultural policy at the federal and provincial levels has been very supportive of these developments— even at the cost of biodiversity, natural landscapes, chemical pollution, and the ethical treatment of animals. As the facts stand, we need to grow food for ourselves and for the world. So farmers face immense pressure to produce more food with less land and water. Trade-offs are very common in agricultural policy; thus, more public debate is needed as the complexities of genetic engineering, pollution, water management, urbanization, immigration, globalization, biodiversity loss, and climate change increase.

The Federal Government and Agriculture

Agriculture and Agri-Food Canada (AAFC) is the department of the federal government responsible for policies governing agricultural production, overseeing agricultural research and development, and regulating the inspection of animals and plants (for import and export). It was created in 1868, just one year after Confederation. That should indicate the importance and centrality of agriculture to the country. For almost as long as Canada has existed, it has had a department of agriculture.

Today, as always, the AAFC is responsible for overseeing all federal policies relating to food and agriculture in Canada. That includes a plethora of policies and laws, such as the Prairie Farm Rehabilitation Act, the Farm Products Agencies Act, the Farm Income Protection Act, the Farm Credit Canada Act, the Experimental Farm Stations Act, the Canadian Dairy Commission Act, the Canadian Wheat Board Act, the Canadian Grain Act, the Animal Pedigree Act, and the Agricultural Products Marketing Act. All these are important pieces of federal legislation, and most were developed in the twentieth century (see Skogstad 2013 for a good overview). But one of the most important agricultural policies dates to the 1872 Dominion Lands Act that offered pioneers the opportunity to homestead up to a quarter section (64.75 hectares) of land for a $10 filing fee. This land policy attracted people to Canada's Prairie provinces and settled the western frontier of the country (Marchildon 2009).

Once the government settled the West, it became somewhat responsible for maintaining the livelihood of the farmers and ranchers in the area. A major test of commitment for both the settlers and the government was the Prairie drought of the 1930s. The Prairie Farm Rehabilitation Administration (PFRA) was established by a 1935 act of Parliament as a response to the widespread drought and land degradation of the "Dust Bowl" era (see Marchildon 2011 for a good history of agriculture in the Prairies). The original mandate was to "secure the rehabilitation of the drought and soil drifting areas in the Provinces of Manitoba, Saskatchewan and Alberta, and to develop and promote within those areas systems of farm practice, tree culture, water supply, land utilization and land settlement that will afford greater economic security" (AAFC 2013; Prairie Farm Rehabilitation Act, R.S.C., 1985, c. P-17, s. 4). The act was both economic and environmental in nature.

Also in 1935, the Canadian Wheat Board (CWB) was created as a marketing board for the wheat and barley grown in Western Canada and to further assist in establishing economic security for Canadian farmers (Marchildon 2011). The Board would buy Canadian grain and sell it on the international or domestic market for profit. It became mandatory for Western farmers to sell their wheat and barley through the Canadian Wheat Board; in fact, it was illegal to sell it through any other market or channel. This monopoly ended in 2012 (Bill C-18 passed in 2011). The Board became unpopular with some farmers in Canada, although a 2011 non-binding survey of Prairie farmers voted in favour of keeping the CWB monopoly (CBC 2011b). The monopoly was also a source of criticism from American farmers, even though the CWB was reformed under the North American Free Trade Agreement (NAFTA) to meet free trade requirements. Today, the Board continues to operate with two major caveats: farmers can sell their own grain directly to other buyers, and the majority shareholder of the Board is now a private company. In April 2015, the federal government sold 50.1 per cent of the CWB to G3 Global Grain Group, a joint venture between Bunge Canada, a subsidiary of the American company Bunge Ltd., and SALIC Canada, a wing of the Saudi Agricultural and Livestock Investment Co. (McGregor 2015).

Another initiative related to agricultural lands is the **Agricultural Policy Framework** (APF) Agreement (and its corresponding implementation agreements) signed by the Government of Canada and all provinces and territories (AAFC, 2005). The goal of the APF is "to make Canada as the world leader in food safety, innovation *and environmentally responsible agricultural production*" (AAFC, 2005, vii; emphasis added). Its five components are business risk management, environmental programs, food safety and food quality, science and innovation, and the renewal of soil, agri-business, and international trade. With regard to the environment, the objective of the program is "to help the agriculture and agri-food sector achieve environmental sustainability in the areas of soil, water, air and biodiversity" (AAFC 2005: 11).

The various policies aimed at landowner management practices range from voluntary measures to subsidized economic measures. Here, the government is using multiple policy tools and strategies to address agricultural issues. APF agreements also involve a large communicative aspect because the federal government needs to facilitate the sharing of information on agricultural management practices that have a less negative impact on the environment. This sharing aims to create "best practices" and prevent "worst practices" across the provinces. Finally, APF agreements have supported new environmental technologies that help to safeguard water and soil quality while minimizing chemical and air pollution (AAFC 2005).

There are about a dozen federal environmental programs under the APF and many more provincial ones, but several national initiatives may have a direct influence on agricultural producers' impact on water quality and quantity. These include Environmental Farm Planning, the National Farm Stewardship Program, and Greencover Canada. All of these programs are voluntary and non-binding on stakeholders. Moreover, these programs are interconnected. Environmental Farm Planning (EFP) is a form of risk assessment and risk management for farming operations. The entire process is voluntary and confidential, so farmers can understand how their present behaviours and farming practices are helping or harming the environment, such as soil and water. The purpose is to build better farm practices one farm at a time.

The APF agreements go far beyond environmental commitments, as the main focus of the policy framework is still economic security and growth. In fact, it can easily be argued that federal agricultural policy has been directed at ensuring economic stability (1867–1950) and growth (1950s–present) for Canada's farmers and ranchers. In 2000, a Liberal federal government called on the Royal Society of Canada to conduct an analysis of a regulatory system for food biotechnology and bioengineered foods. The expert panel made numerous recommendations to the government, including testing GMOs before animal or human consumption, implementing the precautionary principle for new technologies, developing a tracking system for genetically altered animals, a moratorium on genetically engineered fish, and a mandatory labelling system for GMO products (see MacDowell 2012, 232–33; Peekhaus 2014). The federal government never implemented any of these recommendations completely, although it did improve regulatory transparency for products of biotechnology. In most cases, however, the government has made policy to ensure economic growth in the agricultural sector rather than environmental protection; the story provides a good example of the trade-offs that politicians make between the environment and the economy.

The future may see governments making different choices as Canadians become increasingly concerned about food safety and green farming practices. However, the new five-year agricultural policy framework, Growing Forward 2 (2013–18), seems more focused on growing agri-business than on environmental protection. Its programs fund "innovation, competitiveness and market development to ensure Canadian producers and processors have the tools and resources they need to continue to innovate and capitalize on emerging market opportunities" (AAFC 2014). Nevertheless, there is a growing recognition that agriculture is deeply tied to the environment and that, consequently, agricultural policy should be wedded to environmental policy. For example, in the province of Saskatchewan, the Growing Forward 2 funding ($338 million over five years) will provide increasing support to three key environmental programs: Environmental Farm Planning, the Farm Stewardship Program, and Group Planning (Government of Saskatchewan 2015). Similarly, on the other side of the country, Newfoundland and Labrador will use Growing Forward 2 funding to support "environmental sustainability initiatives" that aim to reduce the impact agricultural has in the province. The main priority areas are water management, soil conservation, nutrient management, environmental stewardship, and climate change (see Government of Newfoundland and Labrador 2015, 20–27).

The Provinces and Agriculture

In 2015, Prince Edward Island had 37 separate pieces of legislation (acts) related to agriculture (a list can be found at www.gov.pe.ca/agriculture/). Why so many? A lot of crop and livestock farming takes place on the small island. In fact, the whole island is only 1.4 million acres, but about 594,000 of those have been cleared for agricultural use (PEI Agriculture and Fisheries 2014). What do they grow? The mainstays of production are beef, potatoes, grains, fruit, vegetables, dairy, and pork. There is also a growing organic market on the island. And to manage all of this agriculture, the province has enacted policy for everything ranging from crop rotation to animal health. Prince Edward Island is Canada's smallest province, yet even it has many different acts related to agriculture (PEI

Agriculture and Fisheries 2014). Across the country, over a thousand acts intersect with food production.

A careful examination of Manitoba Agriculture, Food and Rural Development (MAFRD), the provincial department responsible for agricultural policy, illustrates the multifaceted nature of managing agricultural lands at the provincial level. Part of the provincial government's responsibility is to encourage the sustainable use of provincial Crown land for grazing, haying, and cropland. The department's website (www .gov.mb.ca/agriculture) has a section devoted to environmental policy and regulation. It includes an outline of the policies in different but overlapping areas of land management, including climate change, ecological goods and services, soil nutrient management, soil and water quality management, and watershed planning. Although MAFRD policies are not regulatory, they do offer guidelines, and farmers and ranchers can take voluntary actions on their land to benefit the environment. Some published guidebooks include *Farming in a Changing Climate in Manitoba: A Guide to Sustainable Cropping Systems* and the *Soil Management Guide*.

Similar to energy policy, agricultural policy varies across the provinces. It is simply impossible to discuss, or even list, all the provincial policies related to agricultural land use or linked environmental concerns over water, soil, and air or chemical pollution. Instead, what is most important to know is that the federal and provincial governments work together to ensure that Canadian farmers are able to grow food. Governments at both levels desire to maximize growth, which often has environmental consequences, as seen during the Green Revolution. However, there has recently been a more concerted effort to better steward farmland—not so much because of the intrinsic value of the land or of nature but because a well-managed and sustainable farm is a productive farm now and into the future. Effective land stewardship, then, is a good example of a goal in which human interest overlaps with environmental protection—as is sustainable forestry, discussed below.

The Role of Cities

Although it may seem counter-intuitive, cities play a vital role in agriculture. Farmers do not produce food just for themselves; they grow food for the world's urban centres. In Ontario, for example, urbanization and agricultural policy meet in the idea of **food sovereignty** as expressed through the Greenbelt Act. Food sovereignty is a social, political, and environmental movement that focuses on the right of the people who produce and consume food to a just and sustainable food system. It involves coordinated policy that reconciles conflicting interests, for example feeding the hungry and paying farmers decent prices, and that takes into account the global food supply (globalization), urban development, and the economy and immigration (Wiebe and Wipf 2011).

Ontario's Greenbelt is probably Canada's best example of this concept. The Greenbelt was created in 2005 and protects 1.8 million acres of provincial land in the urban area known as the Golden Horseshoe. Within that space, almost 7,000 farms function to provide food to the Greater Toronto Area (Schaer 2011). The intention of the Greenbelt is to protect farmers (provide employment), protect land from city sprawl, bring local food to local people, and grow food that is socially and culturally relevant to the diverse immigrant population in the GTA (OMMAH 2013).

However, Toronto is not the only city playing a role in Canadian agriculture. Urban farming or urban agriculture in the form of community gardens is popping up in hundreds of Canadian cities. In my hometown of Regina, Saskatchewan, an organization called the Grow Regina Community Garden has a mandate to "enhance the social, economic and cultural well-being of Regina residents through community gardening" (http://growregina.ca/about-us/). The benefits of community gardens are countless (for examples, see Firth, Maye and Pearson 2011; Jermé and Wakefield 2013; Zick et al. 2013). First and foremost, it puts the consumer (eater) in close contact with the production of food. Most Canadians have no idea where their food comes from or what went into producing that food. Community gardens also give consumers control over the process of growing—what types of seeds and chemicals are used in the process becomes a democratic and community-based decision. Finally, community gardens can provide fresh and nutritious food at affordable prices—to people or organizations that might not otherwise have the purchasing power. At the end of the day, community gardens represent an alternative to the agricultural business that otherwise operates in Canada. Community gardens are also a lesson in governance (Kirby and Peters 2008). In Regina, for example, the garden is volunteer driven and so lies outside government.

The Role of NGOs

Food safety is an important public health issue. A **genetically modified organism** (GMO) is a plant or animal created through merging DNA from different species. The idea behind this biotechnology was to create crops that did not require pesticides, that were resistant to herbicides, or that would be easier to grow in certain conditions, thereby increasing yearly yields. In Canada, the first GMO approved for public consumption was the Flavr Savr tomato in 1994 (David Suzuki Foundation 2015). Since that time, canola, corn, soya, and sugar beets have become common GMOs produced in Canada. Other GMO products, ranging from milk to papaya, are imported into Canada for human consumption. The health safety of GMOs is a controversial issue (Peekhaus 2014). In Canada, the controversy is intensified because no food-labelling program lets consumers know which foods are genetically modified and which are not. Chances are you are eating GMOs on a regular basis without knowing it.

The Non-GMO Project is non-profit organization that provides third-party verification of non-GMO products. Through the project, a producer can voluntarily have its product certified and labelled as *not* genetically modified, so consumers can purchase non-GMO foods. The organization's history ties the Natural Grocery Company in Berkeley, California, to the Big Carrot Natural Food Market in Toronto, Ontario. In 2005, these two grocery stores teamed up for the Non-GMO Project with a common goal of creating "a standardized meaning of non-GMO for the North American food industry" (Non-GMO Project 2013). The program is voluntary, but, increasingly, consumers can find these certified products in Canadian grocery stores.

Animal rights are another important aspect of agriculture that NGOs have brought to our kitchen tables. Canadian provinces and territories have the primary responsibility for protecting the welfare of animals, including farm animals. And all provinces and territories have laws in respect to animal welfare. But provincial and territorial legislation and regulations tend to be general in scope, covering a wide range of animal welfare interests. Some provinces and territories have regulations that govern specific aspects of animal welfare or are related to certain species. The Criminal Code of Canada prohibits anyone from wilfully causing animals to suffer from neglect, pain, or injury. The law is enforced by police services, provincial and territorial societies for the prevention of cruelty to animals (SPCAs), and provincial and territorial ministries of agriculture. A list of provincial policies to protect and regulate farm animals can be found on the government of Canada's inspection website. Despite the existence of such policies, Canadian NGOs have lobbied for more stringent regulations in certain contexts. For example, the Animal Alliance of Canada and the Canadian Coalition for Farm Animals continue to support legislation to reduce the allowable transport times for farm animals. On October 28, 2009, Bill C-468 was tabled to bring transportation times in line with those enforced in the EU (Animal Alliance of Canada 2014).

The Role of Citizens

Consuming food is a political act. One can easily connect food to issues such as globalization, climate change, land-use policies, animal treatment, pesticides, GMOs, food safety, and food security. When we make these connections, we are left with a question: What should I eat? Deciding to adopt a vegetarian, vegan, or organic diet is a personal choice with numerous environmental and political consequences.

Land farmed organically is on the rise throughout the world (OMAFRA 2014). What is "organic"? That can be a controversial question, and there is no worldwide agreement or certification process. Generally speaking, organic means food that is grown without chemicals (pesticides and fertilizers in the case of crops and antibiotics in the case of livestock) and food that is not genetically modified. According to the federal government's Canadian Organic Standards (proposed in 2006 and implemented through the Organic Products Regulations in 2009), production of organic food includes the following goals:

1. Protect the environment, minimize soil degradation and erosion, decrease pollution, optimize biological productivity and promote a sound state of health.
2. Maintain long-term soil fertility by optimizing conditions for biological activity within the soil.
3. Maintain biological diversity within the system.
4. Recycle materials and resources to the greatest extent possible within the enterprise.
5. Provide attentive care that promotes the health and meets the behavioural needs of livestock.
6. Prepare organic products, emphasizing careful processing, and handling methods to maintain the organic integrity and vital qualities of the products at all stages of production.
7. Rely on renewable resources in locally organized agricultural systems. (Public Works and Government Services Canada 2014, iii)

Thus, from a strictly *environmental standpoint*, eating organic foods is probably best, as doing so means consuming seasonal, locally grown, chemical-free food that does not have to be transported long distances, is rich in produce, and moderate in terms of meat and fish. However, such a diet might not be the most ethical or most healthy or most economical. Those are different questions.

Related to the organic food movement is the local food movement (Pollan [2006] famously brought the two together). The idea behind this second movement is to eat food that is locally grown so as to support local businesses and reduce the transportation impacts of our food choices. In 1986, Carlo Petrini started the "slow food movement" in response to the growth of fast food chains in Italy. The movement now includes millions of people in over 150 countries, including Canada (see slowfood.com). Mostly, slow food encourages people to eat locally grown foods that are natural to the region. The "slow" refers to the cooking process, as we should eat food that takes some time to cook. Reliance on "fast food" is bad for our bodies and bad for the environment. However, locally grown food is not always an option in Canada, especially in the North where almost no agricultural exists.

As consumers, we should measure the environmental footprint of our food choices. Meat-eaters are often blamed for leaving large environmental footprints because farm animals take up a lot of land, eat a lot of food themselves, and produce a lot of mess (and methane). We do not get as much energy (calories) out of farm animals as the energy we put into their production. But before vegetarians can get on a high horse about environmental impact, they need think about where all the tasty plant food comes from. It is not always local. Canada produces beef; Canada does not produce quinoa. Thus, the quinoa has to be flown here on planes. Sure, it does not require refrigeration as does beef, but let's be honest—vegetarian food is not always low impact. Soya comes on planes, although Canada's domestic crop is growing. Produce comes on planes throughout the winter. The only vegetarian food with a low carbon footprint is bought fresh at markets that stock local food. A Canadian vegetarian locavore would be pretty hungry in January as not much food is being grown locally. The point is that trade-offs and controversy are everywhere. The hard part is deciding what we value most.

FORESTRY POLICY

Forestry is an important part of Canadian culture as well as a major economic engine. We have 347.5 million hectares of forest and an additional 49 million hectares of "other wooded land," including wetlands, swamps, and bogs (National Forest Inventory 2013). In addition to being a farming nation, Canada is also a forest nation. In 2007, $33.6 billion worth of forest products were exported from Canada, making it the largest exporter of forest products internationally (Aukema et al. 2009). In the same year, the industry directly and indirectly employed over 290,000 and 450,000 people, respectively (Aukema et al. 2009). All Canadian regions have a forest industry, save Nunavut. Canada has always been a nation deeply tied to its forest. The forests in Canada, including the boreal forest, are government property (with some exceptions), but private companies lease forested land for commercial business and engage in the actual forestry practices (see MacDowell 2012).

In recent decades, Canadians have paid more attention to forest policy (Luckert, Haley, and Hoberg 2012). They have expressed, at various times and in various ways, a desire to protect some forest lands from exploitation. In fact, Canada has experienced recent debates about how forests should be managed, who should manage them, and who should benefit from them. Aboriginal people have also become important actors in forest policy, as Chapter 9 will discuss (see also Tindall et al. 2013). Canada exports pulp, paper, and lumber in vast quantities. That is not going to change in the near future, but how Canada protects this renewable resource has been changing over time. Part of this policy change is driven by climate change. Because forests can absorb vast quantities of CO_2, protecting them has become crucial. The forests of the world sequester over a billion tons of carbon (Malhi, Meir, and Brown, 2003), which helps offset human activities that cause climate change, such as fossil-fuel emissions.

Unlike other areas of environmental and natural resource policy, forestry offers some examples of policy innovation. The provinces have invested money and effort into mixing policy tools and instruments (Luckert, Haley, and Hoberg 2012). Instead of enacting straightforward regulatory policy or self-regulating voluntary policy by industry, some provinces have tried performance standards, incentives, codes of conduct, and certification as well as consultative and participatory policymaking efforts (see Howlett, Rayner, and Tollefson 2009). This innovation makes the study of forestry policy interesting and important for potential spin-off into other areas of resource management and environmental protection.

The Federal Government and Forestry

In the early 1900s, the federal government managed all the forests in Canada's western territories, not just in the North but also on the Prairies. Times have changed. Section 91 of the Constitution does not provide the federal government with much influence over forestry in Canada. The provinces have the constitutional power over, as well as a pattern of hostility toward federal involvement in, forest policy. That said, the federal government does have responsibility for international trade, which is a crucial component of forestry in Canada.

Perhaps the federal government's most well-known role in Canadian forestry has come through the **Canada-US softwood lumber dispute**. This trade dispute is arguably the most significant one between Canada and the United States and one of the most notable trade disputes worldwide in the twentieth century (MacDowell 2012; Yin and Baek 2004; Zhang 2007). Softwood lumber is grown in British Columbia predominately, but the trade of the wood is a federal issue. Thus, the federal government has long been involved in this one area of forestry. The dispute between the United States and Canada arises, in part, because of different patterns of land ownership in the two countries.

In the United States, the market determines the cost of harvesting most wood because most timber is taken from private land. Therefore, one harvester, or company, competes with another for customers, and auctions determine the costs. In Canada, where most timber is harvested from Crown land under provincial control, the price to harvest trees is set by the provinces. The United States claims, therefore, that Canadian lumber is subsidized by the provinces (and, to a lesser extent, by the federal government in the case of forestry on federal lands). The question is whether or not Canada is subsidizing a trade commodity and thereby violating the conditions of NAFTA. Historically, it has fallen to the federal minister of international trade to deal with this dispute (see Zhang 2007).

Beyond trade issues, there are some national policies in place, including the National Forest Strategy (NFS) as developed through the Canada Forest Accord. But these federal policies are not "hard" policies. They are similar to the policies set out in the Canada Water Act—the federal government does not enforce compliance with penalties or fines. Instead, these policies are negotiated agreements between the provinces. The **Canada Forest Accord** is a series of five-year agreements between the provinces and federal government on how to implement sustainable forest management across the country (see Canadian Council of Forest Ministers 1992; 1998). The first accord covered 1981 to 1987, and four subsequent accords have been negotiated as of 2015, the last one covering 2003 to 2008. Each accord was developed through consultation with the forestry community at all levels of government and with actors outside government, such as private industry, Aboriginal groups, and NGOs. The lead authority was the Canadian Council of Forest Ministers (CCFM), which was created in 1985 so federal, provincial, and territorial governments could better cooperate in managing forests. No Canada Forest Accord is presently in operation (nor is there a current policy document with "National Forest Strategy" in its title). Instead, the forest ministers from across Canada agreed to commitments outlined in *A Vision for Canada's Forests: 2008 and Beyond*, which maps out a long-term strategy for sustainable forest management (for more information, see www.ccfm.org).

The Provinces and Forestry

Between 1929 and 1930, Prime Minister Mackenzie King's government transferred to Alberta, Saskatchewan, and Manitoba authority over the Crown lands and natural resources in those provinces. And so ended the era of federal forest management in Canada, as the other provinces already managed their forests (MacDowell 2012). To be clear, the federal government retained authority over national and Aboriginal lands. Also, with the transfer of authority, forests were not sold to private landowners or large corporations but were placed in the hands of provinces to manage on behalf of the public trust (Luckert, Haley, and Hoberg 2012). Today, all provinces regulate forests largely through land management schemas. The provinces will lease provincial Crown lands to industry for a set period, usually 15 to 25 years, and the lease will include specific conditions of tenure—including various management requirements that are monitored by the provinces. This arrangement is known as a **tenure system**. Area-based tenure gives the leaser the right to cut timber within a designated area of Crown land whereas volume-based tenure is the right to cut down a set amount of timber. Most provinces use area-based tenure (Hanna 2010). Regardless of the system, through controlling land tenure, the provinces control the actions of forest companies (Luckert, Haley, and Hoberg 2012).

As with water allocation, how provinces approach tenure, or forestry permits, differs across the country. What constitutes a tenure agreement is very different in British Columbia than in Ontario or Saskatchewan. One reason for this variation is simply that tenure systems were designed at different times and by different governments. The changing context in which forestry permits were negotiated and the fact of interprovincial competition in the forest industry created complexity. Related to the responsibility of negotiating tenure agreements is the provincial or territorial responsibility of determining **stumpage fees**, which is the price a private company has to pay the government for the right to harvest trees. Provincial governments can use numerous factors to set the price, including the economic portfolio of the province, the need to create jobs, or even the need to conserve the forest (see Luckert, Haley, and Hoberg 2012). Obviously, one aspect of provincial responsibility should be to encourage forest companies to be "good stewards" of the forest. But this good stewardship is not the norm across the country. Provinces act independently and create their own regulations.

The Role of Cities

We often think about forestry as something that can happen only in rural or wilderness areas. A "forest" is not something that we imagine exists in a "city." However, urban forestry is growing, both as a field of study and a real-world experiment. Trees play a significant role in urban areas by providing numerous environmental, economic, and social benefits to community residents, businesses, and the general public. These benefits include aesthetics, shade, recreational opportunities, air and water quality, and stress relief from a built environment (Summit and McPherson, 1998). Beginning in the early 1900s, larger cities in the United States initiated urban forestry programs to protect and enhance natural resources in the urban environment (Wolf 2003). Numerous Canadian cities also introduced this practice.

Canada has yet to develop formal, state-led policy on urban forestry. However, an NGO called the Canadian Urban Forest Network (CUFN), created in 2006, has forged a Canadian Urban Forestry Strategy 2013–18 in cooperation with urban forest practitioners across sectors and across the country (see CUFN 2014). At least 54 cities had urban forestry mandates in 2015, according to the CUFN, cities from as far east as St. John's and Charlottetown, to as far north as Thunder Bay and Whitehorse, to as far west as Prince George and Vancouver. Since municipalities conduct all the planning and operations of urban forests, cities must get involved in the maintenance and growth of their forests. Through the CUFN, Canadian cities are put in touch with professional organizations, business associations, educational institutions, community groups, and provincial natural resource agencies. This network helps cities learn best practices and adopt new technologies for urban forestry.

Finally, cities are also tied to forestry because so much of the built and human environment comes from forest products. If you look around your home, office, or workplace, you will see many wood products. We also use paper on a daily basis (although less so than we did 10 years ago). Paint is made from wood by-products, as is asphalt, so chances are you touch and walk on wood products each day. You are also probably eating trees on a regular basis. Cellulose, the material that makes up the walls of tree cells, is used as a food thickener in ice cream, icing, and syrup. It might also be holding your eyeglass frames together. And possibly your toilet seat! These are just a few of the thousands of products we derive from forestry. Most Canadians live in a city, but city life as it is today would not be possible without forestry. Also, because urban populations consume so many forest products, municipal laws can affect forest preservation considerably.

The Role of NGOs

When industry started expanding forestry in the 1970s and 1980s, environmentalists jumped into action. Activists became concerned about forestry in remote regions and began a movement to protect special places. Today we have hundreds of provincial and regional NGOs dedicated to the sustainability of Canadian forests and wilderness areas (a list of the major NGOs working in the forest sector can be found at http://www.canadian-forests.com/non-governmentals.html). One of the most important recent initiatives to come from NGO participation in forestry is the Canadian Boreal Forest Agreement (CBFA). In 2010, the Forest Products Association of Canada (FPAC), its 18 member companies, Kruger Inc., and 7 leading environmental NGOs came together to protect 73 million hectares of public forest. The agreement is entirely voluntary and entirely non-governmental. Environmental groups agreed to stop boycotting forest companies, and, in return, the forest companies agreed to suspend logging operations on almost 29 million hectares of boreal forest—specifically, the area where the boreal caribou is found. (Information about the agreement, its history, and its six ongoing initiatives can be found at http://cbfa-efbc.ca/agreement/.) It is one of the best examples of governance and illustrates the vast potential of NGOs as well as the willingness of Canadian business to steward a natural resource.

The private sector has also participated voluntarily in **forest certification**, which embraces corporate social responsibility. The FPAC, as mentioned, is the "voice of Canada's wood products, pulp, and paper producers nationally and internationally in government, trade, and environmental affairs" (FPAC 2015b). It represents the largest forest producers in Canada, so FPAC participation in the Canadian Boreal Forest Agreement, a forest certification program, is crucial for long-term success. To be a member of the FPAC, a forest company must agree to third-party certification of its forestry practices (FPAC 2015b). The certification is seen as "a voluntary tool available to forestry organizations who want to demonstrate corporate responsibility by having their forest management planning and practices independently certified against a sustainable forest management standard" (BC Forest Service 2013, 31). Beyond following government-led regulatory standards, FPAC members agree to meet requirements for the public disclosure of practices, Aboriginal rights and involvement, the protection of forests from overharvesting, the maintenance of soil and water resources, the conservation of biodiversity, and the protection of special cultural or biological sites (FPAC 2015c). Similar to the non-GMO labelling project, forest certification allows consumers to make responsible choices. When you buy wood products in Canada, you should make sure you are buying certified products (FPAC 2015a).

The Role of Citizens

Canadian citizens can participate in sustainable forestry in Canada by using their purchasing power to endorse sustainable forest products and by participating in projects aimed at protecting urban forests. But other venues for individual involvement in forestry management exist. Provinces conduct public consultation before creating policy and environmental assessments before permitting new forestry projects. In the

realm of forestry, regional advisory committees and local citizen committees seek members who are not just forest experts but also citizens
with an interest in protecting Canada's forests and encouraging sustainable development. The public is also allowed to comment on environmental assessments conducted by the federal or provincial government
when a project that will affect the environment is being considered for
approval (see Environment Canada 2015e for a list of active consultations). Public comments can often be provided online from the comfort
of your home.

Citizens can protect urban forests by getting involved at the municipal
level through community groups and government programs, or just by
visiting forested areas of the city. Using an urban forest signals its importance. One significant and well-used urban forest is Vancouver's famous
Stanley Park. The park was created in 1888 and is the city's oldest and
largest park. Today the park today contains 300 hectares of rainforest
(City of Vancouver 2009). Although the park is an "urban space" (it is
managed by the City of Vancouver), it is also a forest—a prime example
of an urban forest. It is up to Canadians to embrace this forest, which can
be done as simply as by taking urban children to visit the park, thereby
instilling in a new generation of Canadians the value of trees.

URBAN LAND POLICY

In 1871, Canada's population was 3.7 million people in total. Of that,
only 19 per cent lived in a city. By 1951, Canada's population had grown
to 14 million, with 62 per cent living in cities. In 2011, Canada's population was 33.5 million, a whopping 81 per cent lived in an urban area,
and only 19 per cent lived in rural parts of the country. Thus, in less
than 150 years, the urban-rural split completely reversed itself in Canada
(Statistics Canada 2011a). Its largest metropolitan areas are Toronto,
Montréal, Vancouver, Calgary, and Edmonton. Each of those cities has
more than a million people. Canada's next largest cities, those with more
than 200,000 people, include Ottawa, Québec City, Winnipeg, Hamilton,
Kitchener-Waterloo, London, Halifax, Oshawa, Victoria, Windsor (ON),
Saskatoon, and Regina. Out of the country's 18 largest cities, 7 are in
Ontario. Clearly, this province, more than any other, has had to deal with
urban land policy.

The problem with rapid urbanization is **urban sprawl**, a situation marked
by low population density, segregated land uses, and dependence on automobiles (Eidelman 2010). This sprawl brings associated challenges, including
the loss of time through commuting and lack of exercise for residents,
smog, habitat destruction and fragmentation, the blighting of aesthetics,

and individualism and loneliness. Massive suburbanization and urban sprawl have had several negative implications for the environment. This low-density form of development requires an enormous amount of land, diminishing the amount of green space and farmland available while, at the same time, threatening biodiversity and the natural habitats of species at risk. Through its excessive consumption of land, energy, and other resources, suburbia continues to be a major source of water contamination, deforestation, biodiversity depletion, and land erosion (Eidelman 2010).

Other more pressing impacts have gained global attention, including urban sprawl's contribution to air pollution and climate change. The automobile dependency established by urban sprawl, along with the resulting traffic and congestion, means that city-dwellers are some of the biggest polluters of air quality, their vehicles being one of the largest sources of emissions of greenhouse gases (Worldwatch Institute 2001). In 2001, the United States alone, possessing some of the world's most auto-reliant cities, consumed "roughly 43 percent of the world's gasoline to propel less than five percent of the world's population" (Worldwatch Institute 2001). According to the World Resources Institute, about 13 per cent of GHG emissions come from transportation, and land-use changes from natural to built-up environments contribute an additional 18 per cent, both of which are a partial consequence of suburban sprawl (Wheeler 2011). Clearly, this form of urban development is unsustainable.

Smart growth has developed as a response to sprawl. The indicators of smart growth include denser, mixed land-use development; increased transportation choices; affordable housing options; preserved agricultural lands; and preserved ecosystems (Filion 2003). Essentially, living in a smart-growth city means living in a place "where schools, parks, shops, churches, neighbourhood centres and amenities are close to our homes and transit" and where "all people, including low- and moderate-income families, singles and seniors, can find safe and suitable housing within reasonable proximity to jobs and essential services" (City of Burlington n.d.). What does this have to do with the environment? A smart-growth city is a community that is sustainable and green. By bringing everything and everyone in a community close together, a city can reduce its ecological footprint; having goods and services close to urban residents limits air pollution or takes up less green space.

Provinces, Cities, and Urban Land

The federal government does not own or manage any urban land in Canada. So urban policy is left to the provinces and municipal governments entirely. Nothing in the Constitution provides the federal government with powers over urban land use. That said, the federal government does influence urban infrastructure and environmental programs through two significant methods: immigration and the federal budget. Immigration to Canada is the major driver of urbanization, and this is partly a federal responsibility because the national government approves new residents and citizens. Nevertheless, how cities grow in response to immigration is a provincial and municipal issue. Through the federal budget, the government can allocate funding (or not) for things such as public transportation, and these allocations can have a large impact on urban development. So although it does not manage urban land, the federal government does have a role in shaping or influencing urban policies.

Ontario has always been a bit of a trailblazer in urban planning. Already in the 1940s, the province was laying the groundwork for land use and watershed planning through the Conservation Authorities Act of 1946 and the Planning Act of 1946 (Frisken 2008; Solomon 2007). In 2005, Ontario passed the Greenbelt Act to manage growth in Canada's (and North America's) fastest growing urban areas: the Golden Horseshoe that stretches along Lake Ontario from Niagara Falls to Oshawa (Pond 2009). In 2012, the Greater Golden Horseshoe was home to around 9 million people, and that number is expected to rise to 11 million by 2031, putting immense pressure on urban development in the Toronto region (Greenbelt Foundation 2015; Tomalty 2012, 5).

As mentioned, the Greenbelt Act protects 1.8 million acres of environmentally sensitive land and farmland (Amal 2008) and creates one of the largest greenbelts in the world. Affording this protection is significant because the Golden Horseshoe is home to some of Canada's most productive farmland that is also near Canada's most densely populated urban area (Caldwell and Hilts 2005). Urban sprawl in the region, therefore, was threatening both agriculture and the area's ability to produce food for its residents (Gayler 1991). Thus, the Greenbelt Act essentially prevents urbanization from taking over productive farmland and natural and forested areas that not only provide recreational opportunities for city-dwellers but also offset the effects of greenhouse gases (Caldwell and Hilts 2005; OMMAH 2005).

Transportation is a central issue for provinces that are confronting urbanization. Why? Transportation is important for commerce; people have to get to work, food has to get to grocery stores, and supplies have to get to offices. Transportation is also a critically important environmental issue because who and what Canadians move around this large country has implications for CO_2 emissions, habitat fragmentation, water runoff, and public health, to name a few areas of concern. In

2003, the Council of Deputy Ministers Responsible for Transportation and Highway Safety established a national Urban Transportation Task Force to examine urban transportation. The task force comprised representatives from the provinces, the territories, and the federal government. It concluded its multi-year study with the recommendation that "all governments should pursue opportunities to promote awareness of the importance of sustainable urban transportation and transportation choices to the economy, the environment and social lives of Canadians" (UTTF 2005, 3). Unfortunately, this goal has yet to come to fruition in Canadian provinces and cities.

Toronto and Montréal are famous worldwide for their traffic congestion and long commute times. Both cities commonly make the list of "20 worst world commutes" (Florida 2010). It is also not surprising that Toronto and Montréal have problems with smog and air pollution. In fact, they suffer many of the negative externalities of urban sprawl. City councils and the provincial governments need to work together to address the issue—likely by extending subway systems and funding other forms of public transportation. Other Canadian cities are going to face these problems in the next few decades. Urbanization is happening quickly, but Canada should be able to draw on the experiences of Toronto, Montréal, and Vancouver to create best and avoid worst practices. Likewise, Canadian municipalities can look to the south and learn from American cities that experienced similar urbanization 15 to 25 years ago. Smart growth needs to come to Canada quickly.

The Role of NGOs

Smart Growth Canada Network is a national NGO founded in May 2003 that advocates for smart-growth principles in Canada's cities. It provides numerous resources, including online courses for municipal executives who want to learn more about smart growth. The network's "ten principles of smart growth" are for cities to create affordable housing, to develop walking communities, to encourage smart building design, to prefer urban renewal rather than new urban development, to use green infrastructure, to preserve and enhance green space and farmland, to undertake integrated planning, to provide green transportation options, to support participatory democracy and community involvement in smart growth, and to offer incentives to facilitate private-sector investment in smart-growth principles (www.smartgrowth.ca/home_e.html). Like a typical interest group, Smart Growth Canada conducts research, educates, spreads awareness, and lobbies municipal governments. It partners with over 20 other NGOs, from Farm Folk/City Folk to Sierra Club to the West Coast Environmental Law Association. Because smart growth is an issue that encompasses environmental protection, public health, public safety, and economic development, numerous NGOs are involved.

The Canadian Urban Institution (CUI) is another non-profit NGO that focuses on urban life in Canada and internationally. Primarily a research institution, this Toronto-based organization affects planning and policy in Canadian cities as well as in the cities of international partners, such as Jamaica, Ukraine, and the Philippines. The principle research projects focus on transportation, suburban development, integrated water systems, energy mapping, downtown cores, and cultural resource mapping. Working with city planners, academic institutions, other NGOs, and engaged citizens, the CUI is able to significantly change how we design and live in cities. For example, the CUI worked with the City of Hamilton to develop a master plan and infrastructure plan to stabilize and revitalize its downtown core. Similarly, the institute has helped to map water use and improve water efficiency in the cities of Toronto, London, Hamilton, Barrie, and Guelph.

Another NGO involved in urban planning is the Council for Canadian Urbanism (CanU). Established in 2009, CanU connects architects, city planners, engineers, private industry, commercial property owners, and city governments. The primary research and case studies of CanU thus far have been specific communities inside Halifax, Montréal, Hamilton, Toronto, Ottawa, and Winnipeg. In each case, CanU develops a new urban design plan that integrates smart growth and new urbanism into the cities' long-term development plans. The organization is an NGO, but it is open only to professionals who engage in research and hands-on city planning. Nevertheless, the NGO does serve to promote awareness of and to advocate for smart-growth principles.

The Smart Growth Network, the Canadian Urban Institute, and the Council for Canadian Urbanism are just three examples of the hundreds, if not thousands, of NGOs working on urbanization issues. Part of the challenge for these NGOs is coordination and collaboration. Because urbanization raises so many issues, from social justice to green space, ecologically "smart" urban design attracts a lot of interest. Consequently, thousands of people in hundreds of cities are working on the same issues. Resources are likely wasted because inadequately connected groups do not share best and worst practices or other research. To improve this situation, the Smart Growth Network tries to bring together lots of smaller NGOs in a more coordinated effort. Saskatoon should be able to learn from Halifax, just as Winnipeg should be able to share information with Edmonton. All Canadians want to live in healthy and sustainable communities. The coordinated work of NGOs can help to make this happen.

The Role of Citizens

Chances are if you are reading this book, you live in a city. But do you live downtown or in the suburbs? Too few Canadians are choosing to live downtown, for a variety of reasons. Urban sprawl is the aggregate result of individual choices. For many complicated social and economic reasons, individuals, with their families in tow, decide to move outside the urban core. The desire for a bigger house or a larger lawn drives many to suburban growth areas (Moos and Mendez 2013, 2014). From an environmental perspective, this is not good development. Urban dwellers use significantly less carbon for transit than do suburban dwellers—perhaps as much as 70 per cent less carbon (Johnston, Nicholas, and Parzen 2013). Urban dwellers also use less space and compete for less farmland or forested land. Thus, one thing urban Canadians can do is think urban, not suburban.

The personal decision to own a home in the city rather than in suburbia, then, can be important in battling suburbanization and the consequent loss of green space and biodiversity. Where you decide to live affects every ecosystem. Choosing a small home close to work is the ideal environmental choice. Unfortunately, not everyone has that option. Homes in a city's downtown core can be extraordinarily expensive. Citizens have to work with municipalities to ensure that affordable housing exists. And if citizens do decide to buy a home outside the downtown, then considerations about size, green space, green infrastructure, and green transportation should be part of the decision process. Quality of life is linked not only to the size of one's house but also to the size of one's ecological footprint.

Green decisions about transportation can also battle air pollution and the loss of biodiversity. Not everyone has the luxury of walking to work. Those of us who have to travel a long distance need to consider options such as cycling; taking the bus, metro, or train; or carpooling rather than driving by ourselves to work. Often, public transportation is not a convenient or low-cost option. In this circumstance, individuals should consider moving closer to work or getting a job closer to home. Sometimes, however, neither option is realistic. Citizens must therefore demand affordable and accessible public transportation in their cities. And citizens must try to use that transportation where it exists.

The math is simple: slightly more than 80 per cent of Canadians live in a city and slightly less than 20 per cent live in a rural area (Statistics Canada 2011a). How the 80 per cent choose to live is going to have the biggest impact on the sustainability of Canada. These choices are particularly important in cities that compete for farmland, such as Toronto and Vancouver. Canada's population is growing, and new immigrants are moving into our cities every year (Statistics Canada 2011b). We can expect more cities to get larger in the next few decades. Places such as Regina and Saskatoon, which held their populations at under 200,000 through the 1990s and early 2000s, are now quickly growing. Instituting smart-growth planning will be essential. But citizens need to be the driving force behind this effort. It is citizens who buy houses and cars—the two purchases most related to urban sprawl. Thinking urban should mean thinking small—small homes, small cars, and small ecological impact. It is the only way that sustainable development is going to work in Canada.

CONCLUSIONS

Canada has always been a farming nation. In modern times, the techno-logical advancements of the agricultural industry changed the Canadian landscape and raised many ongoing concerns about food security and biodiversity loss across the country. Many people argue that current agricultural practices are not sustainable and pose significant health risks to humans and environmental risks to ecosystems and plant species. We will need to make agricultural and food policy that balances food safety, wildlife habitat preservation, and food production growth in the coming decades.

This challenge will be compounded by the realities of climate change, which will also impact forestry across the country. Unpredictable variation in weather is not optimal for growing food or growing forests. It is likely true that, if Canada got warmer, the growing season could be extended, enabling producers to produce more goods overall. However, the likelihood of warmth being the only effect of climate change is very small. Climate change will also bring fluctuating patterns of precipitation and drought—unpredictable pat-terns and in unpredictable ways. These shifts will leave farming and forestry vulnerable and make each a risky investment.

It is essential to keep in mind what connects cities, farms, and forests: land. An expanding urban population competes with agri-business and the forestry industry for land. The struggle to grow food for growing cit-ies around the world is challenged by the need to preserve green space and ample room for forests inside and outside of metropolitan areas. Canada is a big country, but Canadians often find themselves competing for the same parcels of land. Sound municipal policy is an absolute necessity for managing urban sprawl in the face of agricultural and forestry needs. Moreover, municipal policy should also create space to bring agriculture and food production into urban areas to create sustainable cities and a beneficial human-environment connection. A city is where social, eco-nomic, and environmental goals can come together. Land policy is largely dictated at the provincial level. But multilevel governance is popping up everywhere across all land parcels. Forestry is the most progressive industry in terms of environmental sustainability and clearly illustrative of the potential for private stewardship and NGO leadership.

Key Terms

Green Revolution; Agricultural Policy Framework; food sovereignty; genetically modified organism (GMO); Canada-US softwood lumber dispute; Canada Forest Accord; tenure system; stumpage fees; urban forestry; forest certification; urban sprawl; smart growth

Discussion Questions

1. What did you have for lunch today? Do you know where all the ingredients in your meal came from? Try to make a list of the different provinces and countries that provided ingredients for your lunch. Also note if your lunch included genetically modified foods.
2. Thinking about only the environment (and not about public health), what are the pros and cons of eating a vegetarian diet?
3. How are water allocations and lumber tenure systems similar? Different?
4. Have you ever visited an urban forest? Why are urban forests important for the environment and public health?
5. From an environmental standpoint, why is it better to live downtown in a city than in the suburbs of a city?

Suggested Readings

Canadian Biotechnology Action Network. 2015. *Where in the World Are GMO Crops and Foods: The Reality of GM Crops in the Ground and on Our Plates.* Ottawa: CBAN. http://gmoinquiry.ca/wp-content/uploads/2015/03/where-in-the-world -gm-crops-foods.pdf.
Congress for the New Urbanism. [1993] 2011. "Charter of the New Urbanism." In *The City Reader*, 5th ed., edited by Richard T. LeGates and Frederic Stout, 356–59. Abingdon, UK: Routledge.
McAllister, Mary Louise. 2009. "Sustaining Canadian Cities: The Silos and Systems of Local Environmental Policy." In *Canadian Environmental Policy and Politics: Prospects for Leadership and Innovation*, edited by Debora L. VanNijnatten and Robert Boardman. New York: Oxford University Press.
McLeman, Robert A., Juliette Dupre, Lea Berrang Ford, James Ford, Konrad Gajewski, and Gregory Marchildon. 2014. "What We Learned from the Dust Bowl: Lessons in Science, Policy, and Adaptation." *Population and Environment* 35 (4): 417–40. http://dx.doi.org/10.1007/s11111-013-0190-z.

Mitchell, Bruce, ed. 2010. *Resource and Environmental Management in Canada: Assessing Conflict and Uncertainty*. Oxford: Oxford University Press.

Nikiforuk, Andrew. 2011. *Empire of the Beetle: How Human Folly and a Tiny Bug Are Killing North America's Great Forests*. Vancouver: Greystone.

Page, Justin. 2014. *Tracking the Great Bear: How Environmentalist Recreated British Columbia Coastal Rainforest*. Vancouver: UBC Press.

Pembina Institute. 2008. "Urban Sprawl Threatens Ontario's Climate Change Targets." *Pembina Institute Media Releases*, March 19.

Pond, D. 2009. "Institutions, Political Economy and Land-Use Policy: Greenbelt Politics in Ontario." *Environmental Politics* 18 (2): 238–56. http://dx.doi.org/10.1080/09644010802682619.

Rosenzweig, Michael L. 2003. *Win-Win Ecology: How Earth's Species Can Survive in the Midst of Human Enterprise*. New York: Oxford University Press.

Wheeler, Stephen. 2011. "Urban Planning and Global Climate Change." In *The City Reader*, 5th ed., edited by Richard T. LeGates and Frederic Stout, 458–67. London: Routledge.

Wittman, Hannah, Annette Aurélie Desmarais, and Nettie Wiebe, eds. 2011. *Food Sovereignty in Canada: Creating Just and Sustainable Food Systems*. Halifax, NS: Fernwood Publishing.

Chapter 8

Energy Policy and Climate Change

FEDERALISM IN LARGE PART explains energy politics in Canada. The Constitution grants provinces jurisdiction over the "development, conservation, and management of sites and facilities in the provinces for the generation and protection of energy." Plainly put, provinces are responsible for electrical supply and land use. The federal government has responsibility for environmental protection, international trade, and international agreements—all of which situates Ottawa deep inside energy and climate change policy decisions.

This chapter begins with an overview of Canada's energy needs—in terms of both production for trade and consumption across the country. According to Natural Resources Canada (2014f), the energy sector accounted for approximately 10 per cent of Canada's GDP in 2013. The energy sector's share of the GDP was at or close to this percentage for the decade preceding 2013 (IMF 2014, 3). Energy is a big economic player. It is also deeply tied to the environment because the burning of fossil fuels causes air pollution and climate change. After discussing the types of energy that exist in Canada, this chapter explores federal and provincial governance of energy and climate change policy.

CANADA'S ENERGY NEEDS

Energy is everywhere. And everyone needs energy. From a societal standpoint, energy is needed in the residential, commercial, industrial, and transportation sectors. We often think about energy when we are turning on our lights or warming up our cars in the winter.

But we should be thinking about energy when we eat an avocado too. How did the avocado get to us? It was probably flown into the country on a plane (fuel), transported by truck to the grocery store (more fuel), and then purchased and driven to a home (even more fuel). We should also think about energy when we listen to our iPods. How did Apple make that little metal music machine? And how did it get to Canada? Finally, we should think about energy when we walk into a mall or a university that is heated or cooled to an appropriate temperature and that has the lights on day and night. Every city in Canada has a mall and a school. That is a lot of energy. Canadians get their energy from fossil fuels, nuclear power, and renewable energy sources.

Fossil fuels are formed by buried dead organisms, ones that died over a million years ago. These compressed, decomposed organisms consist of carbon, which is the building block of oil, coal, and natural gas. Together, these three sources comprise about 80 per cent of the world's energy supply and are found all over the world (US Energy Information Administration 2013, 1). For example, there is oil abundance in the Middle East and North America, and natural gas abundance in North America and Russia. Coal and other fossil fuels can be found in the United States, Russia, China, and India, as well as numerous other countries.

Fossil fuels are **non-renewable resources**. Once we use them up, they are gone.[1] Unfortunately, we cannot know or even estimate with any accuracy how much fossil fuel the world contains. Instead, we know only how much is in "proved reserves"—at least in the reserves of countries that have the technology and ability to measure their carbon stores. British Petroleum, one of the largest fossil fuel companies in the world, estimates that, at the end of 2014, the world had in reserve 891.5 billion tons of coal, just over 187.1 trillion cubic metres of natural gas, and just over 1,700 billion barrels of crude oil. At today's current level of extraction, these proven coal reserves will be exhausted in the next 110 years, natural gas reserves will last until 2068–69, and oil will last until 2066–67 (BP 2015).

Will we actually run out of natural gas and oil? If the world lasts long enough, the answer is "yes." But how long reserves will last is difficult to say as more are continually being found. Moreover, proved reserves only include those that can be extracted given today's technology and economic conditions (e.g., oil prices). Those variables are likely to change over time, resulting in new "proved reserves" as oil prices rise, for example. The bottom line is that it is excessively alarmist to suggest that the earth will run out of these resources in our lifetime. A more significant problem is that we have too many fossil fuel resources—if we burn them all, we are in big trouble as a result of the ensuing climate impacts. Another important point is that, as they decrease in quantity, oil and gas will get increasingly expensive, creating hardship for many people.

Fossil fuels also tend to be dirty; their extraction and use cause a lot of pollution. For example, extraction in the form of offshore drilling for oil creates risks for aquatic ecosystems (NRDC 2009). And, in the case of a spill during extraction, as witnessed in the Deepwater Horizon spill in the Gulf of Mexico in 2010, the consequences can be catastrophic for marine life (Cardinale 2010). Another example of risky extraction processes is hydraulic fracturing (fracking) for natural gas. This method threatens water quality and water supply and poses threats to wildlife (Osborn et al. 2011; Souther et al. 2014). To extract natural gas from rock formations, high-pressure water mixed with chemicals is blasted into rock, causing pollution as well as small earthquakes (US Department of Energy 2009). Beyond extraction, the use of fossil fuels is also a very dirty endeavour. Primarily, pollution comes from the combustion of fossil fuels, which produces air pollutants such as carbon dioxide, sulphur dioxide, nitrogen oxides, and heavy metals. Moreover, air pollutants fall back to earth through acid rain. There is no getting around the fact that oil and gas extraction and use pose numerous threats to the environment and public health.

Renewable energy is any energy source that produces almost no waste or greenhouse gas emissions.[2] These include hydro, geothermal, wind, and solar power (Natural Resources Canada 2014a). Like fossil fuels, this type of energy is also found all over the world, but, unlike oil or coal, renewable energy sources will not run out. In 2010, only about 11 per cent of world energy consumption came from renewable sources (US Energy Information Administration 2013, 2). That said, wind energy production in particular is on the rise throughout the world, especially in China, which is emerging as a global leader in wind power production (Urban and Nordensvard 2013). According to the Pembina Institute, the benefits of wind energy are vast: it is cost competitive when compared with traditional power generation, it has low cradle-to-grave impacts, wind is abundant and most readily available during the day when consumption is highest, and wind turbines can coexist with farms (and supply additional income to farmers). However, there are also drawbacks: wind energy causes significant local visual impact, it requires a consistent and considerable amount of wind, the turbines' moving parts require maintenance and upkeep, bats and birds can be affected or struck by turbines, and power output is variable and needs overall system integration (Anderson and Thibault 2012). Moreover, some people also have concerns about potential health impacts of turbines, although there is no definitive evidence to support such claims.

Biofuels are fuels that come from living organisms (plants and micro-algae). Technically, biofuels are a form of renewable energy, as we can always grow more plants. The fuel in biofuel is created through biomass conversion, which happens either through chemical conversion, thermal conversion, or biochemical conversion (Somerville 2007). Biofuels require a lot of energy and resources to produce—for example, cropland, soil, and water—so experts debate whether producing them is a good use of farmland (see, for example, Davis, D'Odorico, and Rulli 2014; Hill et al. 2006). However, by using corn and sugarcane for fuel, we are able to mass-produce an economically profitable and low-carbon kind of energy. Thus, biofuels remain part of the energy system in Canada and other parts of the world.

Nuclear power is neither a fossil fuel nor a renewable energy source. Instead, the energy created from the nuclear process comes mainly from uranium, which is a very common element in Earth's crust. Nuclear fission occurs when the nucleus of a particle is split into smaller parts creating gamma rays (free neutrons and photons) that release large amounts of energy. In 2011, about 10 per cent of the world's electricity came from nuclear power plants; by 2012, that number had climbed to almost 11 per cent, making it the second-largest source of low-carbon electricity (IEA 2014, 2015). The International Atomic Energy Agency (IAEA) reports that, at the end of 2013, 434 nuclear power reactors were in operation in 30 countries, and 72 nuclear power reactors were under construction—29 of them in China (IAEA 2014, 113). Because nuclear energy does not create air pollutants, it is seen as a "clean energy" and thus, by some, as a better way (than coal) for countries to meet their energy needs while reducing their carbon footprints. However, the process of building and supplying production plants requires a lot of GHG emissions by way of other forms of energy—trucking infrastructure supplies to the power plant location, for example. Of course, building infrastructure to supply non-renewable energy also pollutes.

Ontario has phased out coal-fired power plants and now relies on nuclear energy for roughly half its energy needs. The benefit of this, aside from low operating costs, is that nuclear power generation, once the facility is already built, does not cause the type of emissions that lead to smog, acid rain, or climate change. As of February 2015, about 15 per cent of Canada's energy is nuclear, and Ontario supplies almost all of it (World Nuclear Association 2015). Québec had two nuclear generating stations, but they closed in 1979 and 2012. New Brunswick, the only province other than Ontario to generate nuclear power, has one reactor a few kilometres away from Point Lepreau. Today, Ontario has five operating stations: two in Pickering, one in Darlington, and two in Kincardine (Bruce Power). The only *major* accident to happen at one of these stations was in 2009 when about 200,000 litres of radioactive water spilled into Lake Ontario.

There is no question that Japan's Fukushima Daiichi nuclear accident in 2011 changed the public's perception of nuclear energy (see US Energy Information Administration 2013, 5–6, for data and discussion). A 9-magnitude earthquake hit the northeast coast of Japan on March 11, 2011. Even though the nuclear power plant was shut down automatically during the quake, the tsunami that followed the earthquake disabled the power plant's cooling capabilities. The result was a series of explosions and the release of radiation. The Japanese government called for the evacuation of people living within 20 kilometres of the plant (Jones 2011). The long-term results of the crisis are elevated levels of radiation in the air and also in the food grown or raised in the area, including wild fish stocks (Health Canada 2014). It was the worst nuclear disaster since the Chernobyl accident in 1986 in Ukraine. The immediate impact in Japan and worldwide was skepticism about the safety of nuclear power. In fact, Japan shut down 50 other nuclear reactors in 2011–12; increased coal, oil, and natural gas power generation; and implemented conservation measures (US Energy Information Administration 2013, 95). Outside of Japan, China halted approvals for new reactors until safety reviews could be completed, and Germany and Switzerland each announced plans to phase out nuclear energy protection by 2022 and 2034, respectively (US Energy Information Administration 2013, 6).

Even before the disaster in Japan, nuclear energy was considered controversial because it generates nuclear waste (Ferguson 2011). How society chooses to manage and dispose of highly radioactive material created during the production of nuclear power is hotly debated (Alley and Alley 2013). Nuclear waste remains deadly to human beings (and other living things) for thousands, if not millions, of years, so it must be carefully stored. We can safely say that disposal of nuclear waste is the "Achilles' heel of the industry" (Montgomery 2010, 137). Just because nuclear energy produces no greenhouse gas emissions does not make it "good for the environment." There are environmental trade-offs between producing CO_2 emissions and producing nuclear waste. Ontario currently produces a lot of nuclear waste while Alberta produces a lot of CO_2 emissions. Which form of pollution is less harmful? Canada will have to confront the consequences of these decisions in the future.

ENERGY PRODUCTION AND CONSUMPTION: REGIONALISM IN CANADA

We now know what forms of energy exist, both renewable and non-renewable. And we know that Canada's energy supply is mixed, coming from coal, oil, natural gas, wind, solar, hydro, biofuel, and nuclear sources. But where do average Canadians really get most of their energy? What kind of energy do Canadians use the most? Answering these questions is difficult. First, answers depend on where a person lives in Canada, as different regions rely on different sources of energy. Second, answers are affected by what the energy is used for—electricity or transportation or something else. In each province, a resident likely will use one type of energy to turn on the lights and another type to power a car. Third, the form and amount of energy used depends on whether that use is domestic or commercial. Private homes in the city of Calgary get most of their energy for electricity from coal and natural gas; the oil sands industry gets most of its energy for extraction purposes from oil and natural gas. Clearly, "energy" is a complicated and multifaceted economic good and environmental challenge.

Alberta has a large deposit of a substance called **bitumen** from which oil can be extracted. Bitumen is not oil but a thick, sticky, black sand-like petroleum (Bott 2011). The product can be refined into oil once it is extracted from the ground. There is so much bitumen in Alberta that the province is now Canada's largest exporter of oil (CAPP 2015). And Canada is now consistently the largest foreign supplier of oil to the United States (EIA 2015). The bitumen industry is very destructive and dirty. It initially required the deforestation of part of Alberta's boreal forest. Today, extraction more often happens through deep-water injection methods that melt the bitumen below ground and suck it out without cutting down as many trees (Bott 2011). Nevertheless, high-pressure water injection requires not just a lot of water but also a lot of natural gas to power the high-pressure injection. The extraction also requires other heavy machinery powered by fossil fuels. The industry contributes 8.5 per cent of Canada's greenhouse gas emissions (Environment Canada 2015c, pt. 1, 63).

How Alberta's bitumen gets to a refinery and to the international market is a very controversial topic in Canada right now. Presently, bitumen that is not piped through existing networks of pipelines is sent by truck or train to refineries in Canada and the United States. This method of transporting oil is dangerous because spills happen too frequently (Lemphers 2013). However, political support is strong, especially amongst Conservatives, for the construction of a number of new pipelines. One is the Keystone XL pipeline that would take bitumen south from Alberta to Nebraska, where it would link with other pipelines. Another is the Northern Gateway pipeline that would take diluted bitumen west from Alberta through to the BC coastline, where it would be shipped on oil tankers. Yet another is the Energy East pipeline that would transport crude oil from Alberta to terminals in New Brunswick and Québec. And so as not to neglect northward pipeline development, the National Energy Board approved the Mackenzie Gas Project, which would bring natural gas from the North to the oil sands. Each pipeline is a serious possibility, and each has its supporters and its critics. These pipelines will be discussed below and again in Chapter 11.

Other parts of Western Canada, such as British Columbia and southern Alberta and Saskatchewan, do not have any bitumen to speak of and have only modest amounts of conventional oil, but they do have large deposits of shale rock from which natural gas can be extracted through hydraulic fracturing, or fracking. Fracking entails blasting large volumes of water, sand, and chemicals at high pressure down a well to crack the rock and free up natural gas. The process has been around for more than 60 years but has only been used extensively in the past decade, with horizontal drilling opening the door to difficult-to-reach gas deposits (Goodine 2011). As mentioned, the main environmental issues related to fracking include the amount of water used, the way that waste water is disposed of and the possibility of groundwater contamination, and air pollution from the methane gas being extracted (Osborn et al. 2011; Souther et al. 2014). These dangers have led Québec, Newfoundland, and Nova Scotia to impose moratoriums until further scientific study is completed. Some countries also have moratoriums or bans, including France, the Netherlands, and South Africa. In the United States, Vermont, Maryland, Texas, California, Ohio, parts of Colorado, and New York have had a moratorium in place as of 2015 (see "List of Bans Worldwide" at http://keeptapwatersafe.org/).

FEDERAL ENERGY POLICY

Canada's energy policy is "guided by a series of principles, agreements, and accords" (Natural Resources Canada 2014c; see Doern and Gattinger 2003 for a good historical account of energy politics and policy in Canada). According to Natural Resources Canada, the main principles of the federal government's energy policy are market orientation and respect for jurisdictional authority (Natural Resources Canada 2014c). In other words, the federal government considers the market to be an efficient way to determine supply and demand and set prices. Moreover, the federal government generally recognizes and respects the role of provinces as direct managers of their own natural resources, such as coal or bitumen.[3] Not surprisingly, then, the federal energy framework is held together by several provincial accords, or voluntary cooperative agreements.

For example, the Western Accord is an agreement between the governments of Canada, Alberta, Saskatchewan, and British Columbia on oil and gas pricing and taxation. These same Western provinces have also entered into the Agreement on Natural Gas Markets and Prices. On the other side of the country, the Atlantic Accords comprise an agreement between Nova Scotia and Newfoundland and Labrador, which includes the establishment of jointly managed offshore boards for the oil industry. These agreements demonstrate how the federal and provincial governments co-manage energy production and market or trade issues.

Canada also has international responsibilities related to energy. Because energy is a globally traded commodity, trade issues and the emissions associated with the production and use of energy are the subjects of many international agreements. The North American Free Trade Agreement (NAFTA) is probably the most important trade policy for energy in Canada. The new Comprehensive Economic and Trade Agreement (CETA) between Canada and the European Union (EU) will also affect Canada's energy markets. Managing trade agreements is under the purview of the federal government, but it requires cooperation from the provinces, which ultimately produce the energy marketed for trade.

The National Energy Board

Part of the responsibility for cooperation between governments in Canada rests with the **National Energy Board** (NEB), which is an independent federal agency created in 1959 that regulates the energy industry. The NEB is independent from Parliament and serves as part of the federal bureaucracy (Doern and Gattinger 2003). Headquartered in Calgary, the NEB is responsible for overseeing the interprovincial and international aspects of oil and gas production. Have you ever wondered who is responsible for the construction of thousands of kilometres of power lines across our huge country? The answer is the NEB. The board's purpose is to promote safety, environmental protection, and efficient infrastructure and markets in the Canadian public interest within the mandate set by Parliament for the regulation of pipelines, energy development, and trade (NEB n.d.). With respect to specific energy commodities, the board regulates the export of natural gas, oil, natural gas liquids (NGLs), and electricity; it also regulates the importation of natural gas (NEB n.d.).

However, since 1985, the board does not set prices for oil and natural gas. The provinces of Saskatchewan, Alberta, and British Columbia decided to regulate prices and control them independently (Plourde 2010). In addition, the NEB regulates oil and natural gas exploration and development on frontier lands and in offshore areas not covered by provincial or federal management agreements. As part of that duty, it provides a view of Canadian energy requirements and of trends in the discovery of oil and natural gas. The board periodically publishes assessments of Canadian energy supply, demand, and markets in support of its ongoing market monitoring. These reports can be found on the NEB's website. Ultimately, the NEB reports to the minister of natural resources who is then responsible to the Parliament of Canada (NEB n.d.).

Why does the federal government not regulate energy directly? The role of the federal government in energy politics is controversial and often fraught with tension (Doern and Gattinger 2003; Plourde 2010). Problems date back to the Liberal Party's 1980 **National Energy Program** (NEP), which many provinces and Canadians saw as the federal government overextending its power. The NEP was part of the first Liberal budget after the 1980 federal election. It was a response to two oil crises, the embargo of 1973–74 and the "shock" caused by the Iranian Revolution of 1979, which resulted in a massive increase in world oil prices (a 160 per cent increase in 1979–80). During the 1970s, there had been tension between Ottawa and Alberta regarding the sharing of energy (oil) profits (Plourde 2010). And the higher price of oil aggravated this tension because it meant an even larger wealth transfer from consumers to producers. In Canadian terms, wealth went from Ontario and Québec (which accounted for 58 per cent of Canada's oil consumption) to Alberta, which produced 86 per cent of Canada's oil in 1980 (Bregha 2006a). More wealth was also transferred abroad, especially to the United States. In 1973, foreign-controlled companies took in about 90 per cent of petroleum revenues in Canada (Bott 2009). Thus, the NEP set out to create and foster energy security (oil self-sufficiency), wealth redistribution toward consumers and the federal government, and increased Canadian ownership of the oil industry (Bregha 2006b). To reach these objectives, the government adopted a wide-ranging set of measures. Among these measures were grants to encourage oil drilling in remote areas, grants to consumers to convert to gas or electric heating, a two-price policy for energy resources with preferential pricing for Canadian consumers, new taxes on the oil industry, restrictions on energy exports, an expanded role for the Crown corporation Petro-Canada, and a 25 per cent government share of all oil and gas discoveries offshore and in the North (Bregha 2006b).

One of the main follies of the thinking informing the NEP was the assumption that inflated oil prices would not only continue but actually rise indefinitely. That did not happen—in fact, oil prices fell. This drop made the NEP problematic, and it came under heavy criticism from the Progressive Conservative Party, many Canadians (especially those in the West), and Alberta (Doern and Gattinger 2003; Plourde 2010). As a province, Alberta resented having to share more profits with the federal government because provinces "own" their natural resources. To some extent, this debate is ongoing today in light of the booming oil sands industry. The Progressive Conservative Party dismantled the NEP after it won the 1984 election. It has been over 20 years since the rise and fall of the NEP, but hard feelings remain. The Western provinces in particular are deeply mistrustful of the federal government when it comes to oil and energy. The possibility of a new national energy strategy is not completely off the table but would likely be fraught with tension.

PROVINCIAL ENERGY POLICY AND POLITICS

As stated in the Constitution, provinces own their natural resources, including fossil fuels. Thus, it is largely up to the provinces to manage and regulate fuel production. Such regulation for oil and natural gas, including pipelines, is the responsibility of provincial utility boards. A utility board is a governing body that regulates the service and rates of a public utility, for example, electricity (Duffy et al. 2012).

In many provinces, the public utilities are Crown corporations, meaning that they are operated and owned by the province on behalf of the people (Stastna 2012). Manitoba Hydro and SaskPower are examples. Hydro-Québec is also provincially owned. In some provinces, Crown corporations operate in tandem with private companies to provide power, as happens in Newfoundland and Labrador, for example. In the case of Alberta and Nova Scotia, private utility companies provide energy services, although some of these companies are wholly or partially owned by municipalities. In Ontario, energy is generated and distributed by a complex mix of private utilities (e.g., Bruce Power) and government-owned utilities such as Hydro One, a Crown corporation that is in the process of being sold to private interests; Ontario Power Generation, a provincially owned corporation; and the Ontario Power Authority, a non-profit corporation. Through these government-owned or Crown corporations (or through departments of energy or energy boards or utilities commissions), provinces individually grant permits to mine for energy, and they also grant licences to construct and operate energy facilities, such as nuclear plants and hydroelectricity stations. Different provinces have different rules and regulations. There are far too many policies in place to discuss or even list here.

For example, if you look at the New Brunswick Energy and Utilities Board website (http://www.nbeub.ca/index.php/en/acts-a-regulations), you will see that policy is categorized as acts and regulations related to energy, electricity, gas distribution, pipelines, petroleum products, motor carriers, and, finally, motor vehicles. If you click any of the acts or regulations listed, you will be redirected to a bill passed in the New Brunswick Legislative Assembly. In total, the website lists 23 current acts and regulations related to energy, and the provincial utilities board oversees the implementation of all of these policies. That is a big job. And New Brunswick is a small province.

Given the regional nature of energy production, it makes sense that provinces are responsible for regulating their own energy production and use. The role of the National Energy Board, as stated, is to ensure interprovincial and international energy relations are managed legally. The federal government oversees energy, and it does co-manage some energy production with the provinces and First Nations. It also receives royalties from energy projects on federal Crown land in the country (which is mainly in the North). Perhaps more important, the federal government provides subsidies to various forms of energy production (including the production of biofuels and renewables as well as fossil fuels), and it plays a role in financing some provincial energy projects (e.g., the loan guarantee for the Maritime Link project building a subsea cable between Nova Scotia and Newfoundland). Nevertheless, you can see that provinces have the lion's share of responsibility for creating and implementing energy policy in Canada.

CLIMATE CHANGE AND ENERGY POLICY

In 1896, a Swedish scientist named Svante Arrhenius described how burning fossil fuels such as coal would lead to an increase in the earth's temperature (Arrhenius [1896] 2012). In 1938, British scientist G. S. Callendar provided the empirical evidence to confirm Arrhenius's theory (Callendar [1938] 2012). Though initially called the "Callendar Effect," the phenomenon we now call the **greenhouse effect** is a natural mechanism by which certain gases retain the heat emitted from the earth's surface. A range of different gases act as greenhouse gases, and their common characteristic is that each can absorb heat emitted from Earth and re-emit that heat—keeping it on our planet longer (IPPC [1995] 2012). The earth's average temperature is 14° Celsius, so the greenhouse effect keeps the planet warm and liveable. Without the greenhouse effect, Earth would be too cool, and nothing could survive. Thus, greenhouse gases are good things—but only up to a point. Humans have added more than their fair share of greenhouse gases (GHGs) into the atmosphere and are now heating Earth too much and too quickly (Hansen [1988] 2012). This human-caused, or "anthropogenic," greenhouse effect is caused mostly by high concentrations of the so-called "long-lived" greenhouse gases, such as CO_2, methane, nitrous oxide, and chlorofluorocarbon (CFC) gases (IPCC [1995] 2012).

Climate change is related to the greenhouse effect. In fact, climate change is defined as the observed changes to Earth's climate that are due to the additional anthropogenic GHGs retaining and emitting heat. Climate change is a broader phrase than "global warming," which focuses on only the "warming" aspect of the GHG effect. Climate "change" focuses on the wide-ranging effects of GHGs, such as drought, flooding, melting ice caps, eradication of weather patterns, and so on. There is global scientific consensus that continued emissions of GHGs are causing climate change (IPCC [1995] 2012, 2013). Canadians are already experiencing some of the effects of anthropogenic GHGs, including severe weather (e.g., the Alberta floods of 2013) and increased temperatures in the North. Uncertainty over climate change comes from our inability to predict future changes or the costs and benefits of different policy responses to these changes (Vaughn 2011). At the global level and, to a certain extent, at the federal and provincial levels of government in Canada, debate has been extensive over the policy tools necessary to respond to climate change. Chapter 11 will focus on international efforts to address climate change and discuss the United Nations Framework Convention on Climate Change and the Intergovernmental Panel on Climate Change (IPCC). The remainder of this chapter will examine federal and provincial policy in Canada to address climate change.

Federal Climate Policy

Following the 2009 United Nations Framework Convention on Climate Change meeting in Copenhagen, the Canadian federal government committed to a GHG emission reduction target of 17 per cent (relative to its 2005 emission levels) by 2020. That was Canada's goal until the Conservative government announced its plan to cut GHG emissions to 30 per cent below 2005 levels by 2030 (Gollom 2015). How is the federal government planning on reaching this new target, especially as, in 2013 (more than halfway to 2020), total emissions were only 3.1 per cent less than they were in 2005 and creeping upward? (See the government's latest submission to the UN Framework Convention on Climate Change for details; Environment Canada 2015c.) What policies are in play to reduce GHG emissions in Canada?

The federal government prefers a "sector" approach to reducing GHG emissions (Government of Canada 2014c). Specifically, the government has targeted primarily transportation, electricity, and technology. As the transportation sector makes up roughly 23 per cent of Canada's emissions, targeting this sector of the economy for possible GHG reductions makes sense (Environment Canada 2015c, pt. 1, 25). Consequently, the Harper government created new emission standards for cars and heavy trucks. There are now regulations to reduce GHG emissions for model years 2011–16 with the expectation that doing so will bring down emissions by 50 per cent compared to those produced by 2008-model cars (Government of Canada 2014c). The government has also released regulations to reduce GHG emissions from passenger cars and light trucks for model years 2017 and beyond. In conjunction with this, gasoline must now contain an average 5 per cent renewable content (2 per cent for diesel fuel; Government of Canada 2014c).

In the electricity sector, which produces about 12 per cent of Canada's GHGs, Ottawa provides funding for renewable energy and residential energy retrofit programs. It has also set aside funding for carbon capture and storage technologies in an effort to clean up both coal-fired power generation and oil sands carbon emissions.

For example, the Boundary Dam carbon capture and storage project in Saskatchewan, to which the Government of Canada provided $240 million, is now complete (Lorinc 2014). The only federal regulatory policy in place in 2015 that limits GHGs, aside from regulations enforcing emission standards for vehicles and for the composition of fuels, is the limit on emissions from coal-fired power plants (but not oil and gas emissions). This reduction is applied and implemented through the Canadian Environmental Protection Act, 1999 (Government of Canada 2015c). For further information on GHG emissions regulation, see the "Greenhouse Gas Emission Regulations" section of Environment Canada's website (www.ec.gc.ca/).

Market Mechanisms to Reduce GHG Emissions

There are many possible policy tools to reduce GHG emissions in society, including voluntary agreements, regulations, financial incentives, and information instruments. A lot of attention has been given to market mechanisms because they are widely considered the most effective means of quickly curbing emissions. Once such market mechanism is called the **cap-and-trade system** (also called emissions trading). A cap-and-trade system is a regulatory program under which government sets a cap on the quantity of GHG emissions, distributes permits for emissions allowable given that cap, and enables firms to buy and sell these permits after the initial distribution. Regulated sources must pay allowances at the end of a given period equal to their emissions. The price for emission allowances (the carbon price) is determined by supply and demand for allowances in an emissions trading market. Another market mechanism is a **carbon tax**. A carbon tax or a tax on GHG emissions imposes a direct fee (the carbon price) on emission sources based on the amount of GHG they emit but does not set a limit on GHG emissions. In a manner similar to cap-and-trade options, the tax could be imposed upstream or downstream. It could require importers, producers, and distributors of fossil fuels to pay a fixed fee on the carbon dioxide contained in fuel sold; in addition or alternatively, it could require emitters to pay based on their actual emissions. (For further information about cap-and-trade systems and carbon taxes, see Center for Climate and Energy Solutions 2011; Dion 2013; Forge and Williams 2008; Suzuki 2014.)

Prime Minister Harper has made it clear that he wants Canada to harmonize its regulations with the United States for the purposes of trade and energy commerce (Government of Canada 2012b). As of 2011, the Canada-United States Regulatory Cooperation Council was working to "increase regulatory transparency and coordination between the two countries" (Government of Canada 2011, 3). The consequence is that, in 2015, Canada was in a holding pattern waiting for the United States to create national standards for emission reductions such that Canada will be able to adjust to those standards. The United States has never passed federal climate change policy outside of the Clean Air Act and accompanying regulations to limit vehicle emissions and fuel additives, and, although it signed the Kyoto Protocol, the Bush administration announced that it would not implement the agreement, which was never ratified. Various GHG regulatory bills have been approved by the House of Representatives but not by the Senate, for example, the American Clean Energy and Security Act of 2009. Also, in November 2014, President Obama announced an agreement with China whereby the United States would reduce carbon emissions by 26–28 per cent below 2005 levels by 2025 and China agreed to reduce emissions beyond 2030 (Kerry 2014). Canada has not yet agreed to meet the US goal (McCarthy 2014b). However, it is important to note that Obama can only set a goal, not create law. Instead, the US Congress will need to create a bill and pass it in both chambers for the bill to become legally binding in the United States.

Provincial Climate Policy

The provincial track record for policy designed to reduce GHG emissions is marked by inconsistencies. Some provinces, such as British Columbia and Québec, have taken an aggressive approach to emission reduction while others have done very little to target GHG emissions (Holmes et al. 2012). Here it is worth focusing on the handful of provinces that have specific policies in place to address GHG emissions: Alberta, British Columbia, Québec, and Ontario.

In 2007, Alberta became technically the first jurisdiction in North America to implement a carbon price, but this law (the Specified Gas Emitters Regulation [SGER]) should not be confused with the stringent carbon tax implemented by British Columbia or with the carbon tax in Québec. Although all three provinces are using a form of economic regulation, the Alberta government requires a mandatory 12 per cent reduction in GHG emissions for all large industries in the province, including the oil sands industry (ESRD 2015). For coal-fired power plants, which Alberta still has and, unlike Ontario, is not phasing out, the regulation requires a percentage reduction in CO_2 emissions per kilowatt-hour generated. For the oil sands facilities, the policy requires a percentage reduction in CO_2 emissions per barrel of oil produced. The SGER seems like a radical regulatory policy for the Alberta government. The reason the policy is actually more economic and more voluntary than might first be realized is that failure to comply results in a small fee of $15 for each ton of excess emissions. If industry meets the target then it pays nothing. More important, the Alberta policy allows industry to avoid the fine by either buying credits from industries that "outperform" and are under their regulated amount or by purchasing offset credits from unregulated entities, such as farmers, who ostensibly reduce their emissions (Jaccard 2013; Partington 2013; Severson-Baker 2014). Even so, as of April 9, 2015, the government reported $577.9 million in the Climate Change and Emissions Management Fund that collects payments for emissions over the targets (ESRD 2015).

Not too long after Alberta passed its emissions policy, British Columbia implemented a **revenue-neutral carbon tax**. The law passed in 2008, and the final scheduled tax increase took effect on July 1, 2012. Generally speaking, a carbon tax is considered any tax on GHGs caused by burning fuel. It works by putting a price, as determined by government, on each ton of GHG produced (BC 2014). In this sense, it works like other taxes in society. For example, smokers pay a tax on each pack of cigarettes purchased, and industry pays a tax on each ton of emissions it produces in British Columbia. And all industries are subject to the tax—it is not aimed at only coal or oil (BC 2014). Any industry that produces and emits

GHGs into the atmosphere is subject to the policy. The purpose of the tax is to manipulate behaviour through economic incentives. If something costs a lot, people or firms will do less of that costly activity. The province is expecting that CO_2 emissions will decrease because industry will find ways to either reduce GHG emissions in current energy production or produce energy that creates no or not as much greenhouse gas. There is some evidence that GHG emissions are decreasing in the province (see Elgie and McClay 2013; Beaty, Lipsey, and Elgie 2014).

So what makes the tax "revenue neutral"? All the money collected through the carbon tax (from industry) is used to reduce public taxes in other areas, so the government cannot use it for new spending or new programs (BC 2014). The carbon tax is not a "money-grab" for the province. Industry pays taxes on carbon emissions, and the public benefits from that money because of reductions in costs elsewhere, in income taxes, for example. This public benefit is important because, in British Columbia, the carbon tax actually costs the consumer more money for energy. Why? An industry that is being taxed will pass that cost along to the consumer by raising energy prices. Because of this, the province also implemented a refundable Low Income Climate Action Tax Credit to help low-income individuals and families offset the increased cost of their energy (BC 2014).

Québec also has a tax on carbon emissions produced by coal, natural gas, and petroleum production. Compared to BC's policy, Québec's imposes a very small tax rate that is not revenue neutral. Whatever tax revenue the province collects, it can keep and put toward whatever government officials decide is reasonable. The money collected does not have to be returned to the public or spent on reducing taxes. In total, the province collects only about $200 million a year from the tax. The amount is so small partly because only the 50 largest energy companies are required to pay the tax (Holmes et al. 2012). Nevertheless, both Québec and British Columbia are using the tax as part of a larger climate policy agenda. In neither province is the tax the only strategy used to address the challenges presented by climate change.

Beyond a carbon tax, Québec also has a carbon market partnership with California (see Québec 2014a). In 2012, the province developed a GHG emission cap for all emitters such that the combined emissions of all industries in the province can only amount to so much carbon each year. Based on the amount of this cap, a specific number of permits are available, and each industry must obtain enough permits to release its CO_2 into the atmosphere. Starting in 2015, the cap and the number of permits will begin to decrease such that, each year, overall emissions will decrease. Businesses whose GHG emissions are higher than the number of permits they have must either buy more permits from businesses in Québec or California that have extra ones, or they must purchase offsets, such as funding the planting of trees to absorb the excess carbon they will emit. Businesses that have found a way to decrease their emissions may sell their unused permits to any interested party in Québec or California (see Québec 2014a for details). This partnership grew out of the Western Climate Initiative that developed among 11 states and provinces before the 2008 recession. Only Québec and California have gone ahead to establish a carbon market, which officially began January 1, 2014. The success of this partnership will likely affect the viability of a larger integrated North American carbon market.

Last, Ontario does not have a carbon tax or any price on carbon, although the government announced in 2015 that the province would join Québec and California in their cap-and-trade emission reduction commitment (Taber and Morrow 2015). The province has made commitments to reduce GHG emissions in other ways, however (OME 2015). Most notably, the province phased out coal-fired power in 2014. This change will significantly reduce CO_2 emissions across the province. Electricity in the province will rely mainly on renewable sources and those that emit less greenhouse gas.[4] Ontario has subsidized and promoted alternative energy production, such as solar and wind power, by the use of **feed-in-tariff policies** that allow renewable energy producers, including individual homeowners, to sell their electricity to the grid for a fixed and often inflated price. Thus, for example, Joan, living in Peterborough, could put solar panels on her roof and sell the energy she produces back to the Ontario power grid. As a result, other users, such as Joan's next-door neighbour, might be paying for solar energy and not even know it (Ontario Power Authority 2014).

The Role of Cities in Climate Change Policy

Canadian cities have a large role to play in energy policy. Local governments have direct or indirect control of 45 per cent of Canada's greenhouse gas emissions (EnviroEconomics 2009), and, in some provinces (e.g., British Columbia), cities are already expected to meet GHG reduction targets. Through measures such as strengthened building codes, better land use planning, public transit development, and capturing waste heat from landfill and sewage infrastructure, many Canadian municipalities have been trailblazers, reducing energy consumption and cutting GHG emissions. At the same time, local governments have been constrained in these efforts by the downloading of responsibilities without adequate support from higher levels of government. Better tools and more resources to help municipalities reduce GHG emissions and conserve energy are crucial to any national climate change strategy.

During the 1990s and early 2000s, the City of Toronto rose as a climate change policy leader in Canada. In fact, it made significant progress in a very short time. Toronto adopted and implemented several climate change mitigation strategies to reduce greenhouse gas emissions, including the Better Buildings Partnership and the Toronto Atmospheric Fund (TAF). The Better Buildings Partnership provided zero-interest loans for building retrofit projects for up to two-thirds of the project cost. As of September 2014, the program had delivered $37 million in incentives and $34 million in loans for projects that were estimated to reduce over 3 million Megawatt-hours (MWh) of electricity demand and 570,000 tons of CO_2 emissions (City of Toronto 2014a, 2014b).

The Toronto Atmospheric Fund, originally endowed with $23 million in 1991, had invested approximately $60 million by 2013 "in local solutions to climate change and air pollution" (TAF 2014). Notably, the fund's grants and loans created Canada's first municipal trigeneration (heat, power, and cooling) system and North America's first urban wind turbine. Between 1991 and 2011, the TAF saved the City of Toronto over $20 million in energy and maintenance costs, and reduced the city's CO_2 emissions by 500,000 tons (C40 2011).

In 2007, when Mayor David Miller created the Climate Change Clean Air and Sustainability Energy Action Plan, he said, "I feel strongly that since the federal government has abdicated its responsibility on climate change, it's up to cities to lead" (quoted in Summit 2012, 6). As part of this plan, Toronto's city council set a target to reduce the city's energy consumption from its 2007 levels by 21 per cent before 2030 (City of Toronto 2007). And it also developed the first by-law in North America that allowed private properties to use renewable energy. No other city in Canada has done so much in so little time for climate policy in Canada. As Toronto illustrated in the 2003–10 period, cities can lead in the area of environmental policy.

The Role of NGOs in Climate and Energy Policy

The Pembina Institute is credited with drawing Canada's attention to the dire environmental consequences of the Alberta tar sands (Hoberg and Phillips 2011), although other environmental groups such as Greenpeace and the David Suzuki Foundation play an important role as well. The Pembina Institute is a think tank more than an interest group. What is the difference? Both are non-governmental organizations in the sense that they exist outside the purview of the government and do not run candidates for election. **Think tanks** are research institutions that do not have members or encourage specific citizen actions. Instead, they produce well-researched and highly regarded reports and policy analyses. Because such reports often get media coverage and influence government policy-makers, they can be seen as fulfilling an important "interest group–like" function in climate governance in Canada. It is best to consider think tanks as non-state actors or non-government actors—but not necessarily as interest groups. Nevertheless, the Pembina Institute is a very important NGO in Canada, and all non-governmental organizations, whether think tanks or activist interest groups, have become part of the overall climate debate in the country.

Hundreds of NGOs that *are* considered interest groups work on issues related to climate change and energy policy in Canada. Climate Action Network Canada (CANet), which dates back to 1989, brings together and works with Canadian groups focused on climate change. CANet assists the Canadian government in finding experts working on climate change who are not public servants, and it selects NGO members for Canadian delegations to international climate negotiations. The network is able to pool scarce NGO resources and produce pragmatic and visionary reports, such as *Kyoto and Beyond*, published with the David Suzuki Foundation in 2002 (Krajnc and Wartel 2004). See the organization's website for updated information on Canadian policy to address climate change (climateactionetwork.ca).

Greenpeace Canada is also very active in Canadian climate politics and policy. Specifically, the organization acts within three inter-related and overlapping policy areas related to climate change: oil sands, nuclear power, and Arctic issues. With over 90,000 members in Canada and 2.9 million members worldwide in 2015, Greenpeace provides important outreach and educational opportunities (www.greenpeace.org). In its role as a watchdog, Greenpeace Canada targets operations in the tar sands as well as the policy (in)action of the federal and Alberta governments. The group's recent Energy [R]evolution project is directed at spreading awareness of and encouraging policy for clean and renewable energy use across the country. Unlike some other environmental NGOs in Canada, Greenpeace has a strong anti-nuclear platform, which dates back to its founding in 1971 during first-wave environmentalism. Greenpeace would like to see Canada reduce GHG emissions without turning to nuclear energy or creating nuclear waste.

The David Suzuki Foundation (DSF) has been deeply involved in Canadian climate issues for more than two decades. Like CANet and Greenpeace Canada, the DSF fits the classic interest-group model and fulfils the five functions discussed in Chapter 3. Education and outreach are critically important to the foundation, so it maintains an updated website and blog, and supports the publication of numerous scholarly and nonfiction books in partnership with Greystone Books. The foundation also works to get climate issues on government agendas across the country. Finally, as a watchdog, the DSF has worked with Aboriginal citizen groups to monitor the implementation of policy and regulations in the oil sands as well as the implementation and outcomes of climate initiatives at all levels of government.

The Role of Citizens in Climate and Energy Policy

The Canadian government provides citizens with a list of the "top ten things you can do to help" with climate change mitigation and adaptation (Government of Canada 2012c). These would be considered "voluntary policy" and act as guidelines for individual behaviour. The list includes these suggestions:

1. Reduce energy use by turning off lights, using energy-efficient bulbs and appliances, and turning off your computer and unplugging electronics when they are not in use.
2. Change the way you think about transportation. The government encourages you to walk or take your bike whenever you can. If you can do neither, take public transportation, and, if you must use a vehicle, choose one that is fuel efficient, ride with others, and avoid excessive braking and quick acceleration.
3. Insulate your home to avoid unnecessary heat loss or cooled-air loss and related increases in energy use.
4. Conserve water whenever possible by taking shorter showers, turning the water off while you are brushing your teeth, or following other simple methods.
5. Cool wash your clothes and hang them to dry to conserve energy.
6. Use energy efficient appliances, such as those with ENERGY STAR ratings, which is an international standard for energy-efficient consumer products.
7. Switch to green power if possible, and encourage your energy provider to obtain more energy from renewable resources.
8. Recycle.
9. Repurpose your used products by giving them to charity or selling them at garage sales, so fewer consumer products end up in landfills.
10. Plant greenery, such as a tree that can shade or cool your home while also soaking up carbon from the atmosphere.

The energy saved and the pollution averted if one were to follow the activities on this list might seem like a drop in the bucket when compared to the amount of pollution coming from oil sands and shale gas development in the Western provinces. However minimal the results of following these suggestions, doing something will give you a sense of control and help raise the public's awareness of climate issues, as well as maintaining their salience. You can also influence climate policy through your actions as a voter and consumer. As individual citizens, we have very little control over where our energy or electricity comes from, but, as groups of consumers of energy, our power, both political and economic, drives the system.

We all need to eat and keep our homes liveable, and most of us have to get to work or school every day. Those actions are going to require energy of some kind. But the choices we make do matter. Deciding to use public transportation signals to governments (and to society) that this mode of transportation is important and should be funded. Deciding to buy a hybrid car signals to the economy (and to fellow drivers) that this technology is important and in demand. If no one bought SUVs or Hummers, companies would stop producing those vehicles. It can be that simple.

But exercising individual choice is never going to be enough. If Canadians do not get involved in politics and do not tell their governments that the environment should be protected or that CO_2 emissions should be reduced, elected officials are not going to develop or implement policies that achieve these aims. So make informed decisions as a consumer and a voter, communicate those decisions to businesses and to your political representatives at all levels of government, and vote with your dollars and your ballots for the changes you want to see.

POLICY OPTIONS AND OBSTACLES

Overall, Canada has not been effective at reducing GHG emissions (Environment Canada 2013c, 2014b). Numerous policy tools to reduce GHG emissions have been created, and some have been tested in Europe, in the United States, and even in Canadian provinces. These mechanisms include eliminating fossil fuel subsidies, implementing pollution (carbon) taxes or emissions trading (cap-and-trade) rules, and, more broadly, encouraging voluntary action (by industries and citizens) and providing more information and education. Another option is to implement strict regulatory policies that prohibit specific actions and behaviours. Related policy tools also exist to promote the development and use of renewable energy. These tools include subsidies, guaranteed prices, feed-in tariffs, set quotas, and taxes, as well as the same broad strategies of encouraging voluntary action, offering education, and imposing regulation (see Bernstein et al. 2008; VanNijnatten, Craik, and Studer 2013). It is very unlikely that any one of these policies will work on its own. Instead, a mix of policy tools must be implemented at different levels of government across the country. If we know the policy mix that will likely work, why isn't Canada doing more to reduce GHG emissions and conserve energy or use alternative energy sources? To answer this complicated question, we must examine the obstacles to implementing this range of policy mechanisms in our country.

Federalism and regional differences are the most obvious and perhaps the most substantial obstacles or challenges (Harrison and Sundstrom 2007; MacDonald 2009). The fact that the provinces own their natural resources means that national policy will require coordination among all provinces. The regional nature of energy production and consumption further complicates that already difficult task. Alberta uses coal for consumption but relies on the oil sands for energy production and profit. In Saskatchewan, coal is consumed, but natural gas and oil are produced. On the other side of the country, Newfoundland uses hydroelectricity but relies on offshore oil drilling for profit. So, although there are some similarities amongst provinces, there are many regional differences. Coordinated policy is challenged by these differences because a reduction in CO_2 emissions, for example, will have huge consequences for the provincial budgets of the Western provinces but comparatively few for those of Ontario or Québec. Thus, the burden of reforming energy use must be shared in different ways to make it more equal and fair.

The structure of the economy is a related concern. As mentioned in previous chapters, Canada has an economy based on the sale of natural resources (a staples economy). Canada sells wood, fish, and agricultural products to the world. It also sells oil and natural gas. Therefore, the Canadian economy requires CO_2 emissions. Canadians need to use energy to create the energy they sell. The oil sands are a very profitable business—and one that creates thousands of jobs in Alberta and other provinces (where technology is developed and equipment is built). A reduction of CO_2 emissions could inadvertently damage the Canadian economy—a tough trade-off for elected officials who want to see jobs created and money generated.

CONCLUSIONS

Canadians use a lot of energy and produce a lot of energy. On both ends—production and consumption—Canada has a large energy portfolio that varies regionally. In the Western and Atlantic provinces, respectively, the oil sands and the fracking industry both use and produce large amounts of non-renewable energy. Nuclear energy is relied upon in Ontario, as the province phased out coal-power generation. New forms of renewable energy are developing more slowly across Canada, although hydroelectricity is already big business (both its production and consumption) in British Columbia, Manitoba, Ontario, Québec, and Atlantic Canada.

The federal government has very little direct responsibility for energy management in the country. Provinces are literally the powerhouses in Canada. Utility boards in each province manage the production and delivery of energy in accordance with the regulations and standards set by the National Energy Board. However, the federal government does oversee trade and international treaties, and it has the ability to regulate GHGs in the energy sector (discussed in Chapter 11). Consequently, federalism and multilevel governance are key parts of energy policy in Canada.

It is nearly impossible to discuss energy without linking it to climate change. Global climate change is the most significant challenge facing humanity, and, if left unchecked, it will lead to serious disruptions in weather patterns with devastating effects. Canada is a huge GHG producer. On May 15, 2015, the Harper government submitted to the United Nations Framework Convention on Climate Change its target of reducing GHG emissions to 30 per cent below 2005 levels by 2030 (Climate Action Tracker 2015). However, the country was not on target to reach even the more modest goal agreed to in Copenhagen of reducing these emissions to 17 per cent below 2005 levels by 2020. In fact, in a 2014 report to the United Nations, the Harper government admitted that Canada's CO_2 emissions are expected to rise another 38 per cent by 2030 because of oil sands production (Leahy 2014).

A plan to develop a *national* energy and climate *strategy* would clearly be a step in the right direction. Arguably, there is federal policy in the form of GHG regulations for coal-fired power plants, but Canada has no agreed-upon national law to regulate oil and gas emissions. The federal government, it seems, will not likely decide to regulate oil and gas unilaterally, but a national strategy that brings the provinces and territories together to agree on best practices and specific targets is certainly possible. The director of the Canadian-based Columbia Institute, Charley Beresford, argues that an overarching vision to encourage cooperation toward common goals, such as climate change mitigation, energy security, environmental sustainability, and a more diversified economy would benefit all Canadians (Beresford 2013). However, federal policy is not the only way to achieve these goals in Canada—although a stronger national energy policy could be very helpful. Success will come when all government actors at all levels of government determine best practices and common strategies and targets for energy production and consumption in Canada. As the City of Toronto showed in the early 2000s, a national vision will be stronger if Canada's municipal governments, which have such important stakes in outcomes and key contributions to make, are part of the process.

Key Terms

fossil fuels; non-renewable resources; renewable energy; biofuels; nuclear power; bitumen; fracking; National Energy Board; National Energy Program; greenhouse effect; climate change; cap-and-trade system; carbon tax; revenue-neutral carbon tax; feed-in-tariff policies; think tanks

Discussion Questions

1. How is energy a regional issue in Canada?
2. Why are Alberta's bitumen resources so controversial in Canada?
3. What is your city doing to combat climate change? (Remember to cite your sources—including all data and information obtained from the Internet.)
4. Why don't other provinces in Canada adopt a carbon tax?
5. Do you think nuclear power is a good way to reduce Canada's carbon footprint? Why or why not?
6. What obstacles exist to making stronger climate change policy across Canada?

Suggested Readings

Dyer, Simon, Jeremy Moorhouse, Katie Laufenberg, and Rob Powell. 2008. *Under-Mining the Environment: The Oil Sands Report Card*. Drayton Valley, AB: The Pembina Institute and WWF-Canada. https://www.pembina.org/reports/OS -Undermining-Final.pdf.

Grant, Jennifer, Marc Huot, Nathan Lemphers, Simon Dyer, and Matt Dow. 2013. *Beneath the Surface: A Review of Key Facts in the Oil Sands Debate*. Drayton Valley, AB: The Pembina Institute.

Klein, Naomi. 2014. *This Changes Everything: Capitalism and the Climate*. New York: Simon & Schuster.

MacFadyen, Alan, and G. Campbell Watkins. 2014. *Petropolitics: Petroleum Development, Markets and Regulations: Alberta as an Illustrative History*. Calgary: University of Calgary Press.

Marsden, Williams. 2012. *Fools Rule: Inside the Failed Politics of Climate Change*. Toronto: Vintage Canada.

Nikiforuk, Andrew. 2010. *Tar Sands: Dirty Oil and the Future of a Continent*. Vancouver: Greystone Books.

Rowlands, Ian H. 2009. "Renewable Electricity: The Prospects for Innovation and Integration in Provincial Policies." In *Canadian Environmental Policy and*

Politics: Prospects for Leadership and Innovation, edited by Robert Boardman and Debora L. VanNijnatten, 167–82. New York: Oxford University Press.

Sinclair, Peter R. 2010. *Energy in Canada*. Don Mills, ON: Oxford University Press.

Notes

1 Note that, because energy cannot be destroyed, when we use it, say by burning fossil fuels, the form of the energy changes from something we can access (something we can convert into propulsion or light, for example) into something we cannot.

2 The waste and emissions they do produce come mainly from the processes used to produce the energy, such as creating cement to build dams or mining to get the rare earth minerals used in wind turbines.

3 This is an example of open federalism, discussed in Chapter 2.

4 However, energy for transportation will come from fossil fuels.

Chapter 9

Aboriginal People and the Environment

IT IS PERHAPS TOO EASY to say that environmental policy always comes down to property, but understanding who owns a resource and who has the right to use and exploit that resource is essential (Cole 2002). In Canada, land ownership and access and rights to resources are sometimes uncertain and almost always controversial (Johansen 1991). This chapter provides a very brief introduction and overview of Aboriginal politics in relation to environmental policy in Canada. As citizens, land managers, and resource users, Aboriginal groups are key players in environmental policy creation and implementation. However, given Aboriginal history in the context of Canadian policy and law, Aboriginal groups are a unique set of actors that creates challenges and opportunities for the stewardship of Canada's resources.

Prior to European settlement in North America, millions, if not tens of millions, of First Nations people and Inuit already populated the continent. And the Europeans never "conquered" the indigenous people who once lived in what is now called Canada, through war or even military conflict. (Conquest was more the situation in the United States, where the "Indian Wars" lasted from the colonial period until the early twentieth century.) In Canada, indigenous peoples lost access and use rights to land through treaties and through a dwindling population (from disease) that could not keep pace with the vast number of foreigners coming to work and live on the land (Brandon 2013; Forkey 2013; Sauer 1975). In many cases, the First Nations were just pushed aside, and the land they had been using to hunt or live on was deforested and used for other purposes, such as mining, farming, and forestry (Forkey 2013). Inuit land was less contested until more recently, as discussed in the next chapter.

Present-day Canadian law, which includes the Royal Proclamation of 1763 issued by King George III, recognizes Aboriginal claim to lands and resources in Canada. It is widely accepted that the long-term occupancy of Canada (before the Europeans came and continuing today) denotes and confers substantial claim to land and resources from coast to coast to coast (AANDC 2013e). Thus, in Canada today, Aboriginals have title, which confers access and rights, to land and resources. And in some cases, especially in the North, Aboriginals have "comprehensive" land claims agreements that grant ownership of land and resources (as opposed to just a use right). However, as this chapter will explain, that indigenous Canadians were not conquered and never lost legal claim to their lands does not mean that they always get access to land or natural resources. To protect their rights, Aboriginals have used the court system. In fact, in this area of environmental public policy, the Supreme Court—as opposed to Parliament—has had a large impact.

This chapter begins with an overview of the demographic make-up of the Canadian Aboriginal population. After defining "First Nations" and "Métis" and "Inuit," it provides a very brief discussion of Canadian policy and law pertaining to Aboriginals. The status and lives of Aboriginals have been influenced by the British Crown, the Canadian Parliament, the Supreme Court, and, to a lesser extent, the United Nations. At all layers of government and governance, there is broad agreement that Aboriginals have title to land and access to natural resources—under certain conditions in certain circumstances. The last section of this chapter examines Aboriginal politics in four environmental arenas: oil, fisheries, water, and species at risk. As will become clear, environmental governance has a long way to come if it is to include Aboriginals fully as powerful actors in their own right. Although the Canadian government and non-state actors, such as NGOs, have often engaged in governance of the environment, Canada has yet to acknowledge fully the role of Aboriginal groups in managing land and resources—on reserve or off.

WHO ARE ABORIGINALS?

Aboriginal Canadians comprise three large categories of indigenous peoples: **Inuit, First Nations**, and **Métis** (AANDC 2015a). These three groups have similarities, especially from the state's perspective, but their differences are important—not just culturally or legally but from an environmental standpoint. As the next chapter will explain in greater detail, Inuit are a culturally similar group of people who inhabit the Arctic and sub-Arctic regions of Canada (as well as of Alaska and Greenland). Inuit are culturally and linguistically distinct from both First Nations and Métis.

First Nations people, or "Indians" (in the legal sense), are the original inhabitants of Canada outside of the North. There are over 600 different recognized bands, and only some are culturally or linguistically similar (see AANDC 2013a). That is to say, Canada comprises **indigenous** groups such as the Cree, Ojibwa, and Sioux, which then can be divided into smaller regional tribes. For example, the Sioux are a confederation of seven tribes. One of these is the Lakota, which itself comprises seven bands. Two Sioux groups, the Dakota and Lakota, continue to live in Saskatchewan (Stonechild 2007). Canadians sometimes overlook some of these distinctions as we use just two words to describe all these people together: First Nations. Part of the complexity and part of the challenge for non-indigenous Canadians involve coming to appreciate and respect these differences and understand the myriad peoples that compose our country. Making policy that affects "First Nations" is not something done with a wave of a hand. It requires a much more detailed and nuanced understanding of the cultural and linguistic differences and core knowledge, beliefs, and traditions of these distinct peoples.

"Métis" is the word used to describe Canadians who can trace their origins to mixed First Nation and European heritage (AANDC 2015a). When settlers first arrived in Canada, a mixing of cultures and peoples occurred, resulting in a new and unique group: the Métis. As the Canadian state evolved, the Métis presented somewhat of an identity challenge for the government: Are they Indians? The answer is important because recognized Indians, or status Indians, are offered specific benefits and protections under the Indian Act, as will be discussed. For most of Canada's history, Métis have been considered Aboriginal but not Indian. But, in May 2013, a Federal Court judge released his long-awaited ruling that approximately 600,000 Métis and non-status Indians fall under federal jurisdiction as "Indians" (Canadian Press 2013b; see *Daniels v. Canada*, [2013] F.C.R. 6). Consequently, they can now negotiate access to the federal programs and services long denied them. However, Ottawa appealed the decision in 2014, and the Supreme Court of Canada will be tasked with making a final decision as to who should be defined as "Indian" (Canadian Press 2014b).

The Métis never had "reserve land" save in the province of Alberta, which is still (as of 2015) the only province to recognize Métis title to the land. The Alberta Métis Population Betterment Act of 1938 established land for Métis communities in central Alberta, known as "settlements." Initially 10 settlements were established, although at present there are only 8. The largest is Paddle Prairie at 169,909 hectares cubed with a 2008 population of approximately 700 people (Ouellet and Hanson 2009). However, things might change in Manitoba soon because, in March 2013, the Supreme Court of Canada ruled with the Métis by finding that the federal government failed to live up to its constitutional obligations in parcelling out land to children of the Manitoba Métis in the 1870s. Enormous tracts of land may potentially be open for negotiation across the provinces as a result of this decision (Rennie 2013; see *Manitoba Métis Federation et al. v. Canada (Attorney General) et al.,* [2013] S.C.J. No. 14).

Demographics and Geography

The three Aboriginal groups combined represent about 4.3 per cent of Canada's population, according to the National Household Survey of 2011 (Statistics Canada 2014a). Of those people reporting an Aboriginal identity in 2011, 60.8 per cent identified themselves as a First Nations person (North American Indian), 32.3 per cent as Métis, and 4.2 per cent as Inuit. The remaining 2.7 per cent reported more than one Aboriginal identity (Statistics Canada 2014a). The Aboriginal population, then, is quite small. And, more important for policy, the Aboriginal population is unevenly distributed across the country. Ontario has the largest number of Aboriginal people, with 21.5 per cent of Canada's total Aboriginal population. However, as a region, the West also has a very large population; nearly 6 in 10 (57.6 per cent) Aboriginal people live in one of the four Western provinces. In 2011, 16.6 per cent of the Aboriginal population lived in British Columbia, 15.8 per cent in Alberta, 14.0 per cent in Manitoba, and 11.0 per cent in Saskatchewan. In the North, Aboriginal people make up the largest shares of the population in Nunavut and the Northwest Territories. In Nunavut, 86.3 per cent of the population are Aboriginal people (almost entirely Inuit), and, in the Northwest Territories, the percentage is 51.9 (in this region, Aboriginal peoples are a mixture of Dene, Métis, and Inuvialuit, who are a specific subgroup of Inuit indigenous to this area of Canada). In Yukon, Aboriginal people accounted for 23.1 per cent of the population; most are First Nations people (see Statistics Canada 2014a for these figures).

According to the 2011 census, almost three-quarters (73.1 per cent) of Inuit in Canada live in Inuit Nunangat. This area of land stretches from Labrador to the Northwest Territories and comprises four regions: Nunatsiavut, Nunavik, Nunavut, and the Inuvialuit region of the Northwest Territories (see Map 9.1). In 2011, there were roughly 27,000 Inuit in Nunavut, which has the largest land mass and the biggest Inuit population within Inuit Nunangat. In fact, Inuit living in Nunavut made up nearly half (45.5 per cent) of the total Inuit population in Canada. In terms of geographical distribution, Canada's Aboriginal population

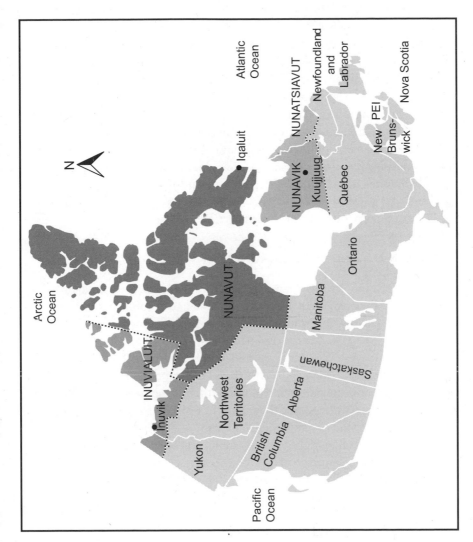

MAP 9.1 Inuit Nunangat in Northern Canada, 2009

is clearly split, with Inuit residing mainly in Nunangat and First Nations and Métis living mainly in the Western provinces and Ontario (Statistics Canada 2014a).

Another important demographic fact is that the Aboriginal population is much younger than the non-Aboriginal population, which suggests that Aboriginal peoples are having more children or have a shorter life expectancy. The median age of the Aboriginal population was 28 years in 2011, compared with 41 for the non-Aboriginal population. (The median age is the age at which exactly half of the population is older and half is younger.) Inuit had a median age of 23 and were the youngest of the three Aboriginal groups. The median age was 26 for First Nations people and 31 for Métis. Children (those aged 14 and under) account for more than one-quarter (28.0 per cent) of the Aboriginal population, compared with 17 per cent among the non-Aboriginal population. These data have important ramifications for future generations because the Aboriginal population is growing more quickly than the non-Aboriginal population. Although Aboriginal groups comprise 4.3 per cent of Canada's population today, we can expect that percentage to increase over time (Statistics Canada 2014a).

ABORIGINALS AND THE ENVIRONMENT

If Aboriginals comprise less than 5 per cent of the total Canadian population, why do they play such an important role in environmental politics and policy? This section will focus on three of the many reasons: land management, self-government, and democratic inclusion.

Aboriginals were the first people to inhabit Canada. First Nations signed **treaties** and made alliances with various Dutch, French, British, and Canadian governments before and after Confederation in 1867. No two treaties are identical, but they usually provide for certain rights, including reserve lands, annuities (a small sum of money paid each year), and hunting and fishing rights. For example, several treaties were signed after the Royal Proclamation of 1763 but before Confederation in 1867, including the Upper Canada Treaties (1764–1862) and the Vancouver Island Treaties (1850–54). Under these treaties, the First Nations surrendered their interest in lands located in what are now known as the provinces of Ontario and British Columbia.

Between 1871 and 1921, the Canadian federal government entered into treaties with various First Nations that enabled it to pursue agriculture, settlement, and resource development of the Canadian West and the North. These treaties were numbered 1 through 11 and are now referred to as the "Numbered Treaties." As you can see in Map 9.2, the Numbered Treaties cover northern Ontario, Manitoba, Saskatchewan, Alberta, and

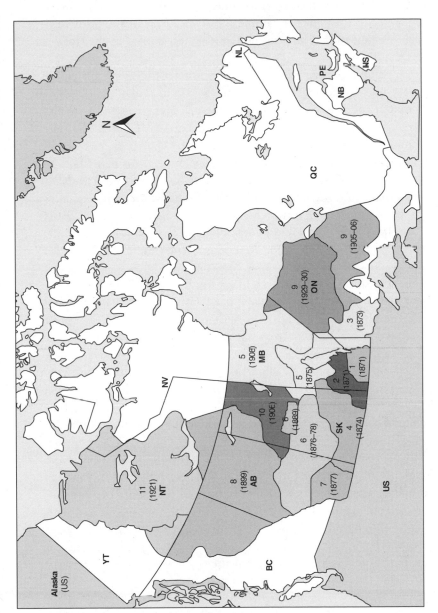

MAP 9.2 The 11 Numbered Treaties in Canada

Source: "Map of Numbered Treaties of Canada," *Wikimedia*, March 26, 2011, http://upload.wikimedia.org/wikipedia/commons/5/5d/Numbered-Treaties-Map.svg.

parts of Yukon, the Northwest Territories, and British Columbia. Like other treaties, these provided for such things as reserve lands and other benefits, including farm equipment and animals, annual payments, ammunition, clothing, and certain rights to hunt and fish. The Crown also made some promises, such as maintaining schools on reserves or providing teachers or educational help to the First Nation named in the treaties (AANDC 2010b).

When thinking about treaties and the impact they have on policy today, we must remember that, for many years in Canada and still to some extent today, there was a fundamental disagreement as to the nature and meaning of the treaties (see Asch 2014; Miller 2009). The Canadian government considered treaties to be land-transfer deals in which the Indians sold their land in return for certain benefits. The indigenous perspective was that the treaties were peace and friendship treaties whereby Aboriginal peoples agreed to share lands and resources with settlers and the government. This divergence in perspective is linked to broader cultural and philosophical differences. For example, many indigenous peoples in the Americas at the time of contact with Europeans had no conception that someone could "own" a parcel of land or, accordingly, have the right to sell it. As well, documentary evidence shows that the promises in the written treaties (which were often signed by a First Nation representative who did not even speak English) were quite different from the oral promises made by the "treaty parties"—the people sent by Ottawa to get the treaties signed. Today, these treaties are recognized as part of our history, and their contents have been upheld in court. In the 1996 *R. v. Badger* case, the Supreme Court ruled that the government must consider the Aboriginal understanding of the treaty at the time it was signed (*R. v. Badger*, [1996] 1 S.C.R. 771; see Table 9.2).

Why do treaties matter for environmental policy? Treaties make Aboriginals important land managers in Canada. A **reserve** is "land set apart and designated as a reserve for the use and occupancy of an Indian group or band" (AANDC 2010a). A reserve is not to be confused with a First Nation's **traditional territory**. Although reserve borders were imposed on First Nations, many have continued hunting, gathering, and fishing in the off-reserve locations that they have used for many generations. In part, they made use of traditional territories because the reserves chosen by the government were often very small and left to the First Nations because settlers did not want the land (it was not productive farm land, for example). In addition, important ceremonial sites may be located outside a reserve but continue to be significant for a band's cultural and spiritual practices (AANDC 2013a).

First Nations do not own land in the same sense that one owns private property. The Constitution of 1867 gives Parliament authority over "Indians and lands reserved for the Indians." The Indian Act, in place since 1876, was passed by Parliament under this authority and sets out the land management responsibilities of the minister of Aboriginal Affairs and Northern Development Canada (AANDC) for much of the reserve lands in Canada. AANDC provides land management services to more than 600 First Nations and covers more than 2,800 reserves with over 3 million hectares of reserve land across Canada. Land management generally includes activities related to the ownership, use, and development of land for personal, community, and economic purposes. Simply put, the federal government oversees all reserves in the country (AANDC 2013d).

Third, First Nation and Inuit communities have a legally recognized right to **self-government** in Canada, a right that includes making their own environmental policy (see AANDC 2014b). In August 1995, the Government of Canada adopted an approach to "negotiating practical and workable arrangements with Inuit and First Nation people to implement their inherent right to self-government" (AANDC 2010a). These arrangements recognize the rights of Inuit and First Nations peoples to make decisions about matters internal to their communities; integral to their unique cultures, traditions, and languages; and connected with their relationship to the land and resources.

Under federal policy, Inuit and First Nations groups may negotiate self-government arrangements for different things, such as government structure, land management, health care, child welfare, education, housing, and economic development. Negotiations are held between Aboriginal groups, the federal government, and, in areas affecting its jurisdiction and interests, the relevant provincial or territorial government. Self-government arrangements may take many forms, based on the diverse historical, cultural, political, and economic circumstances of the Inuit and First Nation groups, regions, and communities involved (AANDC 2015b, 2015d). Self-government regimes can be far-reaching in their powers and jurisdictions. And they can also vary widely in their degree of exclusivity—in the degree to which participation (e.g., voting or holding office) and services are restricted to Aboriginal peoples.

Last, Aboriginal Canadians are important for environmental policy in Canada because they bring a unique voice to the democratic table. The diversity amongst Aboriginal groups in Canada makes it difficult for them to speak in a unified voice. But, in spite of their differences, many Aboriginal societies do have "deeply held principles of respect for the earth and its resources, restraint, and obligation" (Parson 2001, 366;

see also Doyle-Bedwell and Cohen 2001). Obviously, one must be cautious about romanticizing Aboriginal views of the environment. First Nations and Inuit have been both protectors and plunderers of Earth at times (Forkey 2013). As Canadians, their learned history and traditions as well as their present-day right to earn livelihoods and participate in governance makes their inclusion in environmental policy setting absolutely critical. Of notable importance is Aboriginal traditional knowledge, discussed in Chapter 5 and here, as well as in Chapter 10.

UNDERSTANDING CANADA'S ABORIGINAL LAW

Laws and policy that affect Aboriginal peoples in Canada have four main sources: British law, Canada's Parliament, the court system and its rulings, and domestic treaties and comprehensive land claims and international treaties. Each of these will be discussed in turn.

In 1763, King George III of England issued a royal proclamation that has had lasting impacts on Canada's indigenous population. Following the French and Indian War in North America (1754–63), England wanted to organize its North American territory and make peace with indigenous people, especially for the purposes of the fur trade and western settlement. For the much later Canadian government (established in 1867), the Royal Proclamation had four important effects, of which echoes are still felt today: (1) it identified that Aboriginal "title" of land existed through use and occupancy (a very English conception of land in the eighteenth century that is directly related to the theories of John Locke); (2) it set the stage for the reserve system; (3) it defined the process for extinguishing title by permanent sale to the federal government; and, (4) it created a "fiduciary responsibility" whereby the government had, and continues to have, a responsibility to act in the best interests of First Nations in any dealings it undertakes on their behalf (Booth and Skelton 2012; McNeil 1997).

After the Royal Proclamation there have been three major acts of Canada's Parliament that directly affect Aboriginal Canadians. These are summarized in Table 9.1. When Canada East and Canada West joined and outlined federal powers in the Constitution Act of 1867, the federal government was granted responsibility for Indians and the Indian land established under the Numbered Treaties (reserves). This circumstance, perhaps more than anything, has had a lasting impact on Canada-Aboriginal relations and on relations between Aboriginal communities and the environment. Any time policy involves Aboriginal Canadians or their lands, the federal government must be involved in the policymaking process. Only it has jurisdiction in this area, although territories and provinces

TABLE 9.1 Acts of Parliament and Their Effect on Aboriginal Canadians

ACT OF PARLIAMENT	EFFECT ON ABORIGINAL CANADIANS
Constitution Act (BNA Act), 1867	• Made federal government responsible for Indians and reserves
Indian Act, 1876	• Laid out who was recognized as an Indian and the conditions under which "status" could be gained or lost
Constitution Act, 1982	• Section 35 recognizes and guarantees Aboriginal rights and treaty rights but does not define them
	• Métis and Inuit are included as "Aboriginals" in Canada

can get involved in the decision-making process. Map 9.2 illustrates the date and number of these treaties and gives a rough outline of the land affected by each. You can see that treaty lands cross provincial borders. Reserve land established inside these treaty areas is considered part of the "Federal House." Thus, a province cannot make policy regarding reserve land inside its boundaries, for example.

After the Constitution Act of 1867 (the British North America Act), the 1876 **Indian Act** was passed by Canada's Parliament. This act, which remains in effect today (albeit amended), establishes who qualifies as "Indian" in Canada and how qualified Indians can register with the government for benefits and legal protections. When Canada updated its Constitution in 1982, Section 35 of the new Constitution Act categorized the Métis and Inuit as "Aboriginals" and formally recognized that Aboriginals have specified rights, which stem from the continued occupation of lands by Aboriginal peoples since before European settlement, the Royal Proclamation, and subsequent legal decisions vis-à-vis the courts. However, although the Inuit and Métis are Aboriginals for the purposes of the Constitution Act of 1982, neither group was classified as "Indian" or covered under the Indian Act. As already discussed, Métis groups have been fighting to be considered "Indians" since 1999, and, in April 2014, the Federal Court of Appeal largely upheld an earlier decision that recognized them as "Indians" under the Constitution. The issue was before the Supreme Court in 2015.

Since the 1970s, the Supreme Court of Canada has heard several cases and made a number of decisions about Aboriginal rights and land title that bear significance on federalism and the environment across Canada. Table 9.2 provides a brief synopsis of these cases and decisions. Remember that these are not acts of Parliament—the legislative branch of the government did not make these policies. Instead, these are court cases, yet the final decisions carry the weight of law in the country.

TABLE 9.2 Major Supreme Court Cases: Aboriginals and Environmental Policy in Canada

YEAR	SUPREME COURT CASE	OUTCOME/RULING
1973	*Calder v. British Columbia*	For the first time, the Canadian legal system acknowledged the existence of Aboriginal title to land and that such title existed outside of, and was not simply derived from, colonial law. Calder lost the case, but three justices accepted Calder's case, and it was clear that future decisions were likely to affirm title.
1990	*R. v. Sparrow*	The case set out criteria to determine under what conditions the government could infringe on Aboriginal rights, providing that these rights were in existence at the time of the Constitution Act, 1982. These criteria are known as "the Sparrow Test."
1996	*R. v. Van der Peet; R. v. Gladstone*	In these two cases, the court's decision went beyond the earlier Sparrow ruling (1990) to define particular Aboriginal rights regarding fishing. The ruling also resulted in what is known today as the "Van der Peet Test," or the "Integral to a Distinctive Culture Test," which determines how an Aboriginal right is to be defined. Specifically, the right must be proven to be integral to the culture of the claimant. The test outlines 10 criteria that must be met in order for a practice to be affirmed and protected as an Aboriginal right pursuant to Section 35.
1996	*R. v. Badger*	The court held that treaty interpretation has to consider the Aboriginal understanding of the treaty at the time it was signed and held that the onus of proving that a treaty or Aboriginal right had been extinguished was on the Crown.
1997	*Delgamuukw v. British Columbia*	The court decided that oral tradition and testimony merit consideration in assessing legal cases. Also, First Nations had to prove that they had exclusive use and occupation of land at sovereignty or continued use of land to claim title.
1999	*R. v. Marshall*	The court decided that Aboriginal fishing rights date to treaties signed with Britain in the 1760s but that Aboriginal treaty rights are subject to Canadian law.
2004	*Haida Nation v. British Columbia (Minister of Forests)*	The court recognized and defined the Crown's duty to consult Aboriginal groups before exploiting lands to which they may have claims.
2004	*Taku River Tlingit Nation v. British Columbia*	The court held that the Crown has a duty to consult and accommodate Aboriginal peoples with a claim to land even if Aboriginal title and rights have not been proved in court.
2014	*Tsilhqot'in Nation v. British Columbia*	The court granted the Tsilhqot'in title to more than 1,700 square kilometres of land. It agreed that a "semi-nomadic" tribe can claim land (so long as the land was used regularly for hunting, fishing, or other activities before European contact and the tribe did not surrender the land through an existing treaty). A three-point test to determine land titles was developed: occupation, continuity of habitation, and exclusivity in the area.

SOURCES: Data from Asch (1999) and Hessing, Howlett, and Summerville (2005, 7–91). For more information on these court cases, see CanLII (https://www.canlii.org/en/) and the "Land & Rights" section of the Indigenous Foundations site (http://indigenousfoundations.arts.ubc.ca/home/land-rights.html).

There is no question that the 1973 **Calder case** was a landmark judgment in Aboriginal and environmental law in Canada. In sum, the decision recognized that **Aboriginal title** to land could exist in common law. This judgment goes beyond recognizing Aboriginal rights to "reserve" land to live on. Title ensures the right to benefit monetarily from the natural resources found on the land to which Aboriginals claim title. Consequently, disputes over forestry and hydropower developments on Aboriginal land sprang to the forefront. Which land in Canada Aboriginals had "title" to was unclear because of outstanding disputes between the federal government and various Aboriginal groups. Ottawa understood the land under Aboriginal title to mean "reserve land," and Aboriginal peoples understood it to mean "traditional territory." In response, the Government of Canada developed the Comprehensive Land Claims Policy as a framework to negotiate **Aboriginal land claims** (Wood, Tanner, and Richardson 2010). The policy provided a "world class model for participatory, bi-cultural environmental governance" because it incorporated Aboriginal values and knowledge, and it included Aboriginals in the decision-making process (Wood, Tanner, and Richardson 2010, 998). According to Hurley (2009), a total of 23 comprehensive claims were settled between 1973 and 2009:

- James Bay and Northern Quebec Agreement (1975) and Northeastern Quebec Agreement (1978);
- Inuvialuit Final Agreement, western Arctic (1984);
- Gwich'in Comprehensive Land Claim Agreement, northwestern portion of the Northwest Territories and "primary use area" in Yukon (1992);
- Nunavut Land Claims Agreement, eastern Arctic (1993);
- Eleven Yukon First Nation final agreements through 2008, based on the Council for Yukon Indians Umbrella Final Agreement (1993);
- Sahtu Dene and Métis Comprehensive Land Claim Agreement, Mackenzie Valley, Northwest Territories (1994);
- Nisga'a Final Agreement, Nass Valley, northern British Columbia (2000);
- Tlicho Agreement, North Slave region, Northwest Territories (2003);
- Labrador Inuit Land Claims Agreement, Newfoundland and Labrador (2005);
- Nunavik Inuit Land Claims Agreement, Québec (2006);
- Tsawwassen First Nation Final Agreement, BC Lower Mainland (2007); and
- Maa-nulth First Nations Final Agreement, Vancouver Island (2009)

These agreements were signed by federal, provincial or territorial, and Aboriginal representatives (Hurley 2009).

After the Calder case, numerous other Aboriginal cases were heard before the Supreme Court. As Chapter 3 discussed, the courts can have a large impact on public and environmental policy, and case law concerning Aboriginals and the environment is a good example of the courts' influence. Outside of the acts of Parliament mentioned previously, the House and Senate have made very few policies in this area. The federal government has called for a number of investigations and reports on the topic of Aboriginal peoples, however, especially in the area of land claims.

The year 1991 marked the beginning of the Royal Commission on Aboriginal Peoples, a study of the relationship between Aboriginal and non-Aboriginal people in Canada that took numerous years to complete. In Canada, the government establishes a royal commission to investigate a particular issue (such as health care or education). The investigation is generally completed by a panel of experts who develop a report and submit it to cabinet so that any recommendations made by the commission can be implemented by the executive branch or can form the basis of formal legislation (Fox 2006).

The Royal Commission on Aboriginal Peoples took a total of six years to complete and resulted in a 4,000-page report (for a summary, see Hurley and Wherrett 1999). The report did call for new legislation, including a new Royal Proclamation, but even with over 400 total recommendations, the report's impact has been minimal. The federal government has not wanted to make constitutional changes, nor has the House or Senate wanted to alter Aboriginal-state relations significantly (Doerr 2006). Instead, the courts continue to be at the forefront of defining the legal and policy parameters of Aboriginal rights in the country.

International law is another contributor to the context of Aboriginal and government disputes over land and environmental issues. For example, the UN Declaration on the Rights of Indigenous Peoples (UNDRIP) was created in 2007 as a legally non-binding agreement regarding the political, social, and environmental rights of indigenous peoples throughout the world. Canada, Australia, New Zealand, and the United States voted in the United Nations against the declaration, and Canada did not officially endorse the UNDRIP until November 2010 (AANDC 2015e). The government initially withheld support on the basis that the UNDRIP conflicts with the Charter of Rights and Freedoms and that Articles 26 and 32 of the declaration (see textbox) would require a significant re-examination of already settled land claims across the country. However, under pressure from the Assembly of First Nations and the international community, Canada did issue a "Statement of Support" for UNDRIP.

United Nations Declaration on the Rights of Indigenous Peoples

Article 26

1. Indigenous peoples have the right to the lands, territories and resources which they have traditionally owned, occupied or otherwise used or acquired.
2. Indigenous peoples have the right to own, use, develop and control the lands, territories and resources that they possess by reason of traditional ownership or other traditional occupation or use, as well as those which they have otherwise acquired.
3. States shall give legal recognition and protection to these lands, territories and resources. Such recognition shall be conducted with due respect to the customs, traditions and land tenure systems of the indigenous peoples concerned.

...

Article 32

1. Indigenous peoples have the right to determine and develop priorities and strategies for the development or use of their lands or territories and other resources.
2. States shall consult and cooperate in good faith with the indigenous peoples concerned through their own representative institutions in order to obtain their free and informed consent prior to the approval of any project affecting their lands or territories and other resources, particularly in connection with the development, utilization or exploitation of mineral, water or other resources.
3. States shall provide effective mechanisms for just and fair redress for any such activities, and appropriate measures shall be taken to mitigate adverse environmental, economic, social, cultural or spiritual impact.

Important for the Canadian state is Article 46, which states "nothing in this Declaration may be interpreted as ... encouraging any action which would dismember or impair, totally or in part, the territorial integrity or political unity of sovereign and independent States" (United Nations 2007, 14). In other words, the declaration recognizes Aboriginal title to land only inside sovereign countries, such as Canada, and does not advocate for a separatist movement or recognize Aboriginal governments as sovereign. Finally, it is important to keep in mind that the declaration is voluntary and not legally binding.

ABORIGINAL LAND AND ENVIRONMENTAL POLICY TODAY

Acts of Parliament and international treaties have deemed indigenous people to be Canadian citizens with important historical claims to land and resources. In agreement with this, the Canadian court system, especially the Supreme Court of Canada, has determined that government must respect Aboriginal title to land and, moreover, that the law requires Aboriginal access to traditional lands and natural resources. So if both Parliament and the courts agree that Aboriginals have title to land and resources, what is the problem? Where do these affirmed rights leave Aboriginals vis-à-vis environmental policy today? This section examines the intersection of Aboriginal land or resource claims with three policy areas: pipelines, water, and species at risk.

Pipelines

You may recall from Chapter 8 that the Alberta oil sands comprise a large swath of land north of Edmonton and that proposed pipelines from the oil sands extend west through British Columbian (Northern Gateway Pipeline), south through Alberta and Saskatchewan (Keystone XL), north to the Northwest Territories and Yukon (Mackenzie Valley Gas Project), and east to New Brunswick (Energy East Pipeline). Both the oil sands themselves and these proposed pipeline projects extend across reserve and traditional lands and have negative environmental impacts. Not surprisingly, therefore, some First Nations bands and Métis settlements in these provinces and territories have deep concerns about tar sands exploration and extraction. They also have voiced significant complaints about the lack of consultation built into pipeline projects as well as the lack compensation for damaged lands and resources, such as water and marine life (see Anderssen et al. 2013; Canadian Press 2013c; Kilpatrick 2010).

In British Columbia, the Northern Gateway pipeline, which will extend to about 1,180 kilometres, would cut through the traditional territory of 40 Aboriginal groups—many of which are opposed to the pipeline (Ecojustice 2013a). First Nations' opposition reaffirms the federal moratorium of 1972 on the transportation of oil through the Hecate Strait, which is the body of water between mainland British Columbia and the northern-most islands off the BC coast, Haida Gwaii (Royal Society of Canada 2004). Opposition also reaffirms the declaration of the BC coast as a "voluntary" tanker exclusion zone in 1985 (Transport Canada 2015). In December 2010, 61 BC First Nations groups in Canada signed the Save the Fraser Declaration to ban oil sands projects that would impact traditional territory (West Coast Environmental Law 2012). The declaration states, "We will not allow the proposed Enbridge Northern Gateway Pipelines, or similar Tar Sands projects, to cross our lands, territories and watersheds, or the ocean migration routes of the Fraser River salmon" (savethefraser.ca). In 2013, the mayor of Vancouver, Gregor Robertson, joined the First Nations in opposition to the pipeline and declared December 13, 2012, to be "Save the Fraser Declaration Day" in the city (West Coast Environmental Law 2012).

Premier Christy Clark was initially reluctant to allow the Northern Gateway project to proceed in British Columbia. Her government laid out five conditions that had to be satisfied for pipeline projects in the province: successful completion of an environmental review process; the deployment of world-leading marine oil-spill response, prevention, and recovery systems; the use of world-leading practices for land oil-spill prevention, response, and recovery; the fulfilment of Aboriginal treaty rights; and the allocation to British Columbia of a fair share of the fiscal and economic benefits of a proposed heavy-oil project, one that reflects the level of risk borne by the province (CBC 2012). In early November 2013, the premiers of Alberta and British Columbia reached a framework for an agreement to satisfy British Columbia's conditions. Exactly what the agreement between the two provinces means for First Nations is not clear, but all levels of government have agreed to fulfil Aboriginal treaty rights. We can expect the construction of the Northern Gateway Pipeline to commence only after the First Nations governments and provincial and federal governments have come to an agreement about title—or after the courts have settled the matter. Neither has happened (Hunter and Stueck 2014).

On June 17, 2014, the federal government approved the Enbridge Northern Gateway pipeline project. However, a joint review panel did identify numerous issues that must be resolved in the regulatory process and construction of the pipeline—including necessary consultations with First Nations (National Energy Board 2013). The project will be complicated further by a June 26, 2014, Supreme Court decision that granted BC's Tsilhqot'in First Nation title to over 1,700 square kilometres of land (Cryderman and Jang, 2014; *Tsilhqot'in Nation v. British Columbia*, 2014 SCC 44). For the first time in history, Canada's top court recognized a semi-nomadic tribe's claim to land title, including the right to the benefits associated with the land. It is not yet clear what impact the court case will have on the Northern Gateway pipeline, but it clearly raised red flags in the arena. The construction of the pipeline cannot commence until land claims are settled and the Crown's duty to consult is met (see Chapter 9).

Environmental Justice for Aboriginal Canadians

Environmental justice is a form of social justice. Its central ideas originated in the United States in the context of race and environmental risk in the 1980s. The University of Michigan hosted the 1990 Conference on Race and the Incidence of Environmental Hazards, which served as a focusing event for the environmental justice movement. Shortly after the conference, the Environmental Protection Agency, a federal department in the United States, created an Office of Environmental Justice and provided an official government definition of the term: "Environmental Justice is the fair treatment and meaningful involvement of all people regardless of race, color, national origin, or income with respect to the development, implementation, and enforcement of environmental laws, regulations, and policies" (EPA 2012a). The concept is often linked to the civil rights movement and is especially pertinent for African Americans, who often find themselves living in polluted areas of the country.

In Canada, environmental justice is largely about distributive and procedural equity concerns (Fletcher 2003). It seeks to guarantee that individuals and communities can flourish not just through living in an unpolluted environment but also through obtaining the necessary components for maintaining a clean and healthy environment, such as access to jobs, quality schools and housing, and health care (Bryant 1995). All Canadians should be involved in the process of making decisions that affect the environment and public health (procedural justice), and all Canadians should have a safe and clean space in which to create a life (distributive justice).

Aboriginal Canadians are sometimes excluded from the decision-making process (which is why governments now have a "duty to consult"), and they are often denied a healthy space to live. Reserves have extraordinarily poor water quality, and, in 2005, 75 per cent of the water systems in First Nations communities were estimated to have significant threats to the safety of drinking water (Commissioner of the Environment and Sustainable Development 2005, 15). Aboriginal communities are also deeply affected by the production of oil and gas across the country because industry often pollutes the land and waters that such communities have traditionally relied upon for subsistence. These types of environmental injustices raise concerns not only for the environment of Canada but also for democracy and equality in the country.

Water

Indigenous worldviews constitute water as an essential component of all life, so decisions regarding its use "cannot be made independent of context but, rather, must be made on the land, with an eye to assessing how all life on that land will be affected" (Walkem 2007, 310–11). Furthermore, the indigenous worldview recognizes that it is "human activities that must respond to the environment, not vice versa" (310–11). In contrast to this is the view that water is property and that, in Canada, provinces own the water (Phare 2011). This sentiment can be found in almost every provincial law setting out the regulatory regime for water rights and water management. These laws are based upon the jurisdiction provinces have over "property and civil rights" under Section 92 of the Canadian Constitution Act of 1867. The Prairie provinces (Manitoba, Alberta, and Saskatchewan), which joined Canada as provinces after 1867, have enacted their water laws as a result of the rights they received much later—under the Natural Resources Transfer Agreements in 1930 (NRTAs), discussed in Chapter 6. The agreements transferred all resources (lands, minerals, waters) previously "owned" by the federal government to the Prairie provinces.

The NRTAs set out that, among other things, this transfer of land and resources is subject to existing treaties with First Nations. At that time, all the Numbered Treaties with First Nations in Western Canada had been concluded. The provinces often assert the view that, because these treaty documents do not specifically mention water and because the NRTAs gave water to the provinces, First Nations have no water rights. Because the transfer of lands and waters to the provinces was subject to existing treaties, however, which did not clearly resolve or characterize the water rights of First Nations, who "owns" the water flowing through land to which Aboriginals hold title is debatable. Thus, although the Constitution of Canada generally clarifies whether the federal government or the provinces have "ownership" of and responsibility for waters, it does not settle the scope of the rights and authority of First Nations when it comes to waters on their reserves, waters that flow through their reserves, or waters that are on their traditional territories (Phare 2011).

The issue of Aboriginal water rights was highlighted in 2012 when the federal government passed omnibus bills C-38 and C-45. Together, the bills weaken environmental legislation in Canada by creating a new (but less comprehensive) environmental assessment law, giving sweeping discretionary powers to cabinet, and providing fewer opportunities for public participation (Ecojustice 2012b, 2012c). Specifically, the bills made significant changes to the Fisheries Act, the Indian Act, and the Navigable Waters Protection Act, each of which has wide-ranging implications for First Nations. For example, changes to the Fisheries Act mean that only those species of fish with commercial value, and their habitats, will be protected by the federal government. And decisions pertaining to which fish will be protected and what kind of protection they will receive will be made by cabinet without public input and with very little public scrutiny.

The Indian Act, which guides federal-Indian relations and sets out the mechanism for federal governance of "Indian" affairs through the department of Aboriginal Affairs and Northern Development, was also changed by Bill C-45. The intention of the change was economic in nature. The amendment allows First Nations communities, through a simple majority vote at a meeting or referendum, to lease designated reserve lands. Prior to this, bands required a majority vote from all eligible voters, which was a more onerous and time-consuming hurdle. However, the change is not as fundamentally significant as one might imagine because the federal AAND minister maintains the discretionary authority to call band meetings and to accept or refuse a land designation after receiving a resolution from the band council (McGregor 2012).

As discussed in Chapter 6, the Navigable Waters Protection Act was originally passed in 1882. The law granted the federal government oversight of and control over Canada's waterways, including shipping, navigating, and dumping. The new Navigation Protection Act (its name was changed in the 2012 bill) excludes 99 per cent of Canada's lakes and more than 99 per cent of Canada's rivers from federal oversight. For the few navigable waters that remain regulated under the NPA, the protection offered by the law is significantly weakened (Ecojustice 2012b). The provinces now retain authority over most rivers and lakes in the country—making this legislation a prime example of federal offloading of administrative responsibility. The Constitution, as mentioned, is not always clear on who has responsibility for and stewardship of water or about what water rights rest with First Nations. But the Harper administration has interpreted the Constitution as implying that water is property, so the provinces own water.

While the federal government was giving oversight to provinces, Saskatchewan was busy transforming its Saskatchewan Watershed Authority into a new institution called the Water Security Agency. This new agency "leads management of the province's water resources to ensure safe drinking water sources and reliable water supplies for economic, environmental and social benefits for Saskatchewan people" (SWSA 2012). Why are these facts relevant to a discussion of Aboriginal peoples' role in influencing environmental policy? Neither the Conservative federal government (with a majority in Parliament) nor Saskatchewan's conservative provincial government (with a majority in the provincial legislature) sought consultation or input from affected Aboriginal peoples before making these changes. The two omnibus bills passed, and the Water Security Agency was created without much regard for prior promises or commitments to the First Nations. Thus, in the span of a few months, the ground beneath Treaty 4 Indians shifted significantly. The legislative changes shifted political and economic oversight of water and related economic activities from the federal to the provincial state authorities, loosened administrative oversight at all levels, and created new discretionary powers for federal cabinet ministers.

The response from Treaty 4 Indians, represented by the File Hills Qu'Appelle Tribal Council (FHQTC), was that the federal government had violated the terms of Treaty 4. According to the tribal chairs, these omnibus bills are evidence of the "Federal Government's attack and disregard of their Inherent and Treaty Rights through lack of consultation and unilateral imposition of legislation" (FHQTC 2012). Beyond the issue of consultation, which is significant in its own right, the federal government cannot give authority or even oversight to the provinces because "Indians" (and Treaty 4 itself) do not recognize Saskatchewan as a legitimate source of state authority. The FHQTC never signed any agreement with Saskatchewan pertaining to water or wildlife and fish. Treaty 4 exists strictly between the federal government and Qu'Appelle Indians. Moreover, it is the position of Treaty 4 Indians that they did not "surrender all their powers and land, water and resource rights. This assertion is strongly supported by a brief review of the treaties: no treaties indicate that the signatory First Nations released all their governance powers and all their land, water and resource rights" (Phare 2009).

Environmental Justice and Idle No More

Idle No More is an ongoing social and environmental movement that started in Saskatchewan in November 2012 with a series of "teach-ins." The motivation for the movement was omnibus Bill C-45 and the treatment of indigenous treaty rights by the federal government.

Specifically, Bill C-45 made changes to the Navigable Waters Protection Act and the Indian Act. These changes were made without consulting Aboriginal Canadians and without going through formal debate in Parliament.

As a movement, Idle No More gained momentum quickly, and rallies were held across Canada in December 2012 and early 2013. The movement's vision statement and manifesto are available at the Idle No More website (http://www.idlenomore.ca):

> Idle No More calls on all people to join in a peaceful revolution, to honour Indigenous sovereignty, and to protect the land and water.

The Idle No More movement has been linked to human rights issues and to pipeline politics. Nina Wilson, Sheelah McLean, Jessica Gordon, and Sylvia McAdam are considered the founders of the movement as their initial teach-in event in Saskatoon had the title "Idle No More." Apparently, Gordon first coined the phrase in an October tweet (see http://www.idlenomore.ca/living_history). The founders quickly organized a National Day of Action to coincide with Amnesty International's Human Rights Day on December 10. Many Idle No More rallies were held in conjunction with ongoing protests over the Northern Gateway Pipeline in British Columbia. Thus, these issues became linked. In fact, the Idle No More movement rejects resource extraction on First Nations lands and traditional territory. It is too soon to judge the outcomes or effects the movement. Like many social movements, Idle No More has suffered internal disagreements and has struggled with questions of leadership. Nevertheless, the ongoing presence and persistence of Idle No More keeps salient important Aboriginal environmental issues (see CBC 2013c; Coates 2015; Kino-nda-niimi Collective 2014).

Species at Risk

When Minister of the Environment David Anderson introduced Bill C-5 in the 37th Parliament on February 19, 2001, he said in his opening remarks that "Aboriginal communities are especially important in efforts to protect species at risk since so many endangered or threatened species are found on Aboriginal lands. Aboriginal peoples have been successfully involved in efforts to develop this legislation and they will be involved in the species at risk recovery efforts at every appropriate step" (Anderson 2001). Even though Bill C-5, which would become the Species at Risk Act (SARA), was significantly modified before being passed, Anderson's remarks ring true as Aboriginal people did play a role in shaping the law, and they continue to be a centripetal force in conservation efforts in Canada.

The preamble of SARA makes clear that "the roles of aboriginal peoples of Canada and of wildlife management boards established under land claims agreements in the conservation of wildlife in this country are essential" and, therefore, "the traditional knowledge of the aboriginal peoples of Canada should be considered in the assessment of which species may be at risk and in developing and implementing recovery measures" (Species at Risk Act, S.C. 2002, c. 29). However, the law does not specifically define "Aboriginal peoples" or **Aboriginal traditional knowledge**. A new set of guidelines, released in 2010, addresses what constitutes traditional knowledge (see textbox).

What Is Aboriginal Traditional Knowledge?

The United Nations defines traditional knowledge as "the knowledge, innovations and practices of indigenous and local communities around the world. Developed from experience gained over the centuries and adapted to the local culture and environment, traditional knowledge is transmitted orally from generation to generation. It tends to be collectively owned and takes the form of stories, songs, folklore, proverbs, cultural values, beliefs, rituals, community laws, local language, and agricultural practices, including the development of plant species and animal breeds" (Convention on Biological Diversity n.d.).

It is important to think of Aboriginal traditional knowledge (ATK) and the subset of this knowledge, known as traditional ecological knowledge (TEK), as comprehensive worldviews. Canadian Aboriginals have a different way of knowing things and communicating information. ATK is often contrasted with "Western science." Many non-Aboriginal Canadians know about the world and make decisions based on scientific tools of observation and experimentation. Science is predicated upon validity, causal statements, and generalization. As the UN definition states, ATK tends to rely on different ways of knowing things about the world. Both ATK and Western science are valuable sources of information about the environment in Canada.

When Canada ratified the United Nations Convention on Biological Diversity (UNCBD), it committed to maintaining and preserving Aboriginal knowledge and to including that knowledge meaningfully in conservation practices, as outlined in Article 8(j). This article of the UNCBD states that each county party, "[s]ubject to its national legislation, respect, preserve and maintain knowledge, innovations and practices of indigenous and local communities embodying traditional lifestyles relevant for the conservation and sustainable use of biological diversity and promote their wider application with the approval and involvement of the holders of such knowledge, innovation and practices, and encourage the equitable sharing of the benefits arising from the utilization of such knowledge, innovations and practices" (see Convention on Biological Diversity 2014).

SARA requires that Environment Canada establish a council, to be known as the National Aboriginal Council on Species at Risk (NACOSAR), consisting of six representatives of the Aboriginal peoples of Canada selected by the minister based upon recommendations from Aboriginal organizations. The role of the council is to advise the minister on the administration of SARA and to provide advice and recommendations to the Canadian Endangered Species Conservation Council. NACOSAR meets once a year with the environment minister, where it reports on recovery, stewardship, enforcement, and other areas of concern to Aboriginal peoples.

Beyond NACOSAR, the law also states that COSEWIC (see chapters 1 and 5) "must carry out its functions on the basis of the best available information on the biological status of a species, including scientific knowledge, community knowledge and aboriginal traditional knowledge" (Species at Risk Act, S.C. 2002, c. 29, 15(2)). To accomplish this, COSEWIC must establish a "subcommittee specializing in aboriginal traditional knowledge" (Species at Risk, S.C. 2002, c. 29, 18(1)). In 2010, COSEWIC developed guidelines on how ATK would be received through the subcommittee. These guidelines describe ATK as based on "knowledge of the relationships between humans, wildlife, spirituality, environmental conditions, and land forms in a defined locality and, frequently, over lengthy time periods" (Government of Canada 2012d). The goal of the subcommittee is to provide ATK since "bringing together ATK and Western Science knowledge will benefit species by providing another perspective for COSEWIC's wildlife species assessments" (Government of Canada 2012d). However, neither the express language of SARA nor its subsequent interpretations have provided adequate guidance for how ATK is to be collected or used for conservation purposes.

SARA clearly carves out a large role for Aboriginal peoples. If the law were followed as written, the NACOSAR and the ATK subcommittee would be meaningfully involved in almost every step of conservation. However, when asked to comment on the implementation of SARA, Aboriginal leaders explained that how the law works in practice is much different than how it is written. Moreover, the statutory language of some of SARA's provisions is problematic, so Aboriginal peoples are seeking to amend the law along with ensuring its effective implementation (Olive 2014a).

CONCLUSIONS

Aboriginal peoples have rights to land and resources in Canada. According to AANDC, almost 3.4 million hectares of land in Canada were reserve lands in 2014—with over 17,000 of those being managed by self-governing bands with their own administrative capacity to make independent policies regarding property, water, education, health, and other issues, depending on the band (AANDC 2014b). Also, Aboriginal groups either own outright millions of hectares of land or have extensive authority over that land by virtue of land claim agreements. In 1991, a group of First Nation chiefs approached AANDC with a proposal to allow First Nations to opt out of the Indian Act provisions dealing with land and resources. These discussions resulted in the Framework Agreement on First Nation Land Management (Framework Agreement), signed by Canada and 14 First Nations in 1996. The First Nations Land Management Act, which received royal assent on June 17, 1999, ratified and gave effect to the Framework Agreement. The First Nations that signed the Framework Agreement established a central Lands Advisory Board and a Resource Centre to assist them in implementing their own land management regimes (AANDC 2013b).

The result is that, today, First Nations and Métis are important land managers and resource users in the country. Their rights, primarily set down in a royal proclamation in the eighteenth century, have been reinforced by the Canadian court system's legal judgments. However, neither these legal decisions nor the Royal Commission on Aboriginal Peoples' recommendations have been taken seriously enough by Canada's policymakers. Nevertheless, environmental problems and issues such as fishing and water rights are challenging the government to work more collaboratively with Aboriginal groups.

Indigenous peoples have a long historical claim to Canada's land and natural resources. As the original, or native, inhabitants of the continent, indigenous peoples have a unique relationship to the lands and waters of

North America, and their knowledge of environmental issues is ancient. In the past few decades, the Inuit have settled numerous modern treaties or land claim agreements. These and earlier agreements between Aboriginals and the Canadian government make Aboriginal Canadians significant actors in environmental policymaking. Moreover, they create a new level of governance in Canada, one that negotiates environmental policy differently in different contexts. In many ways, this governance structure also places Ottawa firmly inside environmental policy in Canada.

There is no denying federal involvement in Aboriginal environmental policy. In fact, in this one area of environmental policy, provincial authority, responsibility, and autonomy are severely limited. The federal government, and its laws, always trumps the provinces when it comes to Aboriginal affairs because the Constitution clearly gives jurisdiction over "Indians, and Lands reserved for Indians" to Ottawa. Through time, this federal power has evolved into significant environmental regulatory and protection responsibilities. The recognition of treaty land titles, the First Nations Land Management Act of 1999, and the comprehensive land agreements in the North include environmental protection of Aboriginal lands.

However, even though the courts have recognized Aboriginal title and claims, federal policy related to Aboriginals and the environment and the policymaking process in Ottawa have been slow to evolve. Today, many treaty promises are unfulfilled. For example, in many places in Canada, Aboriginal Canadians do not have access to safe drinking water on their reserves. Policy is needed quickly to address this issue. Likewise, the potential for pipelines and oil and gas development threatens Aboriginal lands and traditional hunting and fishing rights. More protection is needed to safeguard treaty rights. The Idle No More Movement is a response to the policy failure of Ottawa. We can expect that, in the next decade, the federal government will have to play policy catch-up because of the court systems' ongoing assurance of Aboriginal rights and claims.

Key Terms

Aboriginal; Inuit; First Nations; Métis; indigenous; treaties; reserve; traditional territory; self-government; Indian Act; Calder case; Aboriginal title; Aboriginal land claims; Aboriginal traditional knowledge

Discussion Questions

1. Why is it important to make a clear distinction between First Nations, Inuit, and Métis when discussing "Aboriginal" environmental policy or law?

2. What is the difference between reserve land, traditional territory, and Aboriginal titled land? In what ways do the differences matter for environmental policy in Canada?
3. Why does the federal government incorporate Aboriginal traditional knowledge (ATK) in species at risk recovery plans?
4. What does Aboriginal self-government mean for the environment?
5. Why has the Supreme Court become so involved in Aboriginal and environmental policy over the past 35 years?

Suggested Readings

Borrows, John. 2006. *Recovering Canada: The Resurgence of Indigenous Law.* Toronto: University of Toronto Press.

Borrows, John. 2010. *Canada's Indigenous Constitution.* Toronto: University of Toronto Press.

McGregor, Deborah. 2002. "Traditional Ecological Knowledge and the Two-Row Wampum." *Biodiversity* 3 (3): 8–9. http://dx.doi.org/10.1080/14888386.2002 .9712586.

McGregor, Deborah. 2004. "Coming Full Circle: Indigenous Knowledge, Environment, and Our Future." *American Indian Quarterly* 28 (3–4): 385–410. http://dx.doi .org/10.1353/aiq.2004.0101.

McGregor, Deborah. 2008. "Anishnaabe-Kwe, Traditional Knowledge, and Water Protection." *Canadian Women Studies* 26 (3–4) 26.

McKenzie, Judith I. 2002. *Environmental Politics in Canada: Managing the Commons into the Twenty-First Century.* Oxford: Oxford University Press.

Schlosberg, David, and David Carruthers. 2010. "Indigenous Struggles, Environmental Justice, and Community Capabilities." *Global Environmental Politics* 10 (4): 12–35. http://dx.doi.org/10.1162/GLEP_a_00029.

Walker, Gordon. 2012. *Environmental Justice: Concepts, Evidence and Politics.* Abingdon, UK: Routledge.

Young, Nathan, and Ralph Matthews. 2010. *The Aquaculture Controversy in Canada: Activism, Policy, and Contested Science.* Vancouver: UBC Press.

Chapter 10

Politics and Policy in the North and Far North

THE ARCTIC IS A MELTING and, thus, rapidly changing place. New policy is needed to manage developing issues from political (sovereignty and co-management) to economic (oil and trade) to environmental (climate change). We have the opportunity for long-term planning. And, in the North, Canada is a major international player. Canada's role is mainly the result of geography; over 40 per cent of the country's landmass lies in the North (Government of Canada 2013). But politically, Canada is also aligning itself as an Arctic power. Why? In part, Canada is making this move because, according to the US Geological Survey, the Arctic may contain 30 per cent of the world's undiscovered natural gas reserves and as much as 13 per cent of its undiscovered oil (USGS 2008a, 2008b). Canada stands to gain a lot from the natural resources in the North. A question remains, however. Will Canada be a good steward of the Arctic environment?

Canada has always been a northern nation on a map. Yet most of its population resides along the country's southern border. In the twenty-first century, we may witness a shift in demography as more Canadians move north—likely for economic opportunities. Recently, Prime Minister Harper has made a concerted effort to put "more boots on the Arctic tundra"—to have Canadians occupy the entirety of their territory so as to make a stronger use claim in sovereignty conflicts (Government of Canada 2009, 9). In a speech announcing the John G. Diefenbaker Icebreaker Project, Harper proclaimed his commitment to Arctic sovereignty: "The True North is our destiny, for our explorers, for our entrepreneurs, for our artists. And to not embrace its promise now at the dawn of its ascendancy would be to turn our backs on what it is to be Canadian" (Harper 2008). This political rhetoric has been a centrepiece of the Harper administration dating to its 2006 ascendancy to government. In fact, in his second Speech from the Throne, Prime Minister Harper made the Arctic a focus, and his government has maintained a heightened economic interest in the region (Privy Council Office 2007).

This chapter opens with a discussion of the geography of the Arctic and of northern Canada, including the North's indigenous inhabitants. Following is a brief history of how Canada came to be a northern nation and the second largest country in the world. This history is critical because Canada continues to make sovereignty claims over vast northern territories and hopes to secure claims to the North Pole and the Northwest Passage. Understanding Canada's history, then, is essential to comprehending the debate over "ownership" in the North. Next, the chapter moves to an overview of government and governance in the North—both domestically and internationally. The Arctic Council is now an internationally recognized governing body in the North, but it faces many governance challenges that will only be magnified as the climate warms. The chapter closes by examining some of the most important issues for the environment in the Arctic: energy politics, including pipelines, and the (Canadian) Northwest Passage.

WHAT IS THE ARCTIC? WHERE IS THE ARCTIC?

The word "arctic" comes from the Greek word *arkitkos* meaning "near the bear," which is a reference to the constellations Great Bear and Little Bear—locators of Polaris, the north star. The arctic is not a "place" so much as an ocean—a frozen ocean to be exact (at least it's frozen now). However, definitions of the **Arctic** are contested (see Grant 2010, 6). It is generally considered to be anything north of the Arctic Circle, or 66° 33'N (as of June 2015; the Arctic Circle shifts because of changes in Earth's axis over thousands of years). Others see the Arctic as a region north of where mean July temperatures are 10° C, and, finally, some consider it as the area north of the natural treeline. Trees do not grow past a certain latitude because the climate is too cold or dry. Some consider the place at which trees stop growing to signify the edge of the Arctic. If definitions were to involve temperatures or treelines, the Arctic would be getting smaller because trees are growing further North as the climate warms (Pearson et al. 2013). This suggests that the latitudinal measurement of the southern boundary of the Arctic Circle is a more robust signifier of the Arctic. From an international geopolitical perspective, then, the Arctic comprises parts of Russia, Canada, the United States, Norway, Sweden, Finland, Denmark (Greenland), and Iceland. Together, these countries are known as the "Arctic 8." In the centre of the Arctic Circle lies the North Pole of Earth. No one "owns" the North Pole or the Arctic Ocean. The Law of the Sea, discussed below, grants sovereign nations a 200-nautical-mile (370-km) claim around their coasts. (See United Nations 2013).

The peoples of the Arctic, those who have lived there for thousands of years, include the Inuit in Canada, the United States, and Greenland; the Sami in Norway, Sweden, Finland, and parts of Russia; the Koryak, Chukchi, Samoyedic, and Ugric peoples and the Evenks in Russia; and the Alutiiq and Yup'ik in the United States. Collectively, these groups can be referred to as "circumpolar peoples" (see Irimoto and Yamada 2004 for a more complete discussion of ethnicity and identity in the North). As Map 10.1 shows, in Canada, most of Nunavut, the northern part of the Northwest Territories, and the very northern tip of Yukon are part of the Arctic. Thus, technically, not all Inuit in Canada live in the "Arctic Circle." For example, Iqaluit, the capital of Nunavut, lies just south of the circle. Nevertheless, Inuit—which means "people" in Inuktitut—have occupied Canada's northern lands and waterways for millennia. As discussed in Chapter 4, long before the arrival of Europeans, Inuit hunters and fishers and their families moved with the seasons and developed a unique culture and way of life deeply rooted in the vast land (Government of Canada 2009).

In the United States, the term "Eskimo" is used to describe groups who are culturally similar to the Inuit of Greenland and Canada, such as the Alutiq and Yup'ik. Groups such as the Aleut are sometimes also referred to as "Eskimos," although they are culturally distinct from Inuit peoples (Williams 2009). The indigenous people of the Scandinavian countries are called Sami and are distinct from the Inuit, although they share a similar lifestyle and a similar political existence in their home countries. These two similarities are also true of Russia's indigenous peoples of the North—the Koryak, Chukchi, Samoyedic, and Ugric peoples and the Evenks—yet these groups are distinct from each other and from the Inuit. (See Irimoto and Yamada 2004 and Hoffecker 2005 for a history of the circumpolar peoples.) Although these indigenous groups are different for one another, they share a deep cultural and physical bond to the Arctic region. Climate change and pollution and resource extraction projects, as well as future trade through the North, will greatly affect these peoples. It is important to keep in mind that the Arctic is now, and always has been, their homeland. Any discussion of the Arctic's environment, politics, and economics must involve an awareness of indigenous peoples in the area.

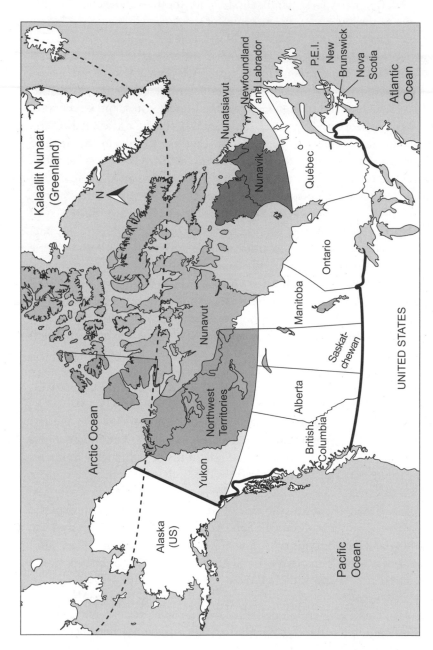

MAP 10.1 Canada's Territorial North, including Yukon, Northwest Territories, Nunavut, Nunavik (Québec), and Nunatsiavut (Newfoundland and Labrador)

It is important to be clear, both geographically and politically, about terms. Northern Canada comprises the three territories: Yukon, Northwest Territories, and Nunavut. Map 10.1 clearly illustrates the size of these three territories. The Far North and the Arctic are interchangeable terms in Canada—both refer to the area north of 66° 33' N. This degree of latitude is marked by the Arctic Circle line on Map 10.1. Canada has a "Northern Strategy" that lays out domestic policy for the three territories, including the Arctic, which is considered part of the North. The inhabitants of Canada's North include First Nations people and Inuit. In the Arctic, or the "Far North," there are mainly Inuit. Therefore, it is possible to talk about the North without specifically making reference to the Arctic. In fact, the capital cities of all three territories lie outside the Arctic. Likewise, it is possible to talk about the Inuit without referring to the Arctic. In general, however, when Canadians say **northern policy**, they mean policy in the three territories—including the Arctic (Natural Resources Canada 2015b).

As the North stretches across a vast geography, it is difficult to speak of one "northern" or even "Arctic" environment. Most of the Far North in Canada, the part beyond the treeline, is ice tundra. Most of the Canadian North is flat like the plains of Saskatchewan, but there are mountains in Nunavut and the Northwest Territories called the Innuitian Mountains (part of the Arctic Cordillera). Because it is so cold in this part of the world, these mountains remain virtually unexplored by humans (Natural Resources Canada 2015b). As mentioned in chapters 5 and 6, many Canadian rivers flow north into the Arctic Ocean. The Arctic Ocean watershed drains a large portion of Alberta and northern British Columbia and Saskatchewan, as well as part of Yukon, the Northwest Territories, and Nunavut. The Hudson Bay watershed, the largest ocean watershed in Canada, also empties into the Arctic Ocean eventually, after travelling through Manitoba.

Despite the cold, desert-like conditions, the North is full of life. The polar bear has become the international symbol of the Arctic and represents the challenges presented in the North by climate change. But the North contains more than just polar bears and seals. About 67 species of land mammals and 35 species of marine mammals inhabit the region, at least seasonally (Reid, Berteaux and Laidre 2013). Most of them have been central to the Inuit diet for thousands of years. There are also 200 species of birds that migrate through the North each year; species range from the common ruddy turnstone to the endangered ivory gull (Ganter and Gaston 2013). There is very little vascular plant life in the North, but moss, lichen, and algae are somewhat common (Daniels, Gillespie, and Poulin 2013). A reason for the relatively poor vascular plant flora is that soil is very thin in the North and often covered with ice or snow. And though there are four seasons in the North, winter and summer predominate. Winter is marked by almost 24 hours of darkness and summer by 24 hours of light. These extremes make it difficult for life to survive in an already cold climate.

One of the largest threats to life in the Arctic is climate change (AMAP 2012). As the planet warms, the sea ice melts—a phenomenon that is happening faster than expected and in ways not yet fully understood by climate science. Climate change resulting from human activity is widely accepted as fact by scientists and the consensus of the community is represented by the Intergovernmental Panel on Climate Change, as discussed in Chapter 8. However, some phenomena related to climate change in the North are not yet scientifically understood. For example, as ice melts in the Arctic, it releases long-stored methane from the ice. Methane is a known greenhouse gas (GHG). Thus, GHG emissions from carbon use in the south cause ice to melt in the North, which causes the release of more methane. How quickly will this additional release of GHG speed up climate change? Such complex interactions are difficult for experts to model (Corell et al. 2008; McGuire et al. 2010). Moreover, scientists know that permafrost, soil that stays below the freezing point of water for at least two years, can absorb GHGs such as methane, but how much and how quickly is not known (McGuire et al. 2010; Tarnocai et al. 2009). And will higher temperatures see the retrenchment of permafrost, which now covers most of the North? Simply put, climate change is affecting the North—but how and how quickly is an ongoing scientific study. We do know that climate change is affecting all life in the North. And the warmer climate is bringing more people and more resource extraction possibilities to the area. In the twenty-first century, the Canadian Arctic will experience iceless summers during which shipping through the Arctic Ocean will be easier than at any time in recorded history.

"DISCOVERY" AND SOVEREIGNTY

Sir Martin Frobisher laid claim to land in the Arctic for England in 1576, when he reached Baffin Island on his expedition in search of the Northwest Passage. During this first voyage, he did encounter Inuit living on the land, but this part of the map was nevertheless considered *terra nullius*, or "land belonging to no one" because no European nation had claimed it (see Grant 2010 for an excellent history of sovereignty in the North American Arctic region). Thus, this part of the Arctic and the parts visited by Frobisher during his two subsequent voyages in 1577 and 1578 were claimed by England, which financed voyages to the region for decades after this European discovery. Although there were government-funded expeditions to the North in the sixteenth through the nineteenth centuries, many were financed by private traders. (Frobisher's first voyage was backed by the Muscovy Company, a group of English merchants trading with Russia.) During the sixteenth century, the rising merchant class in Europe was able to provide private funding and resources for world exploration. So Frobisher had plenty of company in North American waters, most notably Danes.

The Hudson's Bay Company (HBC), a private company originally based on the trade of furs, was established in 1670 (see Binnema 2014 for a history of the HBC). The company became a very large land-owner in the North American Arctic and essentially held title to what was known as Rupert's Land. In fact, the HBC came into existence when King Charles II, claiming he had every right to do so, gave "the Governor and Company of Adventurers of England" an exclusive trading monopoly over all the lands whose rivers and streams drained into Hudson Bay (HBC 2015b). Affected was an area of about 3 million square miles. For almost 100 years, the HBC was a very profitable trading company and established many outlets in the North. Even today, if you travel through the Canadian North you can see old HBC buildings left standing, such as the one in Apex, just outside Iqaluit, that was originally established in 1670. Map 10.2 of northern North America in the nineteenth century just after Canadian Confederation depicts the vast size of Rupert's Land.

During the decade before Canadian Confederation, the HBC faced increasing criticism, however. Settlers were moving westward, and proponents of Canada's growing expansionist movement saw the company as an impediment to development. Added to Canadian and British desires to settle the West were fears of American expansionism. By the mid-1800s, the US Monroe Doctrine of 1823, proclaiming that further European advancement or meddling in the Americas (North or South) would be considered acts of aggression, had combined with the notion of Manifest Destiny, which argued that it was the duty of the United States to expand westward its form of democracy and culture, and that this duty was both obvious (manifest) and certain (destiny). A practical expression of this ideology was a series of explorations of the American West in 1853–55 to find possible routes for the first transcontinental railroad across North America—expeditions supported by the US Department of War. Although the American Civil War relieved fears of American expansionism in the early 1860s, the US purchase of Alaska from the Russians in 1867 (for $7.2 million) revived them. Under pressure from the British Colonial Office, the HBC entered into complicated three-way

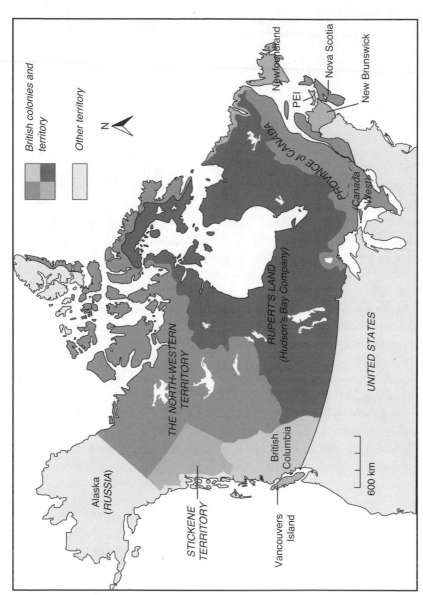

MAP 10.2 Map of Northern America in 1862, before Canadian Confederation

SOURCE: *Canadian Geographic*, "Historical Maps of Canada," Map 1862, http://www.canadiangeographic.ca/mapping/historical_maps/1862
.asp. Reprinted by permission.

negotiations to sell Rupert's Land, which it did in 1869 for the bargain price of $1.5 million. The HBC kept title over 120 of its posts and about 5 per cent of the territory, but it surrendered the rest of this huge territory to the British Crown, which in turn ceded the land to Canada (HBC 2015a). The new country picked up the tab, with the help of a loan guarantee from Britain.

During this period, the United States was also in the business of acquiring Arctic territory. In the nineteenth century, Russia had control over present-day Alaska. However, by mid-century, Russia was at war with Britain, France, and Turkey in Crimea, and it could neither supply nor defend Alaska because of Britain's naval dominance. Also, Russia had very little money and could not easily profit from the Alaskan trade when relations with Britain were frosty. Thus, even though the Crimean War ended in 1856, the decision was made to sell Alaska to the Americans. On March 30, 1867, the United States agreed to Russia's offer to sell Alaska for $7.2 million (see Naske and Slotnick 2011 for a thorough history of Alaska). This price was quite high, considering Canada would pay only $1.5 million three years later for a much larger and more profitable swath of North America (Rupert's Land).

The day before this agreement, March 29, 1867, Queen Victoria signed the British North America Act and created "Canada." Keep in mind that Canada, at this time, was actually quite small, as Map 10.2 illustrates. It was during the next 100 years, beginning in 1869–70 with the acquisition of Rupert's Land, that Canada became the second largest country in the world with the largest coastline in the world. This development is somewhat surprising given that Canada did not have many people and relied on Britain for its military and for any ships capable of Arctic navigation until the early twentieth century. (The Royal Canadian Navy did not come into being until 1911.)

Yet Canada survived and developed into an advanced industrial capitalist economy. How did this happen? How was Canada able to maintain control over such a vast territory? We must remember that Canada began life as the Dominion of Canada and is still part of the Commonwealth. This connection with Britain was a significant help geopolitically in early years. But what about more modern times? How has Canada, with only about 35.5 million people as of 2014, claimed such a significant portion of Earth's landmass? It was in large part because of the United States—its friendship, political influence, military support, economic trade, and desire to maintain peace, security, and control in North America.

AMERICAN INFLUENCE ON CANADA'S ARCTIC

There is no denying that Canada's Arctic has been shaped by American military history (Grant 2010). The Americans brought people and infrastructure to the North, including Canada's North and Greenland. During the early years of World War II, when the fighting looked as if it might spread to North America, Canada and the United States signed the Ogdensburg Agreement on cooperative defence (August 1940). The agreement created the Permanent Joint Board on Defence to assess and recommend projects beneficial to the defence of North America. After this agreement, the United States built weather and radio stations across Alaska, Yukon, and the Northwest Territories.

Two years after the start of World War II, Canada and the United States issued the Hyde Park Declaration of 1941, which allowed American-produced war materials made in Canada for Britain to be included in the "Lend-Lease" agreement by which US war materials were transferred to Britain and its allies in return for deferred payment. Canada and the United States cooperated in the North to organize supply routes too. Newfoundland (not yet part of Canada) allowed the United States Army Air Force to build its own installations at Gander airport to facilitate air cargo transport to supply Britain. The airport, the largest in the world in 1940, had been turned over to the Canadian military for the duration of the war.

Canada was not the only country to ask for American assistance with defence. Greenland, a colony of Denmark left on its own after the Germans captured that country in 1940, asked for and received the protection of the United States. Iceland, a sovereign kingdom with Denmark's King Christian X as head of state, was also granted US protection. Therefore, during World War II, the United States was deeply involved in the protection of the entire North American Arctic, ranging from Alaska to Iceland. This American presence, which grew immeasurably during the Cold War, is what Shelagh Grant (2010) refers to as US de facto sovereignty of the North.

When Japan bombed Pearl Harbor in Hawaii, the ramifications for Alaska were huge. In some ways, Alaska became front and centre in the US war effort (Grant 2010; Naske and Slotnick 2011). Alaska, too, was bombed by Japan, and some of the remote Aleutian Islands, part of the Alaska Territory, were invaded and occupied in June of 1942. Alaskan forces were increased and activated for wartime duty. Because Alaska was not a US state at the time, but a territory akin to Canada's Yukon, it was under the full direction of the US federal government. Airports across northern Canada and Newfoundland were linked with one another and with Alaska. The Alaska Territorial Guard and the Canadian Rangers, composed mainly of indigenous soldiers, were established and put into full force. World War II changed the North by bringing infrastructure and people to the region. It also put the region on the map and in the minds of many North Americans who had never given much thought to the Arctic.

After World War II, the United States withdrew from the Canadian Arctic—but only for a few years. The Cold War between the United States–led Western Bloc and Soviet-dominated Eastern Bloc, which began in the late 1940s, was also a major influence on Canada's Arctic region (Grant 2010). Because both the Soviets and the Americans possessed nuclear weapons after 1949, the threat of full military engagement was low, thus making the war "cold." Instead, there was a space race, an arms race, and much tension and contempt between the two countries. It can also be considered an ideological war, as American capitalism and democracy went up against Soviet communism and central planning. Unfortunately, Canada and Greenland were geographically between the two warring countries, although allied firmly with the United States. To guard against nuclear attacks from the Soviet Union, Canada and the United States cooperated on a series of early warning systems in the North. The Pinetree Line, completed in 1954, was the first. That same year, the two governments agreed to the construction of the Distant Early Warning Line (DEW Line) along the Arctic coast from Alaska to Baffin Island. The Americans paid for construction but Canada retained ownership of sites located in Canada. The DEW line was a radar system stretching from one station to the next that could detect any air movement and thus warn of any impending airborne attack on the US mainland. Each radar station had its own electricity, heating, and water supply. Because the stations had to be checked by human ground crews every few months, each station also had surrounding communities with recreation areas, homes, and roads. These settlements and military installations brought significant change to the Arctic—changes in transportation, communications, and land use. The need for mutual defence also brought about an era of cooperation, for the purposes of security, between the United States and Canada in the North American Arctic.

Perhaps equally important during the Cold War era, but unrelated to it, was the discovery of oil in Alaska (Naske and Slotnick 2011). In many ways, this discovery also created a fundamental shift in the way Americans saw their northern region. For Native Americans, nothing would ever be the same again. A flood of policy actors entered into the political arena in Alaska, including those from the oil industry, environmental groups, and commercial shipping, as well as developers and interested citizens (Nuttall 2010). The Inuit and Eskimo also started to organize themselves and make land claims and demands for self-government. How the Americans dealt with oil exploration and settled claims with Native Americans differs greatly from the Canadian experience. However, it is important to note that the United States has had an enormous impact on the Canadian North. The US military has often been Canada's first line of Northern defence, and this reliance on the US armed forces poses challenges when Canada makes sovereignty claims against the United States.

LAWS IN THE ARCTIC

Since the seventeenth century, nations have followed a **freedom of the seas** doctrine, a tacit understanding that a state's jurisdiction over oceans and seas extended three nautical miles off its coast and anything beyond that three miles was "international waters" open to everyone and belonging to no one (United Nations 1998). In times of peace, countries enjoyed a basic right of passage in all international waters. In the early twentieth century, states began expressing the desire to extend their territory for security reasons and for mineral and fishing rights (United Nations 1998). In 1949, just four years after it was created, the United Nations recognized the need to address the issue of conflicting claims over territorial waters. Consequently, it decided to convene in 1958 the first United Nations Conference on the Law of the Sea (UNCLOS). Four conventions were adopted at this conference, and these entered into force between 1962 and 1964. At a third conference (1973–82), the **United Nations Convention on the Law of the Sea**, less formally known as the "Law of the Sea" treaty, was created, and it was officially opened for signature in 1982 and entered into force in 1994. This treaty defines the rights and responsibilities of all countries when it comes to the oceans—it also offers environmental and business guidelines (United Nations 2013). Canada is a signatory to this treaty, as are all Arctic nations except the United States. Today, the UN Convention on the Law of the Sea is one of the most important international treaties governing or guiding action in the Arctic Circle. It will likely be tried and tested in the next two decades as more countries commit to resource extraction in the North and as shipping routes begin to open.

Outside of international law in the Arctic, Canada does have at least one domestic policy with potentially huge international consequences. Canada passed the Arctic Waters Pollution Prevention Act in

1970, which declared the country's right to enforce pollution control in offshore Arctic waters. According to Canada, this control includes the ability to limit pollution from oil tankers by regulating their passage through waters made hazardous because of almost year-round ice (Transport Canada 2012). The law is a "zero-discharge" act that states "no person or ship shall deposit or permit the deposit of waste of any type in the Arctic waters" (Transport Canada 2012). Fundamentally, the act is an attempt to regulate traffic through Arctic waters.

In 2008, Harper announced that the definition of "Arctic waters" in the act would be changed to bring it in line with the UN Convention on the Law of the Sea, which allows coastal states to apply pollution prevention laws out to 200 nautical miles from the shore (the original limit imposed by the 1970 act was 100 nautical miles out). For the most part, however, this domestic policy has been ignored by other countries, which believe they can pass through Arctic waters without Canadian permission (Byers 2006). It is true that no ships are depositing waste into Canadian waters, but air pollution from the oil tankers could be beyond Canada's control. This discussion will be taken up again at the end of the chapter, when we turn to considering the fate of the Northwest Passage.

ABORIGINAL CO-MANAGEMENT OF THE NORTH

As mentioned in Chapter 9, the Government of Canada and northern Aboriginal groups have settled various land claims agreements dating back to 1975. These agreements have been termed comprehensive because they detail the arrangement between the Government of Canada and Aboriginal groups. They are recognized by the Government of Canada as modern treaties and enjoy constitutional protection under Section 35 of the Constitution Act, 1982. Of particular importance are the provisions for land and resource management. Almost all land in the territories is Crown land—meaning it is owned and managed by the federal government. Land claim agreements create co-management of land and resources between Aboriginal groups and the Government of Canada in specific geographical areas. In the past 20 years, the Inuit and Canada have negotiated, for example, the creation of Nunavut (1999), Nunavik (2007), and the Labrador Inuit Settlement Area (2008). Each land claim agreement is unique. In general, however, they all involve surrendering title to traditional lands (but not the associated Aboriginal rights) in exchange for cash payment; Aboriginal private (fee-simple) ownership of selected land parcels, with subsurface rights granted for some land parcels; important governance provisions; and a range of economic benefits (see White 2009 for an in-depth discussion).

Co-management is like federalism in the sense that it denotes power sharing. It means that boards that manage programs and resources, including those for wildlife, share power with official territorial governments and Aboriginal organizations. These boards are independent of the territorial governments and intended to be impartial, or non-ideological. Board composition is the most visible and important component of co-management (see White 2009). For example, the Nunavut Wildlife Management Board oversees all decisions relating to hunting quotas, habitat protection, and the monitoring of the region's wildlife. That board has non-Aboriginal and Aboriginal members. In fact, four members out of the nine represent Aboriginal groups. Indeed, many co-management boards in the North have a strong majority of Aboriginal members, although some have 50 per cent or less.

That Aboriginal peoples hold the balance of power in these boards is an important aspect of governance in the North. Co-management boards also strive to include Aboriginal traditional knowledge (ATK) in the decision-making process. As discussed in the sections in chapters 8 and 9 on endangered species, traditional knowledge is the Aboriginal way of knowing and being in the world. It is comprises their culture, including their relationship to all living things, and their way of doing things. ATK, or in the case of the Inuit, IQ (which stands for Inuit Qaujimajatuqangit), is sought from elders who provide knowledge orally. Thus, co-management boards that include ATK or IQ must spend time consulting local communities and their elders to gather knowledge about a specific case, such as water use or polar bear hunting quotas. The challenge of a co-management board is balancing the Aboriginal way of doing things and knowing things with the non-Aboriginal way, which is typically bureaucratic and "scientific." Cooperation is not always easy and often fraught with disappointment and frustration on both sides. Nevertheless, that co-management thrives in the North is crucially important to all.

THE ARCTIC COUNCIL AND ARCTIC GOVERNANCE

Who is responsible for the Arctic, and how will Canada manage Arctic matters in the twenty-first century? On September 19, 1996, representatives from the eight Arctic nations created what is known as the **Arctic Council**. The council is committed to the well-being of the inhabitants of the Arctic, to recognizing the importance of their knowledge, to sustainable development, to protection of the Arctic environment, and to regular intergovernmental consideration of and consultation on Arctic issues (Government of Canada 2009). The first Arctic Council meeting was held in Canada. Together, the eight countries adopted the Iqaluit Declaration, which lays out the rules and procedures of the council, adds observer states and organizations, establishes working groups, creates oil and gas development guidelines, and agrees to assess jointly current and future shipping potential in the Arctic region (see the Arctic Council website for a full description).

Every two years, chairmanship of the council rotates among the eight Arctic nations. In 2013, chairmanship moved from Sweden to Canada, which chaired the council until the end of April 2015, when leadership rotated to the United States. Canadian Minister of the Environment Leona Aglukkaq chaired the council between 2013 and 2015. Aglukkaq is from Nunavut, which is part of the reason she was chosen as chair. That is to say, having a minister of the environment chair the Arctic Council is not standard. The current chair of the council is US Secretary of State John Kerry, for example. The nation with the chairmanship is responsible for maintaining all administrative aspects of the Arctic Council. It organizes and hosts the meetings and produces and distributes all reports and documents. In 2012, the council agreed to create a permanent secretariat in Tromso, Norway.

In addition to the secretariat, the council also has six working groups; each has a mandate, a chair, a management board, and a secretariat. These groups are the Arctic Contaminants Action Program; the Arctic Monitoring and Assessment Program; Conservation of Arctic Flora and Fauna; Emergency Prevention, Preparedness and Response; Protection of the Arctic Marine Environment; and the Sustainable Development Working Group. As research groups, these six bodies produce numerous reports that are publicly available on the Arctic Council website. For example, the Conservation of Arctic Flora and Fauna (CAFF) published *Arctic Biodiversity Trends 2010*, which was one of the first comprehensive reports on this subject. More recently, the group published *Arctic Biodiversity Assessment 2013*. In 2014, the CAFF hosted the Arctic Biodiversity Congress in Trondheim, Norway. The three-day conference brought together scientists, indigenous elders, policymakers, industry representatives, and representatives of civil society to discuss biodiversity in the world's North. The final report of the meeting can be found at http://www.arcticbiodiversity.is.

Table 10.1 presents the make-up of the Arctic Council. The eight member nations hold the legal power, as council decisions can be binding if agreed to by all member states. The permanent members, the six representatives from indigenous groups, are intended to provide Aboriginal representation in the council. (Only Iceland does not have indigenous peoples). The Arctic Inuit have been moderately successful at asserting their rights to land and to oil revenue. This success dates

TABLE 10.1 Member States and Organizations Affiliated with the Arctic Council

MEMBER NATIONS	PERMANENT MEMBERS	OBSERVER STATES	INTERGOVERNMENTAL ORGANIZATIONS
Russia	Arctic Athabaskan	France	International Federation of
United States	Council	Germany	Red Cross & Red Crescent
Canada	Aleut International	Netherlands	Societies
Norway	Association	Poland	International Union for the
Finland	Gwich'in Council	Spain	Conservation of Nature
Sweden	International	United Kingdom	Nordic Council of
Denmark	Inuit Circumpolar	**Added (2012)**	Ministers
Iceland	Council	China	Nordic Environment
	Russian Association	India	Finance Corporation
	of Indigenous Peoples	Italy	North Atlantic Marine
	of the North	Japan	Mammal Commission
	Saami Council	South Korea	Standing Committee of
		Singapore	the Parliamentarians of
		Ad Hoc	the Arctic Region
		EU	UN Economic Commission
		Turkey	for Europe
			UN Development Programme
			UN Environment Programme

to the creation of the Inuit Circumpolar Council (formerly the Inuit Circumpolar Conference), founded in 1977, which has since grown into a major international non-governmental organization representing approximately 150,000 Inuit of Alaska, Canada, Greenland, and Chukotka (Russia). The principal goals of the ICC are "to strengthen unity among Inuit of the circumpolar region; promote Inuit rights and interests on an international level; and develop and encourage long-term policies that safeguard the Arctic environment" (Arctic Council 2011a). Today, the ICC represents an important permanent member in the Arctic Council alongside the other five indigenous groups.

Permanent member groups of the Arctic Council may address the member nations and raise issues or objections that must be addressed by the chair. These groups may also help set the agenda for meetings, and they may participate in Arctic Council projects. However, it is important to note that permanent member status does not confer legal status or official recognition of the Inuit or other indigenous groups as sovereign peoples. Moreover, these permanent member groups do not vote on substantive policy matters—only the eight member nations can participate in those decisions (see www.arctic-council.org for a description of the council and for the set procedures for different member nations and organizations).

When the Arctic Council was first created, six non-Arctic countries were granted "observer status" so that they could attend the biannual ministerial meetings. However, these countries cannot participate in the meetings and have no power or votes in any decision-making process. In 2012, six more countries were granted observer status. The EU requested full observer status in 2009, but it was denied by Canada on the basis that some EU countries oppose seal hunting, which is a controversial issue internationally (Coffey 2013). In Canada, Inuit and non-Inuit participate in an annual seal hunt in which up to 468,200 seals are harvested for meat and pelts (the 2015 quota is 400,000 harp seals, 60,000 grey seals, and 8,200 hooded seals; Fisheries and Oceans Canada 2015). Canada's export market is mainly Norway, followed by Germany, Greenland, China, Finland, France, Greece, and South Korea. Despite active trade in seal goods by some EU countries, in 2009 the EU passed a law banning the promotion of imported seal products (Hossain 2013). The law was approved without debate, sparking controversy between Canada and the EU. Thus, the EU has "ad hoc" observer status, meaning that its representatives must ask for prior permission to attend meetings of the Arctic Council. In 2014, the EU agreed to exempt indigenous seal products from the European ban, and Canada agreed to "lift its reservations concerning the EU's observer status in the Arctic Council" (Depledge 2015). However, in its April 2015 meeting, the Arctic Council postponed observer status applications for another two years, so the EU remains an ad hoc observer (Haines 2015).

Finally, the council also includes non-governmental organizations that can attend meetings but not participate or vote. As illustrated in Table 10.1, these groups are very diverse and have different reasons for interest in the Arctic. For example, the International Union for the Conservation of Nature is particularly interested in the work being done by the working groups on the conservation of Arctic plants and wildlife, the protection of the marine environment, and sustainable development. The UN Environment Programme, discussed in Chapter 11, is interested in the same working groups, as well as in avenues for cooperation among the eight Arctic nations, which are each important and powerful members of the larger body of the United Nations. Remember, these intergovernmental organizations can only listen and watch. They do not create policy in the North or directly participate in the council.

The Arctic Council is not a peacekeeping forum. In fact, when it was created in 1996, issues of security were completely left out of its mandate. The Council was never intended to handle geopolitical issues or settle questions of sovereignty and land title (Arctic Council 1996). However, more and more the council is being forced to confront some of these issues. At the seventh meeting of the Arctic Council in Greenland in 2011, the member nations signed the Nuuk Declaration, which, in part, recognizes "the importance of maintaining peace, stability and constructive cooperation in the Arctic" (Arctic Council 2011b). While this declaration is not legally binding, it does suggest that the eight nations have concerns about Arctic security and want to create a precedent for working cooperatively. Iceland has no military capability at all, but other Arctic nations have been actively pursuing a militarization strategy in their Arctic territory. Military confrontation in the Arctic is a very unlikely outcome, but military posturing is an important aspect of foreign diplomacy (Huebert 2013). Also of note is one of the stated focus areas for the term of the US chairmanship of the council: "Arctic Ocean safety, security and stewardship" (Arctic Council 2015).

The Arctic Council was not created to address climate change and for many years remained silent on the issue. However, it officially agreed at the 2011 meetings in Greenland that substantial cuts in emissions of GHGs are the backbone of meaningful global climate change mitigation efforts. Consequently, the Arctic Council urged action in climate summits (Pelaudeix 2013). Taking this position is precarious for the Arctic Council. Obviously, climate change is of the utmost concern to the council, but, at the same time, it has as members two of the world's largest GHG emitters: Canada and the United States. Because the council works by requiring unanimity—all eight nations have to agree on policy—taking a coherent policy stance on climate change is very difficult, if not impossible. Canada and the United States do not have strong national climate policies, and both are interested in resource extraction (of oil and gas) in the North—as are other Arctic nations. For these reasons, matters of climate change will not likely be the primary focus of the Arctic Council's work. That said, the United States has indicated that, under its chairmanship (2015–17), the council will focus on "addressing the *impacts* of climate change" (emphasis added). In other words, climate change is taken as a given in the Arctic, and the United States wants to lead discussion (and perhaps policy) on how the council will cope with the effects of climate change in the North. This is new ground for the Arctic Council, but, as Chapter 11 will discuss, the 2015 Conference of the Parties to the United Nations Framework Convention on Climate Change (COP21) is poised to have policy ramifications for all eight members of the Artic Council—and to change the way the world interacts on issues related to the mitigation of and adaptation to climate change.

So, has the Arctic Council actually made any policy? To date, it has produced only two legally binding agreements: the Agreement on Cooperation on Aeronautical and Maritime Search and Rescue in the Arctic and the Agreement on Cooperation on Marine Oil Pollution Preparedness and Response in the Arctic. The first agreement coordinates emergency response in the Arctic by specifying the search and rescue responsibilities of each state. The second, signed in 2013, aims to strengthen cooperation so as to prevent and respond to oil spills that could potentially happen through oil and gas extraction in the North or through oil tankers travelling through Arctic waters. These agreements may seem like small potatoes given the magnitude and number of issues confronting the North. However, it is important to keep in mind that cooperation among these eight nations should not be taken for granted. As recently as 2014–15, relations between Russia and the other member countries have been strained by what those countries characterize as Russian military "aggression" in Ukraine. Other tensions involve differing historic alliances or memberships. Norway, for example, is not part of the European Union, but Denmark, Finland, and Sweden are EU states. Greenland was granted home rule from Denmark in 1979 and has never been part of the EU. It is likely that Greenland will seek independence from Denmark in the coming years as Greenland's economy grows (Vidal 2014; BBC 2015). The politics of the Arctic countries are complex and marked by histories that are difficult to overcome. Any collaboration amongst these countries should be applauded and encouraged, because more cooperation than ever will be required in the twenty-first century if the environment is to be protected in the rapidly melting Arctic.

DOMESTIC POLICY: CANADA'S NORTHERN STRATEGY

Independent of the Arctic Council, each of the eight nations has an "Arctic Strategy" or a "Northern Strategy" that maps out domestic and foreign policy from that nation's perspective (these can each be found on the Arctic Council's webpage). Canada created its **Northern Strategy** in 2009, and it can be found on the website of the Government of Canada (www.northernstrategy.gc.ca). Its four themes are exercising Canada's Arctic sovereignty, promoting social and economic development, protecting the North's environmental heritage, and improving and devolving northern governance. The first theme, the one involving sovereignty, is arguably the most significant. Why does Canada make such a big deal about sovereignty? The answer is that such a small proportion of the Canadian population resides in Canada's North—despite the fact that it represents nearly 40 per cent of the country's landmass (Carnaghan and Goody 2006). If Canadians are not using it and not living there, what makes it theirs? Here is the claim made in *Canada's Northern Strategy: Our North, Our Heritage, Our Future*: "Canada's Arctic sovereignty is longstanding, well-established and based on historic title, founded in part on the presence of Inuit and other Aboriginal peoples since time immemorial" (Government of Canada 2009, 9). These statements are true, but they provide a shaky footing for Canada's Arctic sovereignty given the ambiguity expressed by the Canadian government about Inuit citizenship in the early twentieth century and the fact that the Inuit did not have the right to vote in Canada until the 1950s (Grant 2010).

Questions around Inuit citizenship in a historical context are one reason Canada's Northern Strategy goes on to acknowledge that "in a dynamic and changing Arctic, exercising our sovereignty includes maintaining a strong presence in the North, enhancing our stewardship of the region, defining our domain and advancing our knowledge of the region" (Government of Canada 2009, 9). This is a basic "use or lose it" approach to sovereignty. In practice, this approach has meant a government-led effort to put "more boots on the Arctic tundra" (Government of Canada 2009, 9). The government does not want to rely on historical claims in the territory but instead increase present-day population and thereby have unquestionable sovereignty by occupation. The Harper administration supports Arctic research and development and is interested in growing northern economies so as to attract new workers and residents to the area. If Canada can make a stronger "use-claim" to the North, its sovereignty arguments have greater weight. What is the big deal? Is anyone really challenging Canada's sovereignty or its claim to own the "Canadian" Arctic? Yes.

Canada has an outstanding dispute with Denmark over Hans Island, a tiny, uninhabited island between Nunavut and Greenland (Carnaghan and Goody 2006). This dispute is ongoing but has been on a "diplomatic track" following the Joint Statement of September 2005 between Canada and Denmark (Government of Canada 2009). Yet, in June 2013, Canada suspended military operations in the vicinity of the island, so as to ensure it did not "create friction in an otherwise friendly relationship" (Dawson 2013). This dispute is about only the island, not the waters, seabed, or the control of navigation. Canada and Denmark also disagree about the maritime boundary in the Lincoln Sea, and there are disputes, or "managed disagreements," between the United States and Canada regarding the maritime boundary in the Beaufort Sea. Overall, sovereignty disputes are managed through diplomatic channels, and there is no real threat of Canada losing any of its northern territory.

Although the Northern Strategy makes little specific reference to the need to militarize the Arctic for the purpose of defending Canadian sovereignty, it does mention specific investments in new capabilities on the land, which include establishing an Army Training Centre in Resolute Bay on the shore of the Northwest Passage, expanding and modernizing the Canadian Rangers, and updating the Canadian Coast Guard icebreaker fleet. Recently, the Harper government also approved funding for stealth snowmobiles (Cudmore 2013). Canada is not planning to go to war over the Arctic or its resources. Indeed, it does not have the military capacity to do so, as its military spending is a fraction of that of the United States or Russia and, at least according to the CIA (2015), lower than that of either Denmark or Norway as a percentage of the country's GDP. Still, as mentioned, military posturing is an important part of diplomatic relations. A show of force is often necessary to be taken seriously in the international arena. In this posturing, Canada is acting no differently than Russia, the United States, Norway, or Denmark vis-à-vis the North.

ENERGY POLITICS IN THE NORTH

As part of the 2009 Northern Strategy, the Government of Canada announced a significant new geo-mapping effort called "Geo-Mapping for Energy and Minerals" (see Natural Resources Canada 2014d and explore the maps yourself). The goal is to combine the latest technology and geo-scientific analysis methods to highlight areas of mineral and petroleum potential, which will lead to more effective private sector exploration investment (Natural Resources Canada 2014d). One of the most important environmental and social developments in the North is the building of pipelines to transfer natural gas from the Arctic southward and to transport oil from southern Canada through the Arctic to the Northwest Passage, where it can be loaded onto cargo ships for trade. Two proposed pipelines are important to the North: the Mackenzie Valley pipeline and the Alaska-Canada pipeline. Both are worth briefly describing here.

The Mackenzie Gas Project

The **Mackenzie Gas Project** (MGP) is a joint proposal between ConocoPhilips Canada, Exxon Mobil, Imperial Oil Resources Ventures, and the Aboriginal Pipeline Group. (Initially Shell Canada was a major player in this pipeline project, but, in 2011, the company backed out). The proposed pipeline is intended to carry natural gas from Canada's Mackenzie Delta–Beaufort Sea region through the Northwest Territories, joining the existing patchwork of pipelines in Alberta. Although the project was first proposed in 1970, it has been slower to develop than initially anticipated (CBC 2010; Nuttall 2010).

When a pipeline down the Mackenzie Valley was initially proposed in the early 1970s, it generated considerable controversy. In 1974, the federal government appointed BC Supreme Court Judge Thomas Berger to head an enquiry into the proposed pipeline (Nuttall 2010). Unlike anything before it, the enquiry spent time in many small Aboriginal communities in the North and listened to hundreds of Aboriginal people voice their concerns about the project. In the end, Berger's 1977 report recommended a 10-year moratorium on pipelines until land claims and conservation issues could be settled. By the time the report was published, the declining economics of oil and gas projects led its proponents to abandon the pipeline proposal, but the Berger Inquiry stands as a landmark for recognizing the views of Aboriginal people, who stood to be the most affected by resource development in the area, and for facilitating their participation in the process (CBC 2010; Nuttall 2010).

Chapter 9 discussed land claim agreements in the North and pointed out that many were settled in the 1980s and 1990s. These settlements cleared up controversy over which land was federally controlled and provided the government the opportunity to sell mineral rights on federal lands. ConocoPhillips, ExxonMobil, Imperial Oil, and Shell purchased these mineral rights and began negotiating with Aboriginal groups for access to land and for further mineral rights on Aboriginal lands. In 2001, these corporations signed a memorandum of understanding with the Aboriginal Pipeline Group (APG), which was formed in 2000 to represent Inuvialuit (Inuit living in the NWT) and First Nations in the Sahtu and Gwich'in regions. In 2003, the APG signed an agreement with TransCanada Pipelines Limited and the four producing companies that gave the APG one-third ownership of the pipeline project. This share is in addition to the revenue Aboriginal groups will receive if extraction occurs on Aboriginal land. (On Crown land, the federal or relevant provincial government gets tax revenue). This agreement represents a new era of governance in the North with Aboriginal groups playing a larger role than ever before.

At the dawn of 2015, the pipeline was not operational. The MGP was granted full federal cabinet approval in 2011 (TransCanada 2012). However, the low price of natural gas on the world market makes MGP unnecessary—for now. This news is good for environmental groups, who have long opposed the pipeline. This opposition stems mainly from wildlife groups who fear the pipeline will destroy the boreal forest and negatively affect caribou, grizzly bears, and migratory birds. Other environmental groups oppose the pipeline for reasons similar to those advocating against Keystone XL—increased reliance on fossil fuels and the resulting increase in GHG emissions (CBC 2010). This second form of opposition is especially pertinent in the case of the MGP because a pipeline in the Arctic is somewhat ironic. Pipelines and the fuels they carry are destroying the Arctic through climate change.

The Trans Alaska Pipeline and the Canada–Alaska Pipeline

In the mid-1970s, just following the international oil crisis of 1973, the Alyeska Pipeline Service Company built a 1,288-kilometre pipeline to transport crude oil from Prudhoe Bay to Valdez, Alaska. The oil in Prudhoe Bay was actually discovered by HBC surveyor Thomas Simpson in the 1830s because of seepage up and onto the ground (Naske 1987, 241). But it was not until the 1960s that the existence of the gigantic Prudhoe Bay oilfield was confirmed and declared the largest oil field in North America. Why didn't the Americans just ship oil directly from Prudhoe Bay through the Northwest Passage or around Alaska down the west coast? For one thing, there was dense ice north of Alaska in the 1970s. At that time, no commercially feasible ice-breakers could assist in the commercial transport of oil. Instead, a private company built the Trans Alaska Pipeline directly from the oil field to the closest pack ice–free port, which happened to be Valdez.

The proposal to construct the pipeline met serious environmental objections and opposition from Alaskans (Nuttall 2010). In 1971, President Richard Nixon signed the Alaska Native Claims Settlement Act, which gave Aboriginal groups $962 million and the opportunity to select from 44 million acres of federal land in return for renouncing their substantial land claims in the state of Alaska (Nuttall 2010; US Fish and Wildlife Service 2013). Although Aboriginal groups could choose the federal lands they wanted access to, they could not choose any land already selected to be part of the pipeline. The environmental battle was led on behalf of the pristine wilderness of Alaska, including its wildlife—especially caribou. Perhaps no other animal has been threatened so much by pipelines as the caribou that populate all of northern North America. Citing threats to caribou migration routes, environmental NGOs in the United States brought lawsuits against Aleyska. The result was a 3,500-page environmental impact statement by Aleyska. Both the courts and Congress agreed that Aleyska had done its homework and should be allowed to build the pipeline (Nuttall 2010).

Why is this pipeline significant for the Canadian Arctic? The answer is in part because it helped to create a culture of oil exploration in the North. It also set a precedent for forcing Aboriginal populations to accept deals not in their best interest when they object to construction projects on their traditional lands. More directly, this pipeline matters because of a proposed Alaska-Canada pipeline that would take natural gas from Prudhoe Bay and transport it through Yukon and British Columbia into Alberta, where it would join a network of existing pipelines that integrate the Canadian-US energy systems.

As of 2015, this pipeline is not feasible because of natural gas fracking in the lower 48 states, mainly in North Dakota and Pennsylvania. Fracking has provided the US economy with a surplus of natural gas. In fact, the United States now exports natural gas (Johnson and Lefebvre 2013). Consequently, transporting natural gas from Alaska to the US Midwest is unnecessary. However, the oil sands development in Alberta requires an immense amount of natural gas, as discussed in Chapter 8. It could be feasible to bring natural gas from Alaska to the oil sands—especially if the Mackenzie Valley Pipeline is constructed and put into full operation.

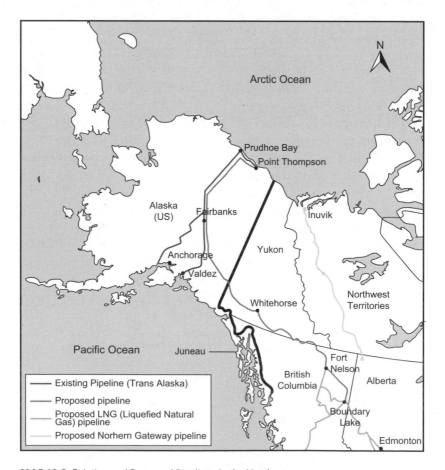

MAP 10.3 Existing and Proposed Pipelines in the North

One way or another, the oil sands will find the natural gas it needs to continue the mass excavation of oil from Canada. The Arctic will be dragged into this development in a myriad of ways—notably through climate change as northern Canada is quickly warming up as a result of CO_2 emissions. The Arctic will also likely provide natural gas and ports for oil outlets. The pipelines necessary to make all of this happen will be constructed by private companies and will cut through wildlife habitat and the boreal forest while threatening groundwater and causing air pollution. The final piece is the Northwest Passage through which Canada and the United States will change the way international trade is conducted. These developments in the North will be like hitting the fast-forward button on globalization.

THE NORTHWEST PASSAGE

The **Northwest Passage** is a sea route along the northern coast of North America—mainly Canada (see Map 10.4). This route connects the Pacific Ocean to the Atlantic Ocean through a series of linked waterways, or passages, that are collectively known as the "Northwest Passage." In December 2009, Canada's Parliament formally named these waterways the "Canadian Northwest Passage." This is a contentious name. Canada considers the waters to be domestic, or internal, waters whereas the United States and the EU consider the waters to form an international strait (see Carnaghan and Goody 2006 for the differing perspectives). Canada's position is that Canada owns and controls access to the passage; the opposing position implies an international right to free passage. The US position is a bit ironic given that these legal designations of "internal water" or "international strait" are enforced with the UN Convention on the Law of the Sea, an agreement that Canada signed but the United States did not (as already discussed). Nevertheless, this issue of who has the right to pass through the (Canadian) Northwest Passage has not been legally settled. From the Canadian standpoint, all vessels must seek permission from Canada to enter these Canadian waters.

On September 17, 2013, a cargo ship left Vancouver and sailed through the Northwest Passage to Greenland (Canadian Press 2013a). This was the first time a cargo ship had made the trip. It took only 10 days, almost 4 days less than the traditional route through the Panama Canal would have taken because the northern route shaves more than 1,000 nautical miles off the journey. This alternate route opens up all sorts of possibilities for shipping goods quickly from Canada and the United States to Europe and Asia. Do you know what

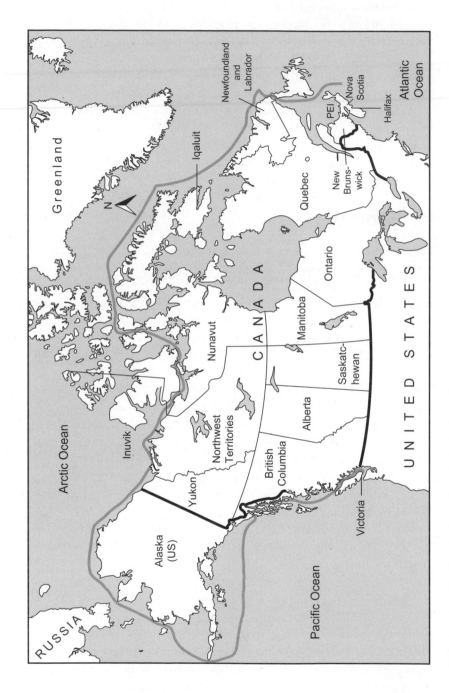

MAP 10.4 Canadian Shipping Route through the Northwest Passage

that very first cargo ship, the 75,000-ton Nordic Orion, was carrying? The answer should not surprise you—it was 15,000 metric tons of coal (Canadian Press 2013a). Yes, its cargo was one of the fossil fuels whose use has caused the melting of Arctic ice and the opening of the Northwest Passage.

Shipping through the (Canadian) Northwest Passage is not a matter of "if" or "when"—it is happening now. This will have unforeseen consequences for northerners and northern ecosystems. Trade through the area will be beneficial to the international economy and likely to the northern economy, however.

CONCLUSIONS

The recent history of Canada's North is marked by two related trends: rapid resource development and climate change. Residents of Yukon, Northwest Territories, and Nunavut will undergo significant life changes in the coming decades as the weather warms and more people move to the area for economic opportunities. For the First Nations peoples and Inuit who have called the North home since time immemorial, these changes threaten traditional ways of life. Animals with habitats in the North are also under threat and are increasingly finding themselves on endangered species lists. Some of these threatened animals include the beluga whale, the Eskimo curlew, and the boreal woodland caribou. In 2015, the polar bear is considered a species of "special concern," and it is expected that it too will be added to the endangered list in the territories and nationally in Canada. All people and all other living things will have to adapt to rapid change.

The Arctic Council is the main international body to guide governance in Arctic matters. Cooperation among its eight member countries is the centrepiece of the council's achievements and of Arctic relations more broadly. However, participation in the council is voluntary, and its scope does not extend to security matters, sovereignty issues, or the causes of climate change. Those are each considered domestic issues. Canada's Northern Strategy does make sovereignty a priority and includes necessary security measures as part and parcel of ensuring it. However, Canada has made it clear on numerous occasions that the reality of climate change is not enough for the country to make strong efforts to reduce GHG emissions. Instead, Canada fully intends to explore natural resource potential in the North and exploit oil and gas where economically feasible. Unfortunately for the environment of the North, Canada's policy approach parallels that of both the United States and Russia.

Key Terms

Arctic; northern policy; freedom of the seas; United Nations Convention on the Law of the Sea; co-management; Arctic Council; Northern Strategy; Mackenzie Gas Project; Northwest Passage

Discussion Questions

1. What is the difference between Arctic policy and northern policy in Canada?
2. Why are there so few laws in Canada's Arctic? Will this change in the next decade?
3. Is Aboriginal co-management the same thing as Aboriginal self-government? Explain what ramifications any differences might have for environmental policy in the North.
4. What purpose does the Arctic Council serve?
5. Look at the list of countries with "observer status" in the Arctic Council. Why would these particular countries want to be observers?
6. What are the most significant environmental issues in the North? How does Canada's Northern Strategy address these issues, if at all?

Suggested Readings

Bennett, John R., and Susan Diana Mary Rowley. 2008. *Uqalurait: An Oral History of Nunavut*. Montréal: McGill-Queens University Press.

CAFF (Conservation of Arctic Flora and Fauna). 2013. *Arctic Biodiversity Assessment: Status and trends in Arctic biodiversity*. Akureyri: Conservation of Arctic Flora and Fauna. http://www.caff.is/assessment-series/10-arctic-biodiversity-assessment/233-arctic-biodiversity-assessment-2013.

Griffiths, Franklyn, Rob Huebert, and P. Whitney Lackenbauer. 2011. *Canada and the Changing Arctic: Sovereignty, Security, and Stewardship*. Waterloo, ON: Wilfrid Laurier University Press.

Henderson, Alisa. 2007. *Nunavut: Rethinking Political Culture*. Vancouver: UBC Press.

Hicks, Jack, and Graham White. 2015. *Made in Nunavut: An Experiment in Decentralized Government*. Vancouver: UBC Press.

Kulchyski, P., and F. J. Tester. 2007. *Kiumajut (Talking Back): Game Management and Inuit Rights 1900–70*. Vancouver: UBC Press.

Laugrand, F. B., and J. G. Oosten. 2010. *Inuit Shamanism and Christianity: Transitions and Transformations in the Twentieth Century*. Montréal: McGill-Queen's University Press.

Nuttall, M. 2010. *Pipeline Dreams: People, Environment and the Arctic Energy Frontier*. Copenhagen: IWGIA.

White, G. 2006. "Cultures in Collision: Traditional Knowledge and Euro-Canadian Governance Processes in Northern Land Claim Boards." *Arctic* 59: 401–14.

Chapter 11

The Canadian Environment in a Global Context

THIS BOOK HAS EXAMINED domestic environmental policy making in Canada. The central focus has been on federalism and understanding authority over environmental issues. This chapter turns outward and examines Canada's environmental policy in a global context. Given Canada's size and its share of the world's natural resources, such as water and oil, the country is almost always part of international environmental policy. The focus of this chapter is on understanding how Canada interacts with other countries to solve environmental problems—namely climate change. Will this chapter be exclusively about the federal government? Not exactly. The Constitution gives the federal government sole jurisdiction to make international treaties. But the federal government does not have exclusive power to implement them the way the national governments of some other countries do (such as France or the United States). Instead, in Canada, the level of government that has jurisdiction over a treaty's subject matter—which often means all 10 provinces—must implement that treaty. Thus, the provinces often have control over how effectively Canada's international treaty obligations are fulfilled (Wood, Tanner, and Richardson 2010).

Canada enjoyed an international reputation for leadership in environmental policy during the 1970–2000 period on the basis of its significant role in global environmental negotiations. It played a vital role in numerous environmental negotiations, including the 1987 Montreal Protocol on Substances that Deplete the Ozone Layer, the 1992 Convention on Biological Diversity, and the 2001 Stockholm Convention on Persistent Organic Pollutants. However, in the last decade, the country has become a laggard state and a bit of an international disappointment. Canada became the first and only country to back out of the Kyoto Protocol, and it dragged its feet on supporting the UN Declaration on the Rights of Aboriginal Peoples, which is deeply tied to environmental justice and to environmental policies around land claims, hunting, fishing, and access to clean and healthy places to live. As Canada has further integrated its energy system with that of the United States, the federal government has made it known internationally that Canada will act in accordance with the United States and not against it. This stance makes climate negotiations more difficult at the global level. What does the twenty-first century hold for Canada's international policy and participation?

This chapter opens with a broad discussion of global institutions and actors in relation to Canada. The focus is on the United Nations, which is still the main body for orchestrating international cooperation. This overview is followed by a summary of some existing international law to which Canada is party. There are hundreds of international agreements that relate to the environment, but there are fewer than 50 core conventions. This paucity of significant international policy is, in part, because of the numerous challenges to making substantive and meaningful environmental law at the international level. Perhaps the most obvious is that environmental law slows in times of increased attention to economic growth—as was readily apparent during the 2008 financial crisis and the world's response to it. Three case studies of international environmental policymaking are presented: biodiversity, toxic substances, and climate change.

GLOBAL INSTITUTIONS AND CANADA'S ROLE

There is no global government and no single global organization for environmental policy. Instead, global governance of environmental issues is fragmented and shared by multiple organizations, some of which overlap, either directly or indirectly. For example, the World Bank and the Global Environment Facility, which the World Bank helped to establish in 1991, have similar goals and directly overlap; both invest in projects that bring environmental as well as economic benefits to developing countries. On the other hand, the World Health Organization (WHO), which is worried about air pollution, indirectly overlaps with the Intergovernmental Panel on Climate Change (IPCC), which is particularly concerned about air pollution in the form of greenhouse gas emissions. Because the environment is such a broad and all-encompassing topic, it tends to intersect with important international issues: poverty, food safety and security, forestry, fisheries, water quality, disease, military waste, and pharmaceuticals, to mention a few. Consequently, global governance is both necessary and cumbersome because of the huge web of intersecting policies, treaties, and relationships.

Consistent and concentrated international involvement in the global environment dates to the United Nations Conference on the Human Environment in Sweden in 1972. The event was attended by 113 countries, including Canada, and is considered the official beginning of an organized international effort to safeguard the environment while at the same time promote economic development across the globe. According to Axelrod, VanDeveer, and Downie (2011) there is now, in a post-1972 world, a system for global environmental governance, and it consists of three main elements: international organizations, financing institutions or mechanisms designed to help fulfil treaty commitments, and international laws and treaties. These will be discussed in turn below.

The most important environmental organization is arguably the United Nations (UN), as it convenes international conferences every year on climate change and hosts a plethora of conventions (treaties) on environmental and social issues. The UN was formed in 1945, but its precursor, the League of Nations, was created in 1919–20 with 42 members (although not the United States); in the mid-1930s, it ceased to function as a collective security organization, but it continued to meet until World War II (there were only 10 members in 1942). After World War II, there was again wide international agreement that wars must be avoided and that a global institution was needed to secure peace and ensure international economic cooperation. As of 2015, there were 193 member states in the United Nations, which is officially headquartered in New York with offices in Geneva, Nairobi, Vienna, and the International Court of Justice in The Hague (United Nations 2015). The UN is funded by the contributions of member states.

Although the main goals of the UN are peace and economic security, these goals are directly tied to the environment because of complex issues such as water security, energy security, food security, human health, and climate change. The main body of the UN is called the General Assembly, and it has a parliament-like function; all member states are represented, and all get a vote. Unlike the "50 per cent plus 1" majority system in Canada, the UN General Assembly requires a two-thirds majority to pass recommendations on issues designated as "important" (General Assembly of the United Nations 2015). These main issues often involve budget matters and international security. However, it is important to note that decisions, even when passed by a two-thirds majority, are never binding on any sovereign nation. The UN has no enforcement capabilities. It is up to member states to implement and respect UN authority.

As mentioned, the United Nations Conference on the Human Environment met in Stockholm, Sweden, in 1972. This meeting was the first time in history all the major powers came together to discuss the global environment. One could say it marked a turning point for international environmental policy. At the conference, the participants adopted 26 principles related to the environment (United Nations 1972). Collectively, these principles are known as the **Stockholm Declaration** and were formally adopted on June 16, 1972. The first principle states

> Man has the fundamental right to freedom, equality and adequate conditions of life, in an environment of a quality that permits a life of dignity and well-being, and he bears a solemn responsibility to protect and improve the environment for present and future generations. In this respect, policies promoting or perpetuating apartheid, racial segregation, discrimination, colonial and other forms of oppression and foreign domination stand condemned and must be eliminated.

This is obviously a (radical) statement about freedom and equality in the world. And it is a good example statement of environmental justice as discussed in Chapter 9. At first glance, the principle seems to have little to do with the environment. However, issues of freedom are central in the global debate because, for hundreds of years, colonizing states reaped the benefits of colonies' natural resources and environmental gifts while polluting the world with waste from manufacturing. The United Nations and the countries agreeing to these principles (including Canada) hold the position that human beings have the *right* to a quality environment—one that allows for dignity, freedom, and equality. The logical implications of this principle are enormous and, to date, no country has lived up to these aspirations adequately.

At the 1972 conference, the **United Nations Environment Programme** (UNEP) was created. Today, it remains one of the most important environmental organizations in the world. UNEP has the broadest representation of any international environmental organization and deals with both policy and scientific issues. It is responsible for overseeing the implementation of international agreements—by way of hosting meetings and otherwise coordinating multi-country participation. UNEP works in six areas: 1) climate change, 2) disasters and conflicts, 3) ecosystem management, 4) environmental governance, 5) harmful substances and hazardous waste, and 6) resource efficiency (UNEP 2015). The organization brings together developed countries, nations whose economies are in transition, and developing nations. We often group countries into the categories "Global North" or "developed" and "Global South" or "developing," depending on the strength of a country's economy. At the UN, the differences between countries' economies in relation to their environments are more nuanced and front and centre.

The UNEP continues to be instrumental in developing international environmental instruments to address global environmental issues, and it hosts the secretariats of several environmental conventions. Most important are the Convention on Biological Diversity, the Convention on International Trade in Endangered Species of Wild Fauna and Flora, the Vienna Convention for the Protection of the Ozone Layer and the Montreal Protocol on Substances that Deplete the Ozone Layer, the Basel Convention on the Control of Transboundary Movements of Hazardous Wastes and Their Disposal, the Rotterdam Convention on the Prior Informed Consent Procedure for Certain Hazardous Chemicals and Pesticides in International Trade, and the Stockholm Convention on Persistent Organic Pollutants. So, although all international environmental policy does not come out of the UN, many major pieces of this policy were arranged and are overseen by the UNEP.

In the past few years, Canada has had a rocky relationship with the United Nations. The country pulled out of the Kyoto Protocol in 2011, and, in 2013, became the only country to withdraw from the UN Convention to Combat Desertification (in Africa). In 2012 Canadian MP Larry Miller, from Bruce-Grey-Owen Sound, received some media attention for his suggestion that Canada should be the first country to leave the United Nations completely. John Baird, Canada's defence minister at the time, responded by assuring Canadians and the world that Canada would continue to participate in UN initiatives. But he also stated that the UN is in "slow decline" and that Canada will voice criticism when necessary (Clark 2012). Prime Minister Harper has acquired something of a reputation for snubbing UN meetings. In August 2011, 2012, and 2013, he decided to skip the opening of the UN General Assembly—even though he was already in New York City for other political meetings (Mackrael 2014). Harper did, however, address the United Nations General Assembly in 2014, for the first time since 2010. And, regardless of the comments of UN detractors, Canada remains party to numerous UN conventions on environmental issues.

Outside of the United Nations, other intergovernmental organizations work on environmental issues. These include forums such as the Arctic Council, the International Union for Conservation of Nature, the International Whaling Commission, the International Atomic Energy Agency, and (literally) hundreds more. A plethora of international non-governmental organizations (INGOs) also address environmental issues (see the textbox "What Are INGOs?"). Additionally, thousands of international organizations research specific environmental issues and lobby for change. The ones that come most readily to mind are Greenpeace, the World Wildlife Fund, Sierra Club, Earthwatch, and the Earth Policy Institute. These are all important actors and institutions at the global level.

What Are INGOs?

As you will recall from Chapter 3, NGOs are organizations that are not part of government but seek to influence government policy through lobbying and mobilizing the public. They are not political parties or related to parties, as they are not trying to elect members to government. Similarly, international non-governmental organizations (INGOs) are not formally part of any government or any governmental organization, such as the UN, but their overarching purpose is to influence global policy—ranging from human rights to climate change to international trade agreements. (See Willetts 2002 for an excellent description of the history of NGOs and the role that INGOs play in international policy.) In 1991, the Council of Europe ratified the European Convention on the Recognition of the Legal Personality of INGOs, which recognized that such organizations "carry out work of value to the international community, particularly in the scientific, cultural, charitable, philanthropic, health and education fields" (UIA 1991). Similarly, the UN has officially recognized the importance of INGOs (most of which developed alongside the UN in the 1960s and 1970s) and has created guidelines for official UN recognition (see DPI/NGO 2014 for criteria for INGO status with the UN).

You are probably already familiar with numerous INGOs, such as Oxfam, Doctors Without Borders, and Amnesty International. These organizations work across borders to provide aid in poor and developing countries. Environmental INGOs that should readily come to mind are the International Union for the Conservation of Nature, Greenpeace, the World Wildlife Fund for Nature, and Rainforest Alliance. These groups have offices in multiple countries, and their work focuses on issues of international concern. As you learned in Chapter 10, INGOs play an important role in the Arctic Council where they attend meetings and influence Arctic policy.

Financial Organizations and Mechanisms

The organizations that orchestrate international cooperation on environmental issues would not be possible (or at least not successful) without the existence of financial organizations and the institutional mechanisms to support the monitoring and implementation of agreements. For example, the World Bank and the Global Environment Facility have been absolutely critical in the development of world environmental law and policy.

The World Bank, head-quartered in Washington, DC, is an international financial institution whose primary mission is to fight world poverty. It does so by providing low-interest loans to countries that invest the money in health care, education, infrastructure, and sustainable development projects. Despite its lofty ambitions, the World Bank is seen with great skepticism by many in the Global South because of its role in imposing neoliberal structural adjustment programs on developing countries. Examples of the World Bank's involvement in the promotion of neoliberal ideologies include its support for the privatization of public services, such as health care or social welfare programs. In other words, the World Bank has a track record of providing aid by way of placing conditional terms such that the receiving government must allow for specific neoliberal policies to be implemented. The World Health Organization, for example, has criticized the World Bank for encouraging cutbacks in government spending on health care as part of structural adjustments to developing countries' economies (World Health Organization 2015).

Although the World Bank was created in 1944, its involvement in environmental projects dates from the late 1980s—and this increased in intensity following the 1992 Earth Summit. The bank has since come under criticism for funding projects with competing goals. Most notably, the bank invests in development projects that involve coal-fired power plants in some countries while, at the same time, managing the UN Clean Technology Fund to make renewable energy lower in cost and more competitive (Axelrod, VanDeveer, and Downie 2011). These conflicting actions are problematic from a global perspective.

Like the World Bank, the Global Environment Facility (GEF) lies completely outside the United Nations even though it is often asked to assist financially with UN initiatives. In 2015, it was a 183-member organization, and its main activity was providing grants (not loans) to sustainable development projects in developing countries. The GEF was established in 1991 and today is the largest funder of international projects that aim to improve the global environment. Initially, the GEF was part of the World Bank, but after the 1992 Earth Summit it became a separate institution. The primary purpose of the GEF is to "facilitate" environmental projects by bringing together the necessary stakeholders to implement these green projects. Its work with the UN includes serving as a financial mechanism for the Convention on Biological Diversity, the Stockholm Convention on Persistent Organic Pollutants, and the United Nations Framework Convention on Climate Change, all of which are discussed in greater detail below.

Last, it should be mentioned that trade agreements are also important financial instruments with effects in the international environmental arena.

For Canada, the most important agreements are the North American Free Trade Agreement (NAFTA) with the United States and Mexico and the Comprehensive Economic and Trade Agreement (CETA) with the European Union. Although neither is environmental by design, both have numerous environmental ramifications, especially because they shape industries such as oil and gas, agriculture, forestry, and fisheries. A supplemental agreement to NAFTA called the North American Agreement on Environmental Cooperation aims to directly address some of the environmental consequences of trade among the three countries. It consists mostly of principles and objectives or goals for protecting the environment and for assisting Mexico in sustainable development.

Nevertheless, Chapter 11 of NAFTA has had serious impact on Canadian oil development and would severely impact water management in Canada if water were ever declared a "tradable good." Essentially, it creates a mechanism by which investors can legally sue Canada (or Mexico or the United States) directly, without first pursuing legal action in another country's court system, for actions taken by the government that affect investment. Initially included in NAFTA to protect American and Canadian investors against corruption in Mexican courts, the measure, critics argue, currently serves to limit governmental control over the environment and labour policies. How does it work? If the Alberta government, for example, decided to cap oil sands production at 3 million barrels a day so as to provide more time for environmental safeguards to be put in place, then oil companies who have invested in the oil sands, such as British Petroleum, could sue the Alberta government for threatening its oil investments (see the textbox on Lone Pine's suit). Thus, Chapter 11 of NAFTA makes it difficult for governments to create environmental policy after investment has been received.

Lone Pine Resources Sues Canada over Fracking

In 2011, the National Assembly of Québec passed Bill 18 and revoked all permits related to oil and gas under the St. Lawrence, including those that would involve fracking. As well, in March of the same year, the government temporarily banned all fracking projects in the province pending further study. Québec wanted to wait until a full environmental review of fracking projects was conducted before approving the practice. Then, in May 2013, the province tabled a bill to ban fracking in the lowlands of the St. Lawrence, Bill 37.

In September 2013, an oil and gas company called Lone Pine Resources filed a $250 million notice of arbitration under Chapter 11 of NAFTA. Its explicit claim was that Québec's moratorium and pro-posed ban violates the company's right to mine for oil and gas under the St. Lawrence River. The company was not notified of the bills or of the moratorium, nor was it compensated for frozen permits. The lawsuit states that

> [we] submit this arbitration on behalf of the Enterprise under Article 1117 of the NAFTA, for the arbitrary, capri-cious, and illegal revocation of the Enterprise's valuable right to mine for oil and gas under the St. Lawrence River by the Government of Quebec without due process, without com-pensation, and with no cognizable public purpose. The Gov-ernment of Canada is responsible for Quebec's acts under the NAFTA and applicable principles of international law.

The lawsuit has not been settled. However, there is public pressure on Lone Pine to drop the case because Québec's moratorium was both legal and publically supported.

SOURCES: Canadian Press (2012); Council of Canadians (2013).

It is too soon to tell what impact CETA will have on the Canadian environment. It is likely that it will increase EU investment in the oil sands. It may also lead to the overexploitation of other resources, for example, fish, for the purposes of trade. This environmental consequence might occur because the agreement is expected to be a boon to Canadian exporters, as it gives better access to EU markets by removing 98 per cent of EU tariffs on a wide range of Canadian products, including agricultural, seafood, metals, and mineral products. Almost 96 per cent of fish and seafood products will be duty free immediately, including live and frozen lobster and frozen shrimp (Foreign Affairs, Trade and Development Canada 2014). After seven years, 100 per cent of the tariffs on fish and seafood products will be eliminated along with almost 95 per cent of agricultural tariffs. Also, tariffs will be eliminated immediately from some agricultural items (including maple syrup, fresh and frozen fruits, cherries, and fresh apples) and cat and dog food. Canadian beef producers will be able to sell 50,000 tons of beef; and pork producers will be able to sell 81,000 tons of pork per year. There will also be duty-free, quota-free access to the EU dairy market (CBC 2013d).

International Law and Canada

Given the existence and nature of international organizations, how does the world actually go about making law? The process is not like the one used to pass legislation in Canada—it is not as simple as someone standing up in the UN General Assembly to introduce a draft bill for consideration, which then goes to a general vote. Instead, the method of making international policy is lengthy and complex, and, at the end of the day, it is not "laws" that are being agreed to so much as rules, guiding principles, and acceptable international procedures for carrying out development and trade. Indeed, Axelrod, VanDeveer, and Downie (2011) define **international law** as the set of principles, norms, rules, and procedures and institutions that countries and other actors create and implement for a specific issue. These words all sound similar and are often used interchangeably, but the distinctions are important. Principles are beliefs of fact and causation; norms are socially accepted standards of behaviours; rules are specific prescriptions for action; operating procedures are the prevailing practices for making decisions; and institutions are the mechanisms and organizations for implementing, operating, evaluating, and expanding policy (Axelrod, VanDeveer, and Downie 2011). At the international level, there is no global government to implement laws and no global police to enforce them. Thus, countries agree to certain standards and operating procedures that they will work toward individually, through domestic policies and laws.

How are agreements about principles or norms made? There is no standard method. Often, the UN (with the assistance of other institutions) convenes an international meeting on a pressing issue. Each country sends delegates to represent its interests. After a week or two of negotiations—which can be complex given world politics and trade—a document is produced and opened for signature. The document, which is called a **convention**, contains a set of principles, rules, and procedures. Sometimes, it includes specific agreements on actions to be taken, such as in the case of climate change negotiations. A convention only comes into effect once enough countries have ratified the document, which is a threshold that is specified in the document (Boardman 2009). For some countries, ratification is as simple as the leader of the country signing the convention. In Canada, the prime minister and his or her cabinet must ratify a convention, or an international treaty, but it can require consent of the provinces if the treaty affects provincial jurisdiction. Consequently, the federal government customarily consults the provinces to gain their approval before ratifying a treaty. Provincial approval is needed for implementation because, more often than not, implementation requires action in areas of provincial jurisdiction. In the United States, ratification requires approval of the Senate. Generally, the US Senate will not ratify a treaty for symbolic purposes because it must be certain the government can implement the rules and procedures at home. These operating procedures in Canadian and US politics sometimes mean that these countries do not ratify a treaty or take a long time to do so.

Once a convention comes into force, it often creates related organizations for the purposes of research, monitoring, or implementation. It can also create related agreements. For example, the UN Conference on Climate Change in Kyoto, Japan, created a separate but related document of international law: the Kyoto Protocol. Therefore, what emerges in international law is a complex web of conventions, protocols, agreements, and the like, which are supported by countless organizations and institutions. And, in the end, it is up to every country to implement policy domestically. The penalties for failure to comply with a ratified treaty are international shaming and, in more extreme cases, trade sanctions or the withholding of financial aid or assistance. Often, however, there are no consequences for signing an agreement and then not following the rules. When Canada backed out of the Kyoto Protocol, the country faced neither fines nor penalties, although the country was shamed by international organizations such as Greenpeace. And perhaps our international reputation for environmental protection was tarnished, but there were no significant consequences for failing to obey the international agreement.

So what international "law" really exists? None per se, but many international rules, policies, agreements, and customs have already been discussed in this book. Instead of looking at laws, we can look to several international principles that, once created, grew into operating norms and became part of international procedures; these principles appear in hundreds of conventions and agreements. We can also explore several issues or topics in international environmental law to see which actors, institutions, and rules are relevant.

International principles can be called **soft laws**; these are largely obeyed and implemented voluntarily. Some of the principles that emerged after the 1992 Earth Summit in Rio de Janerio include the concept of common but differentiated responsibility, the precautionary principle, the polluter-pay principle, and the overarching notion of sustainable development. Most of these have direct origins in the specific principles agreed to by all member nations at the Earth Summit. For example, Principle 7 states that

> States shall cooperate in a spirit of global partnership to conserve, protect and restore the health and integrity of the Earth's ecosystem. *In view of the different contributions to global environmental degradation, States have common but differentiated responsibilities.* The developed countries acknowledge the responsibility that they bear in the

international pursuit to sustainable development in view of
the pressures their societies place on the global environment
and of the technologies and financial resources they command. (United Nations 1992; emphasis added)

The **principle of common but differentiated responsibility** has had significant implications for climate policy negotiations. Similarly the other
principles, which have been discussed in other chapters of this book, have
all influenced Canadian domestic and international environmental policy.
These norms, or international standards of behaviour, are not legally
enforced but are nevertheless recognized as the "right way to behave."

The **polluter-pay principle** is another international soft law that has
emerged since the Earth Summit. Stated as Principle 16, it says, "National
authorities should endeavour to promote the internalization of environmental costs and the use of economic instruments, taking into account the
approach that *the polluter should, in principle, bear the cost of pollution*,
with due regard to the public interest and without distorting international
trade and investment" (United Nations 1992; emphasis added). In practice, this means that, if a private company is going to set up shop, either
domestically or internationally, it should be prepared to pay the cost of
the negative externalities caused by its business. Canada has been slow to
adopt this principle in relation to the oil sands. The cost of reclamation,
or the replanting of trees on the land dug up for oil extraction, was not
initially built into the permit process for industry. However, more recently,
Alberta has started to insist that oil companies cover the cost of replanting the forest. Unfortunately, industry is not being held responsible for
paying the cost of increased CO_2 emissions—the effects of which might
be hard to pin down internationally.

The **precautionary principle**, discussed in earlier chapters, comes from
Principle 15 of the Rio Declaration: "In order to protect the environment,
the precautionary approach shall be widely applied.... Where there are
threats of serious or irreversible damage, lack of full scientific certainty
shall not be used as a reason for postponing cost-effective measures to
prevent environmental degradation" (United Nations 1992). Often this
principle is translated as "better safe than sorry" as it implies that we
should regulate something now rather than be sorry in the future, when
it is too late, that we had not done so. Canada has a mixed relationship
with this soft law as its government sometimes supports and integrates
the principle but, at other times, uses scientific uncertainty to justify policy
inaction. For example, municipalities' bans on the cosmetic use of lawn
pesticides provide a good example of the precautionary principle at work
in Canada. However, the government's refusal to use the principle to justify

regulating bisphenol A (BPA), polybrominated diphenyl ethers (PBDEs), or other chemicals is contradictory. Similarly, Environment Canada has never used the precautionary principle as a rationale for adding a species to the Species at Risk Act. And the country has surely not taken a "better safe than sorry" approach to climate change or energy management.

INTERNATIONAL CASE STUDIES

The international community, led by the United Nations, has come together over the past 40 years to address major international environmental problems such as ozone depletion, biodiversity loss, the use of hazardous chemicals, and climate change. This section examines each of these issues as a case study in international environmental policymaking.

Ozone Depletion

The biggest accomplishment in international environmental law is often considered to be the response to ozone depletion. The 1985 Vienna Convention for the Protection of the Ozone Layer was quickly followed by the 1987 Montreal Protocol on Substances that Deplete the Ozone Layer. The Montreal Protocol, under the auspices of the United Nations Environment Programme (UNEP), aimed to eliminate the global consumption and production of ozone-depleting substances (ODSs) gradually. The Multilateral Fund for the Implementation of the Montreal Protocol was established in 1991 by a decision of the parties to the protocol, and its goal was to provide technical and financial assistance to developing countries so they could achieve their targets in the phasing out of ODSs. Headquartered in Montreal, the Multilateral Fund Secretariat is financed by mandatory contributions from developed countries that are party to the Montreal Protocol, including Canada.

Environment Canada coordinates Canada's overall participation under the Montreal Protocol, including representing Canada internationally and implementing domestic policies and regulations to ensure Canada's compliance with the protocol's requirements, as discussed in Chapter 6. Environment Canada also addresses issues and activities related to the Multilateral Fund, with a view to advancing Canada's strategic interests and objectives regarding implementation of the Montreal Protocol in developing countries. As of 2015, Environment Canada has implemented more than 30 bilateral projects under the protocol in countries such as Bolivia, Chile, India, Jamaica, Mexico, and Uruguay (Environment Canada 2015d). Through these partnerships, Canadians share technology and information to help these countries reduce ozone-depleting substances globally.

However, despite the undeniable success of these international policies, there are reasons to qualify the ozone initiative as a "special case." Dryzek (2013) argues that the ozone convention and protocol cannot be used as prototypes for international policy for at least two related reasons: the stakes were low and material interests guided decision making (not science). More specifically, chlorofluorocarbon (CFC), or the chemical that causes ozone depletion, was useful in refrigeration and as a propellant in aerosol cans, but it could be replaced by comparable substitutes. CFCs are not oil. Moreover, the material interests of key actors were easily brought into line with the environment (Dryzek 2013, 46–47). Importantly, the United States already had a ban on the domestic use of CFCs, so its large chemical companies were already producing a substitute, one they easily would be able to market internationally if there were a global ban. Second, the United States threatened to ban EU products that contained CFCs, making it in the economic interest of the European Union to start using CFC substitutes immediately. In the case of producing international environmental policy to combat ozone depletion, then, success should be recognized and celebrated, but this coincidence of material interest and global environmental concern "should not be expected as a general rule" (Dryzek 2013, 46). In the other case studies, on halting biodiversity loss, the use of hazardous chemicals, and climate change, economic interests do not clearly or neatly align with environmental benefits or protection.

Biodiversity Protection

Canada was the first industrialized nation to ratify the UN Convention on Biological Diversity (UNCBD) in 1992. Thus, it is not surprising that Canada hosts the secretariat of the convention in Montreal. The initial intent of the UNCBD, as mentioned in Chapter 8, was to protect biodiversity in the context of economic development and natural resource extraction in countries across the world. The agreement is geared not so much toward protecting biodiversity for its intrinsic worth but toward ensuring biodiversity can provide necessary ecological services to the world. In fact, in many ways, the UNCBD has become mainly about biotechnology and, more specifically, about the ownership of genetic information stored in species. This focus has numerous and far-reaching ramifications for not just pharmaceuticals but also forestry, agriculture, and fisheries. Through ratification of the UNCBD, Canada agreed to protect biodiversity but also to share the benefits arising from genetic resources in a "fair and equitable way."

To meet its obligations under the UNCBD, Canada must monitor and report its biodiversity. As of 2015, reports are given every two years at meetings of the Conference of the Parties (COP). As Chapter 8 discussed, biodiversity policy presents many challenges for multilevel governance in

Canada. The federal government has jurisdiction only over federal lands, migratory species, and aquatic species. The provincial governments are the major actors in this policy realm—with jurisdiction over provincial Crown land, private property law, and the wildlife found on those land parcels. First Nations' participation is required for wildlife on reserve lands, and Inuit participation is necessary for monitoring and protecting wildlife on Inuit land. Individual managers are important because they are the most intimately connected to the landscape, but environmental NGOs are also critical for education, awareness, and ensuring that governments live up to their legal obligations.

After Canada ratified the UNCBD, the federal government and the provincial and territorial governments signed the 1996 Accord for the Protection of Species at Risk. As discussed in Chapter 8, this agreement pledged its signatories to work together to meet the challenges (and opportunities) of multilevel governance head-on. In 2002, Canada passed the Species at Risk Act (SARA) as well as the National Marine Conservation Areas Act. Parks Canada, responsible for national parks and historic sites, was charged with setting up a national system of marine protected areas. Its National Marine Conservation Areas Program aimed to create protected areas representing the full range of marine ecosystems found in Canada's Atlantic, Arctic, and Pacific waters, as well as in the Great Lakes. Canada has over 243,000 kilometres of coastline along three oceans and another 9,500 kilometres along the Great Lakes—the longest coastline in the world (Yurick 2010). The vast marine ecosystems off these coasts are varied, productive—and precious. Thus, Canadians have a responsibility, both at the national and international levels, to protect examples of this marine heritage for present and future generations.

The National Marine Conservation Areas (NMCAs), are marine areas managed for sustainable use and containing smaller zones of high protection. They include the seabed and the water column above it, and they may also take in wetlands, estuaries, islands, and other coastal lands. NMCAs are protected from such activities as ocean dumping, undersea mining, and oil and gas exploration and development. Traditional fishing activities would be permitted but managed with the conservation of the ecosystem as the main goal. NMCAs are established to represent a marine region and to demonstrate how protection and conservation practices can be harmonized with resource use in marine ecosystems. Their management requires the development of partnerships with regional stakeholders, coastal communities, Aboriginal peoples, provincial or territorial governments, and other federal departments and agencies. Presently, there are only two national marine parks in Canada: one in Georgian Bay, Ontario, and one in Saguenay-St. Lawrence, Québec. The Harper government has made some efforts in this area and, as of 2015, plans are underway for two more: the Lake Superior National Marine Conservation Area in Ontario and the Gwaii Haanas National Marine Conservation Area in BC.

However, apart from its domestic policy, represented by, for example, the Habitat Stewardship Fund for Species at Risk, SARA, and the NMCA program, Canada has struggled to maintain a leadership role at the international level. As mentioned in Chapter 5, provinces are failing to protect biodiversity. And the federal government has not maintained the funding necessary for the programs it is responsible for overseeing. In 2013, the commissioner responsible for the environment and sustainable development portfolio at the Office of the Auditor General of Canada released an audit assessment on biodiversity and Canada's commitments to the UNCBD. The main conclusions of the audit were that "legislative requirements under the *Species at Risk Act* have not been met" and "less than half of the ecosystems Canada assessed in 2011 were in good condition" (Office of the Auditor General of Canada 2013b, 3). Moreover, the auditor pointed out that Environment Canada has completed less than half of the Bird Conservation Region Strategies that it had committed to finishing by 2010. Overall, Canada has not kept up with UNCBD commitments domestically, despite its initial enthusiasm in the early 1990s.

Hazardous Chemicals

The international community recognized the threat posed to humans and the environment by toxic chemicals in 1995 when the UNEP called for global action on persistent organic pollutants (POPs). These are chemicals that persist, or do not break down, in the environment and that bio-accumulate in living organisms, causing adverse effects to human health and the health of other living creatures. According to the UNEP, the health and environmental concerns associated with POPs include persistence for long periods in the environment; travelling long distances and depositing far away from their sources of release; accumulating in the fatty tissues of living organisms, causing complications such as cancer and birth defects; triggering adverse effects on the ecosystem and biodiversity; and potentially disrupting immune and reproductive systems and even diminishing intelligence (EPA 2015b). Emerging from the UNEP's interest in POPs was an assessment of the 12 worst chemicals (the **dirty dozen**) and the development of a set of recommendations on international action, which was undertaken by the Intergovernmental Forum on Chemical Safety.

In 2001, the **Stockholm Convention** to reduce or eliminate the production, use, and release of these 12 chemicals was agreed upon and opened for signature. It went into effect in 2004 (with 128 parties and 151 signatories). Essentially, it aims to protect human health and the environment from the effects of persistent organic pollutants; participants agreed to outlaw or ban most of the dirty dozen chemicals, and to regulate the use of DDT to only malaria control. They also agreed to a process by which new chemicals could be added to the list of POPs to be managed or banned if they met the criteria for persistence and transboundary travel. Finally, the convention also aims to ensure the sound management of stockpiles and waste that contain POPs.

The dirty dozen include aldrin, chlordane, dieldrin, endrin, heptachlor, hexachlorobenzene, mirex, toxaphene, polycholorinated biphenyls, DDT, dioxins, and furans. More recently, in 2010, nine additional POPs were added to the convention, and all signatories must outlaw their production and use or seek exemptions (Stockholm Convention 2008). As of May 2015, there were 179 parties to the convention, including Canada (but not the United States). In fact, Canada was the first country to ratify the convention in 2001 (and has since enacted new chemical legislation in Canada, as discussed in Chapter 6). The Stockholm Convention is considered a very successful international effort to address the threats posed by chemical pollution.

The absence of the United States is a notable exception to the treaty's success. American hesitation comes from the treaty provision that new chemicals can be added to the list of banned chemicals through a review panel on which the United States would not have a veto (CIEL 2006). The Americans perceived this as a threat to US commerce because many of the chemicals that might potentially be added to the list are produced or used in the United States. However, the United States is not without chemical regulation, but the country does not embrace the precautionary principle in the same manner as the EU countries do and requires a greater scientific threshold before it is willing to risk US business (Wiener et al. 2010; Zander 2010). Canada is somewhere in the middle ground between the European Union and the United States when it comes to the precautionary principle. As discussed in Chapter 6, Canada has been rather progressive on chemical pollution but can still drag its feet on commercially important chemicals such as triclosan and polybrominated diphenyl ethers.

Climate Change

In 1990, the United Nations General Assembly began work on convening a climate change convention. At the UN Earth Summit in Rio de Janeiro in 1992, 154 countries signed on to the UN Framework Convention on Climate Change (UNFCCC). Both Canada and the United States were signatories and went on to ratify the treaty domestically. As of 2015, 195 countries and 1 regional economic organization are parties to the UNFCCC. The goals of the convention are to stabilize the amount of greenhouse gas (GHG) in the atmosphere at a level that prevents dangerous human-made climate changes. However, the stabilization must occur in such a way as to give ecosystems the opportunity to adapt naturally while not compromising human safety or endangering sustainable economic development in each country.

Each year, a Conference of the Parties (COP) is held at which all countries that have ratified the convention meet and discuss how the convention's goals can be implemented in practice. To date, the most famous meeting was in 1997 in Kyoto, Japan, at which countries adopted the Kyoto Protocol that committed its parties to internationally binding GHG emission reduction targets. For Canada, this agreement meant a reduction of CO_2 emissions to 6 per cent below 1990 levels by 2012 (other nations had different targets). Canada and the United States both signed the treaty in 1997, but the United States never ratified it at home. However, through the following decade, governments took little action to address GHG emissions in Canada, and, by 2011, it was clear that Canada had failed to meet any of its emission targets. In fact, between 1990 and 2005, greenhouse gas emissions increased by over 20 per cent (see Figure 11.1). The increase is caused not just by the oil sands, as discussed in Chapter 8, but also by Canada's growing transportation sector and other oil and gas industries across the country.

However, despite Canada's less than stellar record, the annual year-end meetings of the COP under the convention have resulted in several major achievements. Table 11.1 summarizes the major outcomes of the

FIGURE 11.1 National Greenhouse Gas Emissions, 1990–2013

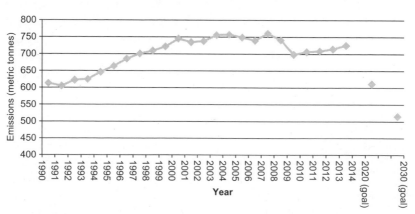

SOURCE: Data from Environment Canada (2015c) *National Inventory Report, 1990–2013: Greenhouse Gas Sources and Sinks in Canada.*

TABLE 11.1 UN Framework Convention on Climate Change: The Outcome of COPs, 1997 and 2009–15

YEAR	LOCATION	SUMMARY OF MAIN OUTCOMES
1997	Kyoto, Japan	Sets binding obligations on Annex I (developed) countries to reduce GHG emissions Kyoto Protocol enters into force in 2005 when it is finally ratified by enough countries (Russia's signature gave it enough signatures to come into effect) Sets timeframe for Kyoto commitments as 2008–12, followed by period two in 2013–20 (which has not entered into legal force)
2009	Copenhagen, Denmark	Agrees to a target of no more than 2° Celsius increase in global temperature Annex I countries commit to economy-wide targets for 2020 Developing countries agree to voluntary actions to reduce CO_2 Green Climate Fund initiated with $30 billion US for 2010–12 and $100 billion a year by 2020 Reducing Emissions from Deforestation and Forest Degradation (REDD+) initiated
2010	Cancun, Mexico	Annex I and II countries formally agree to anchor their 2020 greenhouse gas targets in a parallel manner Official establishment of the Green Climate Fund (first year of money)
2011	Durban, South Africa	Initiated process to develop a new single, comprehensive climate change agreement by 2015 that will include commitments by all major emitters beginning in 2020 Kyoto period one expires and no new protocol is created to replace it
2012	Doha, Qatar	Establishes a timetable for a 2015 accord New commitment period is established for period two of Kyoto Protocol (which has not entered into force)
2013	Warsaw, Poland	Annex I and II countries agree to a timeline to set out their targets on curbing GHG for 2020 New "Warsaw international mechanism" created so victims of disaster can receive aid (but it is not linked to any liability from developed countries) REDD+ completed and $280 million US pledged from the United States, Norway, and the United Kingdom The 48 poorest countries finalize adaptation plans ($100 million US pledged from European countries)
2014	Lima, Peru	All countries agree to reduce carbon emissions March 2015 deadline set for announcing Paris 2015 reduction goals
2015	Paris, France	The Paris Protocol was intended to be binding on signatories and take effect in 2020 (although this was certainly not a guaranteed outcome)

most recent COP meetings. In Copenhagen, Annex I countries (developed nations and economies in transition such as Russia) agreed to economy-wide targets and set 2020 goals for CO_2 emission reductions. Canada set a sector-by-sector regulatory approach in contrast to other Annex I countries, which rely on market-based policies that have proven more effective at real-world emission reductions. In more recent years, Canada has insisted on binding targets for some developing countries (such as China) while denying the historical responsibility for GHG pollution of developed countries. In essence, Canada rejects the "differentiated but equal responsibility" principle.

The 2013 meeting in Warsaw is notable for a few reasons. First, the meeting happened only a few days after Typhoon Haiyan ravaged the Philippines. The typhoon was extraordinary and devastated portions of Southeast Asia, eventually killing over 6,000 people. It is still the strongest storm ever to make landfall in recorded history. Naturally, this event sparked much media attention and international aid effort. It put climate change at the forefront of everyone's mind going into the Warsaw meeting. The reality of climate change victims and refugees (see textbox) was on every television and newspaper round the world throughout the 19th COP—and could also be read on the faces of the Philippine delegates. In part, the typhoon's reminder that climate change can fuel extreme weather helped established the "Warsaw Mechanism," which is a fund created to give assistance to victims of climate change disasters.

Second, Warsaw COP19 is notable because Poland is a coal-dependent nation that is embarking upon the development of new and other dirty forms of energy, such as shale gas. During the talks, Polish Prime Minister Donald Tusk fired Marcin Korolec, his environment minister and the chief of the conference, for his failure to embrace shale gas development in Poland (Sobczak and Doyle 2013). Also, next door to the UN climate change meeting, a coal conference bringing together the largest coal industries was being held. At the time, Poland was planning on building two expansions at an existing coal-fired power plant in the city of Opole. The country already has the biggest carbon-emitting power plant in Europe, the Belchatów power station. The country is dependent on coal for 90 per cent of its electricity (Barteczko and Gloystein 2013). Additionally, the country's decision to allow the coal industry to fund some parts of COP19 and to set up booths inside the meeting corridors, as well as to allow a coal conference to occur in the same city in the same week, was seen as counterproductive by many countries (Associated Press 2013).

Environmental and Climate Refugees

The word "refugee" refers to a person who leaves his or her country of residence due to war or persecution (or fear of persecution) for racial, religious, social, or political reasons. Albert Einstein, for example, fled from Germany after being accused of treason and sought refuge in the United States in 1933. However, today there is a new category of refugee that goes beyond oppression or maltreatment. "Climate refugees" are "people displaced from their homes by the impact of a changing climate" (Goldenberg 2013).

This new category of refugee fits under the older and broader one of "environmental refugees," who are people displaced because of natural disasters (e.g., tsunamis, earthquakes, and floods). The International Red Cross estimates that there are more environmental refugees than political refugees in the world right now (National Geographic n.d.). Human diaspora from climate-devastated areas of the world is occurring across the globe—from small tropical islands in the Pacific to the eastern coast of Africa to remote villages in Alaska (Goldenberg 2013). Becoming a climate refugee might not sound like a concern for those living in Canada or the United States, but some Canadians and Americans are already being displaced and forced to leave their homes and relocate to another part of the country because of climate change.

One area of North America is very sensitive to climate change: the North. Sea levels there are rising as the sea ice is melting. Changes in the northern climate are also causing disruptions in wildlife patterns (which affect hunting) and flooding. According to Susan Goldenberg at *The Guardian*, residents from a few Alaskan villages are "actively working to leave their homes and the lands they have occupied for centuries and move to safer locations" (Goldenberg 2013).

Although the Warsaw talks were generally considered a disaster by most countries and NGOs (some of whom walked out of COP19 in protest), REDD+ became official. REDD+ stands for Reducing Emissions from Deforestation and Forest Degradation in Developing Countries. The basic premise is for Annex I (developed) countries to provide monetary support to Annex II countries so they do not have to cut down their trees. It has been well established that trees can absorb CO_2, so deforestation cuts off a potentially very useful way to reduce these emissions in the atmosphere.

Informally, REDD+ has been operating since 2005 through support of the World Bank, the World Wildlife Fund, and the United States Agency for International Development. In Warsaw, the project came into focus and garnered formal international support. At present, just over $250 million US has been pledged from various countries and economic regions, including Norway, Denmark, and the European Union.

Although some progress was made toward an international agreement to reduce CO_2 emissions at the Warsaw COP, considerable international hope has rested on the Paris meeting in 2015—a new binding agreement was expected. Progress at the international level has been slow for a variety of reasons. Foremost is the immense complexity of the task at hand. There are technological and institutional factors that require time to set in motion. And the backdrop is always new developments in scientific knowledge. As mentioned, climate change is a far more daunting challenge than fixing the hole in the ozone layer. There is no quick or easy fix for climate change. The series of actions that led us to emit too many GHGs cannot be undone quickly, and it is likely that a series of actions to prevent further GHG emissions will be required (as opposed to a single action such as preventing CFCs from entering the atmosphere).

Second, declining public attention to the issue since 2009 has stunted progress on climate change. In Copenhagen that year, COP15 was expected to negotiate a new binding protocol that would be ready for implementation when Kyoto expired in 2012. That did not happen. As a consequence, people have started to pay less attention to the issue—in part because of the frustration of so much talk and so little action, in part because of issue saturation or "issue fatigue," but perhaps mainly because of the preoccupation of the developed world with economic issues after the financial crisis of 2008–09 (Kerr 2009). Most people already know about climate change, and they cannot stay focused on the issue forever, especially when other concerns intrude. The problem with waning public attention is that little pressure is then put on politicians to act. If voters don't care, why should politicians?

This situation made **Paris 2015** even more challenging. The scientific report of the Intergovernmental Panel on Climate Change (IPCC) in 2013 concluded that human beings are the cause of climate change and that only 250–275 GtC (billion tons) of carbon total can be emitted into the atmosphere if we are to limit warming to the agreed-upon 2° Celsius. Human beings are emitting about 10 billion tons of carbon a year—a number that is increasing because of countries like Canada. At this rate, we will use up our "carbon budget" in the next 25 years.

To help ensure an outcome in Paris, the United Nation asked for a pre-meeting to occur in New York in September 2015, where countries were to present their finalized plans to reduce GHG emissions. On January 22, 2014, the European Union became the first party to the UNFCCC to announce its Paris 2015 commitment. It has pledge to reduce CO_2 emissions by 40 per cent below 1990 levels by the year 2030. Because this economic region is the first party to make a commitment, we can consider this percentage as the bar by which we will measure other countries' commitments.

In May 2015, Canada announced its plan to cut GHG emissions by 30 per cent below 2005 levels by 2030. Thus, compared to the commitment of either the EU or the United States, Canada's is weaker. Canada has a longer timeline than that of the United States (which has set 2025 as a target date for reductions from 2005 levels), Canada uses 2005 as the date of comparison rather than 1990, and the country's overall goal is less substantial than that of the EU. The Canadian federal government is also unwilling, and arguably unable, to address the oil sands issue. The new 2030 commitments do not do anything to reduce emissions from the oil sands—largely because that falls under Alberta's jurisdiction. It will be up to that province to decide how to reduce emissions in this sector.

Thus far, international commitments for the purposes of mitigating climate change have been inadequate. This is especially true in the case of Canada. Perhaps no other country contributes so much to GHG emissions and does so little to combat the effects (although Australia would be a contender). Canada's inaction on the issue is leading to much frustration at the international level, especially among countries in the Global South that stand to lose so much. What has Canada done about its UNFCCC commitments? The government does provide GHG emission data on an annual basis as well as report on progress (or lack thereof) in reducing emissions. Canada, like other industrialized countries, also provides financial and technological resources to developing countries. This support is part of the larger UNFCCC framework and is absolutely critical for assisting poor countries not just in adapting to climate change but also in conducting the necessary scientific observations to participate in global monitoring efforts. Canada also participates in the scientific and research initiatives of the IPCC and often provides scientists who aid in the creation of various reports.

With regard to specific policy, Canada agreed in the Copenhagen Accord to reduce its national GHG emissions by 17 per cent from 2005 levels by 2020. This effort was discussed in greater detail in Chapter 8. As indicated in that chapter, Canada is attempting to reach this target through a sector-by-sector regulatory approach. Canada has also committed to harmonizing its climate and energy policy with that of the United States. Nevertheless, Canada remains a significant emitter of CO_2 in the world (on a per capita basis). Unlike international action to prevent ozone depletion and the use of CFCs, the effort to address climate change is far more economically complex. Oil does have substitutes—in the form of alternative energy—but such substitutes do not have the same economic actors in play.

CONCLUSIONS

From world leader to world laggard—Canada's international environmental record has waxed and waned in the past 50 years. The United Nations remains the most important global organization for coordinating state behaviour in relation to economic, social, and environmental issues. The UNEP and IPCC are critical for the environment in a global context. Canada has a mixed relationship with the United Nations and has disappointed the international community in recent decades by refusing to cooperate in large climate change initiatives and by dragging its feet in other areas of commitment, such as the UN Convention on Biological Diversity. By continuously prioritizing trade and its export economy, Canada has fallen behind on the international sustainable development project. The next chapter reflects on Canada's environment in the twenty-first century. As a wealthy, developed, and democratic country, Canada has the potential to lead. And given its vast array of natural resources, it could be argued that Canada has the responsibility to lead.

Key Terms

Stockholm Declaration; United Nations Environment Programme; international law; convention; soft laws; principle of common but differentiated responsibility; polluter-pay principle; precautionary principle; dirty dozen; Stockholm Convention; Paris 2015

Discussion Questions

1. What is international environmental *law*? Why is it so difficult to make global laws for the environment?
2. UN conventions are an important part of international environmental policy. How are they made? What drawbacks or weaknesses exist in the process?
3. Canada has not been a global environmental leader. Provide evidence for that statement.

4. In what ways can we consider the Kyoto Protocol a success—if not for the environment, then for international environmental policymaking?
5. If countries are not legally required to live up to international principles, why do we create them at all?

Suggested Readings

Axelrod, Regina S., and Stacy D. VanDeveer, eds. 2014. *The Global Environment: Institutions, Law, and Policy.* Washington, DC: CQ Press.

Bernstein, Steven, Jutta Brunnée, David G. Duff, and Andrew J. Green, eds. 2008. *A Globally Integrated Climate Policy for Canada.* Toronto: University of Toronto Press.

Brown, Lester R. 2009. *Plan B 4.0: Mobilizing to Save Civilization.* New York: W.W. Norton.

Chasek, Pamela S., David Leonard Downie, and Janet Welsh Brown. 2014. *Global Environmental Politics.* 6th ed. Boulder, CO: Westview Press.

Conca, Ken, and Geoffrey D. Dabelko. 2010. *Green Planet Blues: Four Decades of Global Environmental Politics.* Boulder, CO: Westview Press.

Healy, Robert G., Debora L. VanNijnatten, and Marcela Lopez-Vallejo. 2014. *Environmental Policy in North America: Approaches, Capacity, and the Management of Transboundary Issues.* Toronto: University of Toronto Press.

VanNijnatten, Debora, Neil Craik, and Isabel Studer, eds. 2013. *Climate Change Policy in North America: Designing Integration in a Regional System.* Toronto: University of Toronto Press.

Chapter 12

The Canadian Environment in the Twenty-First Century

FEDERALISM IS THE QUINTESSENTIAL FEATURE of Canadian politics and policy. The Constitution, in Sections 91 and 92, lays down some broad categories regarding the distribution of legislative powers, which the courts have refined over the years. We know that provinces own their natural resources as well as manage their own Crown land and oversee the regulation of private property. This jurisdiction gives them an unquestionably large role in environmental protection and regulation. However, because the federal government has jurisdiction over federal lands, Aboriginal lands and peoples, international treaty making, transboundary water, and everything pertaining to "peace, order and good government," the federal government performs a necessary role in environmental policymaking. But there is more to policy than government. Elected officials are key players—helped out by the judicial branch and the Senate—but, in reality, governance of Canada's environment involves participation by NGOs, citizens, and private industry as well. When it comes to stewardship of this vast nation, all Canadians must take responsibility.

Canada has many challenges and opportunities ahead when it comes to making natural resource and environmental policy in the twenty-first century. To examine both, this chapter, following the major themes already discussed in this book, summarizes how the country has developed and implemented environmental policy over the last 150 years. It begins with a discussion of policy evaluation, the final stage of the policy process, before moving to a more general discussion of environmental policy in the next few decades. Specifically, the chapter focuses on climate change. The limitations and potential of federalism are carefully examined with suggestions for pushing past the laggard status that we have developed in the past 15 years. As well, the prospect of a fourth wave of environmentalism is considered, and, related to that possibility, the roles of responsible citizenship and individual action are highlighted.

POLICY EVALUATION

Canada has many laws in place to regulate natural resources and protect the environment. Are these policies working? Answering this question forms the final stage of the policy process introduced in Chapter 2: **policy evaluation** (Birkland 2011). This stage is reflexive and is about taking stock so that, moving forward, policy can be adaptive and improvements can be made. Policy evaluation is everyone's responsibility. Often, the bureaucracy (the people responsible for implementing policy) collects data on measurable outcomes. For example, is the air cleaner? Did GHG emissions decrease? Is wildlife thriving? Did water quality improve? Various other actors can also help provide answers to these questions—including NGOs and citizens themselves. This section discusses ways policy can be evaluated, including through formal parliamentary review, informal government review, audit reports, judicial review, and public review via elections.

Formal administrative evaluation can occur in a few ways. One important procedural method is the **formal review** of a specific policy after a specified number of years of implementation. For example, as discussed in chapters 7 and 9, the Species at Risk Act was passed in 2002, and the legislative branch of government conducted a formal policy evaluation in 2009 (see Olive 2012). This review was intended to evaluate the policy and assess its weaknesses so these could be addressed moving forward. The House of Commons Standing Committee on the Environment and Sustainable Development evaluated the act and made recommendations to the environment minister on how the implementation of the law could be improved (Government of Canada 2014d). In the case of the Species at Risk Act, a review was conducted, but no amendments were made to the law. A formal policy evaluation does not always result in the termination of or amendments to a policy. Ideally, however, a policy is formally reviewed and weaknesses are confronted via changes, either to the law directly or to the implementation of the law.

Other types of review by government also occur, albeit not formally inside the House of Commons. When the Conservative Party came to office in 2006, it began to examine already existing environmental legislation. Almost every piece of environmental legislation passed in the nine years that followed has been about amending policy. For example, the Environmental Enforcement Act (the bulk of which came into force in 2010) changed the enforcement provisions of nine federal environmental acts. Essentially, the government evaluated policy such as the Canada National Parks Act and the Canadian Environmental Protection Act and decided that enforcement mechanisms needed amending. The government also reviewed the Fisheries Act and the Navigable Waters Protection Act and decided that amendments were necessary. It is quite common for the governing party to assess legislation internally and tweak policy if problems or inadequacies are discovered.

Another type of evaluation can come through the Office of the **Auditor General of Canada**. The auditor can decide to audit any Canadian policy area, program, or department at any time. This evaluation often examines the use of public dollars and determines if a policy, which costs taxpayers money, is achieving its stated goals (Office of the Auditor General of Canada 2014). For example, as discussed in Chapter 11, the Auditor General's Office published a 2013 audit of biodiversity programs in Canada: *Fall Report of the Commissioner of the Environment and Sustainable Development* (see Office of the Auditor General of Canada 2013a for a copy). Because the Auditor General's Office reports to the House of Commons and not to the executive branch of the government, it has the independence to act objectively, and state and non-state actors are likely to respect its findings. In fact, as a form of policy evaluation, an audit by the Office of the Auditor General can be very effective. It is always communicated to the bureaucratic office being audited or to the office responsible for the policy being audited. That office then has the opportunity to respond to the findings. Both the audit and the response to it are published and made publicly available. This sort of policy review is a form of public accountability; the public is the third party, evaluating both the audit and government policy, and the government must publicly respond to any criticism or perceived policy failures. A particularly weak performance in an audit could lead to many policy or institutional changes.

The judicial branch serves as yet another type of evaluator or adjudicator for public policy in Canada. One method of evaluation is through a judicial review of administrative decision making. This review is an important part of Canada's system of checks and balances. The court has the ability to examine the actions and operations of government, namely, how the government conducts its business and creates policy. For example, is it legal for an unelected civil servant to create a new policy, or must policy go through Parliament? Public administrators in the bureaucracy have immense policy reach, yet the courts must determine if that reach is legal and ensure it stays within the reasonable limits of authority. However, the court cannot decide on its own to review a decision, procedure, or policy. A case must be brought to the court through normal channels, or the court must be asked by the government to review a specific decision, commission, or agency. Because the courts are independent of government, the public often holds their findings in high regard. If the courts suggest that a policy or procedure is misguided, then government will often remedy it. One recent and prominent example of a major judicial review occurred in December 2013, when the Supreme Court of Canada determined that the federal ban on prostitution was unconstitutional (*Canada (Attorney General) v. Bedford*, 2013 SCC 72 [2013] 3 S.R.C. 1101). The courts gave Parliament one year to rewrite the law (which it did by June 2014).

The courts can also act as policy evaluators in other types of court cases. In Canada, **public interest lawsuits** are becoming increasingly common. These occur when the people suing the government have no personal stake in the outcome but instead want to protect the environment because it is a shared public resource that benefits all Canadians. Ecojustice has championed this role in Canada. In 2014, Ecojustice had three major cases before the federal and provincial courts. One charged that the federal government broke the law by approving the production of genetically modified salmon. A second case, filed on behalf of the Taku River Tlingit First Nation, challenged the Chieftain Metals' proposed project, which was proceeding based on an outdated environmental assessment. In a third case, Ecojustice asked that the federal government's approval of the Northern Gateway Pipeline be set aside because the environmental assessment on which it was based did not consider the necessary and best available science, as required by law. This last case and the one on genetically modified salmon were still pending as of 2015. In the other case, the British Columbia Supreme Court ruled in favour of the Taku River Tlingit, who must now be consulted as the BC government reconsiders. The court decisions in cases such as these have lasting impact for environmental policy in Canada. If the guidelines and procedures we have in place are illegal, they must be amended. If they are legal but ignored or bent during implementation, the offending governments must be taken to task. That is the policy process at work.

Another way of evaluating policy is by voting. Indeed, it is easy to see elections as the ultimate policy evaluation—if voters do not like a government's policy or think the policies are not improving society, they have the right to try to elect a different government. But elections are not a particularly great way of evaluating policy. Canada's "first past the post" electoral system means that a party can win a majority in the House of Commons although more people voted for other parties. Also, elections happen only every so often. In Canada, federal elections now occur in October on the fourth calendar year after the previous vote, unless Parliament is dissolved or the government loses a non-confidence motion.

Do Canadians have to wait for an election to evaluate a policy? No, but it should be noted that the inclusion of the public at the administrative level is limited and discretionary for the purposes of evaluation. There are few opportunities for public participation in tribunals, forums, or other types of evaluative bodies (Hessing, Howlett, and Summerville 2005). Moreover, there are limited resources to devote to evaluation, and high costs associated with conducting research and gathering data on pollution, public health, and technology. Consequently, the public must rely on either government research or information supplied by industry. Surely this reliance raises issues of accountability and transparency. It is also problematic in terms of procedural justice and accurate measures or evaluation of public policy.

Looking Back and Evaluating

Environmental policy is fluid in Canada. Most major environmental laws flowed into the policy cycle by way of an election promise and were either introduced and legitimatized by the two chambers of the legislative branch (becoming environmental law) or created and implemented by the governing party (forming environmental policy). Major exceptions to this usual process are the policies discussed in Chapter 9 that affect Aboriginal lands and came into being by way of the Supreme Court. Regardless of their legitimization procedure, many environmental policies in Canada falter at the implementation stage. This is mainly for one of two reasons: the federal government has limited powers and loses interest (which happened with the Canada Water Act) or the federal government finds implementation costly and unpopular (as it did with the Species at Risk Act). Table 12.1 illustrates the major environmental policies that were passed in Canada from 1968 to 2014 and who was prime minister at the time of their passage. All of these policies have been evaluated in one or a few of the ways mentioned above. At the very least, the public has had a chance to evaluate each administration at the voting booth.

Second-wave environmentalism put many environmental issues on the government's agenda in the 1970s, a fact clearly illustrated by the number of federal laws passed by Prime Minister Trudeau's administration in the 1968–79 period. During third-wave environmentalism, the Progressive Conservative Party, under Prime Minister Mulroney, made some major progress in the environmental arena, particularly at the

TABLE 12.1 Major Federal Environmental Policy from 1968–2014, by Prime Minister Elect

TIME SPAN	PRIME MINISTER	MAJOR ENVIRONMENTAL POLICY ENACTED
1968–79	Pierre Elliot Trudeau	*Arctic Waters Pollution Prevention Act (1970)*
		Canada Water Act (1970)
		Canadian Environment Week Act/Canadian Pollution Awareness Week (1971)
		Clean Air Act (1971)
		Department of the Environment Act (1971)
		Canada–United States Great Lakes Water Quality Agreement (1972)
		Canada Wildlife Act (1973)
		Environmental Contaminants Act (1975)
		Ocean Dumping Control Act (1975)
1979–80	Joe Clark	
1980–84	Pierre Elliot Trudeau	
1984–84	John Turner	
1984–93	Brian Mulroney	*Canadian Environmental Protection Act (1988)*
		Canadian Environmental Assessment Act (1992)
		Green Plan (1990)
		Canada–United States Air Quality Agreement (1991)
		Ratified UN Convention on Biological Diversity (1992)
		Ratified UN Framework Convention on Climate Change (1992)
1993	Kim Campbell	
1993–2003	Jean Chrétien	North American Agreement on Environmental Cooperation (1994)
		Great Lakes Binational Toxics Strategy (1997)
		Signed and Ratified Kyoto Protocol (1997, 2002)
		Canada-wide Accord on Environmental Harmonization (1998)
		Canadian Environmental Protection Act (1999)
		Canada Foundation of Sustainable Development Technology Act (2001)
		Species At Risk Act (2002)
2003–06	Paul Martin	
2006–15	Stephen Harper	Chemicals Management Plan (2006, 2011)
		Federal Sustainable Development Act (2008)
		Environmental Enforcement Act (2010)
		Canadian Environmental Assessment Act (amendments; 2012)
		Fisheries Act (amendments; 2012)
		*Navigation Protection Act (amendments; 2012)**

*The Navigation Protection Act is the new name for the Navigable Waters Protection Act.

Note: For the purposes of this table, acts are distinguished from other policies by italics.

international level through the ratification of important UN conventions and the passage of the Canada–United States Air Quality Agreement to address acid rain. The Liberal leadership through the 1990s saw fewer substantive environmental regulations and laws enacted compared to the Trudeau and Mulroney eras. The Liberal Party's demise began in 2002 when the auditor general revealed a sponsorship scandal (Jeffrey 2010). This scandal consumed a government that was by no means environmentally proactive, and Prime Minister Jean Chrétien stepped down in 2003. Paul Martin was chosen as party leader and, thus, prime minister. His administration was never able to move past the scandal. The 2002 Species at Risk Act was the last meaningful piece of legislation passed by the Liberal Party, and even it was significantly weaker than initially intended (Illical and Harrison 2007). The electorate spoke in 2004 by voting in a minority Liberal government and then in 2006 by voting in a minority Conservative government.

The Harper Conservatives had not made progressive environmental policy to date, as discussed throughout the book. Most policies were aimed at streamlining federal processes and more efficiently managing the laws already on the books. The government decreased the overall size and budget of the federal government, to the smallest size in 50 years (Flaherty 2014).[1] These cuts have likely hurt Environment Canada's ability to implement and enforce environmental laws. The agency's *Report on Plans and Priorities* states that its budget will decrease from $1 billion in 2014–15 to $7 million in 2016–17 and that its full-time employees will decrease from 6,400 to 5,300 over the same period (Environment Canada 2014l). Thus, Environmental Canada will have to maintain implementation of present policies with fewer resources. The public's evaluation of Harper's government would come in 2015 at the federal election.

Looking Forward and Environmental Leadership

In the past decade, Canada has not shown itself to be an environmental leader on the world stage. On the contrary, Canada is now known as an oil and gas state with rising CO_2 emissions. According to German Watch and Climate Action Network Europe (both think tanks), Canada was a top-10 CO_2 emitter in 2015 and ranked 58th in the world (out of the countries responsible for 90 per cent of the world's CO_2 emissions). Only Kazakhstan, Australia, and Saudi Arabia had worse rankings. The report says of Canada, "nothing has changed and nothing is going forward at state level. Canada is about to miss its 2020 emissions reduction target by about 20 per cent and the only effective policies in place are provincial initiatives" (Burck, Marten, and Bals 2015, 6). During the 1970s and into the 1980s, Canada was known internationally for its "leadership in environmental law reform and progressive stance on environmental matters" (Wood, Tanner, and Richardson 2010, 982). Fast forward to 2015 and Canada is an environmental laggard. It still is a large country with bountiful wilderness, wetlands, forests, and water. But Canadians are no longer great stewards of those natural landscapes.

And Canadians are not just laggards in performance, in living up to existing environmental commitments, but also in enacting and implementing policies and experimenting with policy innovation at the federal level (there has been innovation at local and provincial levels, as discussed in other chapters). The world knows Canada was the first and only state to back out of the Kyoto Protocol. And, in the few years that Canada was a signatory, the federal government did not implement the necessary policies to control GHG emissions.

In 2013, Canada announced its withdrawal from the UN Convention to Combat Desertification, which it signed in 1994 and ratified in 1995. Scholar and career diplomat Robert Fowler, a former Canadian ambassador to the UN, called Canada's withdrawal from the convention "a departure from global citizenship" (Canadian Press 2013e). The world also knows that Canada hesitated on signing the Declaration on the Rights of Indigenous Peoples and equivocated on recent UNCBD discussions over sharing genetic information and resources. (Canada did eventually support the declaration on indigenous rights, but it is not legally binding. See AANDC [2012] for Canada's statement on this declaration.)

Furthermore, while the European Union and other countries experiment with different types of policy mechanisms (voluntary, economic, and regulatory) to address climate change and create sustainable cities, Canada continues to rely, for the most part, on voluntary standards for industry, at least at the federal level of government. Our 2020 GHG emission target will not be met (Harris 2013; McCarthy 2014a). And given Canada's record, some are skeptical about the targets for 2030 announced in 2015 (Climate Action Network 2015). Canadians are also failing to prevent habitat loss for endangered species, as citizens and governments put pipelines and the oil and gas industry before biodiversity. In April 2014, Ottawa removed the North Pacific humpback whale from the list of federally threatened species, but environmentalists suspect this has more to do with approvals for the Northern Gateway pipeline than it does with the whales' secure population (O'Neil 2014). The actions and inaction of Canadian governments are not examples of the kind of leadership needed on environmental policy in this century.

In comparison with the national policies of other nations, Canada's can seem regressive. President Obama has a more progressive climate change strategy than Prime Minister Harper, and we could see the United States pressure Canada to implement more stringent regulatory policies (Clark 2014). In 2013, President Obama released an executive strategy for climate change (White House 2013), which did not pass through Congress into law but became policy by way of a directive from the President's Office; as of 2015, the bureaucracy was implementing it. (Congress can make laws that override this presidential strategy if it so chooses.) Obama was also hesitant to approve the Keystone XL pipeline until Canada agreed to do more about climate-changing GHG emissions from the oil sands (Clark 2014). He also took the lead in achieving a bilateral agreement with China's President Xi Jinping on climate change (White House 2014). China, still a developing country and having no past aspirations of addressing climate change, agreed to slow and then stop emissions by 2030. The United States agreed to reduce GHG emissions by 26–28 per cent by 2025 (Hansen 2014). In North America, the United States is currently the leader on climate change efforts.

Canada has the potential to meet its energy needs through solar, wind, and hydro energy. Yet the top-producing wind power countries are currently China, the United States, Germany, Spain, and India. While the United States was pioneering wind farms in the 1980s and 1990s, Canada was making plans to develop the oil sands. Relying on finite natural resources is not leadership. The largest solar thermal power stations in the world are in California, Arizona, and Spain (IEA 2011). China now manufactures solar panels that are sold at IKEA in UK outlets for domestic use. Although other countries innovate and develop new technologies, Canada continues to grow its oil and gas sectors. Of course, these should not be "either-or" categories, but Canada has been incredibly slow to invest in alternative energy markets, except at the provincial level (especially in British Columbia, Ontario, Québec, Nova Scotia, and Prince Edward Island).

The criticism that Canada is not an environmental leader may leave you asking, why *should* Canada be a leader? The answer rests in the environmental bounty Canada enjoys. The country is the second largest in the world, occupying almost 7 per cent of Earth's landmass and having about 20 per cent of the world's fresh water (but only about 7 per cent of the world's renewable fresh water; Environment Canada 2012). Canada has the largest intact boreal forest in the world, a vast array of biodiversity, and Canadians oversee a large swath of the world's Arctic. Canada was an industrialized, liberal democracy with an educated population and a per capita GDP of $36,000 US in 2012 (Conference Board of Canada 2013a). Canadian universities are some of the best research institutions in the world and have the ability to produce scientists and engineers who can conduct research freely and independently. It is easy to argue that Canadians have an obligation to each other and to the international community to steward the land. Canada also has an obligation to future generations of Canadians and world citizens to safeguard the country's resources and use them sustainably.

If, as a Canadian or a citizen of the world, you do not feel that obligation or believe it matters, then there are still good economic reasons that Canada should be an environmental leader. Dependence on oil and gas is an unstable and short-sighted strategy (Canadian Press 2013d; Clarke et al. 2013). Canada will run out of oil and natural gas. And, when it does, the Canadian economy will suffer a major loss of income and jobs. Canadians can prepare for that future by creating a more diverse energy market—by planning to meet energy needs through nuclear, hydro, wind, and solar power. Canada should also prepare to export those types of energy.

Big Business in Canada

The *Report on Business* magazine published by *The Globe and Mail* issues a list of Canada's top 1,000 businesses by revenue each year (see *Globe and Mail* 2015). In the 2014 rankings, the top 15 revenue-generating Canadian business were

1. Manulife Financial (insurance, financial management)
2. George Weston Ltd. (food supply)
3. Power Corp. of Canada (financial management, originally electric utility company)
4. Loblaw Companies (food supply)
5. Suncor Energy (oil company)
6. Royal Bank of Canada (bank)
7. Power Financial (financial holding company for Power Corp. of Canada)
8. Magna International (automotive)
9. Alimentation Couche-Tard (food supply)
10. Great-West Lifeco (insurance, financial holding)
11. Enbridge Inc. (pipelines)
12. Imperial Oil (oil company)
13. Toronto-Dominion Bank (bank)
14. Bank of Nova Scotia (bank)
15. Husky Energy (oil and natural gas company)

Three of Canada's companies that generated the most revenue in 2014 are oil companies, a fourth supplies oil and gas through pipelines, and none is an alternative energy producer. So sound economic reasons exist for the country to invest in renewable energy.

Suncor Energy, founded in Montreal in 1919 as the Sun Company of Canada and now headquartered in Calgary, had revenue of over $42 billion in 2013 while employing almost 14,000 people. The company is involved in the oil sands business as well as in natural gas production and marketing in Canada and Colorado. Offshore drilling in eastern Canada is also within the company portfolio. It should not be a surprise that environmentalists—and even governments—heavily criticize the company. Suncor has been fined multiple times in the United States and Canada for failing to meet pollution laws (CBC 2009; Christian 2010; Finley 2012). It should be noted that, in an effort to green its business (a form of corporate social responsibility discussed in Chapter 4), the company now operates seven wind power facilities to offset its carbon emissions (see http://www.suncor.com/en/about/217.aspx).

Another economic reason to protect the environment is tourism, which is an important component of the Canadian economy. In 2013, the industry generated an estimated $84 billion in tourism revenue in Canada and accounted for approximately 2 per cent of the GDP (CTC 2013). Canada has 17 World Heritage sites with another 7 cultural and natural sites awaiting review, including the Klondike (Yukon). In 2012, almost 4,000 people visited Yukon and spent an estimated $200 million (CBC 2013e). Banff, Canada's oldest national park and a premier World Heritage site, gets about 3 to 4 million visitors a year (including Canadian visitors), and the park contributes substantially to the Canadian economy (Offin 2015). There is big money in tourism and eco-tourism. In 2012, there were 618,300 tourism-related jobs in Canada (CTC 2013). However, unless Canadians are good stewards of the natural environmental, protecting it in such a way that people want to travel to see it, these economic benefits will dwindle.[2] Of course, tourism cannot replace forestry, oil and gas, or fisheries in the economy, but hard and fast trade-offs between these two economic sectors are not necessary. We can do both at the same time—exploit natural resources in such a way as to conserve them for long-term growth.

Finally, by contributing to climate change and severe weather patterns that devastate foreign countries, Canada is helping to destabilize world markets (Gillis 2011; Schellnhuber 2009). When it is too hot in Europe or Asia to grow food, Canadians suffer because the price of our food increases. In a globalized world we are all interdependent. Canada relies on foreign countries for goods, particularly food. Its export market is dependent upon the ability of countries to buy goods, such as agricultural products, timber, and fish. For all these reasons, Canada should lead in environmental policy creation; doing so is a matter of self-interest. So what are Canada's leadership prospects in the areas of domestic and international policy on climate change?

The Future of Climate Change: Domestic

According to a 2011 Public Policy Forum survey, Canadians do believe that climate change is real and do want political action to address this issue (see Borick, Lachapelle, and Rabe 2011). The main finding of the survey was that 80 per cent of Canadian respondents believe there is solid evidence of global warming. Also, most Canadians believe that both the federal and provincial governments should take actions to reduce global warming. In fact, 73 per cent of Canadians indicated a willingness to pay at least something per year in extra energy costs for increased renewable energy production, and 45 per cent of Canadian respondents would support cap-and-trade systems and carbon taxes even if they imposed increased costs of up to $50 per month in energy expenses (Borick, Lachapelle, and Rabe 2011, 89). So, if the public is willing to go along with a more aggressive approach to climate change, why does Canada have no climate change policy to speak of—either internationally or domestically at the federal level? The answers are plentiful. At the level of domestic national policy, there are really three constraints: voters, federalism, and an economy based on natural resources.

First, if you recall from Chapter 2, in a parliamentary democracy a prime minister and his or her cabinet have considerable authority over policy, especially when the governing party has a majority of seats in the House of Commons. The Conservative Party of Canada, in power at the time of writing and since 2006, supports limited national climate change legislation, as discussed in Chapter 8. Public pressure could change Prime Minister Harper's mind, but, as of the summer of 2015, there had been no overwhelming public outcry on this issue. Even though Canadians do believe climate change is happening and do want laws in place to prevent it, other issues have been more important for voters when making a choice at election time.

Second, as discussed in various chapters throughout the book, important hurdles exist for the implementation of any federal commitments to act on climate change. The most important of these are institutional (Harrison 2013). Provinces own their natural resources and control electricity. The federal government cannot create and implement a national energy strategy or climate change framework without the willing cooperation of the provinces and territories (Belanger 2011).

Third, Canada's economy is natural-resource based. The provincial and federal governments would have to be willing to diversify their energy sectors by adopting more alternative energy and creating new green jobs. Canada will continue to extract its natural resources, including oil and natural gas, until the energy economy has been restructured or these resources run out. The Alberta oil sands are a major revenue and job creator in the country and for the province. Similarly British Columbia and Saskatchewan will engage in fracking to extract natural gas until it is no longer profitable for them to do so. Canadians have always conducted business this way. Economic regionalism has long defined the country (see the ground-breaking 1930 work of Harold Innis, *The Fur Trade in Canada*, which paints a clear portrait of Canada's long history as an economy dependent on natural resources).

Does this mean that Canada will never embrace regulatory climate change policy across the country? Not necessarily. At the domestic level, change may come by way of a shift in energy patterns and a shift in public support. Domestic use patterns of energy in Canada are changing and will likely continue to change. For example, Ontario has phased out the use of coal and replaced it with other forms of power generation, some renewable and some not renewable (such as gas). As discussed in Chapter 8, over the next decade Ontario has plans to diversify its energy sources through integrating more renewable energies. Provinces such as British Columbia and Québec will continue to be major sources of hydroelectricity for both the Canadian and US markets. And there are reasons to suspect that wind and solar projects will pop up in other provinces as well, especially as the price becomes increasingly affordable. In 2015, Canadian Solar is one of the largest producers of solar energy products in the world (Canadian Solar 2015). Though solar energy is not a huge seller in Canada, the company is selling its products to over 70 other countries. It is hoped that, over time, more provinces will invest in this energy source.

The 2015 election provided an opportunity for voters to decide that environmental issues are finally important enough to reinstate the Liberal Party or to give the NDP its first chance at governing the country. Lawsuits by Ecojustice are raising awareness of both environmental issues and the problems associated with procedural justice. Aboriginal groups are also putting environmental issues on the public agenda and calling for change at the federal level. The politics of pipelines, particularly of the Keystone XL project, are keeping climate change a salient issue in Canada. And, finally, citizens in Canada's largest cities (i.e., the census metropolitan areas of Vancouver, Toronto, and Montreal) have been willing to consent to significant environmental legislation for the purposes of climate change mitigation, as discussed in Chapter 8. An estimated 35 per cent of Canadians lived in one of those three census metropolitan areas in 2013 (Statistics Canada 2014b). Their willingness to adopt a carbon tax or phase out coal may suggest a shift in public attitudes. Citizens might yet find a way to champion climate policy in Canada through provincial and municipal action.

The Future of Climate Change: International

At the international level, different constraints impede Canadian action. Indeed, major hurdles exist to the creation of a Paris Protocol that Canada would be willing to adopt. For example, Canada has been unwilling to accept binding conditions that will limit only Annex I, or industrialized, countries but not developing countries such as China or India to reductions in GHG emissions. And Canada has been uncompromising in its pursuit of oil sands expansion. In fact, Canada expects its emissions in the oil sands to rise in the coming decades (Canadian Press 2014a; Climate Action Tracker 2015; Environment Canada 2015b; Leahy 2014). This projection has not stopped the country from announcing as a target a 30 per cent reduction from 2005 GHG emission levels by 2030. These inconsistencies can be construed as Canada pursuing its immediate economic self-interest vis-à-vis the oil and gas industry.

One thing that is very likely to alter Canadian international policy is influence from the United States. As mentioned, in June 2013, President Obama laid out a new climate change strategy for his administration. In roughly 6,000 words, the president reviewed the problems and set out several ideas for solving them. Before the 2016 presidential election, Obama plans on reducing carbon pollution from power plants; increasing funding and support for clean energy; partnering with the automobile industry to advance cost-effective, fuel-efficient cars; cutting energy waste in homes; and reducing other greenhouse gas emissions such as methane (White House 2013). His administration has also begun serious climate adaptation efforts, such as helping the agricultural industry prepare for warmer climates and investing in climate-resistant crops. Regardless of how many of these ideas come to fruition, this plan is the boldest made by any American president on the issue of climate change.

How does the American plan affect Canada? The issue that springs to mind for most Canadians is the Keystone XL pipeline. Does Obama's stance on climate change mean the pipeline will not be approved and built? Obama did not actually say that. It is quite likely that Keystone XL will proceed, and Canada will pipe oil to Texas to be refined. The US position on climate change, however, does make it more likely that environmental safeguards will be put in place. And Canada will experience pressure to commit to a Paris protocol target that is in the line with that of the United States. Given the overwhelming expansion of the oil and gas industry in Canada, it may be difficult for Canada to fulfil its commitments.

More broadly, the Obama plan affects the economy, and that will impact Canada. The US economy is going to embrace more alternative energy and become less dependent on fossil fuels, although the country will obviously continue to drill for oil and frack for natural gas inside its own borders. However, US demand for Canadian oil and gas will decrease. Therefore, Canadian oil will have to find new markets, most likely in India and China. As of 2015, China gets most of its oil from Saudi Arabia but has shown great interest in Canadian oil. The consequences of an increased demand for Canadian oil from China would be both economic and political, as Canada could transition from a US-centric focus to an Asian-centric focus for economic trade.

Provincial-level climate change initiatives with international or continental effects could also expand. Québec and California, for example, are working together in a North American context to confront climate change. As discussed in Chapter 8, on January 1, 2014, the two jurisdictions formally linked their cap-and-trade systems (Québec 2014b). Ontario signed an agreement with Québec in April 2015 that will effectively make it a party to this North American carbon market. Actually, prior to the 2008 recession, 11 states and provinces formed the Western Climate Initiative (WCI) with the goal (among others) of creating a broader North American market for trading carbon. Over time, the other jurisdictions backed out of this particular initiative, although British Columbia and Ontario remained members of the WCI with Québec and California (see http://www.wci-inc.org). For the future, the Québec-California-Ontario partnership will serve as a test case, and there is still the possibility that other states or provinces will join once the program gets up and running.

California has also joined with Washington, Oregon, and British Columbia to coordinate climate policies. An agreement was signed between these three parties in 2013 to better integrate their energy grid, streamline permits for renewable energy, and increase government use of electric vehicles. The agreement is formally known as the Pacific Coast Action Plan on Climate and Energy (Pacific Coast Collaborative 2013). It is similar to the 2001 agreement between six east-coast states and five eastern provinces to address climate change (formally known as the New England Governors/Eastern Canadian Premiers Climate Change Action Plan 2001).

Two of these three North American climate agreements include Québec as a significant participant.[3] And its agreement with California seems unlikely. Roughly 4,900 kilometres separate Sacramento, the capital city of California, from Québec City. These jurisdictions are not neighbours nor are they part of the same "region"—they do not share ecosystems or a watershed. Other than their progressive stance on CO_2 emissions and their willingness to implement an economic policy tool, there is no good reason for these two jurisdictions to cooperate. And yet, they do.

A push-pull effect is at play here. As a nation, Canada is unwilling to reduce CO_2 emissions. But, at the provincial level, Québec is ready to lead the continent. Choosing to work with a US partner is a way to push Canada and US energy markets closer together. But by expanding the oil sands, the national government is pulling China closer. Canada, then, has no coherent or consistent plan at the international level to address climate change. The country's relationship with the United States will continue to affect its actions—domestically and internationally—in the twenty-first century. Likely, where the United States leads, if that country chooses to lead, Canada will follow.

A FOURTH WAVE OF ENVIRONMENTALISM?

In 2001, Edward Parson argued that, in Canada, "[c]itizen concern for the environment has been persistently mixed, labile, and ambiguous, only infrequently reaching and holding the intensity required to provoke major policy change" (373). In the twentieth century, there were three "waves" of environmentalism during which public awareness of environmental issues peaked (turn of the century, 1960s to early 1970s, and 1980s to early 1990s). Will there be a fourth wave of environmentalism? The world is a complex place, far more complex than it was during the first or second wave of environmentalism. It is not clear if the Canadian public can create and sustain a fourth wave of environmentalism.

What we do know about environmentalism is that it coincides with periods of high public salience on environmental issues (Winfield 2012). Moreover, we know that attention to environmental issues coincides with periods of economic prosperity (or at least with periods when people have a feeling of economic stability). When people consider their economic needs to be secure, they turn their attention to other issues: health care, education, poverty, crime, and the environment. Should we expect Canadians to focus on the environment in the next decade? It is hard to say for certain. Our staples economy has most provinces turning out natural resources for immediate sale on the international market. Oil sands production has been an economic boon for the country, but other oil, natural gas, potash, aquaculture, forestry, and agricultural industries can fuel a strong economy. With a strong economy, people can turn their attention to the environment.

The media can also help usher in a fourth wave of environmentalism. Social media especially must play a role, as youth engagement will be necessary for environmentalism to have any hope of achieving a lasting impact. In many ways, social media has already made environmentalism a more salient issue in Canada. We communicate in new ways, allowing us to get access to more information more quickly. Using Twitter, Facebook, Instagram, Pinterest, and mobile applications for news, today's citizens can get instant information about what is happening from coast to coast to coast. For example, when a natural gas pipeline exploded in a rural area of Winnipeg in 2014, I heard about it via Twitter within an hour of the incident. This knowledge is power. Industry will struggle to keep the lid on environmental disasters, even in rural and remote parts of the country.

Modern communications can also foster awareness of the beauty and significance of nature, which could help fuel environmentalism. Social media is not just about communicating disaster. Facebook, Pinterest, and Instagram allow users, predominately young Canadians, to share pictures of Canada and the natural environment. Because most Canadians live in a city, they are far removed from much of Canada's natural environment, such as the Rocky Mountains, the boreal forest, the thousands of lakes and wetlands, and the diverse flora and fauna. Pictures of this environmental bounty can be shared instantly. In fact, social media does not just bring these pictures into our homes; it places them in our hands as we hold our phones and tablets. On buses and subways, in classrooms and offices, Canadians can see images of nature right in front of them. Social media has made recording the environment not just possible but popular.

However, knowing about the environment and doing something about environmental problems are different things. Many people know about climate change and yet act in ways that suggest they neither know nor care (Swim et al. 2009). Inaction might be the result of problems being so big and complex that people do not know what to do. But even in matters requiring only personal choice and individual effort, inaction is common. For example, many people know that eating meat is environmentally unsound and potentially unethical given the nature of its mass production, yet 95 per cent of Canadians eat meat (Garriguet 2004). Why? Individual behaviour is difficult for social scientists to explain. And the relationship between knowledge and behaviour is not always as clear as we would like it to be. Sometimes, for example, the more people are told, the less they act. Issue saturation can mean public apathy. We start to see climate change news everywhere every day, which is exhausting, and soon we being to filter it out (Kerr 2009).

Nevertheless, a fourth wave of environmentalism seems likely to happen because it *has* to happen. Climate change is a reality we cannot escape. Severe weather is already impacting Canadian farmers, fishers, and foresters (Natural Resources Canada 2015a). Eventually, the cost of goods, fuel, and food will increase and affect the average person's bottom line. These and similar circumstances will create the conditions for a fourth wave of environmentalism. People will demand change because they can no longer afford the status quo. It is my hope that we do not wait that long. Too many problems need attention now. And these problems do not necessarily require radical change—at least not yet.

OUR FUTURE AND SUSTAINABLE DEVELOPMENT

Environmental policy is being challenged globally as the economy is monopolizing international agendas. In 2015, Canada had a prime minister who consistently gave the economy preference over the environment. In fact, the marriage of capitalism and globalization makes environmental policy an afterthought. Since around the 1980s, and certainly since 2006, Canada has shifted its model of government away from one in which a strong, independent, and well-funded civil service can initiate state-led efforts and toward one of privatization, even of the public service. This shift includes lessening market controls for the purpose of reducing the regulatory burden on industry, which supposedly creates more opportunities for market growth (Wood, Tanner, and Richardson 2010). This ideology is known as neoliberalism. The effect of this ideology on environmental policymaking is that, instead of instituting environmental regulation, the government removes it and limits policies, or "barriers to growth." This deregulation has affected more than environmental policy; throughout many countries in the world, governments also removed or diminished regulatory policy in other governance areas and markets, such as housing and financial markets. The risks inherent in this model came to light in the 2008 recession, and, consequently, governments worldwide had to intervene in the market to restore stability.

The Canadian government's belief that neoliberalism can coexist with environmental protection comes through as the policy of "sustainable development." If you recall from Chapter 3, Canada passed the Federal Sustainable Development Act in 2008. Unfortunately, Canada has found that sustainable development, though a lofty goal, is hard to implement. The concept is too watered down to offer meaningful guidance. Canada, like other countries, has struggled to translate the idea of sustainable development into real change. Instead, "sustainability" has enabled markets to enjoy significant autonomy and self-regulation while state actors pay lip service to a rhetoric that falsely implies current levels of development can be sustained. Wood, Tanner, and Richardson (2010) argue that environmental policy has prospered in Canada "largely to the extent it was perceived as compatible with a growing economy, such as being able to reduce waste and inefficiency or to create new markets for environmentally-conscious consumers and businesses" (1006). Whenever environmental policy challenged economic growth, it became vulnerable to revisions. For example, 2011 amendments to the Fisheries Act limit the federal government's responsibility of protection to only the fish and habitat of commercially viable species as opposed to all fish and fish habitats.

Ecological modernization is loosely tied to the sustainability discourse that (re)frames ethical and political dilemmas of industrialization as technical and managerial challenges. It posits that environmental challenges can be met with industrial modernity—by harnessing innovative technology and linking it to managerial creativity (Dryzek 2013). Under such a model, green business will benefit economically by improving production efficiency and creating competitive advantages. Essentially, ecological modernization offers a "business case" for sustainability (Wood, Tanner, and Richardson 2010). In this scenario, Prometheans, those who believe in unrelenting human progress, apply technological fixes to environmental problems. For example, instead of slowing down production in the oil sands, policies based on ecological modernization would find more efficient ways to extract bitumen or store wastewater so as to limit environmental damage. More so than sustainable development, ecological modernization is about smart management by engineers, scientists, economists, and politicians.

One reason sustainable development or managerial governance will not protect the environment in Canada is that the country is failing to produce, respect, and support science. In January 2014, the federal government announced it would close 7 of the 11 Department of Fisheries and Oceans libraries (Sisler 2014). This closure is part of a government-led initiative to shrink the size of government. Since 2009, about 2,000 federal scientists have lost their jobs, and funding for hundreds of science programs and institutions has been cut (Sisler 2014). Those scientists that still have a federal job must seek federal approval before sharing research. This policy has led to a debate among academics and public intellectuals that sometimes spills into the wider media as to whether there is a concerted effort to undermine science and scientific creditability in Canada (Evans 2014, for example). If it is the case that the federal government is cutting scientific funding in an attempt to control or manage knowledge, then the environment will certainly suffer. Sound environmental policy must be based on impartial and sound scientific research. Any other foundation dampens the prospect of genuine sustainable development or ecological modernization taking root in Canada.

FEDERALISM AND CANADA'S ENVIRONMENT IN THE TWENTY-FIRST CENTURY

There is no denying that federalism—the sharing of power between Canada's national, provincial, and territorial governments—places numerous obstacles in the path to sound and effective environmental policy. These obstacles do not result from "federalism" per se so much as from the way federalism is organized in Canada. For example, the world leader in environmental policy in the 1970s, the United States, has a federal system. And Germany, widely considered a leader today, also has a federal system. The European Union has adopted something similar to a federal system to manage relations among member states, and it is a relative leader on climate change. Canada itself was widely considered an environmental leader in the 1980s—and federalism did not prevent that. Indeed, federalism creates opportunities for experimentation and innovation that can subsequently lead to leading-edge national policy. Thus, the problem is not federalism itself but the interaction between federalism and other factors in Canada today. Who has authority is not always clear. Who should have authority is even less clear. There is a lack of coordination. There is a lack of accountability. There is an unwillingness to take responsibility. In fact, the biggest impediment to action at all levels of government is political will.

In a federal system, because power is shared so too is responsibility. Consequently, "passing the buck" is an option for all governments at any level of government (Harrison 1996). However, the Supreme Court has repeatedly affirmed a substantial role for the national government in environmental issues because the environment is of national concern. For example, in the 1980s, the court upheld a federal marine pollution statute as a matter of "national concern" (Wood, Tanner, and Richardson 2010). This precedent gives the federal government the power to regulate marine and land-based activities taking place in provinces and territories (albeit Ottawa does not necessarily have responsibility for this regulation). In the 1990s, the courts upheld the national toxic substances legislation under the federal criminal power. More recently, in 2009, the Supreme Court ruled that the federal government must identify critical habitats for species at risk—regardless of where that habitat is located (i.e., inside provinces or territories). This ruling does not give the federal government power to regulate provincial or territorial land, but the clear identification of a critical habitat by the federal government signals to the provinces that the federal government is caretaking all species and makes it easier to invoke the safety-net provision of SARA.

But the Supreme Court has also recognized that environmental leadership can come from any level of government so long as the Constitution and common law are respected. If anyone can lead, what happens when no one wants to? That seems to be the problem plaguing Canada. The federal government has established a norm of deference to the provinces (as part of open federalism) and wants to work inside a framework of cooperation and harmonization. We see the benefits of this approach in the development of Canada-wide standards. However, when cooperation on particular environmental initiatives or standards is difficult, perhaps because of competing interests or ideologies, both the provinces and the federal government get away with doing too little. This inaction occurs, in part, because the public does not demand action. Political actors will act when the rewards are clear: put votes on the line, and politicians will make different decisions.

Do We Need an Environmental Bill of Rights?

The Green Party of Canada, the New Democratic Party, and environmental NGOs such as Ecojustice are pushing to ensure that Canada's Constitution recognizes both the right to live in a healthy environment and the corresponding responsibility to protect it. "Canada is one of a shrinking minority of countries whose supreme law is silent on the environment as environmental rights and/or responsibilities are now found in the constitutions of more than 150 nations" (Boyd 2013a). To this end, Linda Duncan, an MP from the New Democrat Party, introduced Bill C-469, An Act to Establish a Canadian Environmental Bill of Rights, in the House in 2009. The bill was reintroduced in 2010 and referred to the Standing Committee on Environment and Sustainable Development. The committee reported to the House of Commons in February of 2011, asking for more time to study the bill. No further action was taken on Bill C-469. In October 2014, Linda Duncan sponsored a new bill of the same name: Bill C-634, An Act to Establish a Canadian Environmental Bill of Rights. It is true that some provinces have similar legislation, including Québec (1978), Northwest Territories (1988), Yukon (1991), and Ontario (1993), but a lot has changed politically, socially, and economically since those bills passed (Boyd 2013b). A federal environmental bill of rights would require enormous public support.

Neoliberalism has decreased opportunities for public participation and made access to information more difficult. Canada's continued dependence on a resource-based economy, as opposed to a knowledge-based economy,[4] ties Canadian prosperity to that of industries profiting from resource extraction, seemingly aligning the interests of these companies with the public interest. For example, so long as Albertans are dependent upon the oil sands for jobs and economic stability—both of which produce funding for public services such as universities—they will find it extraordinarily difficult to regulate the oil sands for environmental reasons.

Is there a way out of this problem of political will? Reforming our electoral system may go a long way to achieving environmental reform. This is a common refrain among many environmentalists. Presently, we have a first-past-the-post (FPTP) system whereby the person with the most votes in a single riding wins the seat for that riding. If, for example, Canada's three main parties offer candidates in a riding and the Conservative gets 40 per cent of the vote, the Liberal 35 per cent, and the NDP 25 per cent, then the Conservative Party candidate wins that seat—even though 60 per cent of the total votes in the riding went to other candidates. In contrast to this system, **proportional representation** ensures each party a number of seats in the House of Commons in proportion to the share of the vote it wins nationally. In the 2011, election, the Conservative Party won just 39.6 per cent of the popular vote. The reason the party is in power is that, in 166 ridings, Conservatives won more votes than any other candidate. Many people point out that the party has support from only 40 per cent of Canadians.

In 2011, the NDP won 30.6 per cent of the popular vote, the Liberals 18.9 per cent, the Bloc Québécois (BQ) 6.1 per cent, and the Green Party 3.9 per cent. If we were to break those numbers down proportionally, then, out of 308 possible seats, the NDP would have about 92 seats (they have 103), the Liberals 58 seats (they have 34), the BQ 18 seats (they have 4), and the Green Party 12 seats (they have 1). Obviously, proportional representation would tend to give more support and power to the Green Party.

Proportional representation (PR) systems tend to favour environmental concerns in a more systemic way too. If each party knew it would get seats based on the percentage of votes it obtained, fewer candidates might decide to "play to the middle ground" and water down their policy platforms to make them acceptable to the majority. Moreover, voters would not feel as though they were "wasting" a vote by voting for the Green Party, and those wanting a change in government would not have to worry so much that "splitting the vote" between the other two or more contending parties would mean the return of an unpopular administration. In the first-past-the-post system, it makes sense to vote for one of the two (or three) front-running parties to help that party win the entire seat. For example, if there is a close race between a Liberal and an NDP candidate, and you really hope that the Liberal does not win, it makes sense to vote NDP—even when your true preference is the Green Party. In a PR system, each person would just vote for the party he or she wants in office without having to worry about being strategic.

The likelihood of Canada switching to a PR system is very low because this change would have to pass through the House and Senate, where the majority parties stand to lose the most. The Conservative Party of Canada is not going to support PR because, at present, the FPTP system favours the party. Second, electoral reform is controversial and tends to confuse voters. People do not understand PR because they are unfamiliar with it. Maybe if a province, say, British Columbia, adopted a PR system and used it for a few elections, Canadians might be more open to a change at the national level.[5] In the meantime, electoral reform is not the white horse for environmentalists in Canada.

CONCLUSIONS

In *Eating Dirt*, a book about forestry and tree planters, Canadian author Charlotte Gill (2012) describes human nature:

> Perhaps our fatal flaw is inquisitiveness.... If an object exists in this world, it can't stay intact, unexamined, unused. We're biological capitalists. If it lives we've got to make the best of it. We've got to hunt, cook, and taste it. Whatever it is, we've got to harness it and ride it, pluck it and transform it, shave it down and build it up. We just have to glue, mold, freeze, and melt it into something else that hardly resembles that thing in its virgin state. We've got to get our hands on every last scrap and transform it into something useful, even if we have a million of those things already. We've got to cut it down and wring it out until the final ounce is gone (101).

That may have been true about Canadians in the nineteenth and twentieth centuries. But it cannot be true of Canadians in the twenty-first century. The world—yours and mine—can longer sustain this type of human inquisitiveness. Instead, the world needs a new and more directed type of curiosity and human ingenuity. Recognizing that we cannot solve all problems and that we cannot sustain "biological capitalism," we must embrace conservation and sustainability and re-embrace the "three Rs": recycling, reusing, and reducing. How are we going to do this? The creation of sound environmental policy is an essential part of the answer.

Policy innovation is a necessity. We need more than voluntary policy tools. We need all kinds of policies that work in tandem across difference contexts. Historically, Canada has tended to rely on administrative discretion and a consultative style whereby rules are developed and enforced in a largely non-coercive way via closed-door, bilateral negotiations between government and industry (Wood, Tanner, and Richardson 2010). This model will not suffice in the twenty-first century. And yet Canada continues to govern the environment in such a manner. Policy innovation in Canada has meant more market-friendly policy instruments, for example, economic incentives and contractual agreements with industry. In other places, twenty-first century environmental policy has evolved into a diverse array of policy tools—regulatory, voluntary, and economic. This is what the future of environmental governance must entail.

In each chapter you were encouraged to think about the terms introduced in Chapter 2: politics, policy, federalism, and governance. By now you should have a good grasp of environmental policymaking in Canada as well as a framework in which to assess good governance. Politics, or the battle over who gets what, when, and how, leads to an array of public policies. Federalism creates constraints on power and, consequently, the boundaries within which policies can evolve. The constraints established by sections 91 and 92 of our Constitution call for governance—the sharing of power across different levels of government and with non-state actors such as NGOs and citizens. Environmental governance is changing the way we protect our environmental and exploit our natural resources. Multilevel governance is what created the Boreal Forest Agreement and the Mackenzie River Basin Board, for example. Multilevel governance can lead us sustainably through the twenty-first century.

But governance requires **responsible citizenship**. Too many of us care too little about something far too important to overlook—our environment. Politicians lack the political will because the electorate lacks the knowledge, interest, and concern. Thus, more than anything, the twenty-first century is a time for responsible citizenship. As citizens of the world and members of a community, each of us is responsible for the environment, for taking care of the planet and of the places where we live. Today's youth is the most politically disengaged generation of the past 100 years, at least insofar as voting is concerned.[6] If we were to gather together every eligible voter aged 18–24 in Canada, we would expect less than half of them, about 40 per cent, to go out and vote in a federal election. We'd expect fewer in a provincial election.

Yet, young Canadians are more educated and more urbanized than any prior generation of youth in the country. As political scientists, we cannot explain why political disengagement defines young Canadians (Blais and Loewen 2011). But, for the environment, there is no more worrying trend than increasing apathy among the next generation of Canadians, as they will inherit not just Canada's resources but also responsibility for them. They will also inherit many environmental problems of international scope. Environmental policy is not an end in itself but a means to a better, more equitable, more sustainable Canada. Do not underestimate how powerful you are in this world. You have two important policy cards in your own pocket: you are a voter and you are a consumer. So when you cast your ballot or spend your money, do not forget you are a citizen of this planet.

Key Terms

policy evaluation; formal review; Auditor General of Canada; public interest lawsuits; ecological modernization; proportional representation; responsible citizenship

Discussion Questions

1. Why should Canada be an environmental leader from a global perspective?
2. Do you think a fourth wave of environmentalism will happen in the next decade? Why or why not?
3. Why is it unlikely that Canada will adopt proportional representation to better reflect environmental concerns across the country?
4. Thinking about the issues discussed in this book, explain three ways that federalism creates challenges for sound environmental policy in Canada.
5. How would a shift from government to governance create better policy for the environment? Is such a shift already underway?

Suggested Readings

Gill, Charlotte. 2013. *Eating Dirt: Deep Forests, Big Timber, and Life with the Tree-Planting Tribe*. Vancouver: Greystone Books.
Klein, Naomi. 2014. *This Changes Everything: Capitalism vs. the Climate*. New York: Simon & Schuster.
Macdonald, Douglas. 2007. *Business and Environmental Politics in Canada*. Toronto: University of Toronto Press.
Suzuki, David T. 2003. *The David Suzuki Reader*. Vancouver: Greystone Books.

Notes

1 Note, however, that the federal budget is bigger than ever in terms of dollars spent, but as a percentage of the GDP, the government's budget size is at its smallest in 50 years.

2 It should be noted that while tourism can provide a good argument for preserving our natural environment, not all tourism is "green." Eco-tourism can and should be part of the Canadian economy, but we must be mindful about the amount of pollution created through mass tourism.

3 Québec is not part of the Pacific Coast Action Plan.

4 A knowledge-based economy would be one built upon technological development, science, higher education, and financial services. No "economy" is purely knowledge based. Instead, Canada would continue to develop its natural resources but would diversify its economy and have other sectors to rely upon for security.

5 Some provinces have put electoral reform on the table in recent years. BC was one, as was Ontario; both provinces rejected the proposal and retained the FPTP system.

6 Some youth may feel they are engaging in ways other than voting, such as through the Internet. May be young people use Facebook and Twitter to support political action or policy positions. However, this type of "slacktivism" often does not have tangible results.

GLOSSARY

Aboriginal—Umbrella term used in reference to three large categories of indigenous peoples in Canada: Inuit, First Nations, and Métis. "Aboriginal" connotes subjectivity and is a construct of the state vis-à-vis Section 35 of the Constitution Act, 1982.

Aboriginal land claims—Claims to land (and resource rights) made by Aboriginal groups in areas of the country where no prior treaties exist or where no other legal mechanisms are in place to determine use rights.

Aboriginal title—Right to land and resources that goes beyond "reserve" land for Aboriginals to live on. Title ensures Aboriginals the right to benefit monetarily from the natural resources found on the land.

Aboriginal traditional knowledge—Comprehensive worldview that includes the knowledge and practices of Aboriginal peoples. It is developed through historical experience with the land and environment and is passed down orally through the generations.

affluence—An abundance of money and resources (such as property).

Agricultural Policy Framework—Agreements between the federal government and each province or territory to deal with agricultural issues such as business risk, environmental stewardship, food safety, science, soil management, and international trade.

allocations—Pertaining to water, permits or indicators of the right to use a specified amount of water (sometimes for a specific purpose).

alternative energy—Energy that is derived from sources other than fossil fuels: e.g., wind, solar, or nuclear power, or energy from biofuels.

anthropocentrism—Human centred; belief that humans are the most important species on the planet.

Arctic—Polar area located close to the North Pole. Although the exact definition of demarcation is contested, the Arctic is often considered to be the area north of the Arctic Circle.

Arctic Council—Internationally recognized governing body in the North comprised of eight permanent members and six indigenous organizations as well as several observer organizations (other countries and NGOs).

artificial extinction—Extinction of a species caused by human beings (through activities such as overhunting, overfishing, or habitat destruction).

Auditor General of Canada—An independent agency that conducts audits and financial studies of any agency or program in Canada. The audits are presented to Parliament.

bioaccumulation—The state of substances accumulating or becoming concentrated in the body of a living organism. In humans, substances are usually stored in fatty tissue.

biodiversity—Variation in life forms.

biofuels—Fuels that come from living organisms (e.g., plants and micro-algae) and so are renewable.

bitumen—A semi-solid form of petroleum that is often black and sticky.

boreal forest—A vegetation zone in the North dominated by forests of hardy trees, such as pines, larches, and spruces, that can withstand a cold climate. Canada's boreal forest extends across the country and makes up about 24 per cent of the circumpolar boreal forest that rings the Northern Hemisphere (all northern countries have boreal forest, including Russia, Sweden, Norway, and Finland). Although the forest comprises almost one-third of Canada's landmass, only about 10 per cent of Canada's population lives in this region (3.7 million people).

branches of government—Refers to the different sectors of government that together make law and policy. In Canada there are three branches of government: legislative, executive, and judicial.

British North America Act of 1867—Enacted by the Parliament of the United Kingdom, this act established the federal Dominion of Canada and created the structure of the Canadian government (including the three branches of government). See also "Constitution Act."

Brundtland Commission—A group of experts chosen by the United Nations to study and report on "sustainable development" in the world. The formal title of the commission is the World Commission on Environment and Development. The final report by the group, published in 1987, was titled *Our Common Future*.

bureaucracy—A body or organization of non-elected government officials (often referred to as "civil servants"). The bureaucracy is part of the executive branch of government. It includes agencies such as Environment Canada and Natural Resources Canada.

cabinet—A group of elected parliamentarians appointed by the prime minister to oversee the operations of various government departments, and to develop policies and introduce bills. Each cabinet member, or minister, is assigned a portfolio, or area of responsibility, and advises the prime minister on this specific area of policy importance in Canada.

Calder case—A 1973 Supreme Court case (*Calder et al. v. Attorney-General of British Columbia*) that acknowledged, for the first time in Canadian history, the existence of Aboriginal title to land and agreed that such title existed outside of colonial law. Although Calder lost the case, future court decisions made reference to the court's affirmation of title as existing previous to colonial laws as part of "common law."

Canada Act of 1982—The Parliament of the United Kingdom passed the Canada Act and thereby gave Canada the power to amend its own constitution without further approval from the United Kingdom. At this time, the Charter of Rights and Freedoms was added to the Constitution.

Canada Forest Accord—An agreement between governmental and non-governmental stakeholders in the forestry sector usually issued every five years as part of the National Forest Strategy (NFS) developed by the Canadian Council of Forest Ministers (provincial and territorial and federal ministers). The NFS is concerned with how to implement sustainable forest management across the country.

Canada–US softwood lumber dispute—The most significant trade dispute between Canada and the United States. The dispute centres on whether Canada is subsidizing a trade commodity and thereby violating the conditions of the North American Free Trade Agreement.

Canada-wide standards—Intergovernmental agreements through which federal, provincial (but not Québec), and territorial governments agree to harmonize their standards for specific environmental or health regulations.

Canadian Environmental Protection Act—Keystone legislation for chemical management in Canada. The act is jointly administered by Environment Canada and Health Canada.

cap-and-trade system—A market-based approach to controlling emissions and pollution (sometimes called emissions trading). The government or authority sets a cap on how much pollution can be emitted. All firms (emitters of pollution) need a permit to emit pollutions. The transfer of permits, from those who have too many to those without enough, is a trade.

carbon dioxide (CO_2)—Natural chemical compound comprised of two oxygen atoms and one carbon atom. CO_2 is a greenhouse gas as it can trap and re-emit radiation in the atmosphere.

carbon price—Set amount that must be paid to emit 1 ton of carbon dioxide into the atmosphere.

carbon tax—A tax that is put on the release of the carbon dioxide humans create by burning fossil fuels.

central Canada—Although not technically a geographical designation, central Canada comprises Québec and Ontario because the majority of the Canadian population lives in these two provinces and because these provinces have the largest economies in the country.

Charter of Rights and Freedoms—Bill of rights established in 1982 that is part of the Constitution of Canada. The Charter guarantees certain political and civil rights to all citizens of Canada but does not include the right to a healthy or clean environment.

Chemical Valley—A corridor of industry just south of the downtown core of Sarnia, Ontario, that is home to 62 chemical, oil refinery, and power-generating companies. Sarnia has some of the worst air pollution in the industrialized world.

citizen experts—Members of the public who are not elected to government office but have influence over public policy because of their expertise in a given field. For example, a scientist who studies algae blooms may be asked for advice by policymakers when they are setting water quality levels for the Great Lakes.

civil action—A lawsuit in which a private individual sues someone else or sues a company.

civil servants—Individuals who work for government agencies or departments. The civil service functions as the staff of the Canadian state.

class action suits—Lawsuits in which a group of people in a similar situation sue someone or sue a company for damages.

climate change—The changes in weather patterns that are observed on Earth due to the additional anthropogenic greenhouse gases retaining and emitting heat.

closed bargaining—A form of bargaining between the government and private or public agencies that occurs behind closed doors without public consultation or transparency.

co-management—Shared responsibility for and authority over land and resources. The term co-management is usually used to describe an agreement between Aboriginal groups and the Government of Canada in specific geographical areas, e.g., the North.

coalition government—Government by two or more parties that cooperate to form a cabinet, share executive power, and lead the country together. Coalition governments usually occur when no party, on its own, can achieve a majority or a stable minority government and MPs in the House of Commons from several parties have a common interest in forming a government.

constitution—The supreme or fundamental law in a political system that determines not only the relationship between the state and its citizens but also the distribution of powers among different state actors.

Constitution Act—Used to refer to several legal documents that today form the supreme law of Canada. The main document is the Constitution Act of 1982, which incorporated the British North America Act of 1867 (renamed the Constitution Act of 1867 by the Canada Act of 1982) and gave life to the Canadian Constitution as a legal creation of Canada itself.

constitutional litigation—Area of law that deals with the rules of government or procedures that are laid out in a constitution.

constitutional monarchy A form of democratic government in which there is a constitution as well as a monarch who acts a symbolic or non-political head of state. The constitution determines the laws and procedures for the country. The monarch has no legal authority.

convention—An agreement or treaty in international law.

COSEWIC—Committee on the Status of Endangered Wildlife in Canada, a national committee of scientists that assesses wildlife health and distribution and determines which categories of species are at risk of extinction.

Crown land—In Canada, land that is owned by the provinces or the federal government. It can also be referred to as "public lands."

deep ecology—An environmental philosophy founded by Norwegian thinker Arne Naess in 1973. It is predicated on the idea that all living things have intrinsic value *and* inalienable (possibly legal) rights to existence.

devolution of power—The granting of legislative powers (and responsibilities) from higher and more central governments to those at lower levels. For example, a national government could grant power to subnational governments, such as provinces, and these provincial governments could grant power to municipal governments.

dirty dozen—The 12 worst persistent organic pollutants (chemicals) in commercial circulation as determined by the United Nations Environment Programme and the Intergovernmental Panel on Chemical Safety. These chemicals were banned by the signatories to the Stockholm Convention of 2001.

duty to consult—The legal obligation of government to consult with Aboriginal organizations when making decisions that affect Aboriginal land or resources.

Earth Summit—The shorthand name for the United Nations Conference on Environment and Development in 1992, also known as the Rio Summit.

ecocentrism—An environmental philosophy premised on the idea that all of nature has intrinsic worth and should be considered when people make economic and political decisions.

ecological modernization—School of thought that promotes the argument that the economy benefits from environmentalism. The theory suggests that green business will benefit economically by improving production efficiency and creating competitive advantages.

economic instruments—A type of policy that relies on monetary incentive to alter behaviour (such as taxes, charges, rewards, and direct payment).

economic regionalism—The theory or practice of different regions with different resources that are relied upon for economic profit and stability forming regional, rather than central, systems of administration or affiliation. For example, the Pacific NorthWest Economic Region includes British Columbia, Alberta, Saskatchewan, Yukon, and the Northwest Territories, as well as the US states of Alaska, Idaho, Oregon, Montana, and Washington.

economic staple—A single resource, often a natural resource, that a provincial or regional economy depends on for profit. In Canada, these staples have historically included resources such as beaver pelts and forest products. More recent economic staples are shale gas, oil, and hydroelectricity.

Environment Canada—The lead bureaucratic agency responsible for overseeing the administration of environmental law and policy

environmental assessment—A study that must determine the extent to which a project will cause adverse environmental effects.

environmental indicators—Measures that signify what is happening in the environment, such as the measure of air or water quality.

environmental laws—Policy that has formally passed through Parliament and become part of common law in Canada.

environmental policy—Regulations, laws, guidelines, and rules aimed at *protecting* the environment from adverse effects that are the result of development, resource extraction, or consumption.

executive branch—The part of government that is responsible for the development and implementation of laws and policies and for ensuring that public business is carried out efficiently and effectively. In

Canada, this branch includes the monarch, the prime minister and cabinet, and the bureaucracy.

extinction—The end of a species, which occurs when the last member of that species dies.

Federal Sustainable Development Act—A law passed by Parliament in 2008 that guides the implementation of sustainable development across all federal branches of government.

federalism—The principle or actuality of political authority being divided between the national, central government, e.g., in Ottawa, and subnational governments, e.g., the 10 provincial and 3 territorial governments.

feed-in-tariff policies—Policy tools that incentivize investment in renewable energy, typically by allowing energy producers to sell alternative energy at a set amount to the power grid.

First Nations—The people who have occupied Canada (excluding the Inuit and other northern peoples) since time immemorial. In 2015, Aboriginal Affairs and Northern Development Canada recognized over 600 different First Nations communities.

first wave of environmentalism—A movement that began in the United States at the turn of the twentieth century, when the federal government created national parks and started conserving forests and wildlife.

first-in-time, first-in-right system—A system of water allocation based on the seniority of a permit. Essentially, a permit holder gets exclusive right to use water from the date of application.

first-past-the-post (FTPT) system—An electoral system in which the person with the most votes (but not necessarily a majority) in a single riding wins the seat for that riding.

food sovereignty—A social, political, and environmental movement that focuses on global food supply. The idea is that a region should be able to supply its own food through hiring local people to farm local land and sell at local markets.

forest certification—A tool for the forestry industry that verifies, after assessment by a third party, that wood or wood products have been produced using management practices meeting specific environmental (or social) standards.

formal review (of policy)—A systematic and comprehensive assessment of a policy, typically resulting in a report on its effectiveness and implementation. Frequently, a committee in the House of Commons or the Senate (or a joint committee) examines a piece of legislation and its implementation years after it passed in Parliament. Often, formal reviews result in several recommendations to Parliament.

fossil fuels—Fuels formed from buried dead organisms—ones that died over a million years ago. These compressed, decomposed organisms consist of carbon, which is the building block of oil, coal, and natural gas.

fracking—Hydraulic fracturing, or the blasting of large volumes of water, sand, and chemicals at high pressure down a well to crack rock and free up natural gas.

framing—Using how something is presented, often a news story, to emphasize particular aspects of a message, thereby influencing public perception.

freedom of the seas—Doctrine or tacit understanding by all countries that a state extended three miles off its coast and anything beyond that three miles was "international waters," open to everyone in times of peace and belonging to no one.

freshwater supply—Naturally occurring water on Earth (surface or ground) that has low levels of salts.

genetically modified organism (GMO)—Any organism whose genes have been technologically engineered or altered.

governance—The process of governing and decision making. The study of governance examines how elected officials are influenced and mobilized by citizens, the media, or interest groups to act in certain ways at certain times.

governor general—Representative of the monarchy in Canada. He or she is appointed by the monarch on the advice of the prime minister.

grasshopper effect—Environmental process by which certain chemicals or pollutants are transported through cycles of evaporation and condensation.

green consumerism—Purchasing and non-purchasing decisions made by consumers based at least partly on environmental criteria.

Green Party of Canada (GP)—Political party created in 1983 to represent environmental concerns across the country.

Green Revolution—A dramatic increase in global agricultural production that began in the 1940s. It was fuelled both by government policies designed to increase food production and by technological and systematic changes, such as the development of chemical fertilizers and synthetic herbicides and pesticides and of new farming practices (e.g., monoculture crops).

greenhouse effect—A natural mechanism that retains the sun's heat, radiated back from the Earth's surface, so the planet does not become too cold for life. A range of different gases act as greenhouse gases, and their common characteristic is that each can absorb heat emitted from the Earth and re-emit that heat—thus increasing the mean temperature of the planet.

groundwater—Water in the pores and fractures of rock formations under our feet.

House of Commons—In Canada, the lower (elected) chamber of the legislative branch of government.

hypertrophication—The process by which natural and human-generated air and chemical pollutants, such as nitrates, fertilizers, and sewage, enter into water ecosystems and cause an increase in plant or bacteria populations.

Indian Act—A law, originally passed in 1876 by Parliament and amended numerous times, that defines who is considered "Indian" in Canada and sets out the land management and other responsibilities of the federal government in relation to "Indians" and reserves. Currently, Aboriginal Affairs and Northern Development Canada (AANDC) is the responsible department.

indigenous—Means "native to the land" or "original" inhabitants or peoples.

instrumental value—Extrinsic value that material (or non-material) objects can have in the sense that they provide meaning or value to human beings.

interest groups—Organizations or people banded together by a single interest or set of interests and actively working together to try to change public policy.

international law—A complex web of conventions, protocols, agreements, and the like, which are supported by countless organizations and institutions. Each country must implement policy domestically and independently. The penalties for failure to comply with a ratified treaty are international shaming and, in more extreme cases, trade sanctions or withholding of financial aid or assistance.

intrinsic value—Worth that a material (or non-material) object can have in the sense that it is valued for itself and outside of human beings' use or purpose for the object.

Inuit—A culturally similar group of people who inhabit the Arctic and sub-Arctic regions of Canada (as well as of the United States and Greenland). Inuit are culturally and linguistically distinct from First Nations people and Métis.

judicial branch—The judiciary or the body of judges and courts responsible for the non-partisan interpretation of law in Canada. The members of this branch are judges who are appointed federally or provincially.

judicial review of administrative action—A process in which the judicial branch reviews a decision made by someone or some agency with administrative powers, such as ministers, tribunals, bureaucratic agencies, municipal councillors, and so on. The court assesses the decisions or actions to determine if they are lawful (in accordance with common law or the Constitution).

Keystone XL Pipeline—A proposed 1,179-mile pipeline that will carry oil from Hardisty, Alberta, to Steele City, Nebraska. The pipeline will connect to already existing pipelines so that Alberta's oil can reach refineries in Texas.

land claims agreements—Modern treaties that exist between the Government of Canada and Aboriginal organizations (mainly in the North). These agreements establish authority over and co-management boards for land and resources.

legislative branch—The branch of government, often referred to as Parliament, intended to represent the people of Canada. It comprises the House of Commons and the Senate.

Mackenzie Gas Project—Proposed pipeline intended to gather natural gas from Canada's Mackenzie Delta and Beaufort Sea area and carry it through the Northwest Territories, joining the existing patchwork of pipelines in Alberta.

Mackenzie River Basin Board—An intergovernmental body made up of the federal government, the Northwest Territories, Yukon, British Columbia, Alberta, and Saskatchewan that oversees water and environmental issues affecting the Mackenzie River watershed.

majority government—Government by a single party that has not just the most seats in the House of Commons but more than half of all available seats in the House. When a party can form a majority government and govern with a majority mandate, the legislation it proposes passes through the House with frequency and ease because it holds more seats than the rest of the parties combined.

Malthusian catastrophe—The prediction that a population crisis would force a return to subsistence-level conditions.

memorandum of understanding—A commonly used agreement between governments and the private sector to achieve a particular goal.

Métis—The word used to describe Canadians who can trace their origins to both First Nations and European heritage.

minority government—A government formed when no single party has the majority of seats in the House of Commons by the party with the most seats (the party leader becomes prime minister). Minority governments need the support of other parties to pass bills.

multilevel governance—The fact (or theory) of a central or national government's power and decision making being reallocated to or influenced by a broader set of policy actors than the traditional ones. These might include agencies or governments at other levels of power (e.g., international or municipal actors) and Aboriginal bands, citizen groups, and non-governmental organizations.

municipality—A city or town or any urban centre with administrative powers. In the Canadian federal system, municipalities derive their powers from the provinces, and all three levels of government (federal, provincial, and municipal) can share power over certain issues (e.g., water conservation).

myth of abundance—The false sense of security about Canada's water supply and quality.

National Energy Board—An independent federal agency created in 1959 that regulates aspects of the energy industry that are under federal jurisdiction. (It is independent from Parliament and serves as part of the federal bureaucracy.)

National Energy Program—A set of policies created in 1980 by the Liberal Party under Prime Minister Trudeau. The intent of the policy was to foster energy security, a redistribution of wealth toward the federal government and consumers, and Canadian ownership of Canada's oil industry. The program was deeply unpopular in the West and was ended by the Progressive Conservative Party.

natural resources—Material goods or products that are derived from nature, such as wood, oil, freshwater, fish, and sunshine.

neoliberalism—An ideology or set of principles advocating free trade, privatization, open markets, and deregulation. Generally, neoliberal policies include cuts in government spending and a greater reliance on private industry to provide goods and services.

non-governmental organizations (NGOs)—Organizations that are not part of government but seek to influence government policy through lobbying and mobilizing the public. They are not political parties or related to parties, as they are not trying to elect members to government.

non-point-source pollution—Water or air pollution that comes from multiple (and sometimes unknown) sources.

non-renewable resources—Resources, usually with economic value, that, once used, cannot be readily replaced or used again in the same form, such as oil and coal (which, once burned, are transformed).

norms—Informal rules of behaviour shared by a group of people or society at large (such as wearing shoes in public or respecting your elders).

Northern Gateway Pipeline—Pipeline project that will extend twin pipelines from Bruderheim, Alberta, to Kitimat, British Columbia (one pipeline for natural gas and one for diluted bitumen).

northern policy—Policy developed in or for one or more of the Canadian territories (Yukon, Northwest Territories, or Nunavut). The term cannot be used interchangeable with Arctic policy (which refers to policy developed in or for the area north of the Arctic Circle).

Northern Strategy—A policy announced in a 2009 document entitled *Canada's Northern Strategy: Our North, Our Heritage, Our Future*.

The strategy, created by the Harper government, lays out domestic policy in the three territories.

Northwest Passage—A sea route along the northern coast of North America—mainly of Canada. This route connects the Pacific Ocean to the Atlantic Ocean through a series of connected waterways or passages that are collectively known as the "Northwest Passage." In December 2009, Canada's Parliament formally named the passage the "Canadian Northwest Passage."

nuclear power—A form of energy created from a nuclear process using actinide chemicals (metallic chemicals), such as uranium (which is a common element in Earth's crust). When the nucleus of an atom from an actinide chemical is split into smaller parts, gamma rays result. These release large amounts of energy that can be captured and stored for human purposes.

omnibus bill—Any bill that covers a wide range of unrelated topics.

open federalism—A form of governing at the federal level in which the balance of power is tilted toward the provinces and territories by way of reining in federal spending power and responsibilities, recognizing a larger role for the provinces in the international arena, and giving greater respect to the division of powers as stated in the Constitution.

organic—The quality of being naturally derived from plants, animals, or other living organisms. Organic food is grown without chemicals (pesticides and fertilizers in the case of crops and antibiotics in the case of livestock) and is not genetically modified.

Paris 2015—Shorthand for the international commitment on climate change arranged in Paris, France, at the 2015 United Nations Climate Change Conference.

parliamentary democracy—A form of democratic government in which decisions (about law) are made by the elected (and appointed) officials who comprise Parliament.

party whip—The MP or MPP/MLA in each political party whose responsibility it is to ensure that each member of the party attends significant votes and casts his or her ballot along party lines on a given bill.

periphery provinces—The provinces outside of Ontario and Québec (central Canada). Western and Eastern Canadians see their economies and needs as remaining outside of central Canada's economy and political power.

point-source pollution—Water or air pollution from a known site or source.

policy evaluation—Final stage of the policy process. This stage is reflexive and is about taking stock, so policy can be adapted and improvements made, if necessary, or completely revoked and cancelled.

policy process (policy cycle)—A useful description of how policy is made that includes five steps through which a bill passes: agenda setting, formulation, legitimization, implementation, and evaluation.

political party—A group of citizens united by a similar ideological outlook or worldview or historical tradition and seeking control of government to promote their ideas and politics.

politics—According to Harold Lasswell's classic statement, "the art of deciding who gets what, when, and how."

polluter-pay principle—The idea that those who cause pollution should be responsible for paying the cost of cleaning it up or of offsetting the damage it has done to the environment.

Prairie Provinces Water Board—Intergovernmental board made up of the federal government and Manitoba, Alberta, and Saskatchewan that oversees water and environmental issues surrounding shared rivers and runoff.

precautionary principle—Defined as "where there are threats of serious or irreversible damage, lack of full scientific certainty shall not be used as a reason for postponing cost-effective measures to prevent environmental degradation." Often this principle is translated as "better safe than sorry" as it implies that we should regulate something now rather than being sorry in the future.

priming—Exposing the public to a particular point of reference or context to shape people's perceptions of certain people, events, and issues.

principle of common but differentiated responsibility—The idea that countries have contributed differently to global environmental problems and therefore should have different responsibilities for addressing them.

Promethean approach—The idea that the application of science, technology, and research can solve environmental problems. Promethean solutions to resource limitations or pollution, for example, tend to emphasize eliminating inefficiencies or addressing a lack of information (e.g., discovering new procedures or technologies) rather than emphasizing values or conservation. People who subscribe to this approach dismiss the intrinsic worth of nature and instead see the environment as a cache of "resources" for human development.

proportional representation (PR)—An electoral process by which a party gets the number of seats in government (such as in the House of Commons) in proportion to the share of the votes it won nationally.

public interest lawsuits—Legal actions involving people suing a party (e.g., the government or a corporation) for the protection of public interest. The people bringing the suit have no particular personal stake in the outcome but instead want to protect the environment or public health or some public right because doing so benefits all.

public policy—Intentional action or inaction by the government that influences the lives of citizens.

regulatory instruments—Policies that prohibit or require specific actions or behaviours (typically considered "do" and "don't" policies that come with consequences).

renewable energy—Any form of energy that comes from a source that is not completely depleted by the creation or use of that energy, such as wind or solar energy.

reserve—Land set apart and designated as a reserve for the use and occupancy of an "Indian" group or band.

resource policy—Regulation of primary resource extraction, such as policy for oil, forestry, fisheries, mining, fracking, and so on.

responsible citizenship—The position or status of being an individual who accepts the responsibilities of citizenship, including being a good steward of the environment and participating in the democratic process.

revenue-neutral carbon tax—A type of carbon tax whose proceeds would be used to encourage producers and consumers to shift toward renewable energy and not by the government to finance new spending or programs. Revenue-neutral policies do not add or subtract from government revenue.

Rio Declaration—Document signed in 1992 at the Earth Summit in Rio de Janeiro (the UN Conference on Environment and Development) that outlines global political commitments to the environment, human health, sustainable development, and social justice. The declaration includes 27 principles.

riparian rights—Non-transferable rights to access water flow on or bordering property.

risk assessment—An estimate by experts and analysts of the magnitude of risk posed to public health or to the environment. Risk is generally considered to be the product of the probability of an event or exposure and its consequences. The basic question being answered through risk assessment is this: "How much risk *is* there?"

risk management—A process by which people, e.g., politicians or bureaucrats, evaluate the costs and benefits of a risk and decide how society will manage those trade-offs. The basic question being answered is this: "How much risk *should* there be?"

Royal Proclamation—A 1763 document issued by King George III of Britain with the original intent of claiming British territory in North America after Britain won the Seven Years' War with France. It defined Aboriginal title, set the stage for the reserve system, and created government responsibility for Indians (First Nations).

safety net—In the context of Canadian environmental policy, a provision of the Species at Risk Act that grants the federal government authority to regulate species' habitat on non-federal lands when a province fails to protect the species.

second wave of environmentalism—An environmental movement occurring in the 1960s when there was immense public awareness of issues such as air pollution and toxic waste. This wave of environmentalism led to the passage of major legislation in the late 1960s and the 1970s in both Canada and the United States.

Section 91 of the Constitution—Section that sets out the issues and areas that fall under federal authority.

Section 92 of the Constitution—Section that sets out the issues and areas that fall under provincial authority.

self-government (Aboriginal)—The right of Inuit and First Nations peoples to make decisions about matters internal to their communities; integral to their unique cultures, traditions, and languages; and connected with their relationship to the land and resources.

Senate—The upper (non-elected) chamber of the legislative branch of government originally designed to counterbalance representation by population so as to mitigate disparity between regions and between the English and French in Canada.

smart growth—A type of urban development that is more sustainable and greener than the usual urban sprawl. It is generally demarcated by trees, parks, preserved wilderness areas, bike lanes, and affordable housing.

social licence—The granting of political favour (or trust and legitimacy) to a company because of its good behaviour or "good deeds." In exchange for corporate engagement with societal values and issues, a business receives the acceptance it needs to act in ways that might run counter to the public interest (e.g., polluting).

soft laws—Policies that are not legally binding or not backed by any serious threat of punishment. Because no global government or military enforces international laws, such agreements and treaties are often considered soft laws.

staples—Raw resources (e.g., wood, coal, oil, fish, or fur) that Canada sells (or traded, in the early development of the country), often to foreign nations. The exportation of these resources is the driver of economic growth in Canada.

Stockholm Convention—International treaty that was originally signed by 92 countries and the European Community in 2001 in Stockholm, Sweden. Its aim is to regulate persistent organic pollutants such as DDT and PCBs. Over 175 countries had signed the convention by 2015.

Stockholm Declaration—A 26-article declaration adopted by the UN Conference on the Human Environment on June 16, 1972. It is the first document in international environmental law to recognize the right of humans to live in a healthy environment.

stumpage fees—The price that a private firm must pay the government for the right to harvest trees on a specified parcel of land.

sulphur dioxide—A naturally occurring chemical compound. It is a by-product of burning fossil fuels and causes air pollution and acid rain.

Supreme Court of Canada—Part of the judicial branch of government and the highest court of law in Canada.

sustainable development—Generally considered to be the practice of creating economic growth today without jeopardizing the ability of future generations to live in health and meet their own economic needs, although definitions are contested.

tenure system—A system of land holding in which tenants are granted the right to use, control, and transfer land by a higher authority envisioned as owning all land, such as the Crown. In practical terms in Canada, it involves the leasing of public lands to private companies for a set period, often with the right to take resources such as timber from the land.

think tanks—Research institutions that do not have members or encourage specific citizen actions but instead provide studies, data, and information to the general public (and the government).

third wave of environmentalism—Environmental movement occurring during the late 1980s and early 1990s when widespread public awareness grew into public demand for government officials to enact legislation related to issues such as the ozone layer, wildlife preservation, acid rain, sustainable development, and climate change.

traditional territory—Land that was historically used by Aboriginal peoples for hunting and fishing or other economic or cultural practices.

tragedy of the commons—Theory developed by Garrett Hardin suggesting that individuals acting rationally and according to each person's individual self-interest will behave contrary to the best interests of the whole group by depleting or polluting whatever is owned in common.

transboundary water—Water that crosses an international border.

transjurisdictional—A policy area that crosses two or more jurisdictions, such as air or water quality policy.

treaties (Aboriginal)—Agreements between the Canadian government (or the British government before 1867) and Aboriginal bands that usually involved forfeiting title to land in exchange for reserve land, money, hunting weapons, clothing, and rights to hunt or fish.

unicameral legislatures—Legislatures that have only one chamber or level, normally the lower chamber or House of Commons. In Canada, each province has only a lower house in its legislative branch, although Québec did not abolish its upper house until 1968.

United Nations Convention on Biological Diversity—Treaty created in 1992 to bind its signatories to the protection of biological diversity and sustainable ecosystems.

United Nations Convention on the Law of the Sea—One of the most important international treaties governing or guiding action in the Arctic Circle. It defines the rights and responsibilities (both economic and environmental) of all countries when it comes to the oceans.

United Nations Environment Programme—The foundational institution for the environment within the United Nations. Created in 1972, UNEP's main purpose is to promote sustainable development across the globe as well as to facilitate international summits and conferences on issues pertaining to the environment.

urban forestry—The development and maintenance of tracts of land inside cities or surrounding cities that are designated as forests or wooded areas.

urban sprawl—Area surrounding a city that is generally distinguished by low-density, segregated land use and a reliance on automobiles for transport.

urbanization—The process by which people move from rural or remote areas of the country into cities.

voluntary instruments—Policies by which the government asks individuals or companies to change behaviours but does not provide them with direct incentives for doing so (no penalty or payment is applied).

water privatization—To assign to private companies the management of water supply and sewerage on behalf of the public (which owns the water).

watershed—An area of land that is drained by the same water system. All water that is above or below ground (e.g., snow, rain, groundwater) drains into the same place in a watershed region.

western alienation—The state of estrangement experienced by the Western provinces (British Columbia, Alberta, Saskatchewan, and Manitoba), which feel excluded from political power and decision making in central Canada (Ontario and Québec).

REFERENCES

AAFC (Agriculture and Agri-Food Canada). 2005. *Agricultural Policy Framework: Federal-Provincial-Territorial Programs*. Ottawa: Agriculture and Agri-Food Canada. http://publications.gc.ca/collections/Collection/A34-3-2005E.pdf.

AAFC (Agriculture and Agri-Food Canada). 2013a. *Community Pasture Program: Application Process*. http://www.agr.gc.ca/eng/?id=1298391768054. Last modified August 29.

AAFC (Agriculture and Agri-Food Canada). 2013b. *The Canadian Bottled Water Industry*. http://www.agr.gc.ca/eng/industry-markets-and-trade/statistics-and-market information/by-product-sector/processed-food-and-beverages/the-canadian-bottled-water-industry/?id=1171644581795. Last modified July 2013.

AAFC (Agriculture and Agri-Food Canada). 2014. *Growing Forward 2*. Ottawa: Agriculture and Agri-Food Canada. http://www.agr.gc.ca/eng/about-us/key-departmental-initiatives/growing-forward-2/?id=1294780620963. Last modified August 5.

AANDC (Aboriginal Affairs and Northern Development Canada). 2010a. *Frequently Asked Questions about Aboriginal Peoples*. http://www.aadnc-aandc.gc.ca/eng/1100100013800/1100100013801. Last modified September 15.

AANDC (Aboriginal Affairs and Northern Development Canada). 2010b. *Treaties with Aboriginal People in Canada*. http://www.aadnc-aandc.gc.ca/eng/1100100032291/1100100032292. Last modified September 15.

AANDC (Aboriginal Affairs and Northern Development Canada). 2011a. *Aboriginal Consultation and Accommodation—Updated Guidelines for Federal Officials to Fulfill the Duty to Consult* Ottawa: AANDC.

AANDC (Aboriginal Affairs and Northern Development Canada). 2011b. *National Assessment of First Nations Water and Wastewater Systems: National Roll-Up Report*. Orangeville, ON: Neegan Burnside Ltd.

AANDC (Aboriginal Affairs and Northern Development Canada). 2012. *Canada's Statement of Support on the United Nations Declaration on the Rights of Indigenous Peoples*. http://www.aadnc-aandc.gc.ca/eng/1309374239861/1309374546142. Last modified July 30.

AANDC (Aboriginal Affairs and Northern Development Canada). 2013a. *First Nations in Canada*. http://www.aadnc-aandc.gc.ca/eng/1307460755710/1307460872523. Last modified October 21.

AANDC (Aboriginal Affairs and Northern Development Canada). 2013b. *First Nations Land Management Regime*. https://www.aadnc-aandc.gc.ca/eng/1327090675492/1327090738973. Last modified June 26.

AANDC (Aboriginal Affairs and Northern Development Canada). 2013c. *Inuit*. http://www.aadnc-aandc.gc.ca/eng/1100100014187/1100100014191. Last modified September 15.

AANDC (Aboriginal Affairs and Northern Development Canada). 2013d. *Land Management*. https://www.aadnc-aandc.gc.ca/eng/1100100034737/1100100034738. Last modified July 24.

AANDC (Aboriginal Affairs and Northern Development Canada). 2013e. "250th Anniversary of the Royal Proclamation of 1763." *Aboriginal History in Canada*. https://www.aadnc-aandc.gc.ca/eng/1370355181092/1370355203645. Last modified October 8.

AANDC (Aboriginal Affairs and Northern Development Canada. 2014a. *Land Base Statistics*. Ottawa: AANDC. https://www.aadnc-aandc.gc.ca/eng/1359993855530/1359993914323. Last modified March 24.

AANDC (Aboriginal Affairs and Northern Development Canada). 2014b. *Self-Government*. https://www.aadnc-aandc.gc.ca/eng/1100100032275/1100100032276. Last modified June 11.

AANDC (Aboriginal Affairs and Northern Development Canada). 2015a. *Aboriginal Peoples and Communities*. http://www.aadnc-aandc.gc.ca/eng/1100100013785/1304467449155. Last modified April 10.

AANDC (Aboriginal Affairs and Northern Development Canada). 2015b. *Fact Sheet: Aboriginal Self-Government*. https://www.aadnc-aandc.gc.ca/eng/1100100016293/1100100016294. Last modified March 2.

AANDC (Aboriginal Affairs and Northern Development Canada). 2015c. *First Nations*. http://www.aadnc-aandc.gc.ca/eng/1100100013791/1100100013795. Last modified April 7.

AANDC (Aboriginal Affairs and Northern Development Canada). 2015d. *Governance*. https://www.aadnc-aandc.gc.ca/eng/1100100013803/1100100013807. Last modified April 10.

AANDC (Aboriginal Affairs and Northern Development Canada). 2015e. *United Nations Declaration on the Rights of Indigenous Peoples*. https://www.aadnc-aandc .gc.ca/eng/1309374407406/1309374458958. Last modified March 13.

Alam, Shaista. 2010. "Globalization, Poverty and Environmental Degradation: Sustainable Development in Pakistan." *Journal of Sustainable Development* 3 (2): 103–14.

Alley, William M., and Rosemarie Alley. 2013. *Too Hot to Touch: The Problem of High-Level Nuclear Waste*. Cambridge: Cambridge University Press.

Amal, K. Ali. 2008. "Greenbelts to Contain Urban Growth in Ontario, Canada: Promises and Prospects." *Planning, Practice & Research* 23 (4): 533–48. http://dx.doi.org/10.1080/02697450802522889.

AMAP (Arctic Monitoring and Assessment Programme). 2012. *Arctic Climate Issues 2011: Changes in Arctic Snow, Water, Ice, and Permafrost*. SWIPA 2011 Overview Report. Oslo: AMAP.

Amos, William, Kathryn Harrison, and George Hoberg. 2001. "Search of a Minimum Willing Coalition: The Politics of Species-at-Risk Legislation in Canada." In *Politics of the Wild: Canada and Endangered Species*, edited by Karen Beazley and Robert Boardman, 137–66. Toronto: Oxford University Press.

Anderson, David. 2001. "David Anderson on Species At Risk Act." *OpenParliament*, February 19. https://openparliament.ca/debates/2001/2/19/david-anderson-2/only/.

Anderson, Kristi, and Ben Thibault. 2012. Opportunity in the Wind. Calgary: Pembina Institute. http://www.pembina.org/reports/landowner-guide-to-wind-energy-fact-sheet.pdf.

Anderssen, Erin, Gloria Galloway, and Kelly Cryderman. 2013. "First Nations Protests Take Aim at Oil Sands." *The Globe and Mail*, January 13. http://www.theglobeandmail.com/news/national/first-nations-protests-take-aim-at-oil-sands/article7317275/.

Animal Alliance of Canada. 2014. *Farm Animals*. http://www.animalalliance.ca/campaigns/farm-animals.html.

Arctic Council. 1996. *Ottawa Declaration*. http://www.arctic-council.org/index.php/en/document-archive/category/5-declarations.

Arctic Council. 2011a. *Inuit Circumpolar Council*. http://www.arctic-council.org/index.php/en/about-us/permanent-participants/inuit-circumpolar-council.

Arctic Council. 2011b. *Nuuk Declaration*. http://www.arctic-council.org/index.php/en/document-archive/category/5-declarations.

Arctic Council. 2015. *About the United States Chairmanship*. http://www.arctic-council.org/images/attachments/US_Chairmanship/Chairmanship_Brochure_2_page_public.pdf.

Arrhenius, Svante. [1896] 2012. "On the Influence of Carbonic Acid in the Air upon the Temperature of the Ground." In *The Global Warming Reader*, edited by Bill McKibben, 19–32. New York: Penguin Books.

Asch, Michael. 1999. "From Calder to Van der Peet: Aboriginal Rights and Canadian Law, 1973–96." In *Indigenous Peoples' Rights in Australia, Canada, and New Zealand*, edited by Paul Havemann, 428–46. Oxford: Oxford University Press.

Asch, Michael. 2014. *On Being Here to Stay: Treaties and Aboriginal Rights in Canada*. Toronto: University of Toronto Press.

Associated Press. 2013. "UN Climate Talks: Poland Gives Coal a Voice." *The Guardian*, November 8. http://www.theguardian.com/environment/2013/nov/08/un-climate-talks-poland-coal.

Aukema, Brian, Joerg Bohimann, Anne-Christine Bonfils, Daniel Doucet, Ismahane Elouafi, Nadir Erbilgin, Armand Séguin, and Sandy Smith. 2009. *Canadian Forest Health Genomics: Canadian Strengths Address Forestry Challenges*. Ottawa: Genome Canada. http://www.ontariogenomics.ca/sites/default/files/CFHGI - Forest Health Genomics Strategy Paper.pdf.

Axelrod, Regina S., and Stacy D. VanDeveer, eds. 2014. *The Global Environment: Institutions, Law, and Policy*. 4th ed. Washington, DC: CQ Press.

Axelrod, Regina S., Stacy D. VanDeveer, and David Leonard Downie, eds. 2011. *The Global Environment: Institutions, Law, and Policy*. 3rd ed. Washington, DC: CQ Press.

Axelrod, Robert. 1986. "An Evolutionary Approach to Norms." *American Political Science Review* 80 (4): 1095–111. http://dx.doi.org/10.2307/1960858.

Bailey, Ian. 2013. "B.C. Greens' only MLA Doesn't Want Party Leadership." *The Globe and Mail*, August 14. http://www.theglobeandmail.com/news/british-columbia/bc-greens-only-mla-doesnt-want-party-leadership/article13757799/.

Bakker, Karen, ed. 2007. *Eau Canada: The Future of Canada's Water*. Vancouver: UBC Press.

Bank of Montreal. 2012. "Board Diversity." Bank of Montreal Board of Directors' Policies. https://www.bmo.com/corporate-governance/files/en/Extract_Board DiversityPolicy_May2013.pdf.

Barbour, Christine, and Gerald C. Wright. 2013. *Keeping the Republic: Power and Citizenship in American Politics*. 6th ed. Washington, DC: CQ Press.

Barteczko, Agnieszka, and Henning Gloystein. 2013. "Analysis: Poland to Get Dirtier as it Leans toward Lignite Coal." *Reuters*, July 31. http://www.reuters.com/ article/2013/07/31/us-energy-poland-lignite-analysis-idUSBRE96U0L920130731.

Bates, D. 1995. "The Effects of Air Pollution in Children." *Environmental Health Perspectives* 103 (6 Suppl. 6): 49–53. http://dx.doi.org/10.1289/ehp.95103s649.

BBC. 2015. "Greenland Profile–Overview." *BBC News*, February 19. http://www.bbc .com/news/world-europe-18249474.

BC Forest Service. 2013. *BC Timber Sales: Business Plan, 2010/11–2012/13*. Victoria, BC: Forests, Lands and Natural Resources. https://www.for.gov.bc.ca/bcts/about/ serviceplan/BP-10111213.pdf.

BC Ministry of Finance 2014. *Carbon Tax*. Vancouver: Government of British Columbia. http://www.fin.gov.bc.ca/tbs/tp/climate/carbon_tax.htm.

Beal, Brent D. 2013. *Corporate Social Responsibility: Definition, Core Issues, and Recent Developments*. Thousand Oaks, CA: Sage Publications.

Beaty, Ross, Richard Lipsey, and Stewart Elgie. 2014. "The Shocking Truth about B.C.'s Carbon Tax: It Works." *The Globe and Mail*, July 9. http://www.theglobeandmail .com/globe-debate/the-insidious-truth-about-bcs-carbon-tax-it-works/article 19512237/.

Beazley, Karen. 2001. "Why Should We Protect Endangered Species? Philosophical and Ecological Rationale." In *Politics of the Wild: Canada and Endangered Species*, edited by Karen Beazley and Robert Boardman, 11–25. Toronto: Oxford University Press.

Becklumb, Penny 2013. *Federal and Provincial Jurisdiction to Regulate Environmental Issues: Background Paper*. Publication No 2013–86-E. Ottawa: Library of Parliament. http://www.parl.gc.ca/Content/LOP/ResearchPublications/2013–86-e.pdf.

Bélanger, Alexis. 2011. "Canadian Federalism in the Context of Combating Climate Change." *Constitutional Forum* 20 (1): 21–31.

Beresford, Charley. 2013. "Don't Exclude Cities from Canada's Energy Plan." *The Tyee*, May 31. http://thetyee.ca/Opinion/2013/05/31/Canada-Energy-Plan/.

Bernstein, Steven, Jutta Brunnée, David G. Duff, and Andrew J. Green, eds. 2008. *A Globally Integrated Climate Policy for Canada*. Toronto: University of Toronto Press.

Binnema, Theodore. 2014. *Enlightened Zeal: The Hudson's Bay Company and Scientific Networks, 1670–1870*. Toronto: University of Toronto Press.

Birkland, Thomas A. 2011. *An Introduction to the Policy Process: Theories, Concepts, and Models of Public Policy Making*. Armonk, NY: M.E. Sharpe.

Blais, André, and Peter Loewen. 2011. *Youth Electoral Engagement in Canada*. Elections Canada Working Paper Series. Ottawa: Elections Canada. http://www .elections.ca/res/rec/part/youeng/youth_electoral_engagement_e.pdf.

Blanco-Canqui, Humberto, and Rattan Lal. 2010. *Principles of Soil Conservation and Management*. Dordrecht: Springer Netherlands. http://dx.doi.org/10.1007/ 978-1-4020-8709-7.

Boardman, Robert. 2009. "Canadian Environmental Policy in the Global Context: Obligations and Opportunities." In *Canadian Environmental Policy and Politics: Prospects for Leadership and Innovation*, edited by Debora L. VanNijnatten and Robert Boardman, 137–49. New York: Oxford University Press.

Booth, Annie L., and Norman W. Skelton. 2010. "First Nations' Access and Rights to Resources." In *Resource and Environmental Management in Canada*, edited by Bruce Mitchell, 80–103. Don Mills, ON: Oxford University Press.

Borick, Christopher, Érick Lachapelle, and Barry Rabe. 2011. *Climate Compared: Public Opinion on Climate Change in the United States and Canada*. Ottawa: Canada's Public Policy Forum. http://www.ppforum.ca/events/continental-divide.

Bothwell, Bob. 2007. *The Penguin History of Canada*. Toronto: Penguin Books.

Bott, Robert. 2009. "Petroleum Industries." *Canadian Encyclopedia*. http://www .thecanadianencyclopedia.ca/en/article/petroleum-industries/. Last modified March 4, 2015.

Bott, Robert. 2011. *Canada's Oil Sands*. 3rd ed. Calgary: Canadian Centre for Energy Information.

Boulet, D., and S. Melançon. 2013. *Environmental Assessment Report: Air Quality in Montréal, 2012 Annual Report*. Montréal: Ville de Montréal. http://ville .montreal.qc.ca/pls/portal/docs/PAGE/ENVIRO_FR/MEDIA/DOCUMENTS/ RSQA_ASSESSMENT_REPORT_2012.PDF.

Boyd, David R. 2003. *Unnatural Law: Rethinking Canadian Environmental Law and Policy*. Vancouver: UBC Press.

Boyd, David R. 2006. *The Water We Drink: An International Comparison of Drinking Water Quality Standards and Guidelines*. Vancouver: David Suzuki Foundation. http://www.davidsuzuki.org/publications/downloads/2006/DSF-HEHC-water -web.pdf

Boyd, David R. 2013a. "Constitutional Environmental Protection: Moving Forward Instead of Backward." *The Hill Times*, January 28. http://www.flowcanada.org/sites/ default/files/news/Boyd article on right to environment_Hill Times_Jan2013.pdf.

Boyd, David R. 2013b. *The History of the Right to a Healthy Environment in Canada*. Vancouver: David Suzuki Foundation. http://davidsuzuki.org/publications/2013/11/ DSF White Paper 2--2013.pdf.

Boyer, Patrick J. 2014. *Our Scandalous Senate*. Toronto: Dundurn Press.

BP (British Petroleum). 2015. *BP Statistical Review of World Energy, June 2015*. London: British Petroleum. http://www.bp.com/content/dam/bp/pdf/Energy -economics/statistical-review-2015/bp-statistical-review-of-world-energy-2015-full -report.pdf.

Brandes, Oliver M., Linda Nowlan, and Katie Paris. 2008. *Going With the Flow? Evolving Water Allocations and the Potential and Limits of Water Markets in Canada*. Ottawa: Conference Board of Canada. http://poliswaterproject.org/sites/ default/files/09_going_w_flow_1.pdf.

Brandon, William. 2013. *The Rise and Fall of North American Indians: From Prehistory through Geronimo*. Lanham, MD: Roberts Rinehart Publishing.

Bregha, Francois. 2006a. "Energy Policy." *The Canadian Encyclopedia*. http://www .thecanadianencyclopedia.ca/en/article/energy-policy/. Last modified October 20, 2014.

Bregha, Francois. 2006b. "National Energy Program." *The Canadian Encyclopedia* . http://www.thecanadianencyclopedia.ca/en/article/national-energy-program/. Last modified December 16, 2013.

Brock, Kathy L. 2008. "The Politics of Asymmetrical Federalism: Reconsidering the Role and Responsibilities of Ottawa." *Canadian Public Policy* 34 (2): 143–61. http://dx.doi.org/10.3138/cpp.34.2.143.

Brooks, Stephen. 2013. *Canadian Democracy.* 7th ed. Oxford: Oxford University Press.

Brown, Lester. 2009. *Plan B 4.0: Mobilizing to Save Civilization.* Washington, DC: Earth Policy Institute.

Brown, Steven D. 2010. "The Green Vote in Canada." In *Canadian Environmental Policy and Politics: Prospects for Leadership and Innovation,* edited by Debora L. VanNijnatten and Robert Boardman, 14–28. Toronto: Oxford University Press.

Bryant, Bunyan. 1995. *Environmental Justice: Issues, Policies, and Solutions.* Covelo, CA: Island Press.

Burck, Jan, Franziska Marten, and Christoph Bals. 2015. *The Climate Change Performance Index: Results 2015.* Bonn, Germany: Germanwatch. https://germanwatch.org/en/download/10407.pdf

Bushnik, Tracey, Douglas Haines, Patrick Levallois, Johanne Levesque, Jay Van Oostdam, and Claude Viau. 2010. "Lead and Bisphenol A Concentrations in the Canadian Population." *Health Reports* 21 (3). http://www.statcan.gc.ca/pub/82-003-x/2010003/article/11324-eng.pdf.

Byers, Michael. 2006. "The Need to Defend our New Northwest Passage." *The Tyee,* January 30. http://thetyee.ca/Views/2006/01/30/DefendNorthwestPassage/.

C40 Cities Climate Leadership Group. 2011. "Toronto's Atmospheric Fund Makes Sustainability Affordable." *C40 Cities: Case Study,* November 8. http://www.c40.org/case_studies/toronto's-atmospheric-fund-makes-sustainability-affordable.

Caldwell, Wayne, and Steward Hilts. 2005. "Farmland Preservation: Innovative Approaches in Ontario." *Journal of Soil and Water Conservation* 60 (3): 66–69.

Calgary Declaration. 1997. *Premiers' Meeting.* September 14. http://www.exec.gov.nl.ca/currentevents/unity/unityr1.htm.

Callendar, Guy S. [1938] 2012. "The Artificial Production of Carbon Dioxide and Its Influence on Temperature." In *The Global Warming Reader,* edited by Bill McKibben, 33–38. New York: Penguin Books.

Campbell, Karen. 2014. "Water Usage by Fracking Operations Challenged in BC Supreme Court." *Ecojustice: Press Release,* March 14. http://www.ecojustice.ca/pressrelease/water-usage-by-fracking-operations-challenged-in-b-c-supreme-court/.

Campbell, Patricia J., Aran MacKinnon, and Christy R. Stevens. 2010. *An Introduction to Global Studies.* Malden, MA: Wiley-Blackwell.

Canada's Advisory Council for Promoting Women on Boards. 2014. *Good for Business: A Plan to Promote the Participation of More Women on Canadian Boards.* Ottawa: Status of Women Canada.

Canadian Council of Forest Ministers. 1992. *Sustainable Forests: A Canadian Commitment.* Ottawa: Forestry Canada.

Canadian Council of Forest Ministers. 1998. *National Forest Strategy 1998–2002.* Ottawa: Canadian Forest Service.

Canadian Press. 2012. "Ottawa Sued over Quebec Fracking Ban." *CBC News,* November 23. http://www.cbc.ca/news/business/ottawa-sued-over-quebec-fracking-ban-1.1140918.

Canadian Press. 2013a. "Cargo Ship Sails through Northwest Passage and into History Books." *Maclean's,* September 27. http://www.macleans.ca/news/world/cargo-ship-sails-through-northwest-passage-and-into-history-books/.

Canadian Press. 2013b. "Federal Court Grants Rights to Métis, Non-Status Indians." *CBC News*, January 8. http://www.cbc.ca/news/politics/federal-court-grants-rights-to-métis-non-status-indians-1.1319951.

Canadian Press. 2013c. "First Nations Say They Will Fight Oilsands, Pipeline." *CBC News*, March 20. http://www.cbc.ca/news/canada/first-nations-say-they-will-fight-oilsands-pipeline-1.1348611.

Canadian Press. 2013d. "Relying too Heavily on Oil Sands Could be Bad for Canada's Economy, Report Warns." *National Post*, February 21. http://business.financialpost.com/2013/02/21/relying-too-heavily-on-oil-sands-could-be-bad-for-canadas-economy-report-warns/?_lsa=a139-ec73.

Canadian Press. 2013e. "Why Canada Chose to Leave a Global Fight against Desertification." *The Globe and Mail*, March 28. http://www.theglobeandmail.com/news/world/why-canada-chose-to-leave-a-global-fight-against-desertification/article10547365/.

Canadian Press. 2014a. "Canada Falls Short of Its 2020 Climate Change Commitment." *CBC News*, December 9. http://www.cbc.ca/news/business/canada-falls-short-of-its-2020-climate-change-commitment-1.2865992.

Canadian Press. 2014b. "Supreme Court to Hear Landmark Case Involving Métis, Non-Status Indians." *The Globe and Mail*, November 20. http://www.theglobeandmail.com/news/national/supreme-court-to-hear-landmark-case-involving-metis-non-status-indians/article21665992/.

Canadian Solar. 2015. "Corporate Profile." *Investor Relations*. http://investors.canadiansolar.com/phoenix.zhtml?c=196781&p=irol-irhome .

CAPP (Canadian Association of Petroleum Producers). 2015. "Alberta." *Industry Across Canada*. http://www.capp.ca/canadian-oil-and-natural-gas/industry-across-canada/alberta.

Cardinale, Matthew. 2010. "Fears Grow over Oil Spill's Long-Term Effects on Food Change." *The Guardian*, June 1. http://www.theguardian.com/environment/2010/jun/01/bp-oil-spill-wildlife.

Carnaghan, Matthew, and Allison Goody. 2006. *Canadian Arctic Sovereignty*. Ottawa: Parliament of Canada, Political and Social Affairs Division. http://www.parl.gc.ca/Content/LOP/ResearchPublications/prb0561-e.htm.

Carson, Rachel L. 1962. *Silent Spring*. Boston, MA: Houghton-Mifflin.

CBC. 2006a. "Harper Agrees to Send Clean Air Act to Committee." *CBC News*, November 1. http://www.cbc.ca/m/touch/canada/story/1.601441.

CBC. 2006b. "Mulroney Honoured for Environmental Record." *CBC News*, April 20. http://www.cbc.ca/news/canada/mulroney-honoured-for-environmental-record-1.616580.

CBC. 2009. "Suncor Fined $850,000 for Environmental Violations." *CBC News*, April 2. http://www.cbc.ca/news/canada/edmonton/suncor-fined-850-000-for-environmental-violations-1.800377.

CBC. 2010. "Mackenzie Valley Pipeline: 37 Years of Negotiation." *CBC News*, December 16. http://www.cbc.ca/news/business/mackenzie-valley-pipeline-37-years-of-negotiation-1.902366.

CBC. 2011a. *Ontario Votes 2011: Election Day October 6*. http://www.cbc.ca/news2/canada/ontariovotes2011/. Last modified October 7.

CBC. 2011b. "Wheat Board Vote a 'Non-Binding Survey,' Says Ritz." *CBC News*, September 12. http://www.cbc.ca/news/canada/saskatchewan/wheat-board-vote-a-non-binding-survey-says-ritz-1.984620.

CBC. 2012. "B.C. Seeks 'Fair Share' in New Gateway Pipeline Deal." *CBC News*, July 23, http://www.cbc.ca/news/canada/british-columbia/b-c-seeks-fair-share-in-new -gateway-pipeline-deal-1.1205829.

CBC. 2013a. "B.C.'s Greens Win First Provincial Seat." *CBC News*, May 14. http:// www.cbc.ca/news/canada/british-columbia/b-c-s-greens-win-first-provincial -seat-1.1322651.

CBC. 2013b. "Bus-Sized Blob of Fat Found in U.K. Sewer." *CBC News*, August 6. http://www.cbc.ca/news/world/bus-sized-blob-of-fat-found-in-u-k-sewer-1 .1399231.

CBC. 2013c. "9 Questions about Idle No More." *CBC News*, January 5. http://www .cbc.ca/news/canada/9-questions-about-idle-no-more-1.1301843.

CBC. 2013d. "Summary of Canada-EU Free Trade Deal Tabled." *CBC News*, October 30. http://www.cbc.ca/news/politics/summary-of-canada-eu-free-trade-deal-tabled -1.2286695.

CBC. 2013e. "Yukon Tourism up 25 Per Cent in Last 10 Years." *CBC News*, May 8. http://www.cbc.ca/news/canada/north/yukon-tourism-up-25-in-last-10-years -1.1369951.

CBC. 2014a. "Analysis: Drinking Water Contaminated by Excreted Drugs a Growing Concern." *CBC News*, September 22. http://www.cbc.ca/news/health/ drinking-water-contaminated-by-excreted-drugs-a-growing-concern-1.2772289.

CBC. 2014b. "Montreal Air Quality Drops in 2014." *CBC News*, December 30. http:// www.cbc.ca/news/canada/montreal/montreal-air-quality-drops-in-2014-1 .2886981.

CCCE (Canadian Council of Chief Executives). 2014. *Annual Report 2014*. Ottawa: CCCE. http://www.ceocouncil.ca/annual-report/2014/index_en.html.

CELA (Canadian Environmental Law Association). 2011. *Ontario Safe Drinking Water Act, 2002 & Its Regulations: FAQs*. http://www.cela.ca/sites/cela.ca/files/ Water-FAQs-Eng.pdf.

Center for Climate and Energy Solutions. 2011. *Climatic Change 101*. Arlington, VA: C2ES. http://www.c2es.org/docUploads/climate101-captrade.pdf.

Center for Global Development. 2015. *Commitment to Development Index 2014*. Washington, DC: Center for Global Development. Revised January. http://www .cgdev.org/sites/default/files/commitment-development-index-print.pdf.

Center for International Environmental Law. 2006. *U.S. Ratification of the Stockholm Convention: Analysis of Pending POPs Legislation*. Washington, DC: CIEL. http://www.ciel.org/Publications/POPs_Bills_28Feb2006.pdf.

Christian, Carol. 2010. "Suncor Fined for Water Pollutants Released Two Years Ago." *Fort McMurray Today*, December 22. http://www.fortmcmurraytoday.com/ 2010/12/22/suncor-fined-for-water-pollutants-released-two-years-ago.

Christie, Mike. 2010. *Private Property Pesticide By-Laws in Canada*. Ottawa: Coalition for a Healthy Ottawa. http://www.flora.org/healthyottawa/BylawList .pdf.

Chu, Cindy, Charles K. Minns, Nigel P. Lester, and Nicholas E. Mandrak. 2015. "An Updated Assessment of Human Activities, the Environment, and Freshwater Fish Biodiversity in Canada." *Canadian Journal of Fisheries and Aquatic Species*. 72 (1): 135–48.

CIA. 2015. "Country Comparison: Military Expenditures." *The World Factbook*. https://www.cia.gov/library/publications/the-world-factbook/rankorder/2034rank .html.

Cinq-Mars, Jaques. 1979. "Bluefish Cave 1: A Late Pleistocene Eastern Beringian Cave Deposit in the Northern Yukon." *Canadian Journal of Archaeology* 3: 1–32.

City of Burlington. n.d. *Citizens Smart Growth Forum: People.* http://cms.burlington.ca/Asset970.aspx.

City of Toronto. 2007. *Energy Efficiency and Beyond: Toronto's Sustainable Energy Plan.* Toronto: Energy Efficiency Office.

City of Toronto. 2014a. *Better Buildings Partnership: Results.* http://www1.toronto.ca/wps/portal/contentonly?vgnextoid=1556136696f85410VgnVCM10000071d60f89RCRD.

City of Toronto. 2014b. *Environment and Energy Division: 2013 Annual Report.* Toronto: City of Toronto. http://www1.toronto.ca/City Of Toronto/Environment and Energy/Action Plans, Policies & Research/PDFs/A1401668_EED_AnnualReport_TaggedRev_2.pdf.

City of Vancouver. 2009. *Stanley Park Forest Management Plan.* Vancouver: City of Vancouver. http://vancouver.ca/files/cov/Stanley-Park-Forest-Management-Plan.pdf.

City of Vancouver. 2014. *Climate Change Adaptation Strategy.* Vancouver: City of Vancouver. http://vancouver.ca/green-vancouver/climate-change-adaptation-strategy.aspx.

Clamen, Murray. 2013. "The IJC and Transboundary Water Disputes: Past, Present, and Future." In *Water without Borders? Canada, the United States, and Shared Waters*, edited by Emma S. Norman, Alice Cohen, and Karen Bakker, 70–87. Toronto: University of Toronto Press.

Clark, Campbell. 2012. "Tory MP Wants Baird to Consider Yanking Canada out of UN." *The Globe and Mail*, June 6. http://www.theglobeandmail.com/news/politics/ottawa-notebook/tory-mp-wants-baird-to-consider-yanking-canada-out-of-un/article4235343/.

Clark, Campbell. 2014. "US Urges Canada to Act on Climate Change." *The Globe and Mail*, June 3. http://www.theglobeandmail.com/news/politics/aggressive-us-targets-for-reducing-emissions-put-pressure-on-harper/article18957520/.

Clarke, Tony, Diana Gibson, Brendan Haley, and Jim Stanford. 2013. *The Bitumen Cliff: Lessons and Challenges of Bitumen Mega-Developments for Canada's Economy in an Age of Climate Change.* Ottawa: Canadian Centre for Policy Alternatives https://www.policyalternatives.ca/publications/reports/bitumen-cliff.

Clarkson, Stephen. 2011. "Has the Centre Vanished: The Past and Future of the Middle Ground in Canada." *Literary Review of Canada* 19 (October). http://reviewcanada.ca/magazine/2011/10/has-the-centre-vanished/.

Climate Action Network. 2015. "Canada Announces Climate Commitment and It's Weaker than It Looks." *Climate Action News This Week*, May 15. http://climateactionnetwork.ca/2015/05/15/canada-announces-climate-commitment-and-its-weaker-than-it-looks/.

Climate Action Tracker. 2015. "Canada." *Climate Action Tracker.* http://climateactiontracker.org/countries/canada.html. Last modified May 20.

Coates, Ken. 2015. *IdleNoMore: And the Remaking of Canada.* Regina: University of Regina Press.

Coffey, Luke. 2013. "The Arctic Council Rejects the EU—A Boost for Sovereignty and Democracy." *The Daily Signal*, May 16. http://dailysignal.com/2013/05/16/the-arctic-council-rejects-the-eu-a-boost-for-sovereignty-and-democracy/.

Cohen, Bernard C. 1963. *The Press and Foreign Policy.* Princeton, NJ: Princeton University Press.

Cole, Daniel H. 2002. *Pollution and Property: Comparing Ownership Institutions for Environmental Protection.* New York: Cambridge University Press.

Commissioner of the Environment and Sustainable Development. 2005. *Report of the Commissioner of the Environment and Sustainable Development to the House of Commons: Drinking Water in First Nations Communities.* Ottawa: Office of the Auditor General of Canada. http://www.oag-bvg.gc.ca/internet/docs/ c20050905ce.pdf.

Communic@tions Management. 2013. "Daily Newspaper Circulation Trends 2000–2013: Canada, United States, United Kingdom." Discussion Paper. http:// media-cmi.com/downloads/CMI_Discussion_Paper_Circulation_Trends_102813 .pdf

Conca, Ken, and Geoffrey D. Dabelko, eds. 2010. *Green Plant Blues: Four Decades of Global Environmental Politics.* Boulder, CO: Westview Press.

Conference Board of Canada. 2013a. "Income Per Capita." *How Canada Performs.* http://www.conferenceboard.ca/hcp/details/economy/income-per-capita.aspx. Last modified March.

Conference Board of Canada. 2013b. "Municipal Waste Generation." *How Canada Performs.* http://www.conferenceboard.ca/hcp/details/environment/municipal -waste-generation.aspx.

Conference Board of Canada. 2013c. "Sulphur Oxides Emissions." *How Canada Performs.* http://www.conferenceboard.ca/hcp/details/environment/urban-sulphur -dioxide-concentration.aspx.

Conference Board of Canada. 2015a. "Environment." *How Canada Performs.* http:// www.conferenceboard.ca/hcp/details/environment.aspx.

Conference Board of Canada. 2015b. *How Canada Performs.* http://www.conferenceboard .ca/hcp/default.aspx.

Convention on Biological Diversity. n.d. *Traditional Knowledge and the Convention on Biological Diversity.* Montréal: Secretariat of the Convention on Biological Diversity. https://www.cbd.int/doc/publications/8j-brochure-en.pdf.

Convention on Biological Diversity. 2014. *Article 8(j)—Traditional Knowledge, Innovations and Practices.* New York: United Nations Environment Programme. http://www.cbd.int/traditional/.

Conway, Gordon R., and Jules N. Pretty. 2013. *Unwelcome Harvest: Agriculture and Pollution.* New York: Routledge.

Corell, R.W., S.J. Hassol, J.M. Melillo, D. Archer, E. Euskirchen, F.S. Chapin, A.D. McGuire, T.R. Christensen, V.P. Fichelet, K. Walter, et al. 2008. "Methane from the Arctic: Global Warming Wildcard." In *UNEP Year Book 2008*, edited by P. Harrison, 37–48. Nairobi, Kenya: United Nations Environment Programme.

COSEWIC (Committee on the Status of Endangered Wildlife in Canada). 2015. *Wildlife Species Search.* http://www.cosewic.gc.ca/eng/sct1/searchform_e.cfm.

Council of Canadians. 2013. "Lone Pine Resources Files Outrageous NAFTA Lawsuit Against Fracking Ban." *Council of Canadians Media Release*, October 3. http:// www.canadians.org/media/lone-pine-resources-files-outrageous-nafta-lawsuit -against-fracking-ban.

Cox, Robert. 2013. *Environmental Communication and the Public Sphere.* 3rd ed. Los Angeles: Sage Publications.

Crosby, Alfred W. 2004. *Ecological Imperialism: The Biological Expansion of Europe 900–1900*. Cambridge: Cambridge University Press. http://dx.doi.org/10.1017/CBO9780511805554.

CRTC (Canadian Radio-television and Telecommunications Commission). 2013. "CRTC Issues Annual Report on the State of the Canadian Communication System." *CRTC News Release*, September 26. http://www.crtc.gc.ca/eng/com100/2013/r130926.htm#.U10obBZ970c.

Cryderman, Kelly, and Brent Jang. 2014. "Supreme Court Ruling on Native Land Claims Adds to Uncertainty for Pipelines." *The Globe and Mail*, Jun 26. http://www.theglobeandmail.com/report-on-business/industry-news/energy-and-resources/supreme-court-ruling-on-native-land-claims-adds-to-uncertainty-for-pipelines/article19356432/.

CTC (Canada Trade Commission). 2013. *Helping Tourism Businesses Prosper: 2013 Annual Report*. Ottawa: Government of Canada. http://en-corporate.canada.travel/sites/default/files/pdf/Corporate_reports/final_2013_annual_report_en.pdf.

Cudmore, James. 2013. "Harper's Northern Tour Is about Politics as Much as Policy." *CBC News*, August 18. http://www.cbc.ca/m/touch/politics/story/1.1326265.

CUFN (Canadian Urban Forest Network). 2014. *Canadian Urban Forest Strategy, 2013–2018*. Ottawa: Tree Canada. http://media.wix.com/ugd/64e90e_c73381cc7 7f54abb804e91de8845657e.pdf. Last modified August.

Daniels, Fred J. A., Lynn J. Gillespie, and Michel Poulin. 2013. "Plants." *Arctic Biodiversity Assessment: Status and Trends in Arctic Biodiversity*, edited by Hans Meltofte, Alf B. Josefson, and David Payer, 310–53. Akureyri, Iceland: Conservation of Arctic Flora and Fauna.

David Suzuki Foundation. 2015. "Understanding GMO." *Queen of Green*. http://www.davidsuzuki.org/what-you-can-do/queen-of-green/faqs/food/understanding-gmo/. Accessed May 15.

Davis, Kyle F., Paolo D'Odorico, and Maria Christina Rulli. 2014. "Land Grabbing: A Preliminary Quantification of Economic Impacts on Rural Livelihoods." *Population and Environment* 36 (2): 180–92. http://dx.doi.org/10.1007/s11111-014-0215-2.

Dawson, Tyler. 2013. "Canada Suspends Military Operations Near Disputed Hans Island." *Canada.com News*, June 7. http://o.canada.com/news/261064.

De Loë, Rob, and Reid Kreutzwiser. 2007. "Challenging the Status Quo: The Evolution of Water Governance in Canada." In *Eau Canada: The Future of Canada's Water*, edited by Karen Bakker, 85–104. Vancouver: UBC Press.

Dearden, Philip, and Rick Rollins. 2008. *Parks and Protected Areas in Canada: Planning and Management*. Don Mills, ON: Oxford University Press.

Depledge, Duncan. 2015. "The EU and the Arctic Council." *Wider Europe Forum*, April 20. http://www.ecfr.eu/article/commentary_the_eu_and_the_arctic_council3005.

Diamond, Jared. 2011. *Collapse: How Societies Choose to Fail or Succeed*. New York: Penguin Books.

Dickason, Olive Patricia, and William Newbigging. 2010. *A Concise History of Canada's First Nations*. 2nd ed. Don Mills, ON: Oxford University Press.

Dion, Stephan. 2013. "Carbon Taxes: Can a Good Policy Become Good Politics?" In *Tax Is Not a Four-Letter Word: A Different Take on Taxes in Canada*, edited by Alex Himelfarb and Jordan Himelfarb, 171–90. Waterloo, ON: Wilfrid University Press.

Doern, G. Bruce, and Monica Gattinger. 2003. *Power Switch: Energy Regulatory Governance in the Twenty-First Century*. Toronto: University of Toronto Press.

Doerr, Audrey. 2006. "Royal Commission on Aboriginal Peoples." *The Canadian Encyclopedia*. http://www.thecanadianencyclopedia.ca/en/article/royal-commission-on-aboriginal-peoples/.

Dorsey, Kurkpatrick. 1998. *The Dawn of Conservation Diplomacy: US-Canadian Wildlife Protection Treaties in the Progressive Era*. Seattle: University of Washington Press.

Doyle-Bedwell, Patricia, and Fay G. Cohen. 2001. "Aboriginal Peoples in Canada: Their Role in Shaping Environmental Trends in the Twenty-First Century." In *Governing the Environment: Persistent Challenges, Uncertain Innovations*, edited by Edward Parsons, 169–206. Toronto: University of Toronto Press.

DPI/NGO (Department of Public Information Non-Governmental Organizations). 2014. "Membership." *United Nations DPI/NGO*. http://outreach.un.org/ngorelations/membership/.

Dryzek, John S. 2013. *The Politics of the Earth: Environmental Discourses*. 3rd ed. Oxford: Oxford University Press.

Duffy, Patrick G., Bradley B. Grant, Glenn Zacher, and Erik Richer La Flèche. 2012. *Canada: The Energy Regulation and Markets Review*. Toronto: Stikeman Elliot LLP. http://www.mondaq.com/canada/x/202520/Oil+Gas+Electricity/The+Energy+Regulation+And+Markets+Review. Last modified October 19.

Duncan, Linda, and Marie Ann Bowden. 2009. *A Legal Guide to Aboriginal Drinking Water*. Calgary: Alberta Law Foundation.

Eaves, David, and Taylor Owen. 2012. "Liberal Baggage: The National Party's Greatest Burden May Be Its Past." *Literary Review of Canada* 20 (May). http://reviewcanada.ca/magazine/2012/05/liberal-baggage/.

Ecojustice. 2012a. *Failure to Protect: Grading Canada's Species at Risk Laws*. Vancouver: Ecojustice. http://www.ecojustice.ca/wp-content/uploads/2014/08/Failure-to-protect_Grading-Canadas-Species-at-Risk-Laws.pdf.

Ecojustice. 2012b. *Legal Backgrounder: Bill C-45 and the Navigable Waters Protection Act R (RSC 1985, C N-22)*. http://www.ecojustice.ca/wp-content/uploads/2015/03/NWPA_legal_backgrounder_November-20-2012.pdf.

Ecojustice. 2012c. *Legal Backgrounder: Canadian Environmental Assessment Act (2012)—Regulations*. http://www.ecojustice.ca/wp-content/uploads/2015/03/August-2012_FINAL_Ecojustice-CEAA-Regulations-Backgrounder.pdf. Last modified August.

Ecojustice. 2013a. "Conservation Groups Condemn 'Yes' Recommendation from Northern Gateway Review Panel." *Ecojustice Press Release*, December 19. http://www.ecojustice.ca/pressrelease/conservation-groups-condemn-yes-recommendation-from-northern-gateway-review-panel/.

Ecojustice. 2013b. "Federal Government's Failure to Protect Endangered Wildlife Triggers Lawsuit." *Ecojustice Press Release*, March 21. http://www.ecojustice.ca/pressrelease/federal-governments-failure-to-protect-endangered-wildlife-triggers-lawsuit/.

EEA (European Environment Agency). 2014. *Effects of Air Pollution on European Ecosystems*. Luxembourg: Publications Office of the European Union.

EIA (Energy Information Association). 2015. *Petroleum and Other Liquids*. http://www.eia.gov/petroleum/imports/companylevel/.

Eidelman, G. 2010. "Managing Urban Sprawl in Ontario: Good Policy or Good Politics?" *Politics and Policy* 38 (6): 1211–36. http://dx.doi.org/10.1111/j.1747-1346.2010.00275.x.

Elections Canada. 2014. *Survey of Electors Following the 40th General Election.* http://www.elections.ca/content.aspx?section=res&dir=rec/eval/40eval/svy&document=p4&lang=e. Last modified June 2014.

Elections Canada. 2015. *Redistribution of Federal Electoral Districts.* http://www.elections.ca/content.aspx?section=res&dir=cir/red&document=index&lang=e. Modified April 14.

Elgie, Stewart, and Jessica McClay. 2013. *BC's Carbon Tax Shift after Five Years: Results.* Ottawa: Sustainable Prosperity, University of Ottawa. http://www.sustainableprosperity.ca/dl1026.

Employment and Social Development Canada. 2015. "Canadians in Context." *Indicators of Well-being in Canada.* http://www4.hrsdc.gc.ca/d.4m.1.3n@-eng.jsp?did=6. Modified April 19.

Enderlein, Henrik, Sonja Walti, and Michael Zurn. 2010. *Handbook on Multi-Level Governance.* Northampton, MA: Edward Elgar Publishing. http://dx.doi.org/10.4337/9781849809047.

EnviroEconomics. 2009. *Act Locally: The Municipal Role in Fighting Climate Change.* Ottawa: Federation of Canadian Municipalities. http://www.fcm.ca/Documents/reports/Act_Locally_The_Municipal_Role_in_Fighting_Climate_Change_EN.pdf.

Environment Canada. 2007. *Municipal Water Use Report: 2004 Statistics.* Ottawa: Environment Canada. http://www.ec.gc.ca/water-apps/MWWS/pdf/e_mun2004.pdf.

Environment Canada. 2009. *Canada's Fourth National Report to the United Nations Convention on Biological Diversity.* Ottawa: Environment Canada. http://www.cbd.int/doc/world/ca/ca-nr-04-en.pdf.

Environment Canada. 2011. "Atmospheric Carbon Dioxide Measured at Alert, Nunavut." *Climate Change.* https://www.ec.gc.ca/mges-ghgm/default.asp?lang=enandn=E5ACD766–1. Last modified February 14.

Environment Canada. 2012. "Frequently Asked Questions." *Water.* https://www.ec.gc.ca/eau-water/default.asp?lang=En&n=1C100657-1. Last modified February 16.

Environment Canada. 2013a. *Backgrounder: Canadian Ambient Air Quality Standards.* http://www.ec.gc.ca/default.asp?lang=En&n=56D4043B-1&news=A4B2C28A-2DFB-4BF4-8777-ADF29B4360BD. Last modified August 14.

Environment Canada. 2013b. *Backgrounder: Natural Areas Conservation Program.* http://www.ec.gc.ca/default.asp?lang=En&n=FEF1141D-1&news=80AA5B05-B3C8-452F-84A1-593DB066849A. Last modified August 2.

Environment Canada. 2013c. *Canada's Emission Trends.* Ottawa: Environment Canada. https://www.ec.gc.ca/ges-ghg/985F05FB-4744-4269-8C1A-D443F8A86814/1001-Canada%27s%20Emissions%20Trends%202013_e.pdf.

Environment Canada. 2013d. "Great Lakes Quickfacts." *Water.* https://www.ec.gc.ca/grandslacs-greatlakes/default.asp?lang=En&n=B4E65F6F-1. Last modified July 5.

Environment Canada. 2013e. *Groundwater.* https://www.ec.gc.ca/eau-water/default.asp?lang=En&n=300688DC-1. Last modified September 9.

Environment Canada. 2013f. *Planning for a Sustainable Future: A Federal Sustainable Development Strategy for Canada, 2013–2016.* Ottawa: Sustainable Development

Office, Environment Canada. http://www.ec.gc.ca/dd-sd/A22718BA-0107-4B32
-BE17-A438616C4F7A/1339_FSDS2013-2016_e_v10.pdf.

Environment Canada. 2013g. "Vehicle and Engine Regulations." *Air—Pollution
Sources: Transportation*. http://www.ec.gc.ca/Air/default.asp?lang=En&n
=AE4ECEC1-1.

Environment Canada. 2013h. *Wise Water Use*. https://www.ec.gc.ca/eau-water/default
.asp?lang=En&n=F25C70EC-1. Last modified July 23.

Environment Canada. 2014a. *About Environment Canada: Our Mandate*. http://www
.ec.gc.ca/default.asp?lang=En&n=BD3CE17D-1.

Environment Canada. 2014b. *Canada's Emission Trends*. Ottawa: Environment
Canada. https://www.ec.gc.ca/ges-ghg/E0533893-A985-4640-B3A2
-008D8083D17D/ETR_E 2014.pdf.

Environment Canada. 2014c. "Canada's Protected Areas." *Nature Indicators* https://
www.ec.gc.ca/indicateurs-indicators/default.asp?lang=en&n=478A1D3D-1.
Modified August 22.

Environment Canada. 2014d. "Freshwater Quality in Canadian Rivers." *Water
Indicators*. http://ec.gc.ca/indicateurs-indicators/default.asp?lang=En&n
=13307B2E-1. Modified May 8.

Environment Canada. 2014e. "Freshwater Quality in Canadian Rivers: Data Sources
and Methods for the Freshwater Quality Indicator." *Water Indicators*. http://
ec.gc.ca/indicateurs-indicators/default.asp?lang=En&n=5D193531-1. Modified
May 8.

Environment Canada. 2014f. "General Status of Species in Canada." *Nature Indicators*.
http://ec.gc.ca/indicateurs-indicators/default.asp?lang=En&n=37DB2E44-1.
Modified February 10.

Environment Canada. 2014g. *Habitat Stewardship Program for Species at Risk*. https://
www.ec.gc.ca/hsp-pih/. Last modified November 5.

Environment Canada. 2014h. "Land Use Impacts of Freshwater Quality." *Water Indicators*.
http://ec.gc.ca/indicateurs-indicators/default.asp?lang=en&n=88872F95-1. Modified
May 8.

Environment Canada. 2014i. "Soil and Water Quality Indicators for Agriculture."
Water Indicators. https://www.ec.gc.ca/indicateurs-indicators/default.
asp?lang=en&n=30607EED-1. Modified February.

Environment Canada. 2014j. "Sulphur Oxide Emissions." *Environmental Indicators:
Air and Climate*. https://www.ec.gc.ca/indicateurs-indicators/default
.asp?lang=en&n=402A9845-1. Last modified May 8.

Environment Canada. 2014k. *Sustainable Development*. http://www.ec.gc.ca/dd-sd/.
Last modified July 2.

Environment Canada. 2014l. *2014–2015 Report on Plans and Priorities*. Ottawa:
Environment Canada. http://ec.gc.ca/default.asp?lang=En&n=024B8406-1.

Environment Canada. 2015a. *Funding Programs*. https://www.ec.gc.ca/financement
-funding/default.asp?lang=En&n=923047A0-1. Last modified May 4.

Environment Canada. 2015b. "National Greenhouse Gas Emissions." *Environmental
Indicators: Air and Climate Indicators*. http://www.ec.gc.ca/indicateurs-indicators/
default.asp?lang=en&n=FBF8455E-1. Last modified March 17.

Environment Canada. 2015c. *National Inventory Report, 1990–2013: Greenhouse
Gas Sources and Sinks in Canada*. 3 vols. Ottawa: Environment Canada. https://

unfccc.int/files/national_reports/annex_i_ghg_inventories/national_inventories _submissions/application/zip/can-2015-nir-17apr.zip.

Environment Canada. 2015d. *Montreal Protocol Program.* http://ec.gc.ca/ozone/ default.asp?lang=En&n=9090CC46-1.

Environment Canada. 2015e. *Public Participation and Consultation.* http://ec.gc.ca/ consultation/default.asp?lang=Enandn=DB76C34E-1. Last modified May 14.

Environment Canada. 2015f. "Status of Major Fish Stocks." *Nature Indicators.* https:// www.ec.gc.ca/indicateurs-indicators/default.asp?lang=en&n=1BCD421B-1. Modified February 12.

Environmental Commissioner of Ontario. 2009. *The Last Line of Defence: A Review of Ontario's New Protections for Species at Risk.* A Special Report to the Legislative Assembly of Ontario, February. Toronto: Environmental Commissioner of Ontario.

EPA (Environmental Protection Agency). 2012a. "Basic Information." *Environmental Justice.* http://www.epa.gov/environmentaljustice/basics/index.html. Last modified May 24.

EPA (Environmental Protection Agency). 2012b. *What Is Nonpoint Source Pollution?* http://water.epa.gov/polwaste/nps/whatis.cfm. Last modified August 27.

EPA (Environmental Protection Agency). 2015a. "Carbon Dioxide Emissions." *Overview of Greenhouse Gases.* http://www.epa.gov/climatechange/ghgemissions/ gases/co2.html. Last updated April 14.

EPA (Environmental Protection Agency). 2015b. *Persistent Organic Pollutants: A Global Issue, A Global Response.* http://www2.epa.gov/international-cooperation/ persistent-organic-pollutants-global-issue-global-response. Last updated June 29.

ESRD (Energy and Sustainable Resource Development). 2015. *Greenhouse Gas Reduction Program.* http://esrd.alberta.ca/focus/alberta-and-climate-change/ regulating-greenhouse-gas-emissions/greenhouse-gas-reduction-program/default. aspx. Last modified April 27.

Evans, Margaret. 2014. "Time to Lift the Muzzle on Scientific Research." *Chilliwack Progress*, January 21. http://www.theprogress.com/opinion/241323911.html.

Farm Credit Canada. 2014. *Canadian Agriculture and Agri-Food in the Global Economy 2013–2014.* Regina: Farm Credit Canada. https://www.fcc-fac.ca/fcc/ about-fcc/corporate-profile/reports/cage-report/cage-report-2013.pdf.

Ferguson, Charles D. 2011. *Nuclear Energy: What Everyone Needs to Know.* New York: Oxford University Press.

FHQTC (File Hills Qu'Appelle Tribal Council). 2012. "Federal Government Attack on First Nations Rights." *FHQ Tribal Council Media Release*, December 12. http://fhqtc.com/wp-content/uploads/2011/09/Attack-on-First-Nations-Rights .pdf.

Field, Barry C., and Nancy D. Olewiler. 2002. *Environmental Economics.* 2nd Canadian ed. Toronto: McGraw-Hill Ryerson.

Filion, Pierre. 2003. "Towards Smart Growth? The Difficult Implementation of Alternatives to Urban Dispersion." *Canadian Journal of Urban Research* 12:48–70.

Findlay, Megan. 2010. "Grasslands." *Hinterland Who's Who.* http://www.hww.ca/en/ wild-spaces/grasslands.html.

Finley, Bruce. 2012. "Suncor Refinery in Commerce City Will Pay Fine for Air Quality Violations." *The Denver Post*, April 2. http://www.denverpost.com/ci_20308243/ suncor-refinery-commerce-city-will-pay-fine-air.

Firth, Chris, Damian Maye, and David Pearson. 2011. "Developing "Community" in Community Gardens." *Local Environment* 16 (6): 555–68. http://dx.doi.org/10.1 080/13549839.2011.586025.

Fischhendler, Itay, and Eran Feitelson. 2005. "The Formation and Viability of a Non-Basin Water Management: The US-Canada Case." *Geoforum* 36 (6): 792–804. http://dx.doi.org/10.1016/j.geoforum.2005.01.008.

Fischler, Raphael. 2004. "The Problem, or Not, of Urban Sprawl." *Policy Options* 25 (2): 44–48. http://policyoptions.irpp.org/wp-content/uploads/sites/2/assets/po/ canadas-cities/Fischler.pdf.

Fisheries and Oceans Canada. 2015. *Harp Seal and Hooded Seal Competitive Fleet in Newfoundland and Labrador, Quebec, Gulf and Maritimes Regions*. http:// www.dfo-mpo.gc.ca/decisions/fm-2015-gp/atl-002-eng.htm. Last modified February 27.

Flaherty, James M. 2014. *The Road to Balance: Creating Jobs and Opportunities— Economic Action Plan 2014: The Budget in Brief*. http://www.budget.gc.ca/2014/ docs/bb/pdf/brief-bref-eng.pdf.

Flanagan, Erin. 2015. "Tailings Management Framework: A New Chapter in Alberta's Oilsands Story?" *Pembina Institute Blog*, March 16. http://www.pembina.org/ blog/tailings-management-framework-a-new-chapter-in-albertas-oilsands-story.

Fletcher, Thomas H. 2003. *From Love Canal to Environmental Justice: The Politics of Hazardous Waste on the Canada–U.S. Border*. Toronto: University of Toronto Press.

Florida, Richard. 2010. "The World's Worst Commutes." *The Atlantic*, July 1. http://www. theatlantic.com/international/archive/2010/07/the-worlds-worst-commutes/59062/.

FOCA (Federation of Ontario Cottagers' Associations). 2014 "Navigable Waters Protection Act—Overview," *Post Archive*, April. http://foca.on.ca/2014/04/.

Foreign Affairs, Trade and Development Canada. 2014. *Canada-European Union: Comprehensive Economic and Trade Agreement (CETA)*. http://www .international.gc.ca/trade-agreements-accords-commerciaux/agr-acc/ceta -aecg/benefits-avantages/agriculture-agricoles.aspx?lang=eng. Last modified September 26.

Forge, Frédéric, and Tim Williams. 2008. *Policy Options to Reduce Greenhouse Gas Emissions*. Ottawa: Library of Parliament. http://www.parl.gc.ca/Content/LOP/ researchpublications/prb0819-e.pdf.

Forkey, Neil S. 2013. *Canadians and the Natural Environment to the Twenty-First Century*. Toronto: University of Toronto Press.

Foster, John Elgin, Dick. Harrison, and I. S. MacLaren. 1992. *Buffalo*. Edmonton: The University of Alberta Press.

Fox, Paul. 2006. "Royal Commissions." *The Canadian Encyclopedia*. http://www .thecanadianencyclopedia.ca/en/article/royal-commissions/.

FPAC (Forest Products Association of Canada). 2015a. *A Buyers' Guide to Canada's Sustainable Forest Products*. Ottawa: Natural Resources Canada. http://www .fpac.ca/publications/FPAC_Buyers_Guide.PDF.

FPAC (Forest Products Association of Canada). 2015b. *Forest Management Certification in Canada*. http://www.certificationcanada.org/en/home/.

FPAC (Forest Products Association of Canada). 2015c. *Forest Products Association of Canada*. http://www.fpac.ca/index.php/en/.

FPT (Federal, Provincial and Territorial) Governments of Canada. 2010. *Canadian Biodiversity: Ecosystem Status and Trends 2010*. Ottawa: Canadian Councils or Resource Ministers. http://www.biodivcanada.ca/A519F000-8427-4F8C-9521 -8A95AE287753\EN_CanadianBiodiversity_FULL.pdf.

Friesen, Gerald. 1987. *The Canadian Prairies*. Toronto: University of Toronto Press.

Frisken, Frances. 2008. *The Public Metropolis: Political Dynamics of Urban Expansion in the Toronto Region, 1924–2003*. Toronto: Canadian Scholars' Press.

Fuller, Kent, Harvey Shear, and Jennifer Wittig, eds. 1995. "The Great Lakes Today: Concerns." In *The Great Lakes: An Environmental Atlas and Research Book*. Toronto and Chicago: Environment Canada Ontario Region and EPA Great Lakes National Program Office. http://epa.gov/greatlakes/atlas/glat-ch4 .html.

Gagnon, Chantal. 2010. *Montreal Community Sustainable Development Plan 2010—2015*. Montréal: Ville de Montréal. http://ville.montreal.qc.ca/pls/ portal/docs/PAGE/PES_PUBLICATIONS_EN/PUBLICATIONS/VERSION _SYNTHESE_EN.PDF.

Ganter, Barbara, and Anthony J. Gaston. 2013. "Birds." In *Arctic Biodiversity Assessment: Status and Trends in Arctic Biodiversity*, edited by Hans Meltofte, Alf B. Josefson, and David Payer, 143–81. Akureyri, Iceland: Conservation of Arctic Flora and Fauna.

Garriguet, Didier. 2004. *Overview of Canadians' Eating Habits*. Ottawa: Statistics Canada. http://publications.gc.ca/Collection/Statcan/82–620-M/82–620 -MIE2006002.pdf.

Garriguet, Didier. 2008. "Beverage Consumption of Canadian Adults." *Health Reports* 19 (4): 23–9.

Gayler, Hugh. 1991. *The Decline of the Niagara Fruit Belt: Policy Planning and Development Options in the 1990s*. Toronto: Geographical Monographs.

General Assembly of the United Nations. 2015. *About the General Assembly*. http:// www.un.org/en/ga/about/index.shtml.

Gillis, Justin. 2011. "A Warming Planet Struggles to Feed Itself." *The New York Times*, June 4. http://www.nytimes.com/2011/06/05/science/earth/05harvest.html? pagewanted=alland_r-0.

The Globe and Mail. 2015. "Top 1000: Exclusive Rankings of Canada's Most Profitable Companies." *Report on Business*, June 24. http://www.theglobeandmail .com/report-on-business/rob-magazine/top-1000/rankings/canadas-100-biggest -companies-by-revenue/article25020439/.

Goebel, T., M. R. Waters, and D. H. O'Rourke. 2008. "The Late Pleistocene Dispersal of Modern Humans in the Americas." *Science* 319 (5869): 1497–1502.

Goldenberg, Suzanne. 2013. "America's First Climate Refugees: What Is a Climate Refugee?" *The Guardian*, May 13. http://www.theguardian.com/environment/ interactive/2013/may/13/newtok-alaska-climate-change-refugees.

Gollom, Mark. 2015. "Greenhouse Gas Emissions: How Can Canada Cut 30% by 2030?" *CBC News*, May 25. http://www.cbc.ca/news/politics/ greenhouse-gas-emissions-how-can-canada-cut-30-by-2030-1.3080447.

Goodine, Claudia. 2011. "Fracking Controversy." *Canadian Geographic Magazine*, October. http://www.canadiangeographic.ca/magazine/oct11/fracking.asp.

Government of Canada. 2009. *Canada's Northern Strategy: Our North, Our Heritage, Our Future*. Ottawa: Indian Affairs and Northern Development. http://www .northernstrategy.gc.ca/cns/cns.pdf.

Government of Canada. 2011. *Joint Action Plan for the Canada-United States Regulatory Cooperation Council*. Ottawa: Regulatory Cooperation Council. http://actionplan.gc.ca/sites/eap/files/japlan_eng.pdf.

Government of Canada. 2012a. "Canada's Regions." *Discover Canada*. http://www.cic .gc.ca/english/resources/publications/discover/section-13.asp. Last modified July 1.

Government of Canada. 2012b. *Cutting Red Tape ... Freeing Business to Grow*. Ottawa: Red Tape Reduction Commission. http://www.reduceredtape.gc.ca/ heard-entendu/rr/rr-eng.pdf.

Government of Canada. 2012c. "Top Ten Things You Can Do to Help." *Information on Climate Change*. http://www.climatechange.gc.ca/default.asp?lang=en&n= D27052CE-1. Last modified August 23.

Government of Canada. 2012d. *Wildlife Species Assessment: COSEWIC Aboriginal Traditional Knowledge (ATK) Process and Protocols Guidelines*. Ottawa: COSEWIC. http://www.cosewic.gc.ca/eng/sct0/PPG_e.cfm. Last modified April 16.

Government of Canada. 2013. "Canadian High Commission in London Focuses on Canada's Arctic." *The Canadian Arctic*. http://www.canadainternational.gc.ca/ united_kingdom-royaume_uni/bilateral_relations_bilaterales/arctic-arctique .aspx?lang=eng. Last modified March 18.

Government of Canada. 2014a. *Corporate Social Responsibility*. http://www .international.gc.ca/trade-agreements-accords-commerciaux/topics-domaines/ other-autre/csr-rse.aspx?lang=eng. Last modified November 14.

Government of Canada. 2014b. *Growing Forward 2*. Ottawa: Agriculture and Agri-Food Canada. http://www.agr.gc.ca/eng/about-us/key-departmental-initiatives/ growing-forward-2/?id=1294780620963. Last modified August 5.

Government of Canada. 2014c. "Reducing Greenhouse Gases." *Canada's Action on Climate Change*. http://climatechange.gc.ca/default.asp?lang=En&n=4FE85A4C-1.

Government of Canada. 2014d. Species at Risk Public Registry: Parliament Review. https://www.registrelep-sararegistry.gc.ca/default.asp?lang=Enandn=25EC2C4C-1.

Government of Canada. 2015a. "About COSEWIC." *COSEWIC*. http://www.cosewic .gc.ca/eng/sct6/sct6_4_e.cfm. Last updated May.

Government of Canada. 2015b. "How Are Species Listed?" *Species at Risk Registry: Frequently Asked Questions*. http://www.registrelep-sararegistry.gc.ca/about/faq/ default_e.cfm. Last modified April.

Government of Canada. 2015c. *Reduction of Carbon Dioxide Emissions from Coal-Fired Generation of Electricity Regulations*. SOR/2012–167. http://laws.justice .gc.ca/eng/regulations/SOR-2012–167/. Last modified May 22.

Government of Newfoundland and Labrador. 2015. *Growing Forward 2 in Newfoundland and Labrador: Program Guide*. St. John's: Department of Natural Resources. http://www.nr.gov.nl.ca/nr/funding/growingforward2/2013/ gf2_program_guide.pdf.

Government of Saskatchewan. 2015. *Growing Forward 2*. http://www.agriculture.gov .sk.ca/GrowingForward2.

Grant, Shelagh. 2010. *Polar Imperative: A History of Arctic Sovereignty in North America*. Vancouver: McIntyre and Douglas.

Green, Jeff. 2012. "Canada's Population Hits 35 Million." *Toronto Star*, December 6, http://www.thestar.com/news/canada/2012/12/06/canadas_population_hits_35 _million.html.

Green Party of Canada. n.d. *The Green Movement*. http://www.greenparty.ca/en/party/ history.

Green Party of Ontario. 2015. *Party History*. http://www.gpo.ca/about/background/party-history.

Greenbelt Foundation. 2015. *The Greenbelt*. Toronto: Friends of the Greenbelt Foundation. http://www.greenbelt.ca/about_the_greenbelt.

Haines, Lily. 2015. "EU Bid to Become Arctic Council Observer Deferred Again." *Barents Observer*, May 4. http://barentsobserver.com/en/arctic/2015/05/eu-bid-become-arctic-council-observer-deferred-again-04-05.

Hall, Roland I., Peter R. Leavitt, Roberto Quinlan, Aruna S. Dixit, and John P. Smol. 1999. "Effects of Agriculture, Urbanization, and Climate on Water Quality in the Northern Great Plains." *Limnology and Oceanography* 44 (3.2): 739–56. http://dx.doi.org/10.4319/lo.1999.44.3_part_2.0739.

Hanna, Kevin. 2010. "Transition and the Need for Innovation in Canada's Forest Sector." In *Resource and Environmental Management in Canada: Addressing Conflict and Uncertainty*, 4th ed., edited by Bruce Mitchell, 271–300. Oxford: Oxford University Press.

Hansen, James. [1988] 2012. "Statement of Dr. James Hansen." In *The Global Warming Reader*, edited by Bill McKibben, 47–54. New York: Penguin Books.

Hansen, Simon. 2014. "The China–US Climate Change Agreement Is a Step Forward for Green Power Relations." *The Guardian*, November 14. http://www.theguardian.com/commentisfree/2014/nov/14/the-china-us-climate-change-agreement-is-a-step-forward-for-green-power-relations.

Hardin, Garrett. 1968. "The Tragedy of the Commons." *Science* 162 (3859): 1243–8. http://dx.doi.org/10.1126/science.162.3859.1243.

Harker, Brook, John Lebedin, Michael J. Goss, Chandra Madramootoo, Denise Neilsen, Brent Paterson, and Ted vander Gulik. 2004. "Land Use Practices and Changes—Agriculture." In *Threats to Water Availability in Canada*, 49–56. Ottawa: Environment Canada. http://ec.gc.ca/inre-nwri/0CD66675-AD25-4B23-892C-5396F7876F65/ThreatsEN_03web.pdf.

Harper, Stephen. 2008. "Prime Minister Harper Announces the John G. Diefenbaker Icebreaker Project." Speech delivered in Inuvik, NT, on August 28. *Prime Minister of Canada Stephen Harper: Speeches*. http://pm.gc.ca/eng/news/2008/08/28/prime-minister-harper-announces-john-g-diefenbaker-icebreaker-project.

Harris, Kathleen. 2013. "Canada Failing to Meet 2020 Emission Targets." *CBC News*, October 24. http://www.cbc.ca/news/politics/canada-failing-to-meet-2020-emissions-targets-1.2223930.

Harris, Michael. 1998. *Lament for an Ocean: The Collapse of the Atlantic Cod Fishery*. Toronto: McClelland and Stewart.

Harrison, Kathryn. 1996. *Passing the Buck: Federalism and Canadian Environmental Policy*. Vancouver: UBC Press.

Harrison, Kathryn. 2013. "Federalism and Climate Policy Innovation: A Critical Reassessment." *Canadian Public Policy* 39 (s2): S95–108. http://dx.doi.org/10.3138/CPP.39.Supplement2.S95.

Harrison, Kathryn, and Lisa McIntosh Sundstrom. 2007. "The Comparative Politics of Climate Change." *Global Environmental Politics* 7 (4): 1–18. http://dx.doi.org/10.1162/glep.2007.7.4.1.

HBC (Hudson's Bay Company). 2015a. "The Deed of Surrender." *HBC Heritage: Our History*. http://www.hbcheritage.ca/hbcheritage/history/week/the-deed-of-surrender.

HBC (Hudson's Bay Company). 2015b. "The Royal Charter of the Hudson's Bay Company." *HBC Corporate Collections*. http://www.hbcheritage.ca/hbcheritage/collections/archival/charter/home.

Health Canada. 2014. *Additional Information on Radiation from Japan.* http://www
.hc-sc.gc.ca/hc-ps/ed-ud/respond/nuclea/add_info-ren_supp-eng.php. Last
modified October 3.

Health Canada. 2015. "Indoor Air Quality." *Environmental and Workplace Health.*
http://www.hc-sc.gc.ca/ewh-semt/air/in/index-eng.php. Last modified
March 20.

Henriques, Irene, and Perry Sadorsky. 1999. "The Relationship between Environmental
Commitment and Managerial Perceptions of Stakeholder Importance." *Academy
of Management Journal* 42 (1): 87–99. http://dx.doi.org/10.2307/256876.

Hessing, Melody, Michael Howlett, and Tracy Summerville. 2005. *Canadian Natural
Resource and Environmental Policy.* 2nd ed. Vancouver: UBC Press.

Hill, Carey, Kathryn Furlong, Karen Bakker, and Alice Cohen. 2008. "Harmonization
Versus Subsidiarity in Water Governance: A Review of Water Governance and
Legislation in the Canadian Provinces and Territories." *Canadian Water Resources
Journal* 33 (4): 315–32. http://dx.doi.org/10.4296/cwrj3304315.

Hill, Jason, Erik Nelson, David Tilman, Stephen Polasky, and Douglas Tiffany. 2006.
"Environmental, Economic, and Energetic Costs and Benefits of Biodiesel and
Ethanol Biofuels." *Proceedings of the National Academy of Sciences of the United
States of America* 103 (30): 11206–10. http://dx.doi.org/10.1073/pnas.0604600103.

Hoberg, George, and Jeffrey Phillips. 2011. "Playing Defence: Early Responses to
Conflict Expansion in the Oil Sands Policy Subsystem." *Canadian Journal of
Political Science* 44 (3): 507–27. http://dx.doi.org/10.1017/S0008423911000473.

Hoffecker, John F. 2005. *A Prehistory of the North: Human Settlement of the Higher
Latitudes.* New Brunswick, NJ: Rutgers University Press.

Holmes, Miranda, Paul Lingl, Dale Marshall, Ian Bruce, Morag Carter, and Faisal
Moola. 2012. *All over the Map 2012: A Comparison of Provincial Climate
Change Plans.* Vancouver: David Suzuki Foundation. http://www.davidsuzuki
.org/publications/downloads/2012/All Over the Map 2012.pdf.

Hossain, Kamrul. 2013. "The EU Ban on the Import of Seal Products and the WTO
Regulations: Neglected Human Rights of the Arctic Indigenous Peoples?" *Polar
Record* 49 (2): 154–66. http://dx.doi.org/10.1017/S0032247412000174.

Howlett, Michael. 2002. "Do Networks Matter? Linking Policy Network Structure
to Policy Outcomes from Four Canadian Policy Sectors 1999–2000." *Canadian
Journal of Political Science* 25 (2): 235–67.

Howlett, Michael, Jeremy Rayner, and Chris Tollefson. 2009. "From Government to
Governance in Forest Planning? Lessons from the Case of the British Columbia
Great Bear Rainforest Initiative." *Forest Policy and Economics* 11 (5–6): 383–91.
http://dx.doi.org/10.1016/j.forpol.2009.01.003.

Huebert, Rob. 2013. "It's Time to Talk about Arctic Militarization." *National Post,*
May 6. http://news.nationalpost.com/full-comment/arctic-piece-1-for-monday.

Humane Society of the United States. 2014. *Pets by the Numbers.* http://www
.humanesociety.org/issues/pet_overpopulation/facts/pet_ownership_statistics.html.
Last modified January 30.

Hunter, Justine, and Wendy Stueck. 2014. "B.C. Government to Northern Gateway
Pipeline Proposal: 'No.'" *The Globe and Mail,* June 17. http://www.the
globeandmail.com/news/british-columbia/bc-to-northern-gateway-no/
article19213866/.

Hurley, Mary C. 2009. *Settling Comprehensive Land Claims.* PRB 09–16-E.
Ottawa: Parliamentary Information and Research Service, Library of
Parliament. http://www.parl.gc.ca/Content/LOP/ResearchPublications/
prb0916-e.pdf.

Hurley, Mary C., and Jill Wherrett. 1999. *The Report of the Royal Commission on Aboriginal Peoples*. PRB 99–24E. Ottawa: Parliamentary Information and Research Service, Library of Parliament. http://www.parl.gc.ca/content/lop/researchpublications/prb9924-e.htm.

IAEA (International Atomic Energy Agency). 2014. *IAEA Annual Report 2013*. New York: IAEA. https://www.iaea.org/sites/default/files/anrep2013_full_0.pdf.

IEA (International Energy Agency). 2011. *Solar Energy Perspectives*. Paris: International Energy Agency. http://www.iea.org/publications/freepublications/publication/Solar_Energy_Perspectives2011.pdf.

IEA (International Energy Agency). 2014. *Key World Energy Statistics 2014*. Paris: International Energy Agency. http://www.iea.org/publications/freepublications/publication/KeyWorld2014.pdf.

IEA (International Energy Agency). 2015. *FAQs: Nuclear*. http://www.iea.org/aboutus/faqs/nuclear/.

Illical, Mary, and Kathryn Harrison. 2007. "Protecting Endangered Species in the US and Canada: The Role of Negative Lesson Drawing." *Canadian Journal of Political Science* 40 (2): 367–94.

IMF (International Monetary Fund). 2014. *Canada: Selected Issues*. IMF Country Report No. 14/28. Washington, DC: International Monetary Fund.

Innis, Harold A. 1930. *The Fur Trade in Canada: An Introduction to Canadian Economic History*. New Haven, CT: Yale University Press.

International Joint Commission. 2014. *Canada–United States Air Quality Agreement Progress Report, 2014*. Ottawa: Canadian Section International Joint Commission. https://www.ec.gc.ca/Air/D560EA62-2A5F-4789-883E-9F4DA63C58CD/AQA Report 2014 ENG.pdf.

IPCC (Intergovernmental Panel on Climate Change). [1995] 2012. "Summary for Policymakers: The Science of Climate Change." In *The Global Warming Reader*, edited by Bill McKibben, 55–68. New York: Penguin Books.

IPCC (Intergovernmental Panel on Climate Change) 2013. *Climate Change 2013: The Physical Science Basis—Summary for Policymakers*. Cambridge: Cambridge University Press.

Irimoto, Takashi, and Takako Yamada, eds. 2004. *Circumpolar Ethnicity and Identity*. Osaka: Japón National Museum of Ethnology.

Jaccard, Mark. 2013. "Alberta's (Non)-Carbon Tax and Our Threatened Climate." *Sustainability Suspicions* [blog], April 26. http://markjaccard.blogspot.ca/2013/04/albertas-non-carbon-tax-and-our.html.

James, Simon. 2015. *Environmental Philosophy: An Introduction*. Cambridge: Polity Press.

Jansen, Harold. J, and Lisa Lambert. 2013. "Too Little, Too Soon: State Funding and Electoral District Associations in the Green Party of Canada." In *Parties, Elections, and the Future of Canadian Politics* edited by Amanda Bittner and Royce Koop, 211–30. Vancouver: UBC Press.

Jeffrey, Brooke. 2010. *Divided Loyalties: The Liberal Party of Canada, 1984–2008*. Toronto: University of Toronto Press.

Jermé, Erika S., and Sarah Wakefield. 2013. "Growing a Just Garden: Environmental Justice and the Development of a Community Garden Policy for Hamilton, Ontario." *Planning Theory & Practice* 14 (3): 295–314. http://dx.doi.org/10.1080/14649357.2013.812743.

Johansen, Bruce E. 2002. "The Inuit Struggle with Dioxins and Other Organic Pollutants." *American Indian Quarterly* 26 (3): 479–90. http://dx.doi.org/10.1353/aiq.2003.0041.

Johansen, David. 1991. *Property Rights and the Constitution*. BP-268 Ottawa: Parliament of Canada, Law and Government Division.

Johnson, Keith, and Ben Lefebvre. 2013. "US Approves Expanded Gas Exports." *Wall Street Journal*, May 18. http://www.wsj.com/articles/SB100014241278873 2476700457848913030087645.

Johnston, Sadhu Aufochs, Steven S. Nicholas, and Julia Parzen. 2013. *The Guide to Greening Cities*. Washington, DC: Island Press. http://dx.doi.org/10.5822/978-1-61091-504-5.

Jones, Bryony. 2011. "Timeline: How Japan's Nuclear Crisis Unfolded." *CNN World*, March 20. http://www.cnn.com/2011/WORLD/asiapcf/03/15/japan.nuclear.disaster.timeline/index.html.

Kebe, Amadou, Valentin Bellassen, and Alexia Leseur. 2011. "Voluntary Carbon Offsetting by Local Authorities: Practices and Lessons." *Climate Report* 29 September. http://www.cdcclimat.com/IMG/pdf/11-09-30_climate_report_29_voluntary_carbon_offsetting_by_local_authorities.pdf.

Kenny, Alex, Stewart Elgie, and Dave Sawyer. 2011. *Advancing the Economics of Ecosystems and Biodiversity in Canada*. Ottawa: Sustainable Prosperity (SP), University of Ottawa. http://www.sustainableprosperity.ca/dl534&display.

Kerr, Jeremy T., and Josef Cihlar. 2004. "Patterns and Causes of Species Endangerment in Canada." *Ecological Applications* 14 (3): 743–53. http://dx.doi.org/10.1890/02-5117.

Kerr, Josh. 2013. "Deal Allowing Nestlé to Draw Ontario Water during Droughts under Review." *The Globe and Mail*, August 16. http://www.theglobeandmail.com/news/national/deal-allowing-nestle-to-draw-water-during-droughts-under-review/article13811553/.

Kerr, Richard A. 2009. "Amid Worrisome Signs of Warming, 'Climate Fatigue' Sets in." *Science* 326 (5955): 926–28. http://dx.doi.org/10.1126/science.326.5955.926.

Kerry, John. 2014. "China, America and Our Warming Planet." *The New York Times*, November 11. http://www.nytimes.com/2014/11/12/opinion/john-kerry-our-historic-agreement-with-china-on-climate-change.html?_r=0.

Kilpatrick, Julia. 2010. "First Nations Leaders Bring Oilsands Concerns to U.S. Decision Makers." *Pembina Institute Blog*, September 22. http://www.pembina.org/blog/408.

Kingdon, John. 2010. *Agendas, Alternatives, and Public Policies*. Updated ed. Harlow: Pearson.

Kino-nda-niimi Collective. 2014. *The Winter We Danced: Voices from the Past, the Future, and the Idle No More Movement*. Winnipeg: ARP Books.

Kirby, Ellen, and Elizabeth Peters. 2008. *Community Gardening*. Brooklyn, NY: Brooklyn Botanic Garden.

Klinkenberg, Brian. 2012. "What Is Biodiversity?" *Biodiversity of British Columbia*. http://ibis.geog.ubc.ca/biodiversity/Whatisbiodiversity.html.

Krajnc, Anita, and Larry Wartel. 2004. "Top 10 Canadian NGO Strategies & Tactics to Combat Climate Change." *Canadian Dimension* 38 (1): 29. https://canadiandimension.com/articles/view/top-10-canadian-ngo-strategies-tactics-to-combat-climate-change.

Kuttner, Thomas. 2006. "Administrative Tribunals." *The Canadian Encyclopedia*. http://www.thecanadianencyclopedia.ca/en/article/administrative-tribunals/.

La Roi, George H. 2015. "Boreal Forest." *Canadian Encyclopedia*. http://www.thecanadianencyclopedia.ca/en/article/boreal-forest/. Last modified March 4.

Lake Winnipeg Stewardship Board. 2006. *Reducing Nutrient Loading to Lake Winnipeg and Its Watershed: Our Collective Responsibility and Commitment to Action.* Report to the Minister of Water Stewardship. Gimli, MB: Lake Winnipeg Stewardship Board. http://www.gov.mb.ca/waterstewardship/water_quality/lake_winnipeg/lwsb2007-12_final_rpt.pdf.

Lasswell, Harold. 1936. *Politics: Who Gets What, When, How.* New York: McGraw-Hill.

Leahy, Stephen. 2014. "Canada's Carbon Emissions Projected to Soar by 2030." *The Guardian*, January 14. http://www.theguardian.com/environment/2014/jan/14/canada-carbon-emissions-2030-tar-sands.

LeMarquand, David. 1993. "The International Joint Commission and Changing Canada-United States Boundary Relations." *Natural Resources Journal* 33:59–91.

Lemphers, Nathan. 2013. "Moving Oilsands to Market—by Pipeline or Rail?" *Pembina Institute Blog,* May 23. http://www.pembina.org/blog/732.

Liberal Party of Canada. 2015. "Energy and the Environment." *What We Stand For.* https://www.liberal.ca/what-we-stand-for/energy-and-the-environment/.

Linton, Jamie, and Noah Hall. 2013. "The Great Lakes: A Model of Transboundary Cooperation." In *Water without Borders? Canada, the United States, and Shared Waters,* edited by Emma S. Norman, Alice Cohen, and Karen Bakker, 221–43. Toronto: University of Toronto Press.

Locke, John. [1690] 1988. *Two Treatises of Government.* Ed. Peter Laslett. Cambridge: Cambridge University Press.

Lorinc, John. 2014. "The World's First Carbon Capture Plant Opens in Saskatchewan." *The Globe and Mail*, December 2. http://www.theglobeandmail.com/report-on-business/rob-magazine/the-worlds-first-carbon-capture-plant-opens-in-saskachewan/article21877367/.

Lourie, Bruce, and Rick Smith. 2013. *Toxin Toxout: Getting Harmful Chemicals out of Our Bodies and Our World.* Toronto: Knopf Canada.

Lovelock, Brent, Carla Jellum, Anna Thompson, and Kirsten Lovelock. 2013. "Could Immigrants Care Less about the Environment? A Comparison of the Environmental Values of Immigrant and Native-Born New Zealanders." *Society & Natural Resources* 26 (4): 402–19. http://dx.doi.org/10.1080/08941920.2012.697979.

Luckert, Martin K., David Haley, and George Hoberg, eds. 2012. *Policies for Sustainably Managing Canada's Forests: Tenure, Stumpage Fees, and Forest Practices.* Vancouver: UBC Press.

MacDonald, Douglas. 2009. "The Failure of Canadian Climate Change Policy: Veto Power, Absent Leadership, and Institutional Weakness." In *Canadian Environmental Policy and Politics,* edited by Robert Boardman and Debora L. VanNijnatten, 3rd ed., 152–66. Don Mills, ON: Oxford University Press.

MacDonald, Elaine, and Sarah Rang. 2007. *Exposing Canada's Chemical Valley: An Investigation of Cumulative Air Pollution Emissions in the Sarnia, Ontario, Area.* Toronto: Ecojustice Canada. http://www.environmentalhealthnews.org/ehs/news/2012/2007-study.pdf.

MacDonald, Patrick N. 1977. "Peace, Order and Good Government: The Laskin Court in the Anti-Inflation Act Reference." *McGill Law Journal / Revue de droit de McGill* 23:431–61.

MacDowell, Laurel Sefton. 2012. *An Environmental History of Canada.* Vancouver: UBC Press.

MacIntosh, Constance. 2008. "Testing the Waters: Jurisdictional and Policy Aspects of the Continuing Failure to Remedy Drinking Water Quality on First Nations Reserves." *Ottawa Law Review* 39 (1): 63–97.

Mackrael, Kim. 2014. "Harper to Address UN Assembly for First Time since 2010 on Ukraine, Iraq." *The Globe and Mail*, September 10. http://www.theglobeandmail .com/news/politics/harper-to-address-un-assembly-in-september/article20514477/.

Maclean's. 2013. *Canada Top 50 Socially Responsible Corporations*. http://www .macleans.ca/canada-top-50-socially-responsible-corporations-2013/.

Malhi, Yadvinder, Patrick Meir, and Sandra Brown. 2003. "Forests, Carbon and Global Climate." In *Capturing Carbon and Conserving Biodiversity: The Market Approach*, edited by Ian R Swingland, 15–41. London: Earthscan.

Marchildon, Gregory P., ed. 2009. *Immigration and Settlement, 1870–1939*. Regina: University of Regina Press.

Marchildon, Gregory P., ed. 2011. *Agricultural History*. Regina: University of Regina Press.

Marles, Robin James, and Northern Forestry Centre. 2009. *Aboriginal Plant Use in Canada's Northwest Boreal Forest*. Vancouver: UBC Press.

Max Paris Environment Unit. 2013. "No Federal Plan for Biodiversity, Environment Watchdog Warns." *CBC News*, November 5. http://www.cbc.ca/m/touch/news/ story/1.2355875.

McCarthy, Shawn. 2014a. "Canada Won't Meet 2020 Greenhouse Gas Emission Targets: Report." *The Globe and Mail*, December 8. http://www.theglobeandmail .com/news/politics/canada-wont-meet-2020-greenhouse-gas-emission-targets -report/article21998423/.

McCarthy, Shawn. 2014b. "U.S.-China Climate Deal Presents Challenges for Harper." *The Globe and Mail*, November 12. http://www.theglobeandmail.com/report-on -business/international-business/us-china-climate-deal-presents-challenges-for -harper/article21553685/.

McCombs, Maxwell. 1977. "Agenda Setting Function of Mass Media." *Public Relations Review* 3 (4): 89–95. http://dx.doi.org/10.1016/S0363-8111(77)80008-8.

McGregor, Janyce. 2012. "22 Changes in the Budget Bill Fine Print." *CBC News*, October 26. http://www.cbc.ca/news/politics/22-changes-in-the-budget-bill-fine -print-1.1233481.

McGregor, Janyce. 2015. "Investor G3 Global Grain Group to Take over Wheat Board." *CBC News*, April 15. http://www.cbc.ca/news/politics/investor-g3-global -grain-group-to-take-over-wheat-board-1.3033665.

McGuire, David A., Robie W. MacDonald, Edward A.G. Schuur, Jennifer W. Harden, Peter Kuhry, Daniel J. Hayes, Torben R. Christensen, and Martin Heimann. 2010. "The Carbon Budget of the Northern Cryosphere Region." *Current Opinion in Environmental Sustainability* 2 (4): 231–6. http://dx.doi.org/10.1016/j.cosust .2010.05.003.

McKenzie, Judith I. 2002. *Environmental Politics in Canada: Managing the Commons into the Twenty-First Century*. Oxford: Oxford University Press.

McKitrick, Ross. 2006. "The Politics of Pollution: Party Regimes and Air Quality in Canada." *Canadian Journal of Economics / Revue canadienne d'economique* 39 (2): 604–20.

McNeil, K. 1997. "Aboriginal Title and Aboriginal Rights: What's the Connection?" *Alberta Law Review* 36 (1): 117–48.

Miller, J.R. 2009. *Compact, Contract, Covenant: Aboriginal Treaty-Making in Canada*. Toronto: University of Toronto Press.

Mitchell, Kaitlyn. 2010. "Supreme Court of Canada Refines Environmental Assessment Law in British Columbia Mining Case." *Ontario Bar Association*

Environews 19 (3). http://www.cela.ca/article/red-chris-mine-intervention/ SCC-refines-EA-law-BC-mining-case.

Montgomery, Scott L. 2010. *The Powers That Be: Global Energy for the Twenty-First Century and Beyond*. Chicago: University of Chicago Press. http://dx.doi.org/ 10.7208/chicago/9780226535012.001.0001.

Moore, Dene. 2012. "Environmentalists Sue to Force Ottawa to Protect Species along Northern Gateway Route." *The Globe and Mail*, September 26. http://www .theglobeandmail.com/news/british-columbia/environmentalists-sue-to-force -ottawa-to-protect-species-along-northern-gateway-route/article4568673/.

Moos, Markus, and Pablo Mendez. 2013. "Suburbanization and the Remaking of Metropolitan Canada." In *Suburban Constellations: Governance, Land, and Infrastructure in the Twenty-First Century*, edited by R. Keil, 106–117. Berlin: Jovis Verlag GmbH.

Moos, Markus, and Pablo Mendez. 2014. "Suburban Ways of Living and the Geography of Income: How Homeownership, Single-Family Dwellings and Automobile Use Define the Metropolitan Social Space." *Urban Studies* 20: 1–19. http://dx.doi.org/10.1177/0042098014538679.

Morlan, R. E., D. E. Nelson, T. A. Brown, J. S. Vogel, and J. R. Southron. 1990. "Accelerator Mass Spectrometry Dates on Bones from Old Crow Basin, Northern Yukon Territory." *Canadian Journal of Archaeology* 14:75–92.

Morton, Desmond. 2006. *A Short History of Canada*. 6th ed. Toronto: McClelland and Stewart.

Mott, Maryann. 2004. "U.S. Faces Growing Feral Cat Problem." *National Geographic News*, September 7. http://news.nationalgeographic.com/news/2004/09/0907_ 040907_feralcats.html.

MRBB (Makenzie River Basin Board). 2013. "About Us." *MRBB: Mackenzie River Basin Board*. http://www.mrbb.ca/information/8/index.html. Last modified November 6.

Muldoon, Paul, and Richard Lundgren. 1997. "The Hydro-Quebec Decision: Loud Hurray or Last Hurrah?" *Law Times* (September 29–October 5). http://www.cela .ca/publications/hydro-quebec-decision-loud-hurray-or-last-hurrah.

Myers, Norman, and Jennifer Kent. 1995. *Environmental Exodus—An Emergent Crisis in the Global Arena*. Washington, DC: Climate Institute.

Naske, Claus-M. 1987. *Alaska: A History of the 49th State*. Norman: University of Oklahoma Press.

Naske, Claus-M., and Herman E. Slotnick. 2011. *Alaska: A History*. 3rd ed. Norman: University of Oklahoma Press.

National Energy Board. 2013. *Report of the Joint Review Panel for the Enbridge Northern Gateway Project*. 2 vols. Ottawa: National Energy Board. http:// gatewaypanel.review-examen.gc.ca/clf-nsi/dcmnt/rcmndtnsrprt/rcmndtnsrprtvlm1 -eng.pdf and http://gatewaypanel.review-examen.gc.ca/clf-nsi/dcmnt/rcmndtnsrprt/ rcmndtnsrprtvlm2-eng.pdf.

National Forest Inventory. 2013. *Table 4.1: Area (1000 ha) of Forest and Non-Forest Land by Terrestrial Ecozone in Canada*. https://nfi.nfis.org/publications/ standard_reports/NFI3_T4_FOR_AREA_en.html.

National Geographic. n.d. "Climate Refugee." *Education: Encyclopedic Entry*. http://education.nationalgeographic.com/education/encyclopedia/climate -refugee/?ar_a=1.

National Research Council. 2003. *Cities Transformed: Demographic Change and Its Implications in the Developing World*. Washington, DC: National Academies Press.

Natural Resources Canada. 2014a. *About Renewable Energy*. http://www.nrcan.gc.ca/ energy/renewable-electricity/7295. Last modified April 11.

Natural Resources Canada. 2014b. "Boreal Forest." *Forests: Forest Topics*. http://www .nrcan.gc.ca/node/13071. Last modified December 30.

Natural Resources Canada. 2014c. *Energy Policy*. http://www.nrcan.gc.ca/energy/ energy-resources/15903. Last modified May 5.

Natural Resources Canada. 2014d. *GEM: Geo-Mapping for Energy and Minerals*. http://www.nrcan.gc.ca/earth-sciences/resources/federal-programs/geomapping -energy-minerals/10904#Accessed.

Natural Resources Canada. 2014e. *The State of Canada's Forests: Annual Report 2014*. Ottawa: Natural Resources Canada. http://cfs.nrcan.gc.ca/ publications?id=35713.

Natural Resources Canada. 2014f. *Ten Key Facts on Canada's Natural Resources*. Ottawa: Natural Resources Canada. https://www.nrcan.gc.ca/sites/www.nrcan .gc.ca/files/files/pdf/10_key_facts_nrcan_e.pdf.

Natural Resources Canada. 2015a. "Impacts." *Climate Change*. http://www.nrcan .gc.ca/forests/climate-change/13095. Last modified March 18.

Natural Resources Canada. 2015b. *The North*. http://atlas.gc.ca/site/english/maps/ thenorth.html#physicalgeography. Last modified June 3.

Natural Resources Defense Council. 2009. *Protecting Our Oceans and Coastal Economies: Avoid Unnecessary Risks from Offshore Drilling*. New York: NRDC. http://www.nrdc.org/oceans/offshore/files/offshore.pdf.

NDP (New Democratic Party). 2013. *NDP Policy*. Ottawa: New Democratic Party of Canada. http://xfer.ndp.ca/2013/policybook/2013-04-17-PolicyBook_E.pdf.

NEB (National Energy Board). n.d. *National Energy Board Fact Sheet*. http://www .neb-one.gc.ca/bts/whwr/nbfctsht-eng.pdf.

Neimanis, V.P. 2011. "Crown Land." *Canadian Encyclopedia*. http://www .thecanadianencyclopedia.ca/en/article/crown-land/.

Non-GMO Project. 2013. "History of the Non-GMO Project." *Non-GMO Project*. http://www.nongmoproject.org/about/history/.

Norman, Emma S., Alice Cohen, and Karen Bakker, eds. 2013. *Water without Borders? Canada, the United States, and Shared Waters*. Toronto: University of Toronto Press.

Northwest Territories Executive. 1999. *The Constitutional Development of the Northwest Territories*. Aboriginal Self-Government in the Northwest Territories Supplementary Booklet 2. Yellowknife, NT: Government of the Northwest Territories. http://www.gov.nt.ca/publications/asg/pdfs/cons.pdf.

Nowlan, Linda. 2007. "Out of Sight, Out of Mind? Taking Canada's Groundwater for Granted." In *Eau Canada: The Future of Canada's Water*, edited by Karen Bakker, 55–84. Vancouver: UBC Press.

Nuttall, Mark. 2010. *Pipeline Dreams: People, Environment, and the Arctic Energy Frontier*. Copenhagen: IWGIA.

O'Connor, Ryan. 2014. *The First Green Wave: Pollution Probe and the Origins of Environmental Activism in Ontario*. Vancouver: UBC Press.

O'Neil, Peter. 2014. "Ottawa Removing North Pacific Humpback Whales from List of 'Threatened' Species." *The Vancouver Sun*, April 22. http://www.vancouversun. com/technology/Ottawa+removing+North+Pacific+humpback+whales+from+list+ threatened+species/9760778/story.html.

Office of the Auditor General of Canada. 2013a. *Report of the Commissioner of the Environment and Sustainable Development*. Ottawa: Auditor General of Canada. http://www.oag-bvg.gc.ca/internet/English/parl_cesd_201311_e_38658.html.

Office of the Auditor General of Canada. 2013b. *Report of the Commissioner of the Environment and Sustainable Development: Commissioner's Perspective*. Ottawa: Auditor General of Canada. http://www.oag-bvg.gc.ca/internet/docs/parl_cesd_201311_00_e.pdf.

Office of the Auditor General of Canada. 2014. "Who We Are." *About the OAG*. http://www.oag-bvg.gc.ca/internet/English/au_fs_e_370.html. Last modified July 17.

Office of the Commissioner of Lobbying of Canada. 2014. *Annual Report 2013–2014*. Ottawa: Office of the Commissioner of Lobbying of Canada. http://www.ocl-cal.gc.ca/eic/site/012.nsf/vwapj/AR_2013-14en.pdf/$file/AR_2013-14en.pdf.

Offin, Sarah. 2015. "Why Banff Tourism Is Booming with a Busting Economy." *Global News*, March 6. http://globalnews.ca/news/1869317/why-banff-tourism-is-booming-with-a-busting-economy/.

Olive, Andrea. 2012. "Does Canada's Species at Risk Act Live up to Article 8?" *Canadian Journal of Native Studies* 32 (1): 173–89.

Olive, Andrea. 2014a. *Land, Stewardship and Legitimacy: Endangered Species Policy in Canada and the United States*. Toronto: University of Toronto Press.

Olive, Andrea. 2014b. "The Road to Recovery: Comparing Canada and the US Recovery Strategies for Shared Endangered Species." *Canadian Geographer / Le géographe canadien* 58 (3): 263–75. http://dx.doi.org/10.1111/cag.12090.

OMAFRA (Ontario Ministry of Agriculture, Food and Rural Affairs). 2014. *Introduction to Organic Farming*. http://www.omafra.gov.on.ca/english/crops/facts/09-077.htm. Last modified March 18.

OME (Ontario Ministry of Energy). 2015. *Ontario's Long-Term Energy Plan*. http://www.energy.gov.on.ca/en/ltep/. Last modified February 20.

OMMAH (Ontario Ministry of Municipal Affairs and Housing). 2005. *The Greenbelt Plan, 2005*. Toronto: Ontario Ministry of Municipal Affairs and Housing. http://www.mah.gov.on.ca/Page189.aspx.

OMMAH (Ontario Ministry of Municipal Affairs and Housing). 2013. "Background." *Greenbelt Protection*. http://www.mah.gov.on.ca/Page1381.aspx. Last modified January 9.

Ontario. 2015. *Pesticide License and Permits*. https://www.ontario.ca/environment-and-energy/pesticide-licences-and-permits. Last updated May 1.

Ontario Power Authority. 2014. *FIT Program*. http://fit.powerauthority.on.ca/fit-program.

Osborn, Stephen G., Avner Vengosh, Nathaniel R. Warner, and Robert B. Jackson. 2011. "Methane Contamination of Drinking Water Accompanying Gas-Well Drilling and Hydraulic Fracturing." *Proceedings of the National Academy of Sciences* 108 (20): 8172–76. http://dx.doi.org/10.1073/pnas.1100682108.

Otto, Sarah, Sue McKee, and Jeanette Whitton. 2013. "Saving Species at Risk Starts at the Top: Where Is Our Environment Minister?" *Globe & Mail*, August 21. http://www.theglobeandmail.com/globe-debate/saving-species-at-risk-starts-at-the-top-where-is-our-environment-minister/article13754921.

Ouellet, Rick, and Erin Hanson. 2009. "Métis." *Indigenous Foundations*. http://indigenousfoundations.arts.ubc.ca/?id=549.

Pacific Coast Collaborative. 2013. *Pacific Coast Action Plan on Climate Change and Energy*. http://www.pacificcoastcollaborative.org/Documents/Pacific Coast Climate Action Plan.pdf.

Pacific Institute. 2007. "Bottled Water and Energy Fact Sheet." http://pacinst.org/
    publication/bottled-water-and-energy-a-fact-sheet/

Parks Canada. 2008. *National Parks of Canada: National Parks List*. http://www.pc.gc
    .ca/progs/np-pn/recherche-search_e.asp?p=1. Last modified November.

Parks Canada. 2014. *Canada's Existing World Heritage Sites*. http://www.pc.gc.ca/eng/
    progs/spm-whs/index.aspx. Last modified April 16.

Parliament of Canada. 2011. *Electoral Results by Party*. http://www.parl.gc.ca/parlinfo/
    compilations/electionsandridings/ResultsParty.aspx. Last modified October 7.

Parliament of Canada. 2012. *Appointments to the Senate by the Prime Minister: 1867 to
    Date*. http://www.parl.gc.ca/parlinfo/compilations/senate/Senate_NominationByPM
    .aspx. Last modified January 18.

Parliament of Canada. 2014. *House of Commons FAQ: Committees.* http://www.parl
    .gc.ca/CommitteeBusiness/SiteFaq.aspx?Language=E&Mode=1&Parl=41&Ses=2.

Parson, Edward A. 2000. "Environmental Trends and Environmental Governance in
    Canada." *Canadian Public Policy* 26 (Suppl. 2): S123–43. http://dx.doi.org/
    10.2307/3552575.

Parson, Edward. 2001. *Governing the Environment: Persistent Challenges, Uncertain
    Innovations*. Toronto: University of Toronto Press.

Partington, P. J. 2013. "How Carbon Pricing Currently Works in Alberta." *Pembina
    Institute Blog*, April 5. http://www.pembina.org/blog/708.

Pearson, Richard G., Steven J. Phillips, Michael M. Loranty, Pieter S. A. Beck,
    Theodoros Damoulas, Sarah J. Knight, and Scott J. Goetz. 2013. "Shifts in Arctic
    Vegetation and Associated Feedbacks under Climate Change." *Nature Climate
    Change* 3 (7): 673–7. http://dx.doi.org/10.1038/nclimate1858.

Peattie, K. 1995. *Environmental Marketing Management: Meeting the Green Challenge*.
    London: Pitman Publishing.

Peekhaus, Wilhelm. 2014. *Resistance Is Fertile: Canadian Struggles on the BioCommons*.
    Vancouver: UBC Press.

PEI Agriculture and Forestry. 2014. *Agriculture on Prince Edward Island*. http://www
    .gov.pe.ca/agriculture/AgonPEI. Last modified July.

Pelaudeix, Cécile. 2013. "Arctic Council Kiruna Ministerial Meeting: Strengthened
    Role of the Arctic Council in a Globalized Arctic—China in, the EU on Hold."
    Arctic Forum Foundation. http://eu-arctic-forum.org/publications/arctic-council
    -kiruna-ministerial-meeting-strengthened-role-of-the-arctic-council-in-a-globalized
    -arctic-china-in-the-eu-on-hold/.

Pembina Institute. 2011. *Election 2011: Where Do the Parties Stand on Environmental
    Issues?* Drayton Valley, AB: Pembina Institute. http://www.pembina.org/reports/
    eco-survey-2011-eng-final.pdf.

Peters, Guy. 1999. *American Public Policy: Promise and Performance*. New York:
    Chatham House Publishers.

Pew Research Center. 2015. *The State of the News Media, 2015*. Washington, DC: Pew
    Research Center. http://www.journalism.org/files/2015/04/FINAL-STATE-OF
    -THE-NEWS-MEDIA1.pdf.

Phare, Merrell-Ann. 2009. *Aboriginal Water Rights Primer*. Winnipeg: Phare Law.
    http://www.onwa.ca/upload/documents/aboriginal-water-rights-primer-canada.pdf.

Phare, Merrell-Ann. 2011. *Restoring the Lifeblood: Water, First Nations and
    Opportunities for Change*. Toronto: Walter and Duncan Gordon Foundation.

Pimm, S. L., C. N. Jenkins, R. Abell, T. M. Brooks, J. L. Gittleman, L. N. Joppa, P. H.
    Raven, C. M. Roberts, and J. O. Sexton. 2014. "The Biodiversity of Species and

Their Rates of Extinction, Distribution, and Protection." *Science* 344 (6187): 1246752. http://dx.doi.org/10.1126/science.1246752.

Plourde, Andre. 2010. "Oil and Gas in the Canadian Federation." Buffett Center for International and Comparative Studies Working Paper No. 10-001, prepared for the conference *Canadian-United States Energy Issues after Copenhagen*, May 28, 2010, Northwestern University, Evanston, IL. http://buffett.northwestern.edu/ documents/working-papers/Energy_10-001_Plourde.pdf.

Pollan, Michael. 2006. *The Omnivore's Dilemma: A Natural History of Meals.* New York: Penguin Books.

PPWB (Prairie Provinces Water Board). 2012. *Prairie Provinces Water Board Charter.* http://www.ppwb.ca/information/78/index.html. Last modified October.

Pralle, Sarah. 2009. "Reform, Not Revolution: Pesticides Regulation in Canada." In *Canadian Environmental Policy and Politics*, edited by Debora L. VanNijnatten and Robert Boardman, 3rd ed., 252–66. Oxford: Oxford University Press.

Prime Minister of Canada. 2006. "Canada's New Government Improves Protection against Hazardous Chemicals." *News Release*, December 8. http://www.pm.gc .ca/eng/news/2006/12/08/canadas-new-government-improves-protection -against-hazardous-chemicals.

Privy Council Office. 2007. *Strong Leadership: A Better Canada—Speech from the Throne to Open the Second Session of the 39th Parliament of Canada.* Ottawa: Government of Canada. http://publications.gc.ca/collections/collection_2007/gg/ SO1-1-2007E.pdf.

Public Works and Government Services Canada. 2014. *Organic Production Systems: General Principles and Management Standards.* CANCGSB-32.310-2006. Ottawa: Canadian Standards Board. http://www.tpsgc-pwgsc.gc.ca/ongc-cgsb/programme -program/normes-standards/internet/bio-org/documents/032-0310-2008-eng.pdf.

Québec. 2014a. *The Carbon Market: The Québec Cap and Trade System for Greenhouse Gas Emissions Allowances.* Québec: Ministre du Développement durable, de l'Environnement et de la Lutte contre les changements climatiques. http://www.mddelcc.gouv.qc.ca/changements/carbone/Systeme-plafonnement- droits- GES-en.htm.

Québec. 2014b. "Québec, Ontario, British Columbia and California Unite to Advance the Fight against Climate Change." *Minister of Sustainable Development, the Environment and the Fight against Climate Change Press Release*, December 8. http://www.mddelcc.gouv.qc.ca/communiques_en/2014/C20141208-lima.htm.

Reid, Donald G., Dominique Berteaux, and Kristin L. Laidre. 2013. "Mammals." In *Arctic Biodiversity Assessment: Status and Trends in Arctic Biodiversity*, edited by Hans Meltofte, Alf B. Josefson, and David Payer, 78–141. Akureyri, Iceland: Conservation of Arctic Flora and Fauna.

Rennie, Steve. 2013. "Supreme Court Sides with Metis in Historic Manitoba Land Claim Dispute." *CTV News*, March 8. http://www.ctvnews.ca/canada/supreme -court-sides-with-metis-in-historic-manitoba-land-claim-dispute-1.1187212.

Rosenbaum, Walter A. 2013. *Environmental Politics and Policy.* Washington, DC: CQ Press.

Royal Society of Canada. 2004. *Report of the Expert Panel on Science Issues Related to Oil and Gas Activities, Offshore British Columbia.* Prepared at the request of Natural Resources Canada. Ottawa: The Royal Society of Canada. https://rsc-src .ca/sites/default/files/pdf/fullreportEN.pdf.

Royal Society of Canada. 2010. *Environmental and Health Impacts of Canada's Oil Sands Industry.* Ottawa: The Royal Society of Canada. https://rsc-src.ca/sites/ default/files/pdf/RSC Oil Sands Pane Main Report Oct 2012.pdf.

Russell, Peter H. 2012. *How Agriculture Made Canada: Farming in the Nineteenth Century*. Montréal: McGill-Queen's University Press.

Saier, Milton. 2006. "Pollution." *Environmentalist* 26 (3): 205–9. http://dx.doi.org/10 .1007/s10669-006-7764-6.

Sauer, Carl Ortwin. 1975. *Sixteenth Century North America: The Land and the People as Seen by the Europeans*. Berkeley: University of California Press.

Saunders, J. Owen, and Michael M. Wenig. 2007. "Whose Water? Canadian Water Management and the Challenges of Jurisdictional Fragmentation." In *Eau Canada: The Future of Canada's Water*, edited by Karen Bakker, 119–42. Vancouver: UBC Press.

Schaer, Lillian. 2011. "Greenbelt Farmers Realizing Significant Energy Savings, Survey Shows." *Greenbelt Foundation Press Releases*, May 26. http://www.greenbelt.ca/ greenbelt_farmers_realizing_significant_energy_savings_survey_shows2011.

Schellnhuber, Hans Joachim. 2009. *Climate Change as a Security Risk*. Abingdon, UK: Routledge.

Scheufele, Dietram A., and David Tewksbury. 2007. "Framing, Agenda Setting, and Priming: The Evolution of Three Media Effects Models." *Journal of Communication* 57 (1): 9–20.

Schmidt, Sarah. 2010. "Younger Canadians Have More BPA in Their Bodies than Parents: Study." *Postmedia News*, August 17. http://www.canada.com/health/Younger+ Canadians+have+more+their+bodies+than+parents+Study/3408117/story .html.

Schwartz, Alan M. 2006. "The Management of Shared Waters." In *Bilateral Ecopolitcs: Community and Change in Canada-American Environmental Relations*, edited by Philippe G. Le Prestre and Peter J. Stoett, 133–44. Burlington, VT: Ashgate Publishing.

Semeniuk, Ivan. 2013. "Ontario's Grand River Loaded with Artificial Sweeteners, Study Finds." *The Globe and Mail*, December 11. http://www.theglobeandmail.com/ news/national/ontarios-grand-river-loaded-with-artificial-sweeteners-study-finds/ article15896336/.

Severson-Baker, Chris. 2014. "Alberta's Carbon Pricing not Best-in-Canada Example." *Pembina Institute Blog*, December 19. http://www.pembina.org/blog/albertas -carbon-pricing-not-best-in-canada-example.

Shprentz, D. 1996. *Breath-Taking: Premature Mortality due to Particulate Air Pollution in 239 American Cities*. New York: NRDC.

Simeon, R., and I. Robinson. 1990. *State, Society, and the Development of Canadian Federalism*. Toronto: University of Toronto Press.

Sisler, Julia. 2014. "Research Cutbacks by Government Alarm Scientists." *CBC News*, January 10. http://www.cbc.ca/news/technology/research-cutbacks-by -government-alarm-scientists-1.2490081.

Skogstad, Grace. 2008. *Internationalization and Canadian Agriculture: Policy and Governing Paradigms*. Toronto: University of Toronto Press.

Skogstad, Grace. 2013. "Agriculture and Food Policy." *The Canadian Encyclopedia*. http://www.thecanadianencyclopedia.ca/en/article/agriculture-and-food-policy/.

Smallwood, Kate. 2003. *A Guide to Canada's Species at Risk Act*. Toronto: Sierra Legal Defense Fund.

Smith, Rick, and Bruce Lourie. 2009. *Slow Death by Rubber Duck: The Secret Dangers of Everyday Things*. Berkeley, CA: Counterpoint.

Sobczak, Pawel, and Alister Doyle. 2013. "Polish Minister Fired but Still Heads U.N. Climate Talks." *Reuters*, November 20. http://uk.reuters.com/article/2013/11/20/ uk-poland-environment-government-idUKBRE9AJ0UF20131120.

Solomon, Lawrence. 2007. *Toronto Sprawls: A History*. Toronto: University of Toronto Press.

Somerville, Chris. 2007. "Biofuels." *Current Biology* 17 (4): R115–9. http://dx.doi .org/10.1016/j.cub.2007.01.010.

Souther, Sara, Morgan W. Tingley, Viorel D. Popescu, David T.S. Hayman, Maureen E. Ryan, Tabitha A. Graves, Brett Hartl, and Kimberly Terrell. 2014. "Biotic Impacts of Energy Development from Shale: Research Priorities and Knowledge Gaps." *Frontiers in Ecology and the Environment* 12 (6): 330–38. http://dx.doi.org/ 10.1890/130324.

Sprague, John B. 2007. "Great Wet North? Canada's Myth of Water Abundance." In *Eau Canada: The Future of Canada's Water*, edited by Karen Bakker, 23–36. Vancouver: UBC Press.

Stastna, Kazi. 2012. "What Are Crown Corporations and Why Do They Exist?" *CBC News*, April 1. http://www.cbc.ca/news/canada/what-are-crown-corporations -and-why-do-they-exist-1.1135699.

Statistics Canada. 2005. *Land and Freshwater Area, by Province and Territory*. http:// www.statcan.gc.ca/tables-tableaux/sum-som/l01/cst01/phys01-eng.htm. Last modified February 1.

Statistics Canada. 2006. *The Wealth of Canadians: An Overview of the Results of the Survey of Financial Security 2005*. Pension and Wealth Research Paper Series No. 13F0026MIE—001. Ottawa: Statistics Canada.

Statistics Canada. 2007. *Portrait of the Canadian Population in 2006, 2006 Census*. Number 97-550-XIE. Ottawa: Statistics Canada.

Statistics Canada. 2011a. *Population, Urban and Rural, by Province and Territory (Canada): Summary Table*. Ottawa: Statistics Canada. http://www.statcan.gc.ca/ tables-tableaux/sum-som/l01/cst01/demo62a-eng.htm. Last modified February 4.

Statistics Canada. 2011b. *Immigration and Ethnocultural Diversity in Canada*. http:// www12.statcan.gc.ca/nhs-enm/2011/as-sa/99–010-x/99–010-x2011001-eng.cfm.

Statistics Canada. 2012. *Human Activity and the Environment: Waste Management in Canada*. Ottawa: Minister of Industry.

Statistics Canada. 2014a. *Aboriginal Peoples in Canada: First Nations People, Métis, and Inuit*. http://www12.statcan.gc.ca/nhs-enm/2011/as-sa/99–011-x/99–011 -x2011001-eng.cfm. Last modified March 28.

Statistics Canada. 2014b. "Canada's Population Estimates: Subprovincial Areas, July 1, 2013." *The Daily*, February 26. http://www.statcan.gc.ca/daily-quotidien/140226/ dq140226b-eng.pdf.

Statistics Canada. 2014c. *The Canadian Population in 2011: Populations Counts and Growth*. http://www12.statcan.ca/census-recensement/2011/as-sa/98–310- x/98–310-x2011001-eng.cfm.

Statistics Canada. 2014d. *CANSIM Table 051-0001 Estimates of Population, by Age Group and Sex for July 1, Canada, Provinces and Territories, Annual*. http:// www5.statcan.gc.ca/cansim/a47. Last modified September 25.

Statistics Canada. 2015a. "Agriculture is Growing and Evolving." In *Snapshot of Canadian Agriculture: Census of Agriculture 2011*. http://www.statcan.gc.ca/ pub/95-640-x/2011001/p1/p1-01-eng.htm. Last modified February 18.

Statistics Canada. 2015b. *CANSIM Table 051-0005: Estimates of Population, Canada, Provinces and Territories, Quarterly (persons)*. http://www5.statcan.gc.ca/cansim/a26?lang=eng&id=510005. Last modified June 17.

Stockholm Convention. 2008. *The 12 Initial POPs under the Stockholm Convention*. http://chm.pops.int/TheConvention/ThePOPs/The12InitialPOPs/tabid/296/Default.aspx.

Stonechild, Blair. 2007. "Aboriginal Peoples of Saskatchewan." *The Encyclopedia of Saskatchewan*. http://esask.uregina.ca/entry/aboriginal_peoplesof_saskatchewan.html.

Summit, Ariela. 2012. *Engaging Municipalities: Voluntary Climate Change Action in Canada*. Los Angeles: Luskin Center for Innovation.

Summit, Joshua, and E. Gregory McPherson. 1998. "Residential Tree Planting and Care: A Study of Attitudes and Behaviors in Sacramento, California." *Journal of Arboriculture* 22 (2): 89–97.

Suzuki, David. 2014. *Carbon Tax or Cap-and-Trade?* http://www.davidsuzuki.org/issues/climate-change/science/climate-solutions/carbon-tax-or-cap-and-trade/.

Swim, Janet, Susan Clayton, Thomas Doherty, Robert Gifford, George Howard, Joseph Reser, Paul Stern, Elke Weber. 2009. *Psychology and Global Climate Change: Addressing a Multifaceted Phenomenon and Set of Challenges*. Washington, DC: American Psychological Association. http://www.apa.org/science/about/publications/climate-change-booklet.pdf.

SWSA (Saskatchewan Water Security Agency). 2012. "About WSA." *Water Security Agency*. https://www.wsask.ca/About-WSA/.

Taber, Jane, and Adrian Morrow. 2015. "Ontario Unveils Cap-and-Trade Plans as Provinces Take Lead on Climate Change." *Globe and Mail*, April 14. http://www.theglobeandmail.com/news/politics/wynne-unveils-ontarios-plansto-join-emissions-cap-and-trade-system/article23895069/.

TAF (Toronto Atmospheric Fund). 2014. *Annual Report, 2013*. Toronto: Toronto Atmospheric Fund. http://taf.ca/wp-content/uploads/2014/10/annual-report-2013.pdf.

Tarnocai, C., J.G. Canadell, E.A.G. Schuur, P. Kuhry, G. Mazhitova, and S. Zimov. 2009. "Soil Organic Carbon Pools in the Northern Circumpolar Permafrost Region." *Global Biogeochemical Cycles* 23 (2). http://dx.doi.org/10.1029/2008GB003327.

Tchir, Tara. L., Edward Johnson, and Lawrence Nkemdirim. 2012. "Deforestation in North America: Past, Present and Future." In *Encyclopedia of Life Support Systems (EOLSS) Regional Sustainable Development Review: Canada and the USA*, vol. 1. http://www.eolss.net/sample-chapters/c16/e1–50–10–00.pdf.

Tidwell, Mike. 2009. "To Really the Save the Planet, Stop Going Green All Alone." *Washington Post*, December 6. http://www.washingtonpost.com/wp-dyn/content/article/2009/12/04/AR2009120402605.html.

Tindall, D.B., Ronald L. Trosper, and Pamela Perreault, eds. 2013. *Aboriginal Peoples and Forest Lands in Canada*. Vancouver: UBC Press.

Tomalty, Ray. 2012. *Carbon in the Bank: Ontario's Greenbelt and Its Role in Mitigating Climate Change*. Vancouver: David Suzuki Foundation.

Toronto-Dominion Bank. 2015. *TD Forests: Forest Conservation Map*. http://www.tdforestsmap.com/#.

TransCanada. 2012. "Mackenzie Gas Project." *Key Projects: Natural Gas Pipelines*. http://www.transcanada.com/mackenzie-valley.html. Last modified December 18.

Transport Canada. 2012. "Arctic Waters Pollution Prevent Act (AWPPA)." *Arctic Shipping: Acts and Regulations*. https://www.tc.gc.ca/eng/marinesafety/debs -arctic-acts-regulations-awppa-494.htm. Last modified July 19.

Transport Canada. 2015. *Tanker Safety and Spill Prevention*. http://www.tc.gc.ca/eng/ marinesafety/menu-4100.htm. Last modified April 4.

Trudeau, Justin. 2014. "Justin Trudeau Statement." *CBC News*, January 29. http:// www.cbc.ca/news/politics/justin-trudeau-statement-senate-is-broken-and -needs-to-be-fixed-1.2515374.

Turcotte, Martin. 2011. "Commuting to Work: Results of the 2010 General Social Survey." *Statistics Canada Social Trends*, August 24. http://www.statcan.gc.ca/ pub/11-008-x/2011002/article/11531-eng.pdf.

Turner, Chris. 2013. *The War on Science: Muzzled Scientists and Wilful Blindness in Stephen Harper's Canada*. Vancouver: Greystone Press.

UIA (Union of International Associations). 1991. *European Convention on the Recognition of the Legal Personality of INGOs*. http://www.uia.org/archive/ legal-status-4–11.

UNEP (United Nations Environment Programme). 2014. *Urban Biodiversity*. http:// www.unep.org/urban_environment/issues/biodiversity.asp.

UNEP (United Nations Environment Programme). 2015. *UNEP Priorities*. http://www .unep.org/about/Priorities/tabid/129622/Default.aspx.

UNESCO World Heritage Centre. 2015. "Canadian Rocky Mountain Parks." *World Heritage List*. http://whc.unesco.org/en/list/304.

United Nations. 1972. *Declaration of the United Nations Conference on the Human Environment* [Stockholm Declaration]. http://www.unep.org/Documents .Multilingual/Default.asp?documentid=97&articleid=1503.

United Nations. 1992. *Rio Declaration on Environment and Development*. http://www .unep.org/Documents.Multilingual/Default.asp?documentid=78&articleid=1163.

United Nations. 1998. *The United Nations Convention on the Law of the Sea: A Historical Perspective*. New York: United Nations. http://www.un.org/depts/los/ convention_agreements/convention_historical_perspective.htm.

United Nations. 2004. *World Urbanization Prospects: The 2003 Revision*. New York: United Nations.

United Nations. 2007. *United Nations Declaration on the Rights of Indigenous Peoples*. New York: United Nations. http://www.un.org/esa/socdev/unpfii/ documents/DRIPS_en.pdf.

United Nations. 2013. *United Nations Convention on the Law of the Sea of 10 December 1982: Overview and Full Text*. New York: United Nations. http://www .un.org/depts/los/convention_agreements/convention_overview_convention.htm. Last modified August 22.

United Nations. 2015. "Overview." *About the UN*. http://www.un.org/en/sections/ about-un/overview/index.html.

Urban, Frauke, and Johan Nordensvärd. 2013. *Low Carbon Development: Key Issues*. London: Routledge.

US Census Bureau. 2010. "State Area Measurements and Internal Point Coordinates." *Geography*. http://www.ccnsus.gov/geo/reference/state-area.html.

US Census Bureau. 2015. "California." *State & Country QuickFacts*. http://quickfacts .census.gov/qfd/states/06000.html.

US Department of Energy. 2009. *Modern Shale Gas Development in the United States: A Primer*. Washington, DC: United States Department of Energy. http://energy .gov/sites/prod/files/2013/03/f0/ShaleGasPrimer_Online_4-2009.pdf.

US Energy Information Administration. 2013. *International Energy Outlook 2013*. Washington, DC: EIA. http://www.eia.gov/forecasts/ieo/pdf/0484(2013).pdf.

US Fish and Wildlife Service (Division of Congressional and Legislative Affairs). 2013. "Alaska Native Claims Settlement Act." *Digest of Federal Resource Laws of Interest to the U.S. Fish and Wildlife Service*. http://www.fws.gov/laws/lawsdigest/ ALASNAT.HTML. Last modified January 10.

USGS (US Geological Survey). 2008a. *Circum-Arctic Resource Appraisal Assessment: Estimates of Undiscovered Oil and Gas North of the Arctic Circle*. Menlo Park, CA: U.S. Geological Survey http://pubs.usgs.gov/fs/2008/3049/fs2008-3049.pdf.

USGS (US Geological Survey). 2008b. "90 Billion Barrels of Oil and 1,670 Trillion Cubic Feet of Natural Gas Assessed in the Arctic." *USGS Newsroom*, July 23. http://www.usgs.gov/newsroom/article.asp?ID=1980#.VZSxoqbuDu0.

UTTF (Urban Transportation Task Force). 2005. *Urban Transportation in Canada: Needs and Opportunities*. Ottawa: Council of Ministers Responsible for Transportation and Highway Safety. http://www.comt.ca/english/urbantrans.pdf.

Van Dolah, F.M. 2000. "Marine Algal Toxins: Origins, Health Effects, and Their Increased Occurrence." *Environmental Health Perspectives* 108 (s1): 133–41. http://dx.doi.org/10.1289/ehp.00108s1133.

VanNijnatten, Debora, Neil Craik, and Isabel Studer, eds. 2013. *Climate Change Policy in North America: Designing Integration in a Regional System*. Toronto: University of Toronto Press.

Vaughn, Jacqueline. 2011. *Environmental Politics: Domestic and Global Dimensions*. 6th ed. Boston, MA: Wadsworth Publishing.

Venter, Oscar, Nathalie N. Brodeur, Leah Nemiroff, Brenna Belland, Ivan J. Dolinsek, and James W. A. Grant. 2006. "Threats to Endangered Species in Canada." *Bioscience* 56 (11): 903–10. http://dx.doi.org/10.1641/0006-3568(2006)56 [903:TTESIC]2.0.CO;2.

Vidal, John. 2014. "Climate Change Brings New Risks to Greenland, Says PM Aleqa Hammond." *The Guardian*, January 23. http://www.theguardian.com/ environment/2014/jan/23/climate-change-risks-greenland-arctic-icecap.

Vig, Norman J., and Michael E. Kraft. 2012. *Environmental Policy: New Directions for the Twenty-First Century*. Washington, DC: CQ Press.

Walkem, Ardith. 2007. "The Land Is Dry: Indigenous Peoples, Water, and Environmental Justice." In *Eau Canada: The Future of Canada's Water*, edited by Karen Bakker, 303–20. Vancouver: UBC Press. Print

Warren, Fiona J. 2004. *Climate Change Impacts and Adaptation: A Canadian Perspective*. Ottawa: Natural Resources Canada. http://www.cfs.nrcan.gc.ca/ bookstore_pdfs/27428.pdf.

Webb, Sam. 2014. "Fatberg the Size of a Jumbo Jet Strikes Central London." *Daily Mail*, September 1. http://www.dailymail.co.uk/news/article-2739743/Fatberg -size-jumbo-jet-strikes-central-London-Eighty-metre-mass-congealed-fat-wet -wipes-streets-Shepherd-s-Bush-took-four-DAYS-break-up.html.

West Coast Environmental Law. 2012. "First Nations and BC Mayors Stand Together against Threat of Oil Tankers and Pipelines." *Environmental Law Alert Blog*, December 18. http://wcel.org/resources/environmental-law-alert/ first-nations-and-bc-mayors-stand-together-against-threat-oil-tank.

Weston, Anthony, ed. 2003. *An Invitation to Environmental Philosophy*. New York: Oxford University Press.

White, Graham. 2009. "Aboriginal People and Environmental Regulation: The Role of Land Claims Co-management Boards in the Territorial North." In *Canadian Environmental Policy and Politics: Prospects for Leadership and Innovation*, edited by Debora L. VanNijnatten and Robert Boardman, 123–36. Don Mills, ON: Oxford University Press.

White, Jen. 2013. "THM Troubles Grow in N.L. Water Supplies, Tests Show." *CBC News*. February 12. http://www.cbc.ca/news/canada/newfoundland-labrador/thm-troubles-grow-in-n-1-water-supplies-tests-show 1.1341437.

White House. 2013. *The President's Climate Action Plan*. Washington, DC: Executive Office of the President. http://www.whitehouse.gov/sites/default/files/image/president27sclimateactionplan.pdf.

White House. 2014. *US–China Joint Announcement on Climate Change*. Washington, DC: Office of the Press Secretary. http://www.whitehouse.gov/the-press-office/2014/11/11/us-china-joint-announcement-climate-change.

Wiebe, Nettie, and Kevin Wipf. 2011. "Nurturing Food Sovereignty in Canada." In *Food Sovereignty in Canada: Creating Just and Sustainable Food Systems*, edited by Hannah Wittman, Annette Aurelie Desmarais, and Nettie Wiebe, 1–19. Halifax: Fernwood Publishing.

Wiener, Jonathan B., Michael D. Rogers, James K. Hammitt, and Peter H. Sand. 2010. *The Reality of Precaution: Comparing Risk Regulation in the United States and Europe*. Washington, DC: RFF Press.

Wilcove, David S., David Rothstein, Jason Dubow, Ali Phillips, and Elizabeth Losos. 1998. "Quantifying Threats to Imperiled Species in the United States: Assessing the Relative Importance of Habitat Destruction, Alien Species, Pollution, Overexploitation, and Disease." *Bioscience* 48 (8): 607–15. http://dx.doi.org/10.2307/1313420. [

Willetts, Peter. 2002. *What Is a Non-Governmental Organization?* London: Civil Society Networks in Global Governance, City University. http://www.staff.city.ac.uk/p.willetts/CS-NTWKS/NGO-ART.HTM#Part2.

Williams, Maria Shaa Tiaa, ed. 2009. *The Alaska Native Reader: History, Culture, Politics*. Durham, NC: Duke University Press. http://dx.doi.org/10.1215/9780822390831.

Wilson, Jeremy. 1992. "Green Lobbies: Pressure Groups and Environmental Policy." In *Canadian Environmental Policy: Ecosystems, Politics, and Processes*, edited by Robert Boardman, 109–25. Toronto: Oxford University Press.

Winfield, Mark. 2012. *Blue-Green Province: The Environment and the Political Economy of Ontario*. Vancouver: UBC Press.

Wojciechowski, Stephane, Sue McKee, Christopher Brassard, C. Scott Findlay, and Stewart Elgie. 2011. "SARA's Safety Net Provisions and the Effectiveness of Species at Risk Protection on Non-Federal Lands." *Journal of Environmental Law and Practice* 22 (3): 203–22.

Wolf, K.L. 2003. "Introduction to Urban and Community Forestry Program in the United States." *Landscape and Horticulture* 4 (3): 19–28.

Wolman, Gordon M. 1993. "Population, Land Use, and Environment: A Long History." In *Population and Land Use in Developing Countries*, edited by Carole L. Jolly and Barbara Boyle Torrey, 15–29. Washington, DC: National Academies Press.

Wood, Stepan, Georgia Tanner, and Benjamin J. Richardson. 2010. "Whatever Happened to Canadian Environmental Law?" *Ecology Law Quarterly* 37 (4): 981–1040.

World Commission on Environment and Development. 1987. *Our Common Future*. Oxford: Oxford University Press. http://www.un-documents.net/our-common -future.pdf.

World Health Organization. 2011. *Database: Outdoor Air Pollution in Cities*. http:// www.who.int/entity/phe/health_topics/outdoorair/databases/cities-2011/en/index .html.

World Health Organization. 2015. *Structural Adjustment Programmes (SAPS)*. Geneva: WHO. http://www.who.int/trade/glossary/story084/en/.

World Nuclear Association. 2015. *Nuclear Power in Canada*. http://www.world -nuclear.org/info/Country-Profiles/Countries-A-F/Canada--Nuclear-Power. Last modified February.

Worldwatch Institute. 2001. *Curbing Sprawl to Fight Climate Change*. http://www .worldwatch.org/curbing-sprawl-fight-climate-change-0.

Yale University. 2015. *Environmental Performance Index*. http://epi.yale.edu.

Yin, Runsheng, and Jungho Baek. 2004. "The US-Canada Softwood Lumber Trade Dispute: What We Know and What We Need to Know." *Forest Policy and Economics* 6 (2): 129–43. http://dx.doi.org/10.1016/S1389-9341(02)00104-1.

Young, Nathan, and Ralph Matthews. 2010. *The Aquaculture Controversy in Canada: Activism, Policy, and Contested Science*. Vancouver: UBC Press.

Yukon Legislative Assembly. 2012. *Information Sheet Number 7: The Differences between Provinces and Territories*. http://www.legassembly.gov.yk.ca/pdf/ 7_diff_between_prov_territories.pdf. Last modified September 17.

Yurick, Doug. 2010. "National Marine Conservation Areas—Extending Parks Canada's Reach into Canada's Oceans and Great Lakes." *The George Wright Forum* 27 (2): 170–79.

Zander, Joakim. 2010. *The Application of the Precautionary Principle in Practice: Comparative Dimensions*. New York: Cambridge University Press. http://dx.doi .org/10.1017/CBO9780511779862.

Zelko, Frank. 2013. *Make It a Green Peace!: The Rise of Counterculture Environmentalism*. Oxford: Oxford University Press.

Zhang, Daowei. 2007. *The Softwood Lumber War: Politics, Economics, and the Long U.S.—Canadian Trade Dispute*. Washington, DC: Resources for the Future.

Zick, Cathleen D., Ken R. Smith, Lori Kowaleski-Jones, Clare Uno, and Brittany J. Merrill. 2013. "Harvesting More than Vegetables: The Potential Weight Control Benefits of Community Gardening." *American Journal of Public Health* 103 (6): 1110–15. http://dx.doi.org/10.2105/AJPH.2012.301009.

INDEX